D1567773

Casualties of Credit

Casualties of Credit

The English Financial Revolution,
1620–1720

Carl Wennerlind

Harvard University Press

Cambridge, Massachusetts

London, England

2011

Library of Congress Cataloging-in-Publication Data
Wennerlind, Carl.
Casualties of credit : the English financial revolution, 1620–1720 /
Carl Wennerlind.
p. cm.
Includes bibliographical references and index.
ISBN 978-0-674-04738-9 (alk. paper)
1. Credit—England—History—17th century. 2. Finance—England—
History—17th century. 3. Economics—England—History—17th century.
4. England—Economic conditions—17th century. I. Title.
HG3754.5.G7 W46 2011
332.0942'09032—dc23
2011017929

To Monica

Contents

Author's Note on Conventions

England followed the Julian calendar until 1752. Dates given in this book are modern, with the year beginning on January 1. However, since the month of publication is rarely listed, I will use the year of publication listed.

Spelling of quotations has not been modernized and original punctuation has been retained.

Casualty, n.

1. Chance, accident (as a state of things).

2.

a. A chance occurrence, an accident; *esp.* an unfortunate occurrence, a mishap; now, generally, a fatal or serious accident or event, a disaster.

b. Used of the losses sustained by a body of men in the field or on service, by death, desertion, etc.

c. Used of an individual killed, wounded, or injured.

3.

a. State of subjection to chance; liability to accident; precariousness, uncertainty.

b. A thing subject to chance.

4.

a. A casual or incidental charge or payment.

THE OXFORD ENGLISH DICTIONARY, 2ND ED., 1989.

Casualties of Credit

Introduction

Of all Beings that have Existence only in the Minds of Men, nothing
is more fantastical and nice than Credit; 'tis never to be forc'd;
it hangs upon Opinion; it depends upon our Passions of Hope
and Fear; it comes many times unsought for, and often goes away
without Reason; and when once lost, is hardly to be quite recover'd.[1]

CHARLES DAVENANT, *DISCOURSES ON THE PUBLICK
REVENUES, AND ON THE TRADE OF ENGLAND*, 1698

Credit is undoubtedly one of mankind's most enigmatic and powerful achievements. As the influential political economist Charles Davenant pointed out in 1698, during the aftermath of the first crisis of
the English Financial Revolution, credit is simultaneously "fantastical
and nice" and dangerously precarious. Based on cooperation, trust, and
honesty, the new system of credit implemented during the Financial
Revolution fundamentally transformed England. Comprised of a long-
term funded national debt, an active securities market, and a widely circulating credit currency, the modern financial system enabled England
to create a powerful fiscal-military state, to forge a dominant global
empire, and to move in the direction of the Industrial Revolution faster
than any other nation.[2]

Davenant recognized that credit not only permits material advancement and imperial expansion, it is in itself a remarkable social accomplishment. For credit to thrive, people have to learn how to respect and
honor contracts and to trust that others will do the same. Commitment
mechanisms and legal frameworks need to be developed and tailored to
assist in the formation of honesty and trust. Formation of such a culture
of credit thus necessitates a considerable behavioral transformation.
Indeed, many early modern philosophers considered the establishment
of such a framework the very essence of modern society.

Yet, despite his praise of its "niceties," Davenant also recognized that
there were several casualties of the English Financial Revolution. In

1

emphasizing that credit "hangs upon Opinion," he highlighted credit's instability, the fact that it is subject to chance, liable to accident and uncertainty—the very meaning of the term *casualty*.[3] Because credit was built on what was so widely recognized as a porous foundation, nothing short of an epistemological revolution was necessary for people to understand and embrace it, and to overcome their trepidations about basing both commerce and the state on what was fundamentally a mental construct.

Although Davenant specified that credit can never be forced, contemporaries were well aware of the role that power played in the Financial Revolution. Safeguarding the nascent culture of credit required debtors' prisons for the insolvent and the threat of execution for clippers and counterfeiters. Moreover, thousands of African slaves were carried in chains to the New World, so that profits from the South Sea Company might bolster people's trust in public credit. An unprecedented number of Englishmen were hurt or killed in wars with France that England would not have been able to conduct on the same scale without the employment of credit. Casualties continued to mount as state authority was employed to stir up people's "Passions for Hope and Fear" in order to ensure that credit flourished.

While credit, in some form or another, has always been part of human societies, the confluence of financial innovations in Europe during the early modern period fundamentally changed the idea of credit and its place in society. Historian Craig Muldrew has shown that by the sixteenth century credit was already central to English social life.[4] But while sixteenth-century credit was based on a complex and intricate network of personal ties, the credit instruments themselves were relatively simple. The vast majority of early credit contracts were based on personal agreements, many of which were struck verbally in face-to-face interactions. Even when credit obligations were more formally recorded on bonds, notes, and pledges, they remained with the creditors until the due date. The short terms of most credit agreements, private and public, limited the capacity of credit to circulate. Because of credit's inability to enter circulation and thus augment the money stock, contemporaries often complained about the backwardness of England's credit system. When added to the continuous frustration with the lack of silver coin, it was clear to all observers that something had to be done to the nation's monetary system if England were to prosper commercially and enhance its geopolitical clout.

The shift from the Renaissance world of credit to that of the Financial Revolution constituted a radical rupture. While the specific timing and contours of the new financial system owed much to the Glorious Revolution in 1688 and the formation of the Bank of England in 1694, this book contends that the conceptualization of a new financial architecture and the grounds for its general acceptance would not have been possible without an earlier revolution in political economy.[5]

Indeed, it is the purpose of *Casualties of Credit* to reveal the intellectual underpinnings of the English Financial Revolution. By drawing on a wide literature of early modern pamphlets, broadsheets, and books, I show how seventeenth-century political economists, social reformers, and government officials envisioned, explained, debated, and sought to influence credit. Each chapter of this book is focused on a separate debate sparked by the need for a solution to a particular monetary or financial crisis. While I offer descriptions of the economic and political conditions contributing to each crisis, and, when possible, provide an account of its resolution and aftermath, the primary focus of this book remains on the discourse regarding credit.[6] I seek to uncover how people conceived of credit and how their understanding was embedded in the seventeenth-century thinking about the universe, nature, matter, agriculture, commerce, manufacturing, politics, class, war, capital punishment, and colonialism. In doing so, I explore how the Financial Revolution evoked changes in attitudes towards concepts such as time, history, progress, knowledge, imagination, and wealth.[7]

The new political economic thinking paving the way for the Financial Revolution was grounded in a radically transformed worldview that drew extensively on developments in natural philosophy and political theory. Leaving behind the traditional notion that mankind exists in a material, social, and economic world that is finite, static, and knowable, mid seventeenth-century political economists embraced the ideas of infinite worlds, nature's perfectibility, and probabilistic knowledge. With these component parts, they constructed a new worldview in which mankind's purpose was to ceaselessly pursue new methods for the infinite improvement of nature, society, and mankind. For such a vision of perpetual progress to materialize, it was essential to these writers that England develop a more sophisticated system of credit. *Casualties of Credit* traces the origins of this worldview and argues that the Scientific Revolution played an integral role in the making of the Financial Revolution.[8]

This book contends that England's first set of proposals for a generally circulating credit currency were developed within an intellectual framework informed by alchemical and Baconian thinking. I am here building on scholarship that explicitly recognizes the importance of natural philosophy for the development of political economy.[9] Scholars in this tradition have established that early modern political economy incorporated important lessons from the Aristotelian tradition, embraced Sir Francis Bacon's call for the pursuit of useful knowledge, and adopted the alchemical conviction that mankind can improve on nature's creations. *Casualties of Credit* extends these insights and argues that alchemical and Baconian thinking was critical to the development of a new culture of credit in England.

Additionally, I seek to enrich the debate about the emergence of probabilistic reasoning. Here the link between natural philosophy and political economy is more complex.[10] A number of scholars have examined the importance of probabilistic thinking to seventeenth-century natural philosophy, law, religion, and literature.[11] It is also widely recognized that aleatory contracts, including games of chance and insurance, which were part of the new efforts to control and harness risk and uncertainty, were designed with the aid of probabilistic thinking.[12] Little systematic effort, however, has been employed in studying how new forms of credit were conceived and assessed within probabilistic frameworks during the second half of the seventeenth century. I argue that political economists drew on the ways in which trust was conceptualized among natural philosophers, as well as the strategies philosophers used to generate trust in their knowledge claims.[13] However, the influence also ran in the opposite direction. The kind of fiduciary ties prevalent in merchant communities that informed how political economists – many of whom were experienced traders – thought about trust had an impact on the philosophical discourse. This interplay between natural philosophers and political economists was essential to the development of probabilistic reasoning.

The discourse about the state as a commercial, fiscal, military, penal, colonial, and protodemocratic body constituted another central theme in the conceptual development of credit. By the second half of the seventeenth century, the development of a new system of credit had become an interest of state. Indeed, England established a national bank to facilitate the nation's commercial expansion and to finance the Nine Years' War (1688-1697) against Louis XIV. Credit increased both England's commercial prowess and military might, the two most essential components of its quest for power and prosperity. But the state could not merely enjoy the benefits of a new system of credit, it had to contribute actively to its formation. Even though most seventeenth-century political economists recognized that credit relied on a general culture of honesty and trust, it was clear to all that the state had to use its authority to develop and safeguard a more advanced system of credit. Not only did the state use its power to tax in order to secure its loans from the Bank and, in extension, to support the exchangeability of the Bank's notes, the state also used its right to punish to protect trust in the Bank's paper money against corruption and counterfeiting. Another feature of the state's power, its colonial authority, was later called into action to ensure the stability of the Financial Revolution. Facing a situation of rapidly deteriorating public credit in 1710, the state dedicated all of the anticipated profits from its newly acquired monopoly on the slave trade to Spanish America in support of the national debt. Hence, in as much as the modern state was fundamentally based on authority and violence—the power to tax, fight, punish, and colonize—so too was the Financial Revolution.

Casualties of Credit also highlights the necessity of the state to influence public opinion. In order to bolster public credit the state patronized a number of writers who authored propaganda pamphlets that were then widely circulated in the public sphere. But like all other forms of power, the state's power to shape public opinion was contested. Having equal access to the public sphere, the opposition criticized, ridiculed, and questioned the party in power. Previously dictated by the interactions between the monarch and a small number of powerful financiers, public credit was now increasingly informed by public opinion, as the party in power sought, with every means possible, to convince the public of its stellar accomplishments and brilliant prospects. At the same time, the opposition tried to sink public credit in order to force a ministerial change. I maintain that as each party sought to shape and spin news in their favor, they devised their own respective political economies through which they hoped to shape economic literacy in ways that supported their cause.

As this book seeks to improve our understanding of the dynamic relationship between the fiscal-military state, the public sphere, and public credit, it also uncovers the critical role of violence and enslavement in the Financial Revolution.[14] First, by exploring the relationship between the 1694 founding of the Bank of England and the 1696 Great Recoinage, I argue that the death penalty was perceived as an essential protection of credit.[15] Second, by studying the architecture of the South Sea Company, I show how the Tory propaganda machine promoted an imaginary of the Atlantic slave trade as an inexhaustible source of profits. This highly selective imaginary was instrumental to the restoration of public credit in 1711 and therefore the continuity of the Financial Revolution.

By conceiving of credit as a complex social, political, philosophical, and economic phenomenon, *Casualties of Credit* contributes to a rich and growing scholarly tradition spearheaded by historians and literary critics, sociologists and economists. While political economists from the Middle Ages to Karl Marx explicitly recognized the cultural, social, and political embeddedness of money, economists since Carl Menger and William Stanley Jevons have focused their efforts on crystallizing the most crucial qualities of money, often by analytically disassociating it from its larger context.[16] This pursuit culminated in 1965, when the Cambridge economist Frank Hahn established that money really has no place in modern general equilibrium economics.[17] In refusing to lose sight of money's inherently social, cultural, and political roles, I join a number of historians who think politically about economic matters.[18]

Before providing a brief chapter outline, I offer a few caveats about the subject matter, scope, and emphasis of this study. First, in offering a history of the intellectual foundation of the English Financial Revolution, this book places a great deal of importance on the power of ideas to transform history.[19] As J. G. A Pocock points out, credit "symbolized and made actual the power of opinion, passion, and fantasy in human affairs."[20] For example, the Hartlib Circle's (ca. 1640–1660) initial redefinition of money as a symbol of value rather than something valuable in itself opened up the possibility for a nonmetallic currency. The vibrant debates that ensued over the next few decades defined the pool of possible designs available for implementation. Even after the new financial infrastructure was in place, ideas, opinions, and imaginings continued to influence the theory and practice of both private and public credit. Indeed, ideas and theory preceded and dictated changes in socioeconomic structures. Just as historians Margaret Jacob and Joel Mokyr have respectively shown that science and practical knowledge were essential to the Industrial Revolution, I suggest similarly that ideas were constitutive of the Financial Revolution.[21] I note also, however, that the fact that credit was based on ideas, opinion, and imagination made it vulnerable in the eyes of some and therefore inappropriate to serve as the foundation for the economy and the state.

Second, I use the term Financial Revolution in a slightly different manner than most historians. While few scholars contest that England did indeed experience a Financial Revolution, they disagree as to what actually constituted its most revolutionary ingredient. While P. G. M. Dickson highlights the introduction of a long-term national debt backed by Parliament's authority to tax as the crucial feature of the Financial Revolution, D. W. Jones focuses instead on William III's success in raising short-term loans, and John Brewer singles out the state's much improved mechanisms for raising taxes.[22] On the other hand, Keith Horsefield stresses the issuance of a new currency, while Larry Neal insists that it was the formation of a liquid and transparent secondary market in securities that had the biggest impact.[23] Douglass North and Barry Weingast famously claim that the shift in power from the monarch to Parliament during the Glorious Revolution enabled, for the first time, the establishment of credible commitments and a firm respect for property rights; a claim that David Stasavage generally concurs with, although he assigns the credit for public credit more specifically to the rise of the Whig supremacy.[24]

Casualties of Credit argues instead that what mattered most to the Financial Revolution was the development of new ways of seeing and understanding money and credit – in short, the emergence of a new political economy. Once this new political economy caught on, it was just a matter of time before a new financial infrastructure was designed and implemented. While there were certainly political disagreements over what kind of credit mechanisms would be most advantageous, few people during the second half of the seventeenth century opposed banks and credit money altogether.[25] Since it took as much as a century to develop and popularize the conceptual framework vital to the implementation of a new financial system, I use the term *Financial Revolution* quite broadly to refer to the years between 1620 and 1720.[26] When the discourse on money and credit in 1622 is compared to that of 1711, it is clear that a radical transformation in the way credit was understood had taken place.[27]

Third, *Casualties of Credit* focuses almost exclusively on England, despite the fact that scholars have recently come to emphasize that to write the history of seventeenth- and eighteenth-century England it is essential to consider not only Scotland, Ireland, and Wales, but also to recognize England's position within a wider European and Atlantic context.[28] This book employs a more narrow focus for the simple reason that the Financial Revolution was first and foremost an economic, political, and social transformation centering on England, and more precisely London. While some forms of credit, such as bills of exchange, are best seen within a global frame, much of early modern credit was organized on a national or even more local level. Indeed, the very problem with sixteenth- and seventeenth-century credit was that it was too local, motivating political economists to search for ways to make credit circulate throughout the nation, or at least within and between its major cities. The debate about credit and the institutions that came to provide the foundation of the Financial Revolution were predominately framed by the nation and the nation-state. In fact, England was largely self-sufficient when it came to ideas about credit. While political economists sought inspiration from the Dutch on all matters commercial, their financial innovations were considered inadequate to answer England's needs and were thus rarely given serious consideration in the English debates.[29] More precisely, because the Dutch did not develop a national debt backed by the nation-state, did not enjoy a liquid secondary market in public debt instruments to complement its stock market, and, most importantly, did not issue a generally circulating credit currency, Dutch finance did not constitute a model that the English sought to emulate directly.[30]

Even though the story of the English Financial Revolution is here told within the national context, it should be noted that since credit is based on anticipations and imaginations, its value was often dictated by phenomena occurring in a temporally and geographically distant place.[31] The imaginary component of credit instruments circulating in the narrow confines of Exchange Alley facilitated connections between London and the far reaches of the Atlantic and Pacific worlds. As in the case of South Sea Company stocks trading hands in London, credit reached out in the world as far as the human imagination allowed. Similarly, credit also forged connections across social boundaries; the world of haute finance could be linked to the lowest echelon of the social hierarchy without there being any physical contact between gentlemen traders and the London riffraff. The Financial Revolution took place in a circumscribed geography, mostly among the middle and upper classes, but since the imagination had no intrinsic limits, it had the power to connect people throughout the world and across the social hierarchy.

I have structured this book in three thematic and chronological parts: (Part One) alchemy and credit (Chapters 1-2) covering 1620-1660, (Part Two) death penalty and credit (Chapters 3-4) covering 1660-1700, and (Part Three) slavery and credit (Chapters 5-6) covering 1700-1720. Chapter 1 explores how England's first school of political economy emerged in the 1620s in response to the stubborn scarcity of money problem. The lack of high-quality coin was blamed for the decade's severe slowdown in commerce, which resulted in widespread unemployment and poverty, as well as a fiscal crisis of the state. Gerard Malynes, Edward Misselden, and Thomas Mun, three prominent neo-Aristotelian political economists, offered a coherent set of principles about money and commerce in response to this crisis. Drawing heavily on Aristotelian notions, these thinkers insisted that money's primary responsibility was to facilitate justice and maintain balance and harmony in society. They argued that when there is enough money in circulation, money plays its proper role as a measure of value and medium of exchange. Society's finite wealth then flows to its appropriate place in the social hierarchy and the balance of power between different segments of society is properly maintained. When, on the contrary, there is an insufficient amount of money in circulation, money loses its capacity to perform its principal responsibilities, thus jeopardizing class hierarchy, the traditional moral order, and social stability. In such circumstances, agricultural, manufacturing, and commercial activities fail to reach full capacity, generating widespread unemployment and impoverishment, and a threat of social unrest. According to the neo-Aristotelian diagnosis, this is exactly what was happening to England in the 1620s. It was therefore necessary to replenish the money stock as soon as possible. Since the neo-Aristotelians were not optimistic about the prospects of a credit currency, their proposed solutions focused on finding ways to reverse the nation's trade balance. Even though they did not contribute directly to the formation of a new discourse on credit, their analyses are important to explore in a book about credit, since the neo-Aristotelian understanding of money was the norm that subsequent thinkers had to consider or transcend in order to make the case for credit money.

Chapter 2 explores the emergence of a radically different political economy during the Civil War (1642-1649). Taking advantage of the relative absence of political and religious authority, progressive social reformers could now more freely disseminate their often revolutionary proposals to an increasingly receptive audience. One of the most ambitious and influential reform groups congealed around the Prussian émigré, Samuel Hartlib. The Hartlib Circle advocated that fundamental social, political, and economic reform was possible if the latest alchemical knowledge about nature and matter was enlisted in a Baconian pursuit of human improvement. As part of their universal reform project, the Hartlibians developed a new political economy. This chapter records how Hartlibian political economy offered a radical reassessment of the role and nature of money. Instead of a device responsible for maintaining balance, harmony, and justice, money was, for the Hartlibian political economists, an instrument with the power to ignite industry and activate nature's, society's, and mankind's hidden and dormant resources. Additionally, since the Hartlibians believed that wealth was potentially infinite, they needed to find a way to expand the money stock proportionally to the ever-expanding world of goods. Their first attempt to achieve this aim, consonant with their overall intellectual grounding in alchemical thinking, was to launch an ambitious alchemical transmutation project. After exploring how their carefully conducted alchemical experiments failed to generate promising results, Chapter 2 focuses on how the Hartlibians shifted their attention to the development of proposals for a widely circulating credit currency. Since these proposals were clearly shaped by the content and spirit of alchemical and Baconian thinking, I argue that these intellectual currents were essential to the formation of the context within which the Financial Revolution eventually developed.

The Hartlibians' insistence that money does not have to consist of silver or gold opened up the possibility for paper notes—backed by a safe asset as security—to serve as money. The problem with this option was of course that people had to learn how to trust such a currency. As part of their efforts to generate trust, political economists employed models of probabilistic thinking developed in the realm of natural philosophy. Their application of these concepts, in turn, informed the ongoing philosophical discussion about trust. Chapter 3 begins with a study of John Locke's philosophical treatment of probability, one of the first of its kind, and continues by exploring the long list of credit money proposals developed with the aid of the new epistemology during the second half of the seventeenth century. Multiple writers offered diverse solutions, from imitations of the Bank of Amsterdam or the Italian merchant banks, to the launch of a nationwide Lombard bank, a version of the land bank scheme initially proposed by the Hartlibians, or a national bank issuing notes on the security of a fractional reserve of silver coin. The key challenge facing all of the architects of these schemes was to design a set of mechanisms that enabled people to comfortably place their trust in the continued exchangeability of the credit notes. Solid security, portability, legal negotiability, incorruptible management, and transparency were considered crucial for a credit currency to circulate widely. In addition, finding ways to prevent distrust caused by clipping, counterfeiting, and forgery preoccupied almost all contributors to the debate. Most commentators, in fact, argued that the liberal use of the death penalty was absolutely necessary to eliminate and deter those who challenged and undermined trust in money.

Chapter 4 describes the various measures implemented to restore trust in both coin and notes. Once the Bank of England was formed in 1694, the notion that the death penalty was necessary for the public to develop trust in money was put to the test. While forgery was made a capital offense soon after the first spurious Bank of England notes were detected, most of the focus was on the rapid increase in clipping of the nation's coin. As the average silver content of the coin fell to 50 percent of its official weight, a serious monetary crisis developed. Not only was the coin rapidly losing value, but since silver coin served as the security for the Bank of England notes, there was a growing fear that the entire monetary system was in danger, unless all coins were called in and restored to their former value. After exploring how contemporaries viewed the relationship between the Financial Revolution and the Great Recoinage, I argue that much of the responsibility for putting an end to the monetary crimes rested on the shoulders of the executioner. The core strategies used to protect England's coin and credit were thus to add new forms of currency manipulation to those already considered capital offences and to vigorously increase efforts to find, prosecute, and execute the perpetrators responsible for the erosion of trust in money. I consider Locke's prominent role in the debate about how to solve the currency crisis and describe how he and Charles Montagu convinced Sir Isaac Newton to leave Cambridge and come to London to take on the responsibility for finding and prosecuting monetary criminals as the Warden of the Mint.

The concluding Chapters 5 and 6 explore the financial crisis of 1710 and the ingenious innovation that Lord Treasurer Robert Harley implemented as a solution: the South Sea Company. While the Financial Revolution had enabled England to successfully wage war against the French without facing financial ruin, the limits of what the new financial configuration could handle were eventually reached. As bond prices fell, there was a growing concern with the stability of the entire financial system. The fact that the status of public credit was now determined by public opinion made the system appear all the more volatile. This also made public credit vulnerable to the ongoing conflict between Tories and Whigs, who were both using the public sphere to manipulate public credit for their own ends. Chapter 5 explores each party's propaganda campaigns and highlights how they sought to provide their followers with a particular economic literacy so that when they traded their stocks and bonds they would do so in ways that promoted the interest of the party.

After an intense year of scheming and propagandizing, employing prominent writers such as Abel Boyer, Jonathan Swift, and Daniel Defoe, Robert Harley launched his financial panacea in May of 1711. The South Sea Company was designed to clear financial markets of a set of deeply discounted, unsecured government bonds in the hope of reviving public credit. In order to make this debt-for-equity and private-for-public swap appealing to the bond holders, the government vouched to pay a yearly interest on the debt absorbed by the company and, most importantly, granted the company a monopoly on England's slave trade to Spanish America. Since the success of the South Sea Company would determine the status of public credit and thus the political future of Harley's ministry, as Chapter 6 reveals, the South Sea Company and its trade in African slaves became the subject of a vibrant debate. As the discourse on credit engaged with one of the most brutal and violent moments of early modern capitalism, the social imaginary of credit brought together the future and the present, the sphere of commerce and the realm of finance, the slave ship and the coffeehouse.

In the epilogue, I briefly discuss what happened to the discourse on money and credit after the South Sea Bubble burst. Given the perception that overconfidence in credit had led to recklessness, many commentators began calling for the abolishment of credit and a return to the safe world of neo-Aristotelianism. While the French largely followed this path, the English restored their new credit system remarkably quickly. Some prominent commentators, like the Irish philosopher George Berkeley, continued to promote the Hartlibian understanding of credit. Others, like the Scotsmen David Hume and Adam Smith, were much more ambivalent about the modern culture of credit. While they were philosophically open to credit money, they had serious concerns about its practical feasibility.

Casualties of Credit highlights a set of links between the development of credit and other important moments of early modern English culture. While these connections might be unexpected to the modern eye, they were integral to the seventeenth-century discourse on credit. Alchemy, natural philosophy, and epistemology were central to the debates surrounding the Financial Revolution. The Glorious Revolution, the origins of political parties, and the maturation of the public sphere were all essential to the discussion about the future of credit. The importance to the Financial Revolution of the death penalty, the enslavement of Africans, and the buildup of England's armed forces were also clearly recognized in the discourse on credit. Indeed, early modern political economists understood credit in an analytical matrix that explicitly recognized the casualties of credit, its potential indeterminacy, precariousness, and violence—its "Passions of Hope and Fear."

—I—

Alchemy and Credit

— 1 —

The Scarcity of Money Problem and the Birth of English Political Economy

Introduction

England emerged from the Elizabethan period with a sense of growing optimism and confidence about its future commercial and geopolitical prospects. The early Stuart monarchs ambitiously sought to modernize the state apparatus to more effectively administer domestic affairs and to play a more prominent role in the European power game. England's rapidly expanding merchant corps were also poised to boost their power by capitalizing on commercial opportunities opening up at home and around the globe. Yet, at the same time, the nation was besieged by a threatening social instability rooted in rural dislocation, perennial unemployment, and widespread poverty.[1]

Tudor officials had instituted various poverty-reducing measures to alleviate the mounting social friction. When these measures failed, seventeenth-century social reformers and public authorities increasingly looked towards commerce to solve England's social problems. If commercial activity expanded, people would find employment, thus shrinking the size of the threatening surplus population. The problem with this solution, however, was that commerce could only expand so much, as it was severely hampered by the inadequate quantity of quality money in circulation. Even with the elaborate system of private credit developed during the sixteenth century, there was simply not enough money in circulation to mediate all transactions.

While modern economic theory does not recognize the possibility of a scarcity of money, seventeenth-century thinkers were consumed by this problem.[2] Historian Joyce Appleby points out, "Theoretically, there is never an insufficient supply of currency. Actually [seventeenth-century] England suffered chronically from coin shortages."[3] The scarcity of money problem resulted from a growing divergence between the expanding amount of economic activity and the relatively fixed quantity of coin in circulation. A century of rapid population growth, combined with a steady expansion of market activity and monetization of taxes, generated a demand for precious metals that the inflow of bullion from abroad was unable to satisfy. As Rice Vaughan, author of an important economic tract in the 1630s, put it, "the greatest part of the Commerce of the Kingdom, and almost all the Inland Commerce, is made in *Silver,* the want whereof doth greatly prejudice the same."[4]

Historians have estimated that during the second half of the sixteenth century demand for money grew by approximately 500 percent, while the supply of coins expanded by only 63 percent.[5] Even though the inflow of gold and silver increased more rapidly after 1600, the divergence between the demand for and supply of coin persisted. Further contributing to the problem was the fact that the quality of the coin in circulation was generally poor. Unsophisticated minting techniques and years of clipping and hammering had led to a situation where high-quality coin was often taken out of circulation to be kept as a store of value or to be used in international exchanges. Full payment with good money was therefore rare in seventeenth-century England, significantly retarding the circulation of goods throughout society.

To cope with the lack and poor quality of silver coin, English merchants, shopkeepers, farmers, manufacturers, and consumers had developed an elaborate credit network based on personal agreements. One historian estimates that by the first half of the seventeenth century, the ratio of personal credit to coin transactions was 11:1.[6] This statistic is further substantiated by Craig Muldrew's study of how people in sixteenth-century King's Lynn, a then-vibrant coastal town north of Cambridge, used a wide array of credit contracts, such as sales credit, bills, bonds, and pledges, to mediate their commercial interactions. The successful employment of such instruments generated an extensive web of credit that connected people throughout the community, sometimes as creditors and sometimes as debtors. More recently, the historian Chris Briggs has argued that it was not only merchants and city-dwellers who engaged in credit transactions, but that the bulk of the English rural population was trading goods on credit as early as the

Middle Ages.[7] However long this system of private credit had been in existence, seventeenth-century observers made it abundantly clear that this kind of credit was woefully inadequate to alleviate the present scarcity of money problem. The primary hindrance was that personal credit instruments did not circulate, at least not widely enough to make a real difference. For commerce, agriculture, and manufacturing to flourish, new sources of money had to be discovered.

By the 1620s, the English state was desperate for an increase in the circulation of money. An increasingly ambitious state needed more money to strengthen its geopolitical clout and to launch the various improvement projects considered essential for the stability, prosperity, and competitiveness of the nation. By improving the liquidity of the economy, not only would there be more transactions to tax, it would also be easier to collect the taxes. To expand the money stock, the state considered, and in some instances pursued, debasements, minting of copper farthings, changing of mint ratios, altering of exchange rates, implementing trade restrictions, and sponsoring campaigns to gain direct access to American mines. Indeed, increasing the money stock was so important that one of the period's most prominent political economists, the merchant Gerard Malynes (d. 1641), proclaimed that "since Moneys have obtained the title of the Sinowes of war, and the life of Commerce: I hope that the accumulating thereof may properly be called The Præheminent Study of Princes."[8]

The scarcity of money problem became particularly acute in the early 1620s, at which point the government launched a number of commissions to investigate the causes of and possible solutions to the money shortage. A number of participants published their analyses and proposed solutions. Most famously, the three merchants Malynes, Edward Misselden (d. 1654), and Thomas Mun (d. 1641) offered a series of systematic analytical treatments of money and trade that laid the foundation for England's first coherent doctrine of political economy. Considering that they developed their analyses within a traditional Aristotelian framework, Malynes, Misselden, and Mun can be grouped together as *Neo-Aristotelian Political Economists*.[9] Although they disagreed on both the causes and preferred solutions, their analyses coalesced around a shared body of ideas and assumptions about the economy and the world in general. Drawing directly on an Aristotelian worldview, they argued that money's primary responsibility was to facilitate justice and maintain balance and harmony in society. When money plays its proper role as a measure of value and medium of exchange, society's finite wealth flows to its appropriate place in the social hierarchy and the balance of power between different segments of society is maintained. When the proper balance is reached it is possible to uphold the social and moral order of the body politic. On the other hand, when there is an insufficient amount of money in circulation, money loses its capacity to perform its principal responsibilities, thus jeopardizing the social hierarchy and the traditional moral order. In such circumstances, agricultural, manufacturing, and commercial activities fall short of their potential, forcing all social classes to conduct their affairs with fewer resources. To avoid such a downturn, it was therefore necessary to replenish the money stock as soon as possible.

Contrary to Adam Smith's famous caricature and dismissal of the neo-Aristotelians, I suggest that they offered a theoretical program that was both coherent and sound when understood within their own worldview.[10] Smith declared that the neo-Aristotelians subscribed to the ideas that:

> To grow rich is to get money; and wealth and money, in short, are in common language, considered as in every respect synonymous. A rich country, in the same manner as a rich man, is supposed to be a country abounding in money; and to heap up gold and silver in any country is supposed to be the readiest way to enrich it.[11]

I will argue, instead, that for the neo-Aristotelians the ideal moral economy and social order could only be maintained if money were allowed to play its proper role as a mediation device. For money to perform this role there had to be a sufficient level of money in circulation, which, as mentioned earlier, was far from the case during the 1620s. This led Malynes, Misselden, and Mun to focus on reversing the nation's balance of payments. Their aim was not to pursue an unlimited amount of money, but rather to restore the appropriate quantity. Nor did they promote a favorable balance of trade as an end in itself, but viewed it as a means to restore the functionality of money and thus the stability of society.

In believing that only precious metals could serve as money, the neo-Aristotelians were limited to policies capable of expanding the quantity of coin in circulation. They thus paid scant attention to credit as a possible solution to the money shortage. Yet despite the fact that the neo-Aristotelians offered few insights as to the formation of credit per se, their thinking nevertheless serves as the essential backdrop to this book in that subsequent credit proponents were forced to reckon with their philosophy of money.

This chapter begins with an overview of England's economic troubles and the social problems contemporaries blamed on the shortage of money. I then briefly explore the various strategies employed by Elizabethan and early Stuart authorities to alleviate the scarcity of money problem, focusing on attempts to attract silver through international trade and the employment of various credit instruments. The remainder of the chapter explores how the neo-Aristotelian political economists tried to come to terms with the commercial crisis of the 1620s and in so doing developed England's first school of political economy, which importantly though indirectly shaped the debate about the future of credit and its social, political, and economic casualties.

The Anatomy of England's Economic Troubles

Commercial innovations had occurred with great regularity in England throughout the medieval and early modern period, enabling English people to enjoy a comparatively sophisticated commercial society as early as the fourteenth century. Subsequent generations experienced an increasingly inclusive, integrated, and complex commercial world.[12] More and more people produced for the market, obtained part or all of their sustenance through the market, and worked in the market itself, as merchants, retailers, shopkeepers, and peddlers. As European and world commerce continued to develop in the sixteenth century, boundaries between regions broke down further and markets mediated transactions between producers and consumers over ever-greater distances. Commercial expansion increasingly generated opportunities for the entrepreneurial classes, facilitated a more sophisticated world of consumption for those who could afford it, and imposed new standards of productivity and efficiency in both agriculture and manufacturing. No longer dictated exclusively by customary patterns, production and consumption were now increasingly influenced by and subject to cosmopolitan trends and changes.

After the demographic slump following the cataclysmic Black Death came to an end, England's population once again started growing. The population expanded from 2.4 million in 1520 to 3.6 million in 1581 and 5.2 million in 1651. This not only contributed to an increase in prices and rents, which by itself stimulated certain parts of the economy, but also generated commercial opportunities for sectors feeding, clothing, and housing the expanding population.[13] The increasing number of city-dwellers throughout Europe provided further economic stimulus to these sectors.[14] These patterns profoundly changed rural life in England. Many landowners turned their possessions into sheep pasture to supply the rapidly expanding woolen industries in England and the Low Countries. The landowners' response to the new economic opportunities caused a great deal of social dislocation. Since sheep pasturage only required minimum oversight, farmers were no longer needed on the land to the same extent as before and were thus forced to seek employment and residence elsewhere. Sir Thomas More, in his *Utopia*, famously decried this process of enclosure as tantamount to sheep devouring men.[15]

Regions in which most of the land remained arable also experienced significant turbulence as a result of the reorientation towards commercial production. Since food production in England had not kept pace with the growth and urbanization of the population and the price of wool had begun to level off by the early seventeenth century, producing food for the market was increasingly profitable.[16] Taking advantage of these market opportunities required more intense labor, new crops, new technologies, and more innovative techniques. Improvements like these, in turn, necessitated more capital and larger production units, leading to the enclosure of common fields and the commons and the reclamation of fens and marshland. This structural transformation, which gathered momentum in the seventeenth century, put the remaining manorial system under significant pressure.[17] The fact that the newly improved agrarian techniques required less labor input meant that additional people were now added to the ranks of the propertyless and unemployed. Although the agricultural revolution would eventually make England a net-exporter of grain by the second half of the seventeenth century, the necessary restructuring of production methods and property relations substantially destabilized Tudor and early Stuart society.

The threatening consequences of the rural displacement were epitomized by the ever-presence of the dreaded vagrant figure, an annoyance at best and at worst, a danger to the entire social order. The natural philosopher and politician Sir Francis Bacon complained that these masterless tramps constituted "a burthen, an eye-sore and a scandal, and a seed of peril and tumult."[18] This often itinerate class of paupers was disdained by polite society for many reasons. Most importantly, urban pickpockets and highwaymen constituted a threat to people's property. Public authorities were also concerned with the social disorderliness of the vagrants. Drunkenness, debauchery, petty violence, and bastardy were thought to be common traits of the dangerous poor. In addition to jeopardizing property and public order, vagrants were increasingly unpopular because of the costs—mandated by the Poor Laws—they imposed on the parishes they visited.

People's fear of the paupers, vagrants, vagabonds, and idle rogues, combined with a growing anxiety that the lower sorts might rise up in armed revolt, generated a widespread hostility towards the poor and unemployed.[19] This culture of fear was particularly palpable in London, where the vagrancy problem was seemingly omnipresent—the result of an estimated twelvefold increase in the population of vagrants between 1560 and 1625.[20] Since England had no effective police force, nor a standing army until the Civil War, government officials and social reformers were forced to experiment with a number of different solutions to the employment problem. An elaborate Poor Law system, intended to relieve the plight of the deserving poor and provide sturdy beggars with work, had been put in place by Tudor authorities.[21] This public benevolence was coupled with the infamous system of punishments—the so-called Bloody Codes. Unemployed beggars, vagrants, and idlers were criminalized and punished by branding, whipping, or periods of personal servitude. The house of correction constituted another attempt by Elizabethan authorities to remove beggars and vagrants from the streets and to instruct them in proper discipline and work habits.[22] Although sometimes momentarily successful in defusing social tension, neither punishments nor alms seemed capable of providing the desired panacea.

Instead, as England moved into the seventeenth century, attention shifted to the promotion of commerce as the preferred solution to the employment problem. If economic activity could be expanded throughout the nation, more people would find work and the vast surplus population would begin to shrink, gradually eliminating the source of most social problems.[23] Inasmuch as commerce constituted the preferred solution, much of the responsibility for its increase fell on the textile industry. This sector, woolens in particular, was by far the largest industrial employer in England and its biggest exporter. As such, the textile sector had the unique capacity to directly reduce unemployment, as well as bring in money from abroad that could stimulate the rest of the economy.[24] This led Misselden to call the woolen industry "the gold of our Ophir, the milk and honey of our Canaan, the Indies of England."[25]

Initially, putting-out entrepreneurs had hired relatively cheap rural workers for part-time work, but as the demand for English broadcloth— so-called Old Draperies—expanded, more people were employed on a permanent basis in towns and manufacturing districts. The type of labor created in the textile industry was particularly appealing to social and moral reformers. The discipline and regularity of the work provided an antidote to the often lax and intermittent agricultural labor practices. Removed from their former autonomy, displaced small landholders and laborers employed in manufacturing were now forced to work every day of the year, at a pace set by the tireless quest for profits. Social and moral reformers and manufacturers pursued every conceivable measure to promote the woolen trade. This meant creating the ideal domestic conditions—legal and economic—for production and distribution, as well as ensuring that the international terms of trade were favorable to English cloth exports. Indeed, most of the early seventeenth-century debates about the balance of trade were centered on the exportation of woolens to the Low Countries and Northern Europe, England's primary trading partners.[26]

The primary problem, however, with relying on commerce to solve the employment problem was that England was unable to expand its commerce rapidly enough. The main limiting factor, according to contemporaries, was the perpetual scarcity of money. This shortage not only hurt the textile industry, but it curtailed economic activity throughout the realm. The scarcity of money also hampered the Crown's quest to centralize and modernize the state. Although part of the problem was attributed to the state's inadequate institutional mechanisms for raising revenues, there was a clear sense that the fiscal crisis of the state might be eased if the quantity of money in circulation could be increased. More money would not only generate more economic activity, which would expand the tax base, but the increased liquidity would make it easier to collect taxes. If England were to keep up with the other European nation-states and thus have any chance at playing a prominent role in the European power game, England had to find a way to attract a larger money stock.

While Elizabeth had been relatively parsimonious, the same is generally not said about James I.[27] In order to keep up with the ongoing arms race unleashed by the military revolution, James spent lavishly.[28] In the spirit of the courtier and explorer Sir Walter Raleigh's famous proclamation that "Whosoever commands the sea commands the trade; whosoever commands the trade of the world commands the riches of the world, and consequently the world itself," James focused his spending on building up a modern navy.[29] He also spent generously on ceremonial occasions, dress, coaches, and buildings to broadcast his power, consonant with the nascent absolutist trend. The extension of the Poor Laws to contain social problems and unrest also added significantly to the state's expenditures. James's total spending amounted to a staggering half a million pounds per year, an amount that he was unable to raise from the population. By 1608, he had thus accumulated a significant debt, which the new Lord Treasurer Robert Cecil was forced to confront with a royal revenue and financial system that was "antique, inadequate, and ambiguous."[30]

The early Stuart monarchs pursued a number of different revenue sources, most of which yielded only modest results. Since Parliament was in control of taxation, by ruling for long stretches of time without consulting Parliament, James and Charles had to rely primarily on their own royal assets for new revenues. In addition to the sale of mineral rights and titles, Crown lands were sold to generate onetime revenue boosts. James also resumed the highly unpopular practice of selling monopoly rights.[31] For James these sales were not only a convenient way to raise money without consulting Parliament, but an expedient means by which he could assert his royal command over society. Perceiving himself as the supreme authority over his subjects, with a God-given responsibility to ensure the common weal, he believed it was only appropriate that he extended his authority over the economy.[32] As a result, monopoly grants became more numerous than ever, creating a material culture in which people were forced to satisfy nearly all of their consumption needs by purchasing monopoly-produced or traded goods.[33]

The early Stuarts also raised money through the nation's antiquated tax system inherited from Elizabeth. This system included taxes on land

and movable goods, the fifteenth, tenth, and subsidies. These assessments of wealth had become notoriously inaccurate, severely limiting the tax base. To access more liquid wealth, many of the taxes that had traditionally been paid in kind—ship money, wardships, coat and conduct money, and purveyance—were transformed, at least partly, into cash payments. However, because of Parliament's unwillingness to adjust rates in accordance with the new fiscal demands and the higher price levels, combined with the fact that it was difficult to collect taxes in money when there was a shortage of coin, the tax system did not yield substantial revenues for the state. England consequently remained a comparatively lightly taxed nation, with Charles enjoying only a tenth of the revenues raised by his French counterpart, Louis XIII.[34] Robert Cecil made a proposal to Parliament in 1609 to rationalize the tax system by eliminating a number of feudal remnants in return for a fixed annual royal revenue.[35] But, because of the stalemate between James and Parliament, this proposal—the Great Contract—failed.

Inadequate Solutions

International Trade

England's lack of mines and its disastrous experiments with debasements during the reign of Henry VIII made international trade the most viable source of additional money. Not only was it effectively the only way to bring in more specie, but trade had the added benefit of directly adding to the state's coffers through the customs payment.[36] The most advantageous trades included those that promoted a favorable balance of trade with other European nations, exports of goods to the Americas that could be exchanged for precious metals, and imports of exotic colonial goods that could be profitably reexported. To establish these kinds of trades, however, England needed to boost its naval power and assert itself around the globe. They thus needed money to bring in more money. Although England was emerging as an economically and militarily stronger and more self-confident power, its worldwide commercial presence paled in comparison to that of Portugal, Spain, and the Dutch Republic. Until the fall of Antwerp in the 1570s, much of the London trade was conducted by foreign merchants—Hanseatic, Low Country, and Italian. To lift England out of its relative commercial backwardness, the Crown embarked on a more aggressive commercial policy. Emboldened by Sir Francis Drake's circumnavigation of the globe in 1577 and the Elizabethan privateers' occasionally grandiose profits, the English sought to build on the success of its seadogs. To this end, the state chartered a number of merchant companies and encouraged the pooling of private resources through the chartering of joint-stock companies, including the Eastland Company (1579), Levant Company (1581), East India Company (1600), Virginia Company (1606), and Newfoundland Company (1610).[37] These commercial-political bodies challenged Iberian control over the oceans and sought to establish a permanent colonial presence.

The English colonial quest was motivated by a diverse set of goals—gaining political prestige and respect, defending English Protestantism from Popish enslavement, finding an outlet for England's troublesome surplus population, and establishing new markets for English textiles among them.[38] Yet, in many instances, finding a solution to the scarcity of money problem was a key motivating factor. Innumerable state-sponsored colonial ventures were launched with the specific intent of finding silver and gold, none more famous in England than Sir Walter Raleigh's venture down the Oronoco River in pursuit of El Dorado. Indeed, explorers and merchants engaged in the early colonization process were often more interested in looking for precious metals than in undertaking the laborious process of clearing, planting, and harvesting new lands.[39] Indeed, a number of important early English colonization attempts—Roanoke, Guiana, and Jamestown—failed or came close to failing because of the settlers' preference of searching for gold over planting tobacco.[40]

Eventually, however, the colonization efforts began to bear fruit. Despite encountering numerous problems during its first decade, most notably resistance from the native population and hostility from the Spanish, tobacco exports from Virginia soon skyrocketed, from sixty thousand pounds in 1620 to fifteen million pounds by the 1660s. Not only did the tobacco boom generate great profits to planters and merchants, Virginia's plantation economy also absorbed a significant number of vagrants and petty criminals sent from England.[41] Cash crops and job opportunities were soon realized on Barbados as well.[42] While the colony was initially settled to produce tobacco and cotton, it emerged as a significant economic resource in the late 1640s, when it began producing commercial levels of sugar. An increasing importation of tobacco and sugar not only satisfied a rapidly growing domestic demand for exotic stimulants, but the reexport trade also attracted much needed specie from elsewhere in Europe.

English merchants also attracted gold and silver directly by selling cloth, in particular the new lighter woolens—or New Draperies—in Seville and Cadiz, and illicitly in New Spain. Once England captured Jamaica in 1655, the levels of contraband trade drastically increased. Yet, despite the fact that trade to the West now started to net some much needed silver, it was counteracted by the outflow of silver to settle the trade to the East Indies. Because of the insatiable demand for Eastern luxuries—mostly textiles and spices—and the lack of reciprocal interest in European exports, the money stock in Europe was continuously depleted by this trade.[43] Hoping to convince authorities to support the trade, representatives of the East India Company argued forcefully that even though silver needed to be exported to obtain textiles from India, the enormous reexport potential would eventually ensure a net inflow of silver to England.

In the end, despite high hopes that global commerce might solve England's problems, the scarcity of money problem continued to plague England throughout the first half of the seventeenth century. In fact, the breakdown of England's international trade in the 1620s was the main reason behind the period's most desperate economic crisis.

Credit

Despite attracting much needed specie from abroad, England was still suffering from a palpable lack of an adequate currency. Historian C. G. A. Clay describes how "demand was affected as it became increasingly difficult for most people either to buy or to sell, and for employers to pay wages."[44] Part of the problem, Clay notes, was that there "was no alternative to the silver coinage for everyday purposes: certainly the lack of confidence in any possible issuing authority made paper money inconceivable."[45] While it is certainly true that there was no widely circulating credit currency in England at the time, credit was far from absent. As historians Eric Kerridge and Craig Muldrew have respectively shown, merchants, tradesmen, shopkeepers, farmers, and laborers developed a number of credit mechanisms to alleviate the effects of the scarcity of money.[46] Indeed, Muldrew claims that credit was so pervasive in early modern England that "almost all buying and selling involved credit of one form or another."[47] Although silver coins were still necessary for certain transactions, such as exchanges between strangers, for payments of rent, tithes, and taxes, as well as for certain overseas exchanges, nearly all people engaged in credit transactions on a regular, if not daily, basis.[48] In fact, Muldrew concludes that the deficiency of coin was so extreme that credit came to serve as the primary means of exchange, while the coinage system operated as the unit of account and final means of settlement.[49]

England, like the rest of Europe, employed a wide array of credit instruments by the seventeenth century.[50] Internationally, the long-serving bill of exchange facilitated both commercial transactions and loans, while personal sales credit was the most ubiquitous form of domestic credit.[51] Sales credit was sometimes recorded in ledgers, but more often based on verbal agreements. When such agreements were struck, either a penny was handed over as a sign of the obligation or an oath was sworn in the presence of a third party. Commercial loans were also commonly extended using bills obligatory, bonds, and pledges. These credit mechanisms generally involved larger sums of money and were more formal than sales credit, in that they were written in a proper legal format by lawyers or scriveners and then signed and sealed by two witnesses. Bills obligatory were essentially promissory notes, in which people borrowed a sum of money on their reputation and committed to paying principal and interest at a certain future date. The sealed bond was a loan agreement with the added security of a penalty clause, which was often substantially greater than the principal and accrued interest. Given that the defaulting borrower would normally not be able to pay the penalty, borrowers were generally asked to designate a third party responsible in the event of a default.[52] An even more secure loan was the pledge, which required the borrower to designate personal property, most often jewelry, plate, or land (mortgage), which would be transferred to the lender in the event of a default.[53]

The aforementioned credit instruments provided much needed relief to the overburdened coinage system. Yet the London money market was still comparatively primitive, with bills, bonds, and pledges enjoying only limited negotiability. Legal obstacles, awkward denominations, and the lack of an impersonal exchange prevented the development of a widely circulating credit currency.[54] If credit were to provide the solution to the scarcity of money problem, an altogether different type of credit instrument had to be developed.

The state also tried to improve its financial flexibility through the use of credit, but experienced only limited success. The amount of loanable funds available in the London money market was too small to satisfy the government's needs and the term structure offered was too short to be of much use to the state.[55] The primary reason, however, why lenders were hesitant to extend loans to monarchs was the latter's immunity from legal redress. The Tudors had therefore been forced to rely on loans from foreign merchants in Antwerp, at least up until the 1570s, after which the English Crown essentially stopped borrowing from abroad, focusing instead on the imposition of forced loans at home. While Elizabeth used this source of revenue sparingly, for example, to finance the war on the Spanish Armada, James and Charles exploited it more extensively. When the early Stuarts managed to borrow in the domestic money market, it was often through some measure of coercion or promises of favors. They targeted noblemen, well-connected individuals at court, and prominent government officials, such as Sir William Russell, Treasurer of the Navy, and Lionel Cranfield, Lord High Treasurer.[56] The state also called on wealthy individuals, like the merchant-financier and unofficial paymaster Philip Burlamachi, syndicates of prominent merchants, and corporations, like the Merchant Adventurers and the Corporation of London, to extend large sums of money. Yet, despite the best efforts of the early Stuarts to raise money, they often fell short of their aspirations. And, even when they did manage to raise some money through credit, the instruments issued were not transferable and thus did not serve to augment the currency.[57] Despite England's relative success in attracting silver from abroad and developing credit mechanisms, the nation was still searching for a way to once and for all put an end to the troubles caused by its inadequate currency.

The Crisis of the 1620s and the Rise of Neo-Aristotelian Political Economy

The outbreak of the Thirty Years' War (1618–1648) and the renewed hostility between the Dutch and the Spanish in 1621 occurred at an especially inopportune moment for England, deepening an already devastating commercial downturn. Not yet recovered from the disastrous Cockayne experiment, the textile industry suffered particularly hard.[58] In 1614, Sir William Cockayne, a prominent merchant and influential royal advisor, had managed to convince the government that England wasted crucial commercial opportunities by exporting mostly unfinished cloth. The prospects of improving the nation's balance of trade by exporting greater volumes of dyed and dressed cloth led the government to put a ban on exports of unfinished cloth and to transfer the export monopoly from the Merchant Adventures to Cockayne's group. But failure to master the technological complexities of dyeing and finishing, combined with the Dutch retaliatory ban on imports of English finished cloth, sent England's most important industrial sector into a tailspin. While the project was quickly brought to a halt in 1616, the damage had already been done. Continental competitors had seized on the opportunity to supply cloth to the textile manufacturers in the Low Countries, revealing that England's competitive strengths in the production of broadcloth had come to an end. The loss of exports quickly generated massive unemployment in the textile-producing areas, which combined with a series of bad harvests and resulting high grain prices during the first few years of the 1620s produced a severe crisis. Faced with the threat of widespread rioting by starving textile workers, social reformers and government officials recognized the need to act.

As the severity of the commercial depression deepened, Parliament and the Privy Council formed a series of investigative committees to explore the causes and possible solutions to the crisis. While a consensus emerged that the scarcity of money was responsible for the crisis, opinions diverged on the reasons for the coin shortage, exemplified by the twenty-one separate explanations provided by a 1621 parliamentary committee.[59] The Privy Council then ordered the formation of a standing trade commission, which drew on the expertise of gentry, merchants, manufacturers, custom officials, drapers, and dyers. While the views expressed before this commission were not recorded for posterity, the debate survived in pamphlets and books published by some of the participating expert witnesses. Most famously, Malynes, Misselden, and Mun engaged in a heated, sometimes highly personal, debate about the causes and solutions to the scarcity of money problem. In addressing these issues, they put forth the first truly systematic analytical treatments on the role, responsibility, and dynamics of money in society

and, as such, established the basic parameters for how future generations conceived and theorized money.

The neo-Aristotelians agreed that emancipating the nation from the
doldrums of the present depression required a solution to the scarcity
of money problem. While they disagreed on the proper solution, they
agreed that money played an absolutely central role in the body politic.
For Malynes, money was the "Soule" that "did infuse life to Traffique";
for Mun, money "hath given life unto so many worthy trades"; while
Misselden claimed that "money is the vitall spirit of trade."[60] Money's
life-engendering qualities were thus essential for commerce to flourish,
for society to realize its potential wealth, and for the surplus population
to find employment.

Merchant, assay master, and former trade commissioner to Antwerp,
Gerard Malynes argued that the shortage of silver coin was caused by
the speculative activities of merchants and bankers in the international
market for bills of exchange.[61] In clearing and settling these bills, foreign coins were systematically overvalued, leading to an outflow of silver
from England. The solution proposed by Malynes was to reestablish the
Royal Exchange and make it responsible for publishing proper exchange
rates and overseeing that all settlements of bills between merchants were
properly conducted. This would ensure that only weight and fineness dictated the exchange rate between coin from different nations and that the
profit incentive to trade or export currencies was therefore eliminated.[62]
Moreover, in addition to stemming the outflow of silver, the reestablish-
ment of the official valuation would restore the "the soueraignty and dig-
nity of the Prince"—a critical concern of the early Stuarts.[63]

Edward Misselden, a prominent member of the Merchant Adventurers and later the East India Company, summarily dismissed Malynes's
explanation.[64] He argued that the outflow of coin was caused, first and
foremost, by a negative trade balance, and secondarily by an underval-
uation of silver vis-à-vis gold at the English mint.[65] The trade deficit was
generated by rising demand for foreign luxuries, excessive competition
between English merchants, inability to sell English goods in India,
pirates operating in the Mediterranean, and Dutch fishing encroaching on English waters.[66] The solutions Misselden advocated involved
the state passing additional sumptuary laws to curtail imports, chartering restricted companies to better organize trade, upholding the Statutes of Employment to prevent foreign merchants from exporting coin,

increasing the price of silver at the mint, and putting an end to all alms given to beggars in order to force them to seek employment.[67]

The prominent East India Company merchant Thomas Mun also contributed to the debate, primarily on his friend Misselden's side.[68] Mun agreed that the shortage of money was created by a negative trade balance, but argued that the trade balance had been caused by a combination of factors posited by Malynes and Misselden. He primarily blamed excessive imports and a lack of domestic industry for the unfavorable trade balance, but he also acknowledged that monarchical manipulations of the coinage on the continent and currency speculations by merchants and bankers added to the problem.[69] While Mun believed that the bimetallic mint ratio and the exchange rate contributed to the outflow of silver from England, he argued that the flow of goods had a greater influence on the flow of money than vice versa.[70] The key, therefore, to resolving the crisis was to reverse the trade balance. Contrary to Misselden, however, Mun did not support efforts to curtail the outflow of silver by legal means, but instead suggested that the English had to "bridle" their affection for foreign luxuries and "stirre up our minds, and diligence, to helpe the naturall Comodities of this Realme by industrie, and encrease of Arts."[71] Instead of interfering with the international flow of goods and money, Mun wanted to reform morals and manners. By allowing silver and gold to circulate freely, Mun argued that trade would flourish and thus benefit "the Kings revenues, our Merchants, Mariners, Shipping, Arts, Lands, Riches."[72] In general, Mun maintained, nations that allow precious metals to circulate freely across their borders rarely suffered from a scarcity of money.[73]

While differing in important ways, Malynes, Misselden, and Mun fundamentally shared the same Aristotelian understanding of money as a balancing device and an instrument of justice. Before exploring the monetary thinking of the neo-Aristotelians further, it is necessary to briefly investigate Aristotle's conceptualization of money. For Aristotle, money's capacity to mediate interactions within a complex social hierarchy was its primary purpose. While it, Aristotle recognized, created some obstacles to social cohesion and peace, hierarchy was essential to the common good as it ensured that all the necessary functions of society were fulfilled. "It is no new or recent discovery of political philosophers," he argued, "that the state ought to be divided into classes, and that the warriors should be separated from the farmers."[74] The challenge of managing a hierarchical society was thus to ensure that a society of unequals was able to live in peace and that each segment was able to fulfill its natural purpose.

Money, for Aristotle, was first and foremost an instrument of justice, binding people together and thus keeping society intact. He argued that "in associations that are based on mutual exchange, the just in this sense constitutes the bond that holds the association together."[75] However, since all people are not equal, nor are the products they produce of equal value, upholding the social bond is not a trivial matter. Recognizing the challenge of binding a diverse set of people together, Aristotle noted that "a community is not formed by two physicians, but by a physician and a farmer, and, in general, by people who are different and unequal. But they must be equalized; and hence everything that enters into an exchange must somehow be comparable."[76]

It was for the purpose of commensurability that money was invented. By establishing "reciprocity in terms of a proportion and not in terms of exact equality," money specifies how many shoes are equal to a house. In so doing, money not only mediates the relationship between the house and the shoe, but more importantly facilitates an orderly interaction between the builder and the shoemaker. As such, money maintains a stable hierarchy, as well as ensures that each segment receives the appropriate amount of value required for the fulfillment of their social roles. Inequality is thus managed in a manner that enables people to uphold justice and proper sociability.[77] Aristotle concluded, "Thus, money acts like a measure: it makes goods commensurable and equalizes them. For just as there is no community without exchange, there is no exchange without equality and no equality without commensurability."[78]

The neo-Aristotelians' understanding of money never strayed far from Aristotle's original articulation. They viewed society as consisting of a finite level of wealth and a static class composition, held together by an intricate balance between its component parts, all of which had their own proper place, rights, duties, and purposes. People's roles in life were strictly circumscribed by the social norms that governed their profession or class. This meant, according to historian Keith Thomas, that not only was each person ascribed "distinctive qualities, virtues, skills, and aspirations" in accordance with their social position, but "an individual's ends in life were predetermined by his or her position in the overall scheme."[79] All people in the social hierarchy had to have access to a certain unequal proportion of the social wealth, appropriate to their continued performance of their social role. Indeed, it was money's primary responsibility to ensure that wealth was appropriately distributed. Capturing the prevailing mode of thought, historian Andrea Finkelstein stresses, "A society in balance was harmonious (a term virtually synonymous with justice), but justice was always simultaneously *commutative* and *distributive*." She continues, "And both meanings revolved around a conception of equity that meant giving to each his *particular* due, making sure each social organ had the privileges and resources it needed to fulfill its duty to the whole."[80]

But what exactly were the qualities that allowed money to infuse life into trade? If additional money stimulated commerce, was more money not always advantageous? Malynes clarified these questions by explaining that money "infuse[s] life to Traffique by meanes of *Equality* and *Equity*, preventing advantage betweene Buyers and Sellers."[81] Hence, the primary purpose of money was to mediate exchanges between qualitatively different goods, to maintain balance between the different spheres of the body politic, and to establish justice throughout society. But for money to be able to play this part, there had to be a sufficient amount of it in circulation. This is the reason why it was so important that the present shortage was eliminated. Only then would money once again be able to mediate the interaction between the king, landowners, manufacturers, merchants, peasants, and laborers in a way that would ensure stability and prosperity. Only then would each segment of the social hierarchy be able to maintain their proper place and perform their allotted social roles. Malynes described how the inhabitants of England had historically lived "by the natruall richesse of the land they were borne unto, or by the artificiall riches they were bred unto, . . . every man using and enjoying his own, & nothing but his own."[82] He continued by specifying that:

> Clergy men and magistrates did live by their revenues and pensions, Noblemen and Gentlemen of their lands, husbandmen by their farmes, merchants and citizens by their trade, artificers by their craft and handy-worke; all of them making a perfect consent and harmony of the governement of a common-wealth.[83]

But when money no longer preserved proportionality, a poisonous social mobility was unleashed. Malynes noted that recently some people had been amassing greater amounts of wealth, reaching beyond their station, while others were failing to maintain riches commensurable to their rank, thus destabilizing the hierarchy and the reciprocity between social classes.[84] Although movements by small degrees up and down the social scale were common in early modern England, as Keith Thomas points out, Malynes and many others still preferred "a customary allocation of resources and rewards which would ensure the perpetuation of the group as a whole."[85] Misselden also complained about the imbalances enabling the social mobility, noting that "now a dayes most men live above their callings, and promiscuously step forth *Vice versa,* into one anothers *Rankes.* The *Countrey mans* Eie is upon the *Citizen:* the *Citizen* upon the *Gentleman:* the *Gentleman* upon the *Nobleman.*"[86]

Malynes blamed the prevailing flux in the social hierarchy on the widespread violation of money's integrity. As Aristotle pointed out, money's only proper role was to serve as a measuring and mediating device, making any other pursuit that "makes a gain out of money itself, and not from the natural object of it," unnatural and therefore a violation of money's principal function.[87] Malynes argued that unprincipled currency speculators had undermined money's role as measure of value by "making of money a merchandize."[88] Not only did this practice compromise money's proper functions, but it also contributed to the outflow of silver and thus the scarcity of money problem. By reducing the quantity of money in circulation, the speculators introduced "inequality betweene the estimation of the natruall riches and the artificiall riches," and thus undermined money's capacity to make goods commensurable. As such, they "overthroweth the harmonie of the strings of the good government of a common-wealth, by too much enriching some, and by oppressing and impoverishing others, bringing the instrument out of tune: when as every member of the same should live contented in his vocation and execute his charge according to his profession."[89] As such, the speculators have made "men generally unable to live by the naturall or artificiall riches whereunto they were borne or bred," jeopardizing the prosperity of the landed elites, the profitability of the merchants, as well as the employment and livelihood of the poor.[90]

Writers in the 1620s also followed in Aristotle's footsteps regarding the proper art of wealth-getting. For Aristotle, the art of householding was based on the recognition that the material world is finite and that each object exists for a particular purpose.[91] Whether on the level of the family or the state, householding therefore implied providing "such things necessary to life, and useful for the community of the family or state."[92] Similar to Aristotle, Mun claimed that the proper end of the "riches or sufficiency of every Kingdome, State, or Common-wealth, consisteth in the possession of those things, which are needful for a civill life."[93] While England had enough natural resources to remain self-sufficient, its people had to be industrious for England to "flourish and grow rich . . . [and] furnish and adorne us with the Treasuree and those necessarie wares, which forreing Nations do afford."[94] The nation should therefore encourage industry among its multitudes, "for where the people are many, and the arts good, there the traffique must be great, and the Countrey rich."[95] Even though both the need and potential for wealth were considered finite, the neo-Aristotelians encouraged industriousness to ensure that the greatest possible level of wealth was actualized and that the bulk of the population was employed in productive pursuits. If society's wealth fell short of its potential, all segments of society would suffer. Hence, for Mun, a well-functioning society produces at full potential and distributes the wealth in a way that allows each segment to reproduce itself.

When money is allowed to operate freely, it regulates the relationship between different people, professions, and ranks. More precisely, money enables people to regulate their own interactions, establishing societal harmony without the need for too heavy-handed an intervention of the state. However, occasionally the maintenance of the proper moral order required the state to intervene. Here Malynes, Misselden, and Mun differed in their suggestions. Malynes, a staunch defender of the idea of absolutism, believed that the economy was integrated in a larger social and political order, all of which was subject to, at least theoretically, the monarch's supreme authority. Consequently, when something was amiss, it was the monarch's responsibility to address it. In the present circumstances, when the currency speculators were threatening to destabilize the social hierarchy and public order, the monarch—or "the father of this great household"—had the God-given right and responsibility to restore order.[96] He suggested, therefore, that the time had come for James to reassert his authority by reestablishing the Royal Exchange to oversee the settlement of bills and to put an end to the merchants' profit-motivated abuse of the unit of account. In essence, he argued that "*Princes* and *Governours*" should be reinstalled "at the *sterne* of the course of *Trade* and *Commerce*."[97] By asserting his authority over the monetary mechanism, James could ensure that money, in turn, disseminated his royal power throughout the realm. As such, the absolute authority of gold and silver in the economy corresponded to the absolutist political authority the early Stuarts so desperately coveted.[98]

Misselden also prescribed an active role for the state, including the reinstatement of sumptuary laws to quell the importation of luxury goods, the chartering of additional merchant companies to make sure that English merchants did not compete against each other in remote areas of the world, and a more dedicated policing of the ban on foreign merchants exporting precious metals from England. The state intervention Misselden was adamantly opposed to were the Poor Laws. He suggested that they undermined discipline and the development of a proper work ethic and that, as long as England was able to restore its stock of money, poverty relief would no longer be necessary.

Mun, on the other hand, believed that the monetary mechanism would operate more smoothly if it were given autonomy from the state. In fact, he believed that it was neither desirable nor possible for the state or any other body to gain operative control over money and commerce. Only when no one had command over money was it possible for it to serve as an incorruptible measure of value and thus provide its disinterested service to society. Although he viewed the commercial realm as largely operating according to its own set of rules, with prices, exchange rates, and interest rates dictated by merchants, he nevertheless advocated for the state to implement laws supporting the commercial system to ensure its prosperity and stability.[99] In particular, he was favorably inclined towards policies that promoted industriousness and innovation, thus minimizing the extent to which people spend "time in Idleness and Pleasure."[100]

Considering that the neo-Aristotelians were not guilty of confusing wealth and money and thus did not advocate an unlimited accumulation of silver, the question remains: by how much should the money stock be expanded? The ideal quantity of money, Malynes argued, was such that there was always "a certaine equalitie," or proportionality, between the amount of commodities and the quantity of money.[101] "Plenty of Money," he noted, just like plenty of "Bloud in the bodie," meant to have an appropriate amount of money to nourish all parts of the body politic.[102] Just as the physical body needed a certain amount of blood, not too much and not too little, to function well, so did the body politic require a certain amount of money. As one of the neo-Aristotelians' predecessors, Bernard Davanzati (1529–1606), proclaimed:

> For as *Blood*, which is the Juice and Substance of Meat in the natural Body, does, by circulating out of the greater into the lesser Vessels, moisten all the Flesh, which drinks it up as parch'd Ground soaks Rain Water; so it nourishes and restores as much of it as was dri'd up and evaporated by the natural Heat: In like manner, Money, which we said before was the best Juice and Substance of the Earth, does, by circulating out of the richer Purses into the poorer, furnish all the nation, being laid out upon those things whereof there is a continual Consumption for the Necessities of Life . . . Hence, it may be easily conceiv'd that every *State* must have a quantity of *Money*, as every *Body* a quantity of *Blood* to circulate therein. But as the *Blood* stopping in the Head or the larger Vessels puts the *Body* naturally into a Consumption, Dropsy, or Apoplexy, &c. so should all the *Money* be only in a few Hands, as in those of the rich for Example, the *State* falls unavoidably into Convulsions, and other dangerous Distempers.[103]

The use of blood as a metaphor for money in the context of Galenic medicine underscores the claim that the neo-Aristotelian thinkers conceived of society as a finite body that functioned best when properly balanced. In the same sense that sickness in the human body was attributed to an imbalance in the humors so too was a breakdown in the social and political order.[104] In addition to the comparison to blood, money was also frequently likened to sinews. For example, when Malynes referred to money as the "Sinowes of war, and the life of Commerce," he was referring to money as providing merchants and the state with a flexible tissue connecting the various parts of the body politic.[105] In a similar sense that the body does not benefit from an unlimited amount of tendons, the neo-Aristotelian thinkers believed that there was an ideal size of the money stock.

A few years later, Rice Vaughan (d. 1672), a lawyer and political economist, heavily influenced by Malynes, Misselden, and Mun, articulated even more clearly the idea of an appropriate stock of money. Vaughan argued that there was a certain amount of money that was the "fittest for the Common-wealth," which meant that it was as possible to have "a too much as a too little."[106] However, like the rest of the writers of his generation, Vaughan did not seriously explore the scenario in which England was troubled by too much money. This was, of course, an irrelevant consideration at a moment when money was defined by its scarcity and the consequences of too much money had already been exhibited by Spain's sixteenth-century experience. In 1640, one of Malynes's disciples, Sir Ralph Maddison (1574-1656), an improving landlord and investor in coal mines, discussed the importance of maintaining an appropriate amount of money, or what he called a "convenient stock of money."[107] Convenient, for him, meant the level that was able to "maintaine the price, and to bear or maintaine our home Commerce."[108] If the money stock fell below this level, people would be unable to carry out their transactions, prices of all commodities and land would fall, impoverish all trades and handicrafts, and thus create conditions ripe for social unrest and rebellions.[109]

For the neo-Aristotelians, credit never figured as a feasible solution to the scarcity of money problem. Yet, they acknowledged that credit might partly be able to alleviate the shortage. Mun pointed out that coins were actually not essential for commerce. He argued that the historical record had shown that barter and credit might serve as adequate substitutes. For him, as for Malynes, the coinage was first and foremost a system of measurement required to facilitate commercial transactions.[110] Its role as medium of exchange could thus be easily assigned to a variety of credit instruments. All three thinkers agreed that the scarcity of money problem could be greatly ameliorated if, for example, bank money was introduced and the transferability of debt instruments, such as bills of exchange, pledges, and bonds, were improved.[111] Referring to the Italian banking practices prevalent since the Middle Ages, Mun pointed out that Genoese, Venetian, and Florentine merchants were able to transfer great sums of money between each other in writing, while "the Mass of Treasure which gave foundation to these credits is employed in Forraign Trade as a Merchandize."[112] While these banks did not issue a circulating currency, they nevertheless expanded the money stock by granting credit to its customers on the basis of a fractional reserve and by allowing them to write payment orders—an early form of checks. Malynes and Misselden, on the other hand, focused on the negotiability of credit instruments in the Low Countries and Germany, suggesting that they provide "an excellent meanes to supply mens wants in course of trade; and tendeth also to the enlarging thereof."[113] Malynes acknowledged that while negotiable debt instruments can produce the same "great matters" as "ready money," properly speaking they did not constitute money.[114] Nevertheless, considering that the commercial depression was so dire, people ought to recognize that "things which are indeede, and things which are not indeede, but taken to be indeed (as this is for payment of moneys) may produce all one effect."[115] Not only would an increased transferability of debts quicken trade in general, but the improved liquidity of the merchants would eliminate many unnecessary bankruptcies caused by a shortage of circulating coin.[116]

As Malynes lamented, the English legal system was not yet equipped to handle an increased negotiability of debt instruments. The fact that the law did not allow anyone but the initial creditor to sue the debtor prevented debt instruments from circulating and credit from easing England's troubles. Hence, while the neo-Aristotelians appreciated the contributions of existing private credit arrangements—praising loans as the cornerstone to the success of merchants and the employment of the poor—the limited potential of existing credit instruments to circulate widely kept them from exploring the idea of credit in a more systematic fashion.[117] Moreover, not only did their political economy not have a place for credit money, their theoretical framework did not acknowledge the feasibility of a currency based on trust.

Money, in practice, meant coined precious metals. The reason why money was valued and circulated was because its "internall value in substance" or "intrinsique value."[118] This meant that metallic coins operated as a special, more liquid, commodity in a sophisticated system of barter. Goods of equal value, whether coin, grain, or meat, exchanged for each other principally because they all embodied the same amount of value. Market exchange was thus always based on *par pro pari*—value for value—and money was the mechanism that allowed for commensurability between qualitatively different commodities. The fact that money had to be comprised of precious metals meant that there was no other way to expand the money stock than to attract silver and gold from abroad. This led the neo-Aristotelian political economists to advocate policies that made it appear, at least to Adam Smith, that they were confused as to the relationship between money and wealth. In reality, I argue, they were trying to engineer an inflow of precious metals to facilitate the rebalancing of the body politic and thus restore order at a moment when England's prosperity and stability were greatly threatened.

As the scarcity of money problem continued to trouble England in subsequent decades, the ideas of England's first political economists survived almost intact to influence later debates.[119] Although commercial conditions improved by the mid-1620s, an outbreak of the plague in 1625 set off another commercial slump. Unwilling to suffer through another prolonged depression, government officials prepared to expand the money stock by debasing the currency.[120] Charles might very well have commenced his reign with a radical alteration of the coin had it not been for the powerful opposition spearheaded by the prominent Parliamentarian and royal advisor, Sir Robert Cotton (1571–1631). Although Cotton acknowledged the possibility that the king might generate some temporary advantages by tampering with the coin, he argued that the only way to consistently attract more money was to maintain a favorable balance of trade. Moreover, Cotton argued that a monarchial manipulation of the currency signaled that something was fundamentally wrong in the nation and that the monarch was incapable of restoring order. In fact, there can be "no surer Symptom of a Consumption in State, than the Corruption in Money." Indeed, the greatness of a kingdom is "best expressed in the measure and purity of their monies."[121]

Charles continued to wrestle with the scarcity of money problem. On the eve of the Civil War, the versatile writer Henry Peacham (1578-1644) noted that "the want of Money, which like an Epidemicall disease, hath over-run the whole Land," now threatened to sap the nation's commercial vitality.[122] While he believed that the slowdown in commerce and the trade deficit were the primary culprits, the practice of melting coin into plate during moments of political and commercial uncertainty had further retarded the circulation of money and goods. Paraphrasing Sir Francis Bacon's famous adage, Peacham pointed out, "Money so heaped up in Chests, and odde Corners is like unto dung, which while it lieth opon an heap doth no good, but dispersed and cast a broad, maketh fields fruitfull."[123]

Peacham, Maddison, and Sir Thomas Roe (1581–1644), among others, continued to debate the causes of the money shortage during the lead-up to the Civil War, but few innovative positions were staked out.[124] Some followed Malynes and blamed the problem on the absence of an authority setting proper exchange rates, while others argued, in the spirit of Misselden and Mun, that the money market should be left alone and all efforts should instead be focused on the establishment of a favorable trade balance. The general discontentedness with Charles I's personal rule (1629–1640), characterized by a series of fiscal exactions that alienated merchants and gentry alike, seemed to have galvanized these writers around the idea that direct monarchical authority over the monetary mechanism was no longer desirable.

Conclusion

Soon it would become clear that only the introduction of a widely circulating credit currency had the capacity to put an end to England's scarcity of money problem. The nation's first school of economic thought, however, did not foresee this possibility and consequently did not contribute directly to the intellectual foundations of the credit system that eventually emerged. While the neo-Aristotelian thinkers acknowledged the importance of various private credit instruments, Malynes, Misselden, and Mun did not view credit as a viable alternative to a metallic currency because of these instruments' limited negotiability. Nor did their theoretical framework allow for a nonmetallic currency based on trust. Instead they argued that the only way to replenish the money stock to the level necessary for money to fulfill its Aristotelian purpose and to mediate exchanges and thus maintain justice and balance in the body politic was to attract more money from abroad. This, it turned out, proved difficult, forcing people and the state to continue operating with a lack of money. The obvious need for an alternate way to expand the money stock soon gave rise to a number of proposals for a generally circulating credit currency. The conceptualization of the credit currency that would eventually revolutionize England's—and soon thereafter the world's—monetary and financial infrastructure was grounded in a fundamental *rethinking* of the neo-Aristotelian philosophy of money. In the next chapter, I will explore the intellectual context within which the Financial Revolution emerged and argue that the new thinking on money was made possible by the adoption of a series of conceptual innovations in natural philosophy by political economists.

— 2 —

The Alchemical Foundations of Credit

Introduction

The scarcity of money problem continued to plague England throughout the Civil War and the interregnum. The failure of neo-Aristotelian political economy to provide a solution to England's troubles motivated a number of suggestions for how to expand the money stock. Some of the most creative and influential proposals were articulated by members of the Hartlib Circle, the period's premier scientific and social reform group. Taking advantage of the relative void in political and religious authority during the Civil War, the Hartlibians articulated a radically new political economy that embraced the period's optimistic and progressive Zeitgeist. Contrary to the neo-Aristotelian emphasis on restoring hierarchy, order, and balance, the Hartlibians were convinced that infinite progress was possible through the continuous pursuit of knowledge, innovation, and industry. Central to this new progressive mentalité were the Baconian and alchemical ideas that mankind can assert control over nature and that nature's inherent development can be accelerated by human intervention. Armed with the proper knowledge it was considered possible for mankind to transmute nature, matter, and even people for utilitarian ends. By promoting innovations in agriculture, horticulture, mining, and manufacturing, and by initiating broadly based educational campaigns, the Hartlibians launched a process of improvement that they hoped would generate an ever-growing prosperity and an eventual solution to England's political, social, and economic problems.

In making human progress central to social life, the Hartlibians insisted that all people can contribute to and benefit from the pursuit of knowledge. They reconceived of the poor as a productive resource, allowed for the class composition to evolve as part of the improvement process, and insisted that history was an open-ended process with progress as its sole telos. Hence, contrary to the neo-Aristotelians' preoccupation with restoring the traditional order, the Hartlib Circle envisioned a future of constant change and improvement. Instead of striving to recreate the future in the image of the past, the Hartlibians insisted that people now be understood as participating in the creation of their own historical reality, in a natural and social topology that shared its lack of fixed limits with that of the universe, which concurrently was being reconceived as an indefinite or even infinite space.[1] As the historian Reinhart Koselleck emphasizes, in the traditional view the "guaranteed futurity of the past effected the closure and bounding of the sphere of action available to the state." But, with the new improvement mentality, "Progress opened up a future that transcended the hitherto predictable, natural space of time and experience, and thence—propelled by its own dynamic—provoked new, transnatural long-term prognoses."[2]

Money played a central role in this infinite improvement process. The Hartlibians believed that by facilitating circulation and engendering productive endeavors, money had the capacity to activate hidden or dormant resources in nature and mankind. Money thus partnered with knowledge and industry as the key ingredients in the infinite expansion of nature and society. Moreover, as the world of goods expanded continuously the money stock had to be able to grow proportionally in order to circulate all the new commodities. Given that wealth was potentially infinite, Hartlibians had to find a method whereby they could add to the money stock indefinitely. Expanding the money stock was therefore no longer about solving a temporary scarcity of money, but rather about the introduction of a monetary mechanism that could facilitate change and growth, *ad infinitum.*

Since their entire worldview was deeply informed by alchemical thinking, it comes as no surprise that the Hartlibians' first attempt to expand the money stock was through alchemical transmutation. If only they could figure out the exact recipe for the magic tincture or convince one of the many allegedly successful adepts to share their secret, the Hartlib Circle would be able to finally grant mankind the power to control and thus to expand the money stock at will. The Hartlibians made many attempts, but their transmutation projects failed. Yet, this failure did not put an end to alchemy's influence on the history of money. In this chapter, I argue that the alchemical and Baconian worldview that inspired the Hartlibians' universal reform and infinite improvement project not only motivated their transmutation project, but also provided the intellectual foundation for their next monetary innovation: a generally circulating credit currency. The fact that England's first proposals for a widely circulating credit currency were *de facto* conceived within a Baconian and alchemical worldview suggests that the Scientific Revolution played a significant part in the development of the Financial Revolution—an unexpected link that historians have hitherto not properly acknowledged.[3]

A number of scholars have emphasized that for seventeenth-century alchemical thinkers the spiritual, philosophical, and economic motives behind alchemical research were both intertwined and inseparable.[4] In the process of restoring alchemy to the center of seventeenth-century knowledge formation, spiritual quest, and social progress, many historians have chosen not to focus on the pursuit of alchemy as a moneymaking project. They have rightfully pointed out that most serious alchemical thinkers scorned those who sought the magic tincture for their own enrichment and indeed tried very hard to ensure that alchemical knowledge was kept secret and out of the hands of such luciferous profiteers.[5] I argue, however, that alchemy's moneymaking potential should not be ignored as it was not only capable of producing private profits, but it also had the capacity to stimulate commerce by increasing the quantity of coin in circulation. I will show that the Hartlibians' insistence on an expanding money stock to facilitate their alchemically-inspired spiritual, social, and economic improvement projects led them to first pursue metallic transmutation and then to promote the establishment of a credit currency.[6] As such, part of this chapter is designed to show that metallic transmutation played a legitimate role in the overall improvement project until it was replaced by credit money as the preferred mechanism to expand the money stock. However, the main point of this chapter is to show that alchemical thinking, combined with Baconianism, contributed importantly to the development of a new political economy within which the first proposals for a credit currency in England were formulated. Additionally, this chapter highlights the central role played by the Hartlib Circle in the development of English political economy, a group that according to the historian Richard Drayton has "not so far received adequate historical attention."[7]

I begin this chapter by exploring the relationship between alchemy and political economy during the first half of the seventeenth century. I discuss how a number of neo-Aristotelian political economists engaged with alchemical ideas, focusing mostly on Gerard Malynes, who was favorably inclined towards alchemy. Yet, because of the neo-Aristotelians' overall worldview and understanding of money, they did not embrace the progressive and dynamic features of the alchemical tradition. It was only after the alchemical understanding of nature was infused with the utilitarian ethos of Baconianism that alchemy began playing a prominent role in political economy. After exploring the basic philosophical foundations of the Hartlibians and the development of their revolutionary political economy, I offer an account of their ambitious transmutation efforts and their ultimate failure. The remainder of the chapter explores the Hartlibians' proposals for a widely circulating credit currency. Much of this discussion focuses on how the Hartlibians reconceived of the body politic and its constitutive parts. As infinite growth and improvement became the overall purpose of society, money's role was now to serve as an instrument of continuous growth. The Hartlibians also reconsidered the nature of money, insisting that it was not the intrinsic value of the coin that allowed money to circulate, but that paper notes partially backed by solid assets could also circulate as long as people were able to put their trust in them. These conceptual innovations contributed to a new understanding of money that made it seem feasible for all commerce—private and public—to be carried out with credit money. This breakthrough, I argue, was essential to the Financial Revolution.

Alchemy and Political Economy

Alchemy enjoyed a prominent position in seventeenth-century European intellectual and political life. Many natural philosophers accepted the alchemical understanding of nature as basically sound and the art of alchemy was actively pursued throughout Europe, in kitchens, laboratories, and courts.[8] In England, royal support of alchemists dates back at least to the reign of Edward IV, who was the dedicatee of one of the period's most famous alchemical tracts by George Ripley.[9] Edward VI and

Elizabeth I continued the support of alchemists, the latter by patron-izing John Dee, the well-known polymath who contributed greatly to the spread of alchemical knowledge in England.[10] Dee's successor, Sir Kenelm Digby, another prominent advocate of alchemical knowledge, gained the support of the two subsequent kings, James I and Charles I.[11] The heightened interest in alchemy during the Civil War continued after the Restoration.[12] Charles II built a clandestine alchemical lab under his bedroom with access provided only by a private staircase and James II engaged with alchemy as both a patron and practitioner.

The motives for pursuing and patronizing alchemy were many and diverse. In addition to the spiritual, medicinal, and industrial aims, the possibility of using alchemy to expand the money stock did not go unnoticed by social reformers interested in solving England's social and economic problems. If the philosopher's stone could be found, not only would the scarcity of money problem be solved once and for all, but the very foundation of the commercial system would change and mankind's control over the commercial world would vastly increase. One of many early seventeenth-century neo-Aristotelian political economists who paid close attention to alchemy was Gerard Malynes.[13] In his most far-reaching treatise on commerce, *Lex Mercatoria*, Malynes put forth an analysis of money that drew on various spheres of knowledge, including Galenic medicine, Copernican astronomy, and Paracelcian alchemy.

Malynes and his contemporaries had access to a vast body of accumu-lated alchemical knowledge. Arabic, pseudo-Aristotelian, Renaissance hermetic, and Neoplatonic philosophy supplied the basic foundation for the alchemical tradition, with figures like Pico della Mirandola, Gior-dano Bruno, Cornelius Agrippa, Jan van Helmont, and Paracelsus play-ing particularly prominent roles.[14] Alchemists eclectically drew on a variety of sources to improve their knowledge, skills, and techniques.[15] Although there were multiple variants of alchemy, the basic alchemi-cal worldview saw the natural world as an organic creation. Nature and everything therein was alive and constantly growing, always incomplete but incessantly striving towards its ultimate nature—seeds maturing into trees, children realizing their potentiality as adults, and base metals striving to become gold.[16] Most alchemists subscribed to a complex cosmology within which all things social, natural, and cos-mological were hierarchically arranged.[17] Each being, from highest to lowest, occupied a fixed place in the hierarchy with a corresponding set of rights and responsibilities. In addition to the connections link-ing each component to that above and below in the hierarchy, there were also correspondences between the different parts of the ladder. As the historian of science John Henry points out, "there might be a cor-respondence between the seven planets and the seven metals; between the noblest men, kings and the noblest metal, gold; between the incon-stant moon and womankind."[18] He concludes that these correspon-dences promoted "the belief that knowledge about, or control of, one thing could be gleaned by study and manipulation of other things even though they might be as remote as a flower and a star."[19]

Influenced by Aristotle, seventeenth-century natural philosophers understood matter in the universe to be comprised of varying propor-tions of the four primary elements—fire, air, water, and earth. Minerals and metals were also comprised of the four elements, but their imme-diate constituents were two exhalations—earthly smoke and watery vapor. The combination of these vapors took place within the bowels of the earth, as a result of the heat and pressure and the celestial influence of the stars. The earthly smoke—philosophical sulphur—consisted of particles that were in the process of turning into fire, while the watery vapor—philosophical mercury—consisted of water in the process of turning into air.[20] As everything in nature had its corresponding coun-terpart in the cosmos, so too did philosophical sulphur and mercury. Sulphur represented the masculine, the sun, and the lion, while mer-cury represented the feminine, the moon, and the lioness. Whenever the perfect union between sulphur and mercury, man and woman, sun and moon, occurred, the most noble offspring—gold—appeared. If there were obstacles to the attainment of perfection, the combination of sulphur and mercury produced only a base metal. Since metals, like all other things in nature, strove for perfection, they would eventually overcome the obstacles and proceed according to their inherent telos and become precious.[21]

In the context of discussing the role of precious metals as the soul of commerce, Malynes offered his own summary of the basic composition of metals. He began his discussion by asserting some basic alchemical principles:

All Philosophers have determined that the sperme, or seed of all things, created of the foure Elements, doth in a secret manner lowre within the

two Elements of Water and Earth; and that Nature doth continually
worke to produce perfect things, but is hindered therein by accidentall
causes, which are the begetters of corruption and imperfection of all
things, whereby we have varieties of things which are delectable to the
spirit of man.[22]

Malynes further noted that all metals are "vegitable things" that:

have their beginning from Sulphur and mercury, *Tanquam ex patre &
matre;* which meeting and concurring together in the veines of the earth,
doe ingender through the heat and qualitie of the Climate by an assidu-
all concoction, according to the nature of the earth wherein they meet,
which produceth the diversitie of the mettalls of Gold, Silver, Copper,
Tin, Lead, and Yron, in their severall natures: and hereupon they have
assigned them under their distinct Planets.[23]

Malynes pointed out that the "Sunne and Moone, and the other Planets
and Starres [played an important role] in the generation of all things."[24]
He continued:

The exhalations of the earth being cold and drie, and the vapours of the
seas being cold and moist, according to their natures, ascending and
meeting in a due proportion and equalitie, and falling upon some hilly
or mountainous countrey, where the influence of Sunne and Moone have
a contiunall operation; are the cause of generation, or properly from it
is Sulphur and *Mercurie* engendered, penetrating into the earth where
there are veines of water, and there they congeale into Gold or Silver, or
into the Ores of Silver, Copper, and all other mettalls, participating or
holding always some little mixture of the best; or being in nature better
or worse according to the said accidental causes.[25]

Many seventeenth-century scientific thinkers influenced by the alchemical worldview believed that humans could intervene in nature's maturation process and speed up its natural progress towards perfection.[26]
Since all things consisted of the same basic elements, in theory any
physical matter could be transformed into another by altering the relative proportions of the primary elements. In practice, this required a
full understanding of the composition of matter and its specific relationship to the celestial sphere, as well as full expertise in laboratory
techniques. In pursuing this complicated and esoteric knowledge, the

adepts' ultimate aim was to obtain the philosopher's stone, which would enable them not only to reveal nature's deepest secrets and access universal medicines and eternal youth, but also to transform any matter into another, including base metals into gold. With the help of the elixir, magic tincture, or philosopher's stone the alchemists sought to harness the powers inherent in nature and to mimic nature's own processes in order to accelerate the pace of its inherent evolution.[27] Alchemists who concentrated their efforts on the transmutation of metals sought to hasten the combination and birth of living metals in the artificial womb of the furnace and to speed up the ripening of base metals into gold. They paid careful attention to the proper proportion between philosophical sulphur and mercury, the appropriate heat of the furnace, and the most favorable alignment of the celestial sphere. Some alchemists even held that it was necessary for the adept to develop an appropriate spiritual rapport with the materials used in the transmutation. Hence, alchemists had to possess both technical and experimental proficiency, as well as a spiritual understanding and purity, in order to be able to enter into the nature–universe nexus and expedite its natural transformations.[28]

Malynes shared the seventeenth-century optimism about the alchemist's capacity to aid nature in obtaining its final perfect form. By removing the accidental obstacles, he wrote, "Art (being Natures Ape by imitation) hath endevoured to performe that wherein Nature was hindered."[29] However, these operations, he continued, "cannot bee done without projection of the Elixar or Quintescense upon mettalls. Hence proceedeth the studie of all the Philosophers to make their miraculous Stone, which (I confesse) is very pleasant, and full of expectation."[30]

Malynes then provided an account of a German physician, of whom he had "been informed by a friend," who successfully carried out a series of transmutations and became a very wealthy man, owning more than "one hundreth houses in that Citie before hee died."[31] He described how his friend had tried to replicate the German adept's transmutation. In accordance with the received wisdom that the sun is "166 times bigger than the whole Globe," he used 166 vials with different combinations of metals and minerals, and carefully exposed them to the right angle of the sun.[32] While Malynes had expressed some skepticism, his friend was fully convinced that he would succeed. He recalled, "Many were the questions between him and me, but hee was confident that there was the Elixar."[33] Unfortunately, the results were never known because the friend died before the seven years required for the development of the philosopher's stone had come to an end. Despite not witnessing a successful transmutation in person, Malynes remained convinced of alchemy's promise. In fact, he believed, "The charge to make it, was little or nothing to speake of, and might bee done in seven moneths, if a man did begin it upon the right day."[34] He thus seemed hopeful that the proper harnessing of the art of alchemy could be successful in creating precious metals.

In believing that alchemical transmutations were feasible, Malynes was in good company. Indeed, the seventeenth century abounded with reports of successful transmutations.[35] Taking stock of these reports in 1707, Thomas Heton noted that while "this Grand Secret in Nature, the *Physical Tincture* or *Elixir*, has been known but to few Persons in the World . . . [and they] have used it very sparingly to what they might have done; but *some* use they have made of it."[36] He listed the people known to have been in possession of the philosopher's stone, including Paracelsus, Van Helmont, Edward Kelley, John Dee, and George Ripley, many of whom, he claimed, carried out their own successful transmutations. Perhaps the most famous and well-respected account of a transmutation was that reported by Johann Schweitzer, generally known as Helvetius, physician to the Prince of Orange, in December of 1666.[37] He described how a stranger presented him with three walnut-size, brimstone-colored pebbles, which he claimed constituted the philosopher's stone. The stranger told Helvetius that the stones could not only be turned into twenty tons of gold, but could also yield multiple benefits to the human body and spirit. He performed an actual transmutation in front of Helvetius, who was fully convinced by the operation. Helvetius pleaded with the stranger to leave him with a sample, but he only managed to obtain a speck of the elixir, enough to carry out just a single experiment. Lacking the patience to wait until he had assembled a set of credible witnesses, Helvetius carried out the experiment on his own that very same evening.[38] He then brought the resulting gold to a local goldsmith and the general assay master of Holland, both of whom attested that this was the most excellent gold they had ever seen. The famous philosopher Baruch de Spinoza heard of this successful transmutation and sought to quell his skepticism by personally visiting Helvetius, a visit that allegedly left Spinoza fully convinced of the veracity of Helvetius's account.[39]

While alchemy was generally considered a legitimate scientific pursuit throughout the seventeenth century, there were many detractors who viewed metallic transmutation as an ethically questionable practice. They accused its practitioners of vulgarizing the noble search for nature's hidden secrets and the pursuit of legitimate applications in agriculture, mining, dyeing, and medicine. These critics complained that the lure of great profits provided by metallic transmutation attracted large numbers of fraudulent practitioners, thus compromising the public image of alchemy.[40]

Yet, despite the presence of these critical voices, there were plenty of well-respected natural philosophers who did not see any ethical or practical problems with metallic transmutation, believing that it was just one of the many ways in which alchemy could contribute to the improvement of the world. Malynes's discussion reveals that alchemical thinking figured favorably in the discourse on political economy from its very inception. His *Lex Mercatoria* remained a popular and influential text, with at least four editions published during the remainder of the century (1629, 1636, 1656, and 1686). Excerpts from his writings on the alchemical understanding of metals were also republished by Samuel Hartlib in *Chymical, Medicinal, and Chyrurgical Addresses* (1655). Yet, it should be noted that Malynes's favorable views on alchemy coexisted with those of political economists who viewed alchemy either as an irrelevant impossibility or a dangerous threat to the functionality of the monetary system. Henry Peacham, one of the neo-Aristotelian political economists encountered in Chapter 1, categorized those searching for the philosopher's stone as projectors motivated by little else than vanity and simple self-enrichment. He compared the search for the philosopher's stone to that for the Adamantine Alphabet and life on the moon, calling them "sundry kinds of useless wilde-fire, Waterworks, Extractions, Destillations, and the like."[41] For Peacham, the only likely outcome of such spurious experimentations was failure and personal impoverishment.

Other political economists expressed the concern that alchemy might undermine the capacity of money to serve as a dependable and incorruptible measure of value. Sir Robert Cotton, for example, argued in 1626 that by patronizing alchemists, English monarchs, in particular Henry VI, had further contributed to the corruption of the purity and stability of silver required for money to accurately express the wealth of the kingdom. Alchemy thus contributed to the "Monster that had so long devoured . . . the Variation of the Standard."[42] Rice Vaughan, another neo-Aristotelian discussed in Chapter 1, also launched an attack on alchemy. To Vaughan, money was primarily useful as a measure of all things and as a universal access point to all commodities. As such, he compared it to the alchemical notion of *Materia Prima*, "because, though it serves actually to no use almost, it serves potentially to all uses."[43] However, when considering the actual pursuit of alchemical transmutation, Vaughan was entirely dismissive. He called the alchemists "foster Fathers" of the counterfeiters, in that they undermined the community's confidence in the monetary standard.[44] As such, alchemy only caused confusion, and confusion could only lead to a worsening of the scarcity of money problem.[45] Hence, even if the alchemists had to date only managed to show "that it is harder to destroy Gold than to make it," they still constituted a dangerous threat to the basic role of money in society.[46]

The Rise of Hartlibian Political Economy

The role of alchemy in political economy changed radically once alchemical knowledge was coupled with the new progressive spirit and the scientific methods promoted by Sir Francis Bacon (1561–1626). A group of scholars, natural philosophers, and social improvers gathered around the Prussian émigré Samuel Hartlib in the 1640s and launched an ambitious alchemical- and Baconian-informed project for the improvement of nature, society, and mankind. Infused with the optimism characteristic of the political climate and inspired by millenarian ideas of an impending final age of Christian civilization, the Hartlibians believed that mankind was on the verge of experiencing a new age of prosperity.[47] While the nature of the final judgment was a matter of theological speculation, the Spiritual Brotherhood—as the historian Charles Webster famously called them—focused on the penultimate stage, when God's Kingdom on Earth would finally arrive and mankind's knowledge and command of nature lost during the Fall would be restored.[48] But because this imminent utopia would not materialize by itself, mankind had to unlock nature's secrets to fully enjoy God's gifts. Alchemy, they believed, offered the source code; Bacon offered the proper method.

Samuel Hartlib (ca. 1600–1662) settled in England in 1628 and soon began collaborating with two of the leading figures in European Protestantism: the promoter of religious unity John Dury (1596–1682) and the champion of universal education Jan Amos Comenius (1592–1670). Their aim was to disseminate and circulate knowledge among natural philosophers, inventors, and social reformers so that mankind could pool its resources and build on each other's breakthroughs, turning natural philosophy into a truly collaborative enterprise with universal reformation as its ultimate goal.[49] Hartlib envisioned that this network would become a permanent, well-funded institution, modeled on the Parisian Bureau d'Adresse, which the Paracelsian physician Théophraste Renaudot (1584–1653) had founded in the 1630s. Hartlib's Office of Address would, in Sir William Petty's words, be a place where "the wants and desires of all may bee made knowne unto all, where men may know what is already done in the businesse of Learning[,] What is already at present in doing, and what is intended to be done."[50]

Even if the Office of Address never fully materialized, Hartlib managed and organized the circulation of ideas between a set of distinguished thinkers and practitioners in what became known as the Invisible College.[51] This cosmopolitan group included future luminaries of the Royal Society such as Robert Boyle (1627–1691), Henry Oldenburg (ca. 1619–1677), and Sir William Petty (1623–1687), as well as other well-known natural philosophers and experimentalists, like Benjamin Worsley (1617–1677), Henry Robinson (d. 1673), Gabriel Plattes (ca. 1595-1644), and George Starkey (1628–1665). In tying together correspondents in London, Paris, Amsterdam, Hamburg, and Stockholm, Hartlib launched a pan-European project dedicated to universal human improvement rather than nationalistic empowerment and aggrandizement.[52] Indeed, the improvement project soon became trans-Atlantic as the future governor of Connecticut and future member of the Royal Society, John Winthrop Jr., implemented an alchemically inspired spiritual and social improvement project in New England.[53]

In addition to their Puritan convictions, the Hartlibians shared a dedication to a Baconian-inspired alchemical worldview.[54] They were all well versed in the latest alchemical knowledge and they were fully committed to the Baconian project of using knowledge to gain control over nature for utilitarian purposes. While Bacon's formalization of the empirical and experimental methods played an important role in the philosophical legitimization of the period's new methods of knowledge formation, historians of science now recognize that empirical and experimental methods were already well established in the vernacular scientific culture of Elizabethan England.[55] The historian Deborah Harkness, for example, shows that while scholars at Oxford and Cambridge were still busy debating "the authority of ancient texts," naturalists, medical practitioners, mathematicians, inventors, and alchemists in London were employing empirical and experimental methods in "constructing ingenious mechanical devices, testing new medicines, and studying the secrets of nature."[56] While Bacon no doubt must have been impressed by these activities, he found the organization of these pursuits inadequate to the task of human advancement. For Bacon, what was wrong with the prevailing approach to natural philosophy was captured by the unregulated empiricism of contemporary alchemists. In its place, he advocated for the establishment of Salomon's House, in which the systematic pursuit of all knowledge would be tightly organized. A college-like campus with libraries, orchards, gardens, laboratories, mines, observations towers, hospitals, and machines would be managed and controlled by a single well-educated person, who in turn answered only to the monarch.[57] If the pursuit of new knowledge were carried out in the proper surroundings under the appropriate leadership, the new scientific methods had the capacity of becoming nothing less than "the propagator of man's empire over the universe, the champion of liberty, the conqueror and subduer of necessities."[58]

In addition to his call for a more formal organization of the pursuit of new knowledge, Bacon's formulation of the overarching aims of natural philosophy also influenced the Hartlib Circle. Bacon infused natural philosophy with a new purpose and a new openness. Instead of the traditional mentality of focusing on knowledge of nature for its own sake or solely for spiritual purposes, Bacon insisted that knowledge had to be instrumentalized and made public.[59] Only then could natural philosophers and inventors "endow human life with new discoveries and resources" that would steadily improve the welfare and convenience of the entire population. Moreover, while traditional natural philosophy was geared towards knowledge that reaffirmed the traditional moral order, the Baconian-inspired scientific pursuits emphasized the capacity of mankind to evolve and improve.[60] Bacon was convinced that his scientific project had the capacity to generate sustained and far-reaching improvements, far greater and more substantial than any political reform. He argued that while "the benefits of discoveries may extend to the whole human race, political benefits only to specific areas; and political benefits last no more than a few years, the benefits of discoveries for virtually all time."[61]

In synthesizing the empirical and experimental methods with the conviction that humanly engineered improvements of nature were possible, Baconianism emphasized features that the alchemical tradition had embraced for centuries.[62] Together, merged into one project by the Hartlibians, the Baconian and alchemical vision of progress gained popularity during the Civil War and the interregnum, enabled by the relative void in political and religious authority. The Hartlibians emerged alongside a wide variety of dissident and radical groups that similarly exploited the laxity in discipline and promoted their own reform proposals and social experiments. These groups, which included the Diggers, Fifth Monarchists, Baptists, Quakers, Muggletonians, Seekers, and Ranters, accused the king of being autocratic, the court corrupt to the core, the Anglican Church insufficiently Protestant, and the landed elites devoid of sympathy for the landless poor.[63] The political and religious establishment could therefore not be trusted to improve the lives of the multitude, leaving Puritan reform groups to shoulder the responsibility for spiritual and social regeneration on their own. That said, the Hartlibians' vision of reform did not necessitate that the world was turned upside down. The existing authority structure and property relations could comfortably coexist with the reform projects they advocated. The application of new knowledge and diligent industry, rather than an extension of the voting charter or the restoration of the common fields, was the proper path to progress.[64]

The Hartlib Circle's general vision of improvement was first articulated by Gabriel Plattes, in his brief utopian tract *A Description of the Famous Kingdome of Macaria*.[65] Intended to be read in the tradition of More's *Utopia* and Bacon's *New Atlantis*, Plattes outlined an ideal kingdom in which peace, stability, and prosperity reigned supreme. In addition to skillfully managing Macaria's husbandry, fishing, trade, and new plantations, the state's most crucial role was to encourage the innovation of new ideas and techniques. He saw opportunities for improvement and growth everywhere; in the soil, vegetables, animal husbandry, metals, children, the poor, and so on. In particular, Plattes believed that recent breakthroughs in alchemical knowledge offered mankind a treasure trove of new practical ideas that could be profitably implemented. The new alchemical insights into the basic composition of matter were particularly promising, as they introduced the possibility of altering the physical world. In exploring the common denominators of all matter in his earlier work, *A Discovery of Infinite Treasure*, Plattes asked, "for what is corne, and fruits, the chiefest of all riches, but the fatnesse of the earth; *Iacobs* blessing elevated by the heate of the Sunne, and turned into vapour by the helpe of the Universall spirit of the world, then drawne together by the Adamantine virtue of the Seeds and Plants, and so congealed into the same forme?"[66] Even gold, he added, "that great Commander, is nothing else but the said fatnesse of the earth, elevated by the said universall spirit, and after depuration congealed into that splendorous Body."[67] By continuously advancing knowledge and systematically looking for practical applications, Plattes argued that the "transmutation of sublunary bodies" had the capacity to generate a radical increase in material wealth so that "the Kingdome may maintaine double the number of people, which it doth now, and in more plenty and prosperity, than now they enjoy."[68]

Plattes believed that alchemical knowledge held the key to making "this Countrey the Paradise of the World."[69] He focused on "the earths fatnesse," which constituted "the Treasure, and indeed the Fountaine of all Treasure and Riches in the World," in that it could "be transformed into what forme the Workman listeth."[70] This "fatnesse" is present in air, as well as in the water, as witnessed "by the infinite increase of Fishes: also in the earth by the infinite and inexhaustible treasure which it produceth continually."[71] However, since this fatness is simultaneously both terrestrial and celestial, it is crucial to find the exact right mix. If the celestial part is insufficient to "lift up the Terrestriall part, then no fruit thereof springeth [and] . . . if the Terrestriall part be not of force to coagulate and harden the other into profitable fruits, then all is turned into smoake."[72] Plattes therefore proclaimed that "all the skill consistheth in the right compounding of these two substances, which in many places, may be done with such facilitie as is wonderfull," even by ordinary people, thus turning simple "Plowmen into Philosophers."[73] By turning the search for knowledge into a collaborative project, the Hartlibians empowered everyone to contribute to and enjoy the fruits of new knowledge. Also crucial to the improvement process was that innovators found ways to disseminate their findings. "For he," Plattes suggested, "that found out the way of fertilizing of Land with Lime or Marle, (though by accident) did a more charitable deed in publishing thereof: then if he had built all the Hospitalls in *England:* for the one feedeth and cloatheth a few hungry and naked persons, the other enableth an infinite number both to feed and clothe themselves and others."[74]

Plattes suggested a number of ways in which alchemical knowledge might offer "good improvements of the earth."[75] His list included proposals for how to improve animal fodder, manure, irrigation, meadows, pasture, hay grounds, and fruit trees.[76] He argued that since something as simple as properly planting and grafting fruit trees had the capacity of enriching the nation by £2 million per year, nothing short of a revolutionary expansion of riches would follow if all of his proposals were implemented. Not only would his suggested improvements bring great affluence to the king, church, landowners, farmers, and tradesmen, but they would be particularly beneficial to the poor and destitute. He pointed out that "the working poore may be imployed in these new improvements, in such manner that they may live twice as well as they doe now; and yet notwithstanding, there may issue out of the benefit of their labours, sufficient maintenance for the impotent poore."[77]

In focusing on the infinite progress made possible by nature's abundance and human industry, Plattes and the Hartlibians mirrored the new cosmography's focus on the infinite and limitless character of the universe. They joined thinkers such as Giordano Bruno and Henry More in promoting the idea that the earth and humanity were no longer fenced in by a closed and fixed universe, but rather existed as part of an infinite space and infinite worlds. Whereas people of the fifteenth century, as the historian Arthur Lovejoy describes, "still lived in a walled universe as well as in walled towns," the new cosmography shattered the outer walls of the medieval universe and asserted "the actual infinity of the physical universe."[78] This revolutionary reconceptualization had profound effects on people's imagination. Mankind now existed in a universe without center, shape, or rational plan, "a formless aggregate of worlds scattered irregularly through unimaginable reaches of space."[79] This must have been bewildering for most, but the Hartlibians focused on how this worldview opened up new possibilities for mankind.[80] If God had infinite power and had created an infinite universe, they imagined everything therein must be potentially infinite. The challenge therefore was to unleash nature's, society's, and mankind's infinite creative powers, which was best done through a continuous advancement in knowledge, incessant industry, and—as will soon be shown—an ever-expanding stock of money.

Plattes's call for the realization of Bacon's Great Instauration was quickly answered by the rest of the Hartlib Circle, who contributed voluminously to the pool of improvement ideas. Apart from their interest in the basic nature of knowledge—methods, language, logic, and learning—they submitted proposals for how to improve the productivity of all sectors of the economy, including new insights about mining, drainage, distillation, gunpowder, navigational technology, fishing, and medicine.[81] Their primary focus, however, was to find ways to enhance the productivity of plant and animal husbandry. They circulated ideas about all aspects of agriculture, including seed refinement, soil enhancement, plowing, planting, fertilization, irrigation, harvesting, and preservation.[82] They also intervened in the debate about landownership. As advocates for the improvement of all available land, including fens, wastes, and forests, they argued that firm property rights were necessary.[83] Since England's land did not even yield "one fourth part of that profit either to private or publique, which they are respectively capable of," the pace of enclosures and land reclamation ought to be accelerated.[84]

Most of the Hartlib Circle members were also dedicated to finding ways to eradicate what was widely considered the greatest source of societal instability and discord—unemployment and poverty.[85] But contrary to many of their contemporaries, they were not satisfied with simply providing employment to the poor. Just as much as they believed that nature could be transmuted with the proper methods, they believed that it was possible to transmute the poor by changing their habits, manners, and character. By introducing them to the primary ingredients of personal improvement—industry, religion, and education—and thus "reforming their ungodly life," the Hartlibians hoped that the multitude might become more serviceable both to themselves and the Commonwealth.[86] Hartlib cooperated with, among others, John Dury and William Petty to formulate proposals for how to improve the quality and reach of education.[87] They discussed everything from reforming the methods of teaching languages and mathematics to the universal education of children, emphasizing practical skills that would serve them—and the nation—well once they reached working age.[88]

Hartlib, moreover, wanted workhouses to take on a more active role in removing beggars, vagabonds, and idlers—and their families—from the streets and reforming their conduct.[89] His motto was to *"Comfort, the honest helples Poor. Reform, the obstinate ungodly Poor."*[90] Workhouses should serve as colleges for the poor, in which they would be instructed in the Puritan gospel, taught rudimentary trade skills, and trained in the proper work ethic. In the event that the workhouses failed in reforming the idle poor, Hartlib proposed that recalcitrant people should be arrested and forcefully committed to houses of correction. Alternatively, they could be employed on fishing vessels in the North Sea or shipped off to the Atlantic colonies.[91] For the poor who were willing to work but experienced difficulties finding employment, a clearinghouse, in which prospective workers and employers could be matched up appropriately, was proposed.[92]

Hartlibian Political Economy and the Alchemical Solution to the Scarcity of Money Problem

As long as a proper spirit of industriousness and inventiveness prevailed, members of the Hartlib Circle were convinced that it was possible for mankind to transcend any problem it might face, for there are "infinite Meanes of Reliefe *and* Comfort, *for all sorts of Calamities to be found in* Nature, *and well ordered* Societies."[93] Yet, even if people marshaled all available knowledge to transform nature and society, the Hartlib Circle also realized that the feasibility of their improvement programs ultimately relied on a healthy circulation of goods and money. To quicken land improvement and to undertake all the various agricultural, horticultural, mining, and manufacturing projects, it was therefore necessary "that people may know where to be furnished with stock at low interest, and that a sufficient quantity of currant money be disperced amongst them."[94] Since the only reasons to hold money, according to the Hartlibians, were as a means of exchange and as a store of value between sale and purchase, an increase in the quantity of money would no doubt stimulate commerce. "The more there is of money in any Nation," they argued, "the quicker also must all those wayes be, wherein money is ordinarily imployed."[95]

By no longer thinking of the world as comprised of finite wealth and static hierarchies, within which money's role was to balance and maintain justice, the Hartlib Circle pioneered a different conceptualization of society and money's role therein. By shifting to a worldview in which the only constant was continuous change, growth, and improvement, the role and responsibility of each component part of nature and society consequently changed. The main challenge was therefore no longer to maintain an appropriate amount of money for the purposes of equilibration, but to expand the money stock in a way that could activate hidden and dormant natural and societal resources. Since the Hartlib Circle believed that resources were ultimately capable of generating an infinite amount of wealth, in order for money to be able to circulate this expanding world of goods, there could be no strict limit to how much the money stock could grow over time. Operating under the discipline of a metallic standard was therefore a major obstacle. To attract money, England "must part with so much of their best Staple-Commodities, as will purchase the Gold and Silver they want, from that great Merchant of Gold and Silver, the King of *Spain*."[96] In addition to the geopolitical drawback, an even greater hindrance to ending the scarcity of money problem by attracting specie from abroad was the fact that "there hath not bin (at least not yet) a sufficient quantity of either [gold or silver], to supply all Nations towards that increase of Trade, which a greater quantity of money (if it could be had) would produce."[97]

Despite the obstacles to attracting money from abroad, Henry Robinson and Benjamin Worsley, both central members of the Hartlib Circle, still believed the state should strive to maintain a trade surplus, alongside other possible strategies.[98] Robinson argued that if the proper measures were taken—such as lighter customs, lower interest rates, increased transferability of bills of exchange, creation of additional merchant corporations, and encouragement of new manufactures— England would be able to avail itself of the world's resources and thus multiply its wealth many times over.[99] He assured his readers that if all his proposals were followed, "I suppose it may appear there will not only bee suddenly found money enough to drive the present trade, but that wee are farther capable to become the wealthiest Nation in all the World."[100] Worsley also focused on global commerce as England's most important strategic interest and called for the implementation of a more aggressive trade policy. He believe that the best way to challenge the economic prosperity of the Dutch was to prevent them from importing strategic commodities for their shipping and naval industry, as well as obstruct the sale of Dutch manufactured goods abroad. This, he promised, would impoverish and weaken the Dutch and thus allow England to establish a greater colonial presence.[101] While Robinson and Worsley suggested a number of specific strategies to improve the balance of trade, they both recognized that their advice did not go beyond that which the neo-Aristotelians had advanced.

The Hartlibians' first attempt at establishing a method to expand the money stock was to employ their alchemical knowledge in the transmutation of lead into gold. The version of alchemy they subscribed to was that promoted by Johann Rudolph Glauber (d. 1670) and Michael Sendivogius (d. 1636). The Hartlibian John French (d. 1657) had translated and synthesized this body of knowledge in *The Art of Distillation* (1651), which informed and influenced many of the other members. In this work he outlined in great detail the composition of metals and the basic methods whereby the adept could alter or refine them. Similar to Plattes, French described how the four elements generate a sperm at the center of the earth, which was then distributed to different areas of the globe. He writes, "The seed, and Sperm of all things is but one, and yet it generates diverse things . . . The Sperm, whilst it is in the center, is indifferent to all forms . . . [it] can as easily produce a tree, as a metal, and an hearb as a stone, and one more precious than another, according to the purity of the place."[102] Hence, the sperm, or humid vapor, was not only the source of metals, but the origin of all matter. What the alchemist had to study was therefore how this vapor turned into different metals as it passed through the layers of the earth. When the earth is subtle, pure, and humid, the vapor or "Mercury of Philosophers," turns into gold; if the earth is impure or cold, baser metals result. If all impurities could be removed from gold, the alchemists would be left with the elixir itself. French thus concluded, "the Elixir, or Tincture of the Philosophers, is nothing else bot gold digested into the highest degree."[103] This meant that if gold "were helped by the industry of the skilful Artist, who knew how to promote Nature to separate these Sulphurous and Earthly impurities from Gold," it would then be possible to obtain a seed that could be infinitely multiplied.[104]

French was enthusiastically optimistic about the potential of alchemy and pleased that it was finally gaining the respect it deserved.

"I rejoyce," he wrote, "as at the break of the day after a long tedious night, to see how this solitary Art of Alchymie begins for to shine forth out of the clouds of reproach, which it hath a long time undeservedly layen under."[105] To him the possibilities of alchemy were endless. The alchemists "may command Lead into Gold, dying plants into fruitfulnesse, the sick into health, old age into youth, darkness into light, and what not?"[106] He also addressed the detractors who were suspicious of this art and questioned why, if the philosopher's stone had already been discovered, there were no infinitely rich alchemists. French answered that it was too dangerous for the philosopher to reveal his secret. He queried, "Can a man that carrieth alwaies about him 10000 pounds worth of Jewels and gold, travel every where up and down, safe, and not be robbed?" Inevitably, the adept would be kidnapped by some prince and thus become "instrumental to their luxury, and tyranny."[107] He also maintained that the true philosopher is not interested in material wealth, but is rather moved by his passion for revealing the unknown.

Plattes had earlier offered a different rationale for why alchemists had not yet produced substantial amounts of gold.[108] He noted there was no point for the aspiring adept to pursue his alchemical skills, because "instead of gaine he shall pay for his learning, by going away with losse."[109] Alchemy was simply not cost-effective.[110] Except, of course, his own alchemical project. In *A Caveat for Alchymists*, he proclaimed that while all other alchemists were laboring in vain, he was the only one who had the requisite knowledge to succeed. "But I having not onely found out the Philosophers stone," he claimed, "but also a sure and infallible way to make *England*, and so the world happy by it, which is ten thousand times better than it, will exalt the praises of God in the superlative degree."[111] Addressing himself to Parliament, he declared that he would be pleased to make his knowledge available to the nation, if Parliament would provide him with a laboratory, similar "to that in the City of *Venice*, where they are sure of secrecy," because no one ever leaves the laboratory for any other reason than to be buried.[112]

Despite warnings from French and Plattes about the obstacles and costs associated with alchemy, the Hartlib Circle launched their own ambitious transmutation project. The responsibility for managing the project was assigned to Benjamin Worsley, one of Hartlib's closest associates and his main source of technical advice after the sudden death of Plattes in 1644. He was not only an active contributor to debates about economic matters, as mentioned earlier, he was also an alchemist, having translated important parts of Glauber's work and promoted a large saltpeter project.[113] In 1648, Worsley was dispatched to Amsterdam to consult with Hartlib's continental associates and to acquire knowledge about chemistry, agriculture, pumps, mills, lens-making, etc. The main aim, however, was apparently to gain the confidence of Glauber so that he would divulge as much of his alchemical knowledge as possible. Although Glauber was a controversial figure, many, including Hartlib, saw him as one of the world's most prominent authorities on alchemical matters.[114]

Teaming up with another Hartlib associate, Johann Moriaen (d. 1668), a German merchant, physician, and alchemist operating out of Amsterdam, Worsley successfully gleaned important information from Glauber. In the end, however, he was frustrated by Glauber's reluctance to reveal all the necessary ingredients and techniques to undertake a transmutation. Some suggested that Glauber was becoming concerned with his growing reputation as a self-enriching gold-maker and merchant of alchemical secrets. Moriaen did indeed acknowledge that Glauber had commercial intentions, but added that there was nothing wrong with making money as long as it was compatible with the overall vision of social progress.[115] Eventually, after Worsely returned to London in 1649, a financial agreement was struck with Glauber, in which he promised to explain how to extract gold from lead. After Moriaen secured funding for the project, the Hartlib Circle was now finally in a position to begin production.

Around the same time, the period's perhaps most revered alchemical expert joined the Hartlib Circle. The enigmatic figure George Starkey, also known as Eirenaeus Philalethes, arrived in London from New England in 1650, rumored to bring along a recipe for the elixir. After arriving on English soil, Starkey enjoyed a meteoric rise to prominence, inspiring and educating many significant scientific thinkers, such as Johann Becher, Robert Boyle, and Sir Isaac Newton.[116] Hartlib did his utmost to encourage Starkey to join the ongoing—and thus far seemingly successful—transmutation project, which now included Worsley, Moriaen, Johann Sibertus Küffler, and a figure referred to simply as the Aurifaber, or gold-maker.[117] In a 1651 letter, Hartlib described how "Worsley, Morian and Aurifaber [were] undertak[ing] to turne that Antimonial silver into Gold. Also to extract Gold out of Tinne (for which they have set up their great Work) and Gold out of Iron in great quantity." He added that, "Stirke [Starkey] is now pidling and toiling for smal quantities, whereas if hee joine, hee cannot but bee a vast gainer by them."[118] Yet, despite multiple invitations from Hartlib and Worsley, Starkey refused to join the gold-making project. Although he acknowledged that he knew an adept who was in possession of both the silver- and gold-making elixirs, Starkey refused to compromise his commitment to the adept and kept his secret regardless of the intensity of the pleading.[119] In a letter to Boyle, Starkey conveyed his irritation with Worsley's repeated overtures: "Some Gentlemen sollicite me to follow extractions of [gold] & [silver] out of [antimony] & [iron], among whom Mr Worsley an ingenious Gentleman did much perswade."[120] Starkey explained his refusal by revealing that he was uninterested in giving up his quest for nature's deepest mysteries in exchange for a life of gold-making, which "might be Compared with that of a Milhorse running round in a wheele to day, that I may doe the same tomorrow."[121] Starkey also revealed his disgust with those who corrupted the alchemical project by selling secrets and thus jeopardizing that they may end up in the wrong hands. In referring to a well-known alchemist, Thomas Vaughan (1621–1666), Starkey proclaimed that "he cheated various greedy people labouring under the sacred thirst for gold of more that two thousand minas, to whom he communicated his secrets for money under an oath of silence, and now, his fraud having been detected, he stinks hugely."[122] He also reproached Glauber, partly for his willingness to sell alchemical secrets and partly because of his lack of alchemical expertise—after having seen one of Glauber's secret recipes, Starkey called it nothing but a "ludicrous, monstrous, stupefying and a tenfold lie."[123]

After having successfully extracted silver, which twenty refiners and goldsmiths allegedly accepted as real, Starkey was offered £5,000 for the secret. Starkey once again declined the offer, proclaiming that he would much rather be a stoic in these matters and that the possession of a secret "is to me more cordially Satisfying than any outward wealth."[124] There was, however, one purpose for which Starkey was willing to share his alchemical secrets. Starkey was fervently opposed to the commercial society developing around him. He detested the kind of power that money conferred and believed that private property and money served to undermine morality and religion in dangerous ways.[125] To that effect, he was interested in sharing his knowledge about the multiplication of gold solely if it would lead to the dismantling of the entire monetary mechanism! Starkey wrote about silver, "I hope and expect that after a few more years money will be common, and this fulcrum of the Antichristian monster will fall down into rubbish, for the populace goes mad, and whole races are insane to have this useless weight rather than God. Will this not attend our imminent and so long expected redemption?"[126]

Both French and Starkey made it clear, in their respective ways, that secrecy was of paramount importance in the world of alchemy.[127] If the magic tincture were found, the alchemical key had to be kept secret and access given only to people of the greatest reputation and dependability in order to preserve the safety of the adept and the integrity of the monetary system. As the famous scientist Robert Boyle pointed out two decades later, if the recipe for gold-making were made widely available, alchemy "would much disorder the affairs of Mankind, Favour Tyranny, and bring a general Confusion, turning the World topsy turvy."[128] Another reason why the pursuit of alchemy had to be kept secret was because alchemical transmutation had been a felony since Henry IV.

Unable to extract the secret from Starkey and discouraged by the lack of progress made in the collaboration with Moriaen, Worsley became skeptical of the feasibility of their experiments. Moriaen recounted in a letter that "Mr Worsley refuses to believe any longer in transmutation."[129] Worsley wrote in a letter to Hartlib, "I have laid all considerations in chemistry aside, as things not reaching much above laborants, or strong-water distillers, unless we can arrive at this key, clearly and perfectly to know, how to open, ferment, putrify, corrupt and destroy (if we please) any mineral, or metal."[130] The only way that the project could bear fruit was if *the key* to operate on metals could be found. If not, the philosopher was reduced to a mere laborant or laboratory worker.[131] While Worsley would later renew his interest in alchemy, his present disillusionment was enough to put an end to the most ambitious attempt by the Hartlib Circle to produce gold.[132]

From Alchemical Transmutations to Credit Money

The failure of alchemical transmutation to provide mankind with a lever to control the money stock and thus solve the scarcity of money problem encouraged members of the Hartlib Circle to focus on another expedient promising to generate the same set of benefits as alchemy. They turned their attention towards finding a way to establish a widely circulating credit currency, either by creating a bank or by reconfiguring the existing network of private credit instruments so that they would circulate more widely. In addition to offering solutions to the same problems, metallic transmutation and credit money shared the same underlying idea of using an expansion in the money stock to launch a process of continuous economic change, improvement, and growth. As such, for the Hartlib Circle, the idea of making money through metallic transmutation or credit were both rooted in the same alchemical and Baconian worldview and were part of the same universal reform project.

Hartlib published two nearly identical pamphlets, one by Sir Cheney Culpeper (1611–1663) and one by William Potter, both advocating the benefits of a credit currency on the basis that its "capacity of inriching this Nation, is in a sort infinite."[133] Culpeper and Potter were both deeply informed by alchemical and Baconian thinking. Culpeper, a wealthy landowner and Parliamentarian, carried out his own alchemical experiments and translated some important tracts by Glauber, in addition to collaborating with and exchanging ideas about alchemy with Hartlib, Worsley, and Küffler.[134] Potter, of whom little is known, revealed his alchemical grounding by giving his most systematic proposal for a credit currency the title *The Key of Wealth, or, A New Way for Improving of Trade*. In alchemical terms, "the key" referred to the knowledge required to transmute one matter into another, thus suggesting an explicit analogy between credit and the philosopher's stone.

Culpeper and Potter proclaimed that all forms of money are, in essence, credit. Money serves as a "kind of securitie which men receive upon parting with their commodities, as a ground of hope or assurance that they shall be repayed in some other commoditie."[135] Historically, gold and silver had served as "Universal credit or [a] *Medium* of Commerce," but as of late the inconveniences associated with these metals had become increasingly obvious. First of all, as mentioned earlier, there simply was not enough gold and silver available in the world to mediate all transactions in a rapidly expanding world economy. Secondly, since the king of Spain was in possession of most of the world's precious metals, for England to acquire the quantities needed, they would have to part with their best commodities and thus add to their rivals' comforts and conveniences. Thirdly, using gold and silver as money forced people to constantly assess the integrity of all coin passing through their hands and exposed them to the manipulation of clippers and counterfeiters. The use of precious metals also provided a constant temptation for thieves and highwaymen. These inconveniences made it abundantly clear that "as the case now stands with us, *the only feasible means, whereby both to receive and multiply the decayed Trade of this Land, is by increasing amongst Tradesmen some firm and known Credit.*"[136]

As we saw in the previous chapter, England had already developed an elaborate network of personal credit instruments. However, since the legal system was not equipped to handle the circulation of bills, bonds, and pledges, these instruments were unable to serve as an alternative currency.[137] On the continent, banks had already transcended the disadvantages associated with the lack of quality coin. The Bank of Amsterdam, founded in 1609, provided traders in the Dutch Republic with a convenient and secure paper currency. However, because the paper currency was fully backed by coin in the vault, the Bank of Amsterdam did not augment the overall money stock, at least not in a significant way. The Italian deposit banks in Venice, Genoa, and Florence also offered their customers an efficient and safe way to conduct transactions without the use of metallic coin. A merchant with an account in a bank could pay for goods delivered by another merchant by instructing the bank to transfer funds from his account to the vendor's account. In some instances, checks or receipts of deposits were also used to convey instructions to the bank, but these instruments rarely, if ever, entered general circulation. Banks also frequently offered merchants a line of credit to trade on, enabling them to make payments beyond their deposits. As such, even though these banks, properly speaking, did not issue a paper currency, they nevertheless added to the amount of money in circulation.

Some of the Hartlibians, including Henry Robinson, appreciated what they saw in the continental banks and advocated that similar enterprises be established in England.[138] Robinson, for example, suggested that the legal code had to be adjusted so that bonds and bills became "irrevocably assignable from one man to another," which would "virtually multiply the stock [of money] of this nation."[139] He also advocated the formation of a merchant bank "capable of multiplying the stock of the Nation, for as much as concernes trading *in Infinitum:* In breife, it is the *Elixir or Philosophers Stone.*"[140] Others, however, pointed out that such banks were "but a lame and short remedy to [the] Inconveniences" presently plaguing England.[141] Apart from limiting their services primarily to merchants, the silver kept in the banks' vaults as security provided a powerful temptation to both foreign and domestic princes to compromise the banks' integrity and expropriate their assets. The primary reason, however, why existing banks were inadequate to answer the present challenges was simply because they were unable to generate "any new *Medium* of Commerce."[142] While some of these banks did actually create *some* credit, the Hartlibians were unimpressed by the extent of the credit expansion, arguing that the banks "are nothing else in effect but places where men pawn or deposite their moneys for obtaining currant credit, as that which they may keep with lesse danger, and assign to another with lesse trouble."[143] Robinson, despite promoting such a bank, acknowledged its comparative sterility, declaring it would be "no more than a Grand Cash-keeper of this whole Kingdome."[144]

For a radical improvement in the well-being of mankind to be possible, a much more flexible credit currency had to be implemented. Potter argued that the only reason why people were willing to part with their commodities in exchange for money was that they would later be able to use the money to obtain other commodities.[145] Money was therefore considered a "Token or Ticket." While coined gold and silver had proven capable of playing the role of money well, Potter was convinced that a credit currency could perform the same role. The key was that the currency was backed by a solid security, making credit money "*in all respects as good as money.*"[146] Credit would then be able to unlock the door to society's "*store-house* of *Riches,*" thus making credit "*the true* Seed *of Riches.*"[147]

Potter's proposal was based on a small number of merchants "of knowne and sufficient credit" joining together to create a new currency. The participating merchants would print a series of £10 bills, payable to the bearer, which the members, upon offering good security, could borrow, free of interest, and use as a means of exchange for goods and services. While the venture could be launched with as few as ten to twenty well-respected merchants, it had the capacity to expand rapidly to include the bulk of the population, at least those with adequate means. Participants committed themselves to jointly redeem these bills for ready money on demand. To that end, Potter suggested a number of rules. First, the merchants had to establish an office to organize the redemption of the bills. When a holder of a bill desired to obtain metallic money in exchange they would present the bill to the office, which would issue a bond for payment within six months. The office would then, once a month, send a ticket to the members informing them of the number of bills presented for redemption. Each member would then be responsible for paying a sum of silver money, proportionate to the number of bills they had initially borrowed, to the office within four months. In order to prevent credit from contracting as bills were redeemed, participating merchants received bills equaling the value of their payment, which they could use as ready money. The only way that credit would contract as a result of a redemption was therefore if a merchant was unable to pay his share in cash and had to forfeit the assets put up as security for the initial loan.

Potter argued that these bills would be as safe as metallic money. Since borrowers were only offered bills on the most secure backing, it meant that if the merchants had no ready money available to redeem the bills, they could always sell the property they put up as collateral and obtain enough money to pay the holder of the bill. In the unlikely event that a merchant's security turned out to be worthless, the responsibility for redeeming the bill would fall on the other merchants. This, in itself, would not be a significant inconvenience, as the responsibility would be spread out among many merchants. Nevertheless, in order to prevent that this might become a burden, Potter suggested that the bills should be insured by a separate company. Such an insurance company would, in exchange for a 1 percent premium on all bills, redeem the insolvent merchant's share. The insurer would also be given a "negative voice" in the lending of bills, creating another layer of oversight that ensured that only people with good security would be allowed to borrow bills.[148]

Even though bills would be conservatively issued, nothing stopped merchants from obtaining bills equal to the value of their entire estates, including houses, ships, goods, and land. By obtaining interest-free credit, they would be able to expand their operations and greatly increase their capital, which, in turn, would allow them to obtain even more credit. While the credit mechanism could be established by a small number of merchants, Potter was convinced that once the rest of the community recognized the benefit of this system, they would venture to join. In fact, competitive pressures would force them to join, as the participating merchants would be able to undersell everyone else.[149] As more, or all, people joined the system and participants monetized more of their estates, a potentially infinite economic expansion could be launched. More precisely, Potter estimated that the credit scheme had the capacity to double England's capital every two years, which meant that £1,000 would grow to more than £1 million after twenty years and £1 billion after forty years.[150] These ideas in Potter's *Key of Wealth* were powerful enough to facilitate the kind of universal reformation the Hartlibians were pursuing.

By launching a secure and universally negotiable credit currency in a nation so well equipped for land improvement, fishing, and global trade, the Hartibians claimed riches would expand "much more then proportionable to such encrease of money, and that without encreasing the price of commodity."[151] Since the increase in money would spark industry and activate unused resources, there would be no upward pressure on prices. While Potter had initially compared the benefits of his scheme to that of discovering a "Myne of gold," he later revised his statement and proclaimed that his credit mechanism was in fact far more advantageous than a gold mine.[152] First, the presence of a gold mine would compromise England's national security, as it provided powerful incentives for other nations to conspire against England. Second, operating a gold mine and producing gold coin was a costly affair, including charges for protection, digging, and coining, which his credit system would avoid. Most importantly, however, was the fact that it is not always possible to produce as much gold from a mine as the economic conditions called for and that, eventually, a gold mine would become exhausted. But with Potter's credit currency, England could acquire operational control over its money stock and would thus be able to generate more money on demand, *ad infinitum*. With Potter's scheme, people could now autonomously expand the money stock independently of authorities—mints, Parliament, and the king—and the prevailing trade balance. As such, the scheme embodied an antiauthoritarian spirit that resonated well with the Hartlibians' preference for organic social improvement processes initiated and conducted outside the purview of traditional powers.

Potter predicted that his plan would bring revolutionary change. By greatly improving trade, fishing, and agriculture, not only would England abound with inexpensive commodities, but it would soon engross the trade of all of Europe. England's geopolitical strength would receive an important boost from its rapidly increasing custom and excise receipts, the presence of additional trading vessels that could easily be mobilized for naval purposes, the ability to properly reward soldiers, and a greater sense of patriotism that came from having great riches to defend. But, like many other social reformers associated with the Hartlib Circle, Potter seemed particularly interested in the moral and social reformation of the body politic. While the exponential growth of the economy would enrich all segments of society, it would most crucially have a transformative effect on the poor. Their exposure to periodic harvest failures could now be eliminated by the maintenance of emergency granaries. His credit scheme also had the potential to contribute to the transmutation of the behavioral characteristics of the poor. By generating vastly more employment opportunities, "*Vagabonds* and idle *Runnagadoes*, . . . [would be] reduced to some order and *discipline*" and their mischievous designs and frequent contributions to public disturbances could be brought to an end. Indeed, many of the most threatening sorts of poor people—rouges, cutthroats, and highwaymen—would soon face extinction as prosperity would eliminate the conditions that encouraged them to embark on a life of crime. So pleased was Potter with the promises offered by his scheme that he queried, "if . . . Gold may be made of Paper without considerable charge, what is it amongst earthly things that may not safely be undertaken?"[153]

Potter also offered a proposal for a land bank, which was remarkably similar to that of Culpeper. Since "Credit grounded upon the best security is the same thing with Money," the key was to establish a bank that used a different asset than precious metals as security backing the credit money.[154] Since land was considered the most concrete and stable commodity at the time, there could be no better security than land to induce people to part with their commodities in exchange. By mortgaging land, which "would serve as well and better for such a pawn," the land bank created a credit currency that would have "as true intrinsick value, as Gold and Silver" and allow for transactions, not just amongst merchants, but throughout the nation.[155] Moreover, this device would allow England to expand its money stock by a factor of ten or more without having to part with any of its domestically produced commodities. The fact that gold and silver would no longer need to "lay dead" in the vault of the bank also meant that the threat of covetous princes was eliminated and the entire stock of gold and silver could enter circulation.[156] A further benefit of a land bank was that once the new currency had been created it would not be removed from circulation, as its lack of intrinsic value eliminated all incentives for people to export it abroad or hoard it as a store of value.[157] This ensured that the expansion of the money stock was sustainable and that the scarcity of money problem would not reappear. As Culpeper concluded, "it plainly appears that the way to remove Poverty, Taxes, and most publique Grievances, and to make this Nation abound in Wealth, Trade, Cities, Shipping, People, and Renown, is neither unpracticeable, nor difficult."[158] Hence, in credit, the Hartlibians had found a panacea similar to the philosopher's stone, but one that required far less effort and expense to develop.[159]

The well-known physician Peter Chamberlen (1601–1683), an affiliate of the Hartlib Circle, suggested another credit scheme that he hoped would help England prosper. Writing just months after Charles's beheading, Chamberlen argued that the present political instability made it necessary for Parliament to quickly establish its authority and popularity. He advised Parliament that the most pressing issue was to provide the poor with compelling reasons to support the new rule. *"Provide for the poor,"* he proclaimed, *"and they will provide for you. Destroy the poor, and they will destroy you."*[160] Not only was Chamberlen arguing that the poor had the power to undermine the new government, but he also claimed that the poor held the key to the nation's affluence and security. "The wealth and strength of all Countries are in the poore," he argued, "for they do all the great and necessary workes, and they make up the maine body and strength of Armies."[161]

Chamberlen proposed that a public stock should be created from the sale of the Royalists' lands, houses, and movable property.[162] In addition, all unwrought mines, as well as commons, wastes, forests, heaths, mores, and fens, should be enclosed and improved to increase the yield. Chamberlen envisioned that this public stock would be capable of serving the nation in many ways, including paying off both Parliament's and the king's accumulated debts within ten and twenty years, respectively; eliminating all taxes except the customs; paying for arrears and provide all the necessities to the armed forces; maintaining the government administration; erecting a public bank similar to that of Amsterdam; feeding and clothe all people in need; providing employment to all able bodies; guaranteeing a place in a workhouse for all thieves and robbers; and offering instruction in academies for the children of the poor.[163] These measures would stabilize the polity, restore prosperity, and launch a long-term process whereby the poor would become "civilized" and made "more tractable to all duties and commands."[164] These poverty-eradicating programs would benefit the whole nation "by improving of Lands that were never improved, by imploying of men that were not onely useless; but a burthen, through idlenesse, or want to imployment, and by converting them into good Common-wealths-men."[165] Since this public stock had the potential to facilitate a universal reformation of society, he called it "*the best Elixir: The* Philosophers *stone.*"[166]

The Politics of Hartlibian Political Economy

The Hartlib Circle's pathbreaking reconceptualization of money and credit was made possible by the new worldview introduced by the period's new scientific thinking. Drawing on alchemical and Baconian ideas, the Hartlibians believed that nature, society, and mankind could be continually and infinitely improved. Exemplifying the emphasis on human agency in engendering progress, Culpeper wrote that the natural philosopher was the means "by which nature, or the spirite of nature, is put into motion, in all those circulations which wee see nature to make & by the reiterated apposition of which, the true Artiste may put nature into those reiterated motions which nature cannot giue her selfe."[167] This very spirit infused all aspects of Hartlibian political economy.

The Hartlibian and neo-Aristotelian political economists both viewed commerce and finance as systems. The neo-Aristotelians thought of the world as existing within a closed, finite, universe, within which all aspects of nature and society had their proper place. In order for harmony and balance to prevail and for the traditional hierarchy to be upheld, it was essential that each person and class be kept to their place and performed their allotted roles. Money's role in this system was to mediate relations between people, both within and between different segments of the social hierarchy. By serving as a measure of value, money made qualitatively different goods commensurable and therefore enabled people to exchange anything and everything. As long as the quality and quantity of money remained intact, money was able to fulfill its role as a measure of value and medium of exchange and thus contribute to the formation of a just society.

The Hartlibians employed a different kind of system, where the parts had a different relationship to each other and to the whole. While they too thought of nature and society in hierarchical terms, they focused less on maintaining balance and order than on improving each component part, whether natural, political, or economic. That is, contrary to the static and finite neo-Aristotelian system, the Hartlibians' system was dynamic and elastic. The role of money in this system was consequently very different. Instead of a balancing device, money for the Hartlibians had the capacity to awaken and activate nature's, society's, and mankind's hidden or underutilized resources. While science would unlock nature's secrets and remove obstacles to progress, an elastic currency was necessary to support the circulation of society's constantly expanding wealth.

In conceiving of the body politic in separate ways, the two schools of thought theorized the social order differently. As noted earlier, the neo-Aristotelians prioritized upholding the traditional hierarchy and moral order. This meant that each segment of the social hierarchy should enjoy a fixed share of society's wealth, because only then would each rank be able to fulfill its social responsibility. The Hartlibians, on the other hand, while not advocating social mobility per se, promoted the advancement and improvement of each segment of the social hierarchy. By encouraging innovation, growth, and progress, they believed that social tensions between ranks could be eased and that prosperity could alleviate the conditions of all. It was also likely that the process of universal reformation would transform the traditional moral order and the associated social hierarchy. To the elites, in particular the landed classes, improvement was consequently considered a threat to their position and privilege. The Hartlibians sought to ease their anxiety by showing that the transformation of the middling and lower ranks of society was in fact something universally beneficial. Instead of using the traditional body politic metaphor, in which the aristocracy was seen as the stomach and the king the heart enriching the rest of the body, Potter imagined a body politic in which all people were mutually reliant on each other.[168] He wrote, "no Member [of the Body Politique] can subsist by itself, without both serving the whole Body, and receiving a competent nourishment from it." He continued:

> no Artificer or Trades-man can accommodate himself, with all things necessary to a comfortable subsistence, by his Industry in any one Calling, without transmitting the overplus of the fruits of his endeavors therein, to other Members of the said Body Politique, and from them receiving instead thereof, a proportionable reflex of the surplusage of their labours and commodities.[169]

The more each person produced, the greater the "Multiplication, Improvement, [and] Distribution" of commodities, and thus the wealthier the entire population would become.

Peter Chamberlen added that increased affluence of the middling sorts is a necessary cause and an inevitable consequence of national prosperity: "The more Merchants, the more Trading, and the more flourishing of Merchants." Any attempt to restrict the number of merchants should therefore be discounted as "the suggestion of the Devill, Covetousnesse and Jelousie."[170]

The segment of the population that the Hartlibians were mostly concerned about improving was the poor. They hoped that their various measures would encourage the transmutation of the poor into respectable, civilized, and polite citizens. In fact, they introduced a new understanding of poverty and the poor.[171] Not only was it possible to turn the poor into productive members of society—an idea that moved the emphasis from getting rid of the surplus population to harnessing their productive potential—but it was conceivable that the poor might be altogether eliminated as a category. Through hard work, education, and proper religious instruction, the manners, habits, and customs of the poor could change in ways that would eventually allow the least affluent people in society to transcend the meaning of poverty and its associated behavior. Hence, while the Hartlib Circle did not seek to turn the world upside down, as some of the more radical Puritan reform groups had advocated, they were indeed open to changes in the social hierarchy that might result from the improvement process they advocated.

The neo-Aristotelians also differed from the Hartlibians in terms of how they viewed the relationship between political authority and money. While Malynes argued that the body politic was subject to the authority of the monarch and that it therefore was the king's responsibility to correct any problems with the monetary mechanism, Mun believed that the monetary mechanism functioned best when given relative autonomy from the polity. In fact, he did not believe that it was possible for anyone to gain operational control over the monetary mechanism. The Hartlib Circle, on the other hand, envisioned a situation in which any industrious and honest person could create money. They argued that anyone who needed money for a transaction should be able to create money by monetizing their assets. Whether through a land bank, Lombard bank, or a generalized transferability of debt instruments, people would gain partial operational control over the money stock and be able to expand it at will—or at least in proportion to their property—to take advantage of commercial opportunities and thus contribute to society's affluence.

The Hartlib Circle recognized, of course, that people could not be given complete control over the money stock. They recognized, as had George Starkey before them, that unlimited access to credit (or the philosopher's stone) would surely undermine the entire monetary mechanism, as well as society itself. Credit had to be checked at any given moment by the commercial conditions and the level of trust built up in society. Consonant with their general disdain towards state power, the Hartlibians completely removed the monarch and the state from any responsibility for managing the monetary system. They believed that in order for an organic process of growth and improvement to gather momentum, it was necessary that all forms of arbitrary authority were eliminated, in trade, politics, and matters of faith. Capturing this spirit, Culpeper wrote in a letter to Hartlib:

> monopolizinge Corporations of Merchantes, may perhaps finde (ere longe) imploymente inought to defende theire paste incroachements upon the liberty of the subjectes & truly the monopoly of trade will proue as great a greeuance (when rightly understoode) as any in this kingdome whatsoeuer, nexte unto that monopoly of Power which the [King] claimes; & beleue it, nowe wee are pullinge downe of suche monopolies wee shall starte a great many which yet ly hid in the bushes but the greate monopoly muste firste downe; & then the monopoly of trade the monopoly of Equity, (a thinge which nowe begins to be lookt into), & the monopoly of matters of conscience & scripture (a very notable monopoly), all these & many more wee shall haue in chace & what

one hownde misses another will happen in the sente of & thus will Babilon tumble, tumble, tumble, tumble.[172]

Conclusion

The Hartlib Circle gradually dispersed towards the end of the 1650s and ceased to exist after the Restoration, when their writings fell out of favor with the political establishment because of their association with Civil War radicalism.[173] However, since many Hartlibians joined the newly founded Royal Society, their improvement program survived in different forms.[174] Hartlibian political economy also continued to influence the progressive side of the political debate. Hartlibian ideas were particularly influential in the debate about England's financial and monetary future. In addition to the members of the Hartlib Circle, such as William Petty—who continued to advocate the creation of land banks and the issuance of credit money—many subsequent authors debating the future of credit drew heavily on the conceptual and theoretical contributions of the Hartlib Circle, as will be discussed in the next chapter.[175] As such, by defining the intellectual framework within which credit money was conceived and debated, Hartlibian political economy paved the way for the Financial Revolution. In that sense, the pursuit of alchemy contributed to the emergence of a credit currency in ways that resemble how Francis Bacon, though an avowed critic of many features of alchemy, envisioned the possible unintended benefits of alchemy. He wrote:

> it must not be denied that alchemists have discovered quite a few things, and given men useful discoveries. They fit quite well in the story of the old man who left his daughters some gold buried in a vineyard and pretended not to know the exact spot; as a result of which they set themselves to dig diligently in that vineyard; and no gold was found, but the harvest was richer for the cultivation.[176]

While alchemical transmutation failed to eliminate the scarcity of money problem, alchemical thinking nevertheless contributed to its eventual solution by inspiring and informing the development of a generally circulating credit currency.

— II —

Death Penalty and Credit

— 3 —

The Epistemology of Credit

Introduction

The Hartlib Circle's rethinking of money sparked a vibrant debate on how to design an English credit currency. In arguing for the feasibility of widely circulating credit notes and highlighting their importance to a modernizing society, the Hartlibians had carefully considered the potential of credit to contribute to the universal reformation of nature, society, and mankind. Yet, despite their systematic reassessment of money and credit, they left perhaps the most essential ingredient of credit—the concept of trust—relatively unexplored. Many subsequent seventeenth-century political economists, such as Sir William Petty, Nicholas Barbon (1637–1698), and Charles Davenant, emphasized the importance of trust—which they viewed as a subset of opinion—to the functionality of credit money. Petty, for example, described credit as founded "upon a good Opinion of the World"; Barbon noted, "Credit is a Value raised by Opinion"; Davenant proclaimed that credit "hangs upon Opinion."[1]

The Hartlibians maintained that the exchangeability of money was determined by people's trust in money's capacity to serve as a pledge and security in market exchanges. As such, they departed from the neo-Aristotelian tradition of conceiving of coin as mediating commerce because it embodied the same intrinsic value as the commodities for which it was exchanged. Instead, they argued that people were willing to accept money in exchange for their goods because they believed that money would enable them to purchase other goods of the same value at a later date. Money's value was therefore determined more by the

future than by the past or the present. A full-bodied coin could successfully operate as a pledge because the silver physically present in the
coin provided excellent security. Indeed, coin often served as a pledge
for a higher value than the silver embodied in it, especially when the
coin was minted by a well-respected state. According to William Potter's
definition, the security backing the medium of exchange did not have
to be physically present, nor did the security have to consist of precious
metal.[2] In fact, a paper note issued by a reputable source and backed by
a considerable asset—whether precious metals, land, or merchandise—
could instill the same level of confidence as a full-weight coin. Notes thus
had the capacity to mediate commerce just as well as coin; but, because
notes were not in short supply as were precious metals, they could easily
be multiplied to solve the neo-Aristotelian scarcity of money problem or
to facilitate the Hartlibian infinite improvement process.

The main challenge facing efforts to create a new currency was to
figure out how to enable the public to trust that an entry in the bank's
ledger or a piece of paper would retain its exchangeability for the foreseeable future. This is the same problematic that famously preoccupied
the sociologist Georg Simmel two and a half centuries later.[3] Like Potter,
Simmel pointed out in his *Philosophy of Money* that money can only
operate satisfactorily if there is "confidence in the ability of an economic
community to ensure that the value given in exchange for an interim
value, a coin, will be replaced without loss."[4] Trust was so essential to
money, Simmel argued, that "money transactions would collapse without trust."[5] Indeed, the fact that people can never be fully assured that the
money they hold will actually entitle them to obtain a certain amount
of goods and services in the future "confirms the character of money as
mere credit."[6] Simmel continued, "for it is the essence of credit that the
probability of realizing it is never one hundred per cent, no matter how
closely it may approach it."[7] Simmel concluded that because coin and
notes are conceptually identical "the development from material money
to credit money is less radical than appears at first."[8]

Seventeenth-century political economists considered a number of
institutional designs to promote the appropriate kinds and levels of
trust. Solid security, portability, legal negotiability, incorruptible management, and transparency—just to mention a few—were considered
crucial for a credit currency to circulate widely. Additionally, finding
ways to prevent distrust caused by clipping, counterfeiting, and forgery

preoccupied most commentators. This was truly a matter of life and death. If trust in money and credit could not be adequately protected from such monetary crimes, the very foundation of English society would be in jeopardy. It was therefore considered necessary that anyone undermining trust in money should be punished by death. While I document in this chapter that most political economists emphasized the importance of the death penalty in shoring up trust in credit, I show in Chapter 4 that the gallows did indeed play a central role in the defense of credit during the monetary turmoil of the 1690s.

The second aim of this chapter is to highlight the productive interplay between natural philosophy and political economy in terms of how trust and opinion were considered. For some time, natural philosophers throughout Europe had recognized that indisputable knowledge was rarely available in most areas of life. Yet they had learned from the ways in which merchants, bankers, and lawyers, as well as agriculturalists, surgeons, and alchemists conducted their affairs, that opinion, beliefs, and probabilistic knowledge provided valuable guidance to their decision-making. In England, philosophers like Thomas Hobbes and John Locke, fully recognizing the centrality of opinion to people's lives, therefore set out to systematically investigate the epistemological content of opinion.[9] Drawing on how trust and opinion operated in commercial societies, Hobbes's and Locke's theoretical expositions provided political economists with useful frameworks for exploring the feasibility of credit money.

This chapter begins by exploring seventeenth-century probabilistic thinking, focusing on how Hobbes and Locke conceived of trust and opinion. Next, I investigate how political economists employed probabilistic epistemologies in designing institutions that would safeguard trust in credit. While I describe the general purpose and logic of each credit scheme proposed during the second half of the seventeenth century, the emphasis will be on how the various mechanisms were designed to foster trust and confidence in the continuous circulation of credit notes.[10]

The Epistemological Foundation of Credit

The kind of qualitative probabilistic reasoning employed by political economists in discussing credit had only recently been formalized.

Seventeenth-century natural philosophers, increasingly aware that the search for absolute truths was largely in vain, had come to realize that their efforts would be better spent looking for ways to navigate a world of radical uncertainty. This led to a breakdown in the strict demarcation between, on the one hand, *scientia*, knowledge and certainty, and, on the other hand, opinion, probability, and appearance.[11] Philosophers now became interested in exploring and assessing different practices of forming knowledge claims that had been employed for quite some time in a number of different areas. Historians of science Lorraine Daston, Ian Hacking, and Barbara Shapiro note three areas of seventeenth-century life in which probabilistic thinking was particularly pervasive: legal reasoning, aleatory contracts, and the new experimental sciences.[12] According to Daston and Shapiro, in legal cases where evidence was partial, legal theorists insisted that close attention be paid to both the intrinsic credibility of the facts presented and to the extrinsic credibility of the witnesses. Once all the available evidence had been properly weighed, an opinion based on the qualitative probability of guilt was formed, providing the basis for judgment.

The issuers of aleatory contracts, including annuities, insurances, and games of chance, also employed probabilistic thinking. They carefully considered the probabilities of deaths, accidents, and winning tickets to make sure that the odds were in their favor. While legal thinking was more amenable to qualitative probabilities, aleatory contracts were well suited to numerical calculations. Yet, long into the eighteenth century, Daston points out, mathematical probability had almost no bearing on the terms on which annuities, insurances, and lotteries were transacted.[13] The early application of probabilistic reasoning was thus almost exclusively conducted in terms of qualitative probabilities.

Hacking locates the emergence of probabilistic reasoning in the new sciences. Arguing that the elevation of empirical evidence over testimony from authorities was the crucial ingredient in making opinion epistemologically respectable, Hacking focuses on what he calls the low sciences, including alchemy and medicine, as the source of the growing popularity of probabilistic thinking. Since the empirical and experimental investigations carried out by alchemists and physicians were rarely amenable to intuitive or demonstrative knowledge, the practitioners were forced to develop alternative modes of proof. This led them to focus on signs as evidence on which to base their opinions. While the resulting understanding of the world never reached the level of certainty sought by earlier natural philosophers, the success of the alchemists and physicians in translating their probabilistic assessments of their evidence into pragmatic ways of understanding and transforming the world inspired many other fields of inquiry to embrace their approach. Hacking concludes: "Doubtless the technology devised by the proto-chemists affected what men did, but the true effect, of lasting importance to the new civilization, may lie in how men thought about what they did."[14]

Thomas Hobbes (1588-1679) was one of the first English philosophers to explore probabilistic reasoning. Although he remained optimistic about the prospects of mathematics and syllogistic reasoning to provide science with demonstrative knowledge, he nevertheless recognized that people were forced to make many of their everyday decisions based on opinion and that their opinion often had to be based on the testimony of others.[15] Indeed, most of what passes as practical knowledge is, according to Hobbes, mere opinion. For example, when people speculate about an unobserved event in the past or the future, the resulting presumption can never rise beyond opinion. Moral discourses about good and evil can also only produce opinions. In fact, whenever a discourse is not based on an axiom or a person's sensory impression, but on "some other contemplation of his own," absolute knowledge is impossible, leaving us to rely on opinion.[16] Matters become even more tenuous when we engage in reasoning based on "some saying of another."[17] In such circumstances the discourse "is not so much concerning the Thing, as the Person; and the Resolution is called BELEEFE, and FAITH: *Faith, in* the man; *Beleefe,* both *of* the man, and *of* the truth of what he sayes."[18] Hence, for Hobbes, beliefs were comprised of two opinions, "one of the saying of the man; the other of his vertue."[19] Ultimately he concluded that "whatsoever we believe, upon no other reason, then what is drawn from authority of men onely, and their writings; whether they be sent from God or not, is Faith in men onely."[20] For Hobbes, the importance of the witnesses' integrity and reputation was thus essential for their credibility.

Despite the fact that most philosophers were suspicious of the veracity of testimonies, the actual process of knowledge formation nevertheless depended in large part on information provided by other people. As the historian of science Steven Shapin has shown, natural philosophers and experimentalists regularly pondered the extent to which it was prudent to believe in the testimonies of others.[21] Since knowledge of the world inevitably relied, to some extent, on other people's testaments, it became important to obtain information about the individuals offering such testimony to judge whether it was appropriate to trust them. Particularly important to determine the credibility of a witness, Shapin suggests, were the social and economic circumstances of the witness. Members of the gentility ranked highest in this respect, since they were believed to embody a different level of honor and virtue, grounded in their socialization, education, and freedom from economic constraints.[22] In scientific circles, such as the Royal Society, gentlemen were thus considered more trustworthy than the rest of the community.[23] In addition to the social position of the witnesses, Shapin also noted that the truth-value of testimonies were determined by the witness's knowledge, skill, integrity, disinterestedness, and confidence-inducing qualities, as well as the information's plausibility, multiplicity, consistency, and immediacy.[24]

The formation of a collective judgment about truth and a shared cognitive order also depended, as Simon Schaffer points out, on "the construction of stable communities."[25] Groups developing shared cultural and intellectual reference points were better able to generate stable knowledge claims in all areas of inquiry, from cosmology to credit.

In turning his attention to credit, Hobbes reiterated the importance of being able to trust other people.[26] However, he famously noted that it was near impossible to trust the sincerity of people's proclamations and testimonies. He pointed out that "since words alone are not adequate signs to declare one's will, other signs of one's will may give words which refer to the future the same force as if they referred to the present."[27] To overcome the inadequacy of language as a commitment mechanism, Hobbes suggested that people can convey their intentions by binding themselves to contracts. In *On the Citizen* he points out that contracts are indispensable when people agree on future performances, as in the case of credit. He noted, "when either or both are trusted, the trusted party promises to make performance later; and a promise of this kind is called an AGREEMENT."[28] At the moment that the trusted party receives a benefit as part of the agreement, the person commits to reciprocate at a later date, thus elevating the promise to the same epistemic level as the transference of a right in the present. Yet, because people have the capacity to renege on promises, trust can never be complete. Therefore, Hobbes believed, some form of punishment had to await those who failed to honor their agreements for trust to be generalized. He concluded, "For he that performeth first, has no assurance the other will performe after; because the bonds of words are too weak to bridle mens ambition, avarice, anger, and other Passions, without the feare of some coërcive Power."[29]

A few decades after Hobbes made his intervention, John Locke offered a more systematic investigation of the role of opinion in human knowledge, considered by some modern scholars to be the first fully articulated philosophy of probabilism.[30] While Locke ranked intuitive knowledge derived from immediate perception and demonstrative knowledge obtained through axiomatic reasoning highest on the epistemic scale, he acknowledged that mankind is most often faced with situations in which indisputable knowledge is not attainable. He claimed that "most of the Propositions we think, reason, discourse, nay act upon, are such, we cannot have undoubted Knowledge of their Truth."[31] The complexity of the world, combined with the intrinsic limits of human understanding, necessitated that people form their own judgment on the basis of the available evidence. Indeed, it would be next to impossible to conduct oneself in the world without relying on belief and opinion. He warned, "If we will disbelieve every thing, because we cannot certainly know all things; we shall do much what as wisely as he who would not use his Legs, but sit still and perish, because he had no Wings to fly."[32] To avoid falling into a paralysis of skeptical despair, it is consequently necessary to form propositions about the world and assign them varying levels of confidence. "The entertainment the Mind gives this sort of Propositions," Locke called "*Belief, Assent,* or *Opinion.*"[33] In forming an opinion about matters involving human agency, there is an unavoidable uncertainty based on the fact that knowledge of another person's intentions and motivations can never be complete and people always have a degree of freedom to disappoint our expectations.[34] But since we cannot access the future, we focus on the past and try to create the best possible picture of how nature, society, or other people have behaved. With the aid of observation and testimonies, probability then helps us assess the reasonableness of our beliefs.

Locke entertained a wide range of opinion, from "full *Assurance* and Confidence" down to "*Conjecture, Doubt,* and *Distrust.*"[35] Dictating where on this spectrum an opinion belongs is the degree of probability a person assigns to the truth of a proposition. Probability thus offers a barometer to assess propositions when certainty is unavailable and people only have "some inducement to receive them for true."[36] When considering whether to trust or not, Locke suggested that people tend to form their opinion on the basis of (1) how well the proposition conforms with their own knowledge, observation, and experience, and (2) what the testimony of others tells them.[37] If the relevant proposition seems to correspond well with that which a person already knows or has personally observed or experienced, the person's confidence in the opinion formed is "proportionably to the preponderancy of the greater grounds of Probability."[38] This probability can be quantitative, but in most of the instances Locke considered, the probability assessment was qualitative. When people rely on information from others to make up their minds about a proposition regarding nature, guilt in a legal case, solvency of a bank, or the credibility of a person, their level of confidence is, according to Locke, dictated by the number, integrity, and skill of the witnesses providing the testimony.[39] That is, if it is possible to access a large number of skilled witnesses of impeccable integrity, the probability assigned to an opinion is all the greater. Yet, Locke insisted, testimonies are never as reliable as a source of information as personal observation or experience.

Locke's epistemic delineation between knowledge and opinion was not a novel intervention; many medieval and Renaissance thinkers subscribed to a similar division. However, the manner in which Locke valorized opinion captured the spirit of the new natural philosophy enveloping Europe. For medieval thinkers, such as Thomas Aquinas, opinion was the product of testimony and authority, not evidence. As Hacking argues, "Testimony and authority were primary, and things could count as evidence only insofar as they resembled the witness of observers and the authority of books."[40] Although Locke acknowledged that testimony was important in influencing opinion, he highlighted that it was not the *authority* of the witnesses, but the *skill* and *integrity* whereby they conveyed their knowledge, observations, and experiences that mattered most.[41] Empirical evidence was thus the basis for both knowledge and opinion, suggesting to Locke that there is a high degree of proximity between knowledge and opinion.[42]

Locke posited four basic categories of opinion, defined by their associated degrees of qualitative probability. The highest degree of probability is when "the general consent of all Men, in all Ages, as far as it can be known, concurs with a Man's constant and never-failing Experience in like cases."[43] In such clear circumstances, empirical and testimonial evidence combine to elevate opinion close to certain knowledge. Locke called opinion held with such a high level of certitude *assurance*. The next range of probabilities corresponds to situations in which "I find by my own Experience, and the Agreement of all others that mention it, a thing to be, for the most part, so; and that the particular instance of it is attested by many and undoubted Witnesses."[44] Once again, firsthand observation and experience are augmented by the testimony of others to generate an opinion based on a high degree of probability. Locke suggested that opinions held with such a degree of probability could be labeled *confidence*. The next level of probability, still high enough to give people little liberty in how they judge the evidence, occurs when "any particular matter of fact is vouched by the concurrent Testimony of unsuspected Witnesses."[45] In cases where the person making the judgment has no direct access to observe the matter at hand—for example, if the event transpired centuries ago—the sensible way to proceed is to rely on the most credible witnesses, in this case the most reputable historians. While opinion based solely on the testimony of others is not as credible as those that are based on firsthand observation or experience, there is no reason for the sensible thinker to discount the only available information, in particular if the source is reputable.[46] Below this degree of probability, opinions were often too weak to serve as an accurate guide to action. Such situations occurred when testimony contradicted common experience and "the reports of History and Witnesses clash with the ordinary course of Nature, or with one another."[47] In such circumstances, what mattered most was the credibility of a "Common Observation in like cases, and particular Testimonies in that particular instance."[48] Since observations and testimonies were liable to so many different circumstances and qualifications, the degree of probability emerging was generally difficult to assess, giving rise to an array of different entertainments of the mind, including *"Belief, Conjecture, Guess, Doubt, Wavering, Distrust, Disbelief,* etc."[49]

Although Locke did not entirely disregard the testimony of others, he argued that the greater the reliance on testimony the lower the probability that can be assigned to an opinion. The least trusted opinions consequently derived from testimonies farthest removed from "the

Being and Existence of the thing it self."[50] In Locke's words, "A credible Man vouching his Knowledge of [the original truth], is a good proof: But if another equally credible, do witness it from his Report, the Testimony is weaker."[51] Locke here challenged those who "look on Opinions to gain force by growing older."[52] His disparaging views on hearsay as evidence linked up with his lack of respect for the collective opinion of the public. He argued that the collective opinion was notoriously inaccurate; "there cannot be a more dangerous thing to rely on, nor more likely to mislead, one; since there is much more Falshood and Errour amongst Men, than Truth and Knowledge."[53] Hence, as will be discussed in Chapters 5, public opinion was a highly contested phenomenon.

In sum, Hobbes's and Locke's epistemological discussion exemplified the new intellectual mind-set that "marked the endeavors of nearly all seventeenth-century Englishmen engaged in philosophy, the investigation of nature, religion, history, law, and even literature."[54] This form of qualitative probabilistic thinking, I will show in the following, was also popular among political economists thinking about opinion, trust, and credit. Political economy was now leaving the certainty of the Aristotelian world defined by finite wealth, a traditional moral order, and fixed hierarchies, in which property was mediated by money of intrinsic value, and entering a world open to infinite improvement and growth, in which symbolic money was entrusted to circulate society's wealth. Since absolute knowledge was inaccessible in this new world of commerce and finance, it was particularly helpful to political economists to have access to a framework within which trust and opinion could be assessed. As such, probabilistic reasoning joined the Hartlibian fusion of Baconian and alchemical thinking to form the philosophical-scientific discourse within which the debate about the future of credit in England was conducted during the second half of the seventeenth century. Before exploring the various credit schemes proposed during this period, I offer a brief outline of the prevailing historical circumstances.

The Future of England's Credit System

General Economic Conditions

After an often difficult first half of the seventeenth century—during which mounting unemployment caused innumerable social problems and a devastating civil war killed some sixty thousand people—England's fortunes began to change after the Restoration.[55] Most importantly, land-improvement campaigns began to generate significantly higher yields.[56] Additional land was enclosed, crop rotations eliminated, seeds refined, and methods and techniques improved, making harvest failures less frequent, and resulting in a downward pressure on grain prices.[57] Grain imports were no longer needed and were in some instances prohibited in order to keep domestic prices from falling too far. In fact, landowners were occasionally offered subsidies by the authorities to export their bumper crops in order to stabilize prices.[58]

An expanding and diversifying manufacturing sector also contributed substantially to England's increasing prosperity. The rebuilding of London after the devastation of the 1666 fire generated much needed economic activity in the capital and so did the Crown's ambitious campaign to ensure that the Royal Navy would never again be embarrassed by foreign ships sailing up the Thames. The Navy became a growth industry, both in terms of the number of people employed and the size of the enterprises developed to provide ships, sails, weaponry, and other supplies.[59] Alongside the recovery of traditional industries, like cloth making and ironworks, the variety of England's manufacturing grew.[60] Spurred by an increase in the standard of living due to falling food prices, the consumption of nonessential goods—domestic, continental, and colonial—expanded rapidly during this period.[61]

The second half of the seventeenth century also witnessed a rapid growth in England's foreign trade.[62] The Cromwellian regime had dedicated itself to the expansion of England's colonial presence, a policy continued by Charles II, who expanded the number of colonies and imposed more direct political control over England's possessions. Charles challenged the Dutch dominance of the Atlantic carrying trade by renewing the Navigation Act, hoping thereby to turn London into the premier European entrepôt for the colonial trade. The resulting expansion in trade greatly contributed to the diversification of England's manufacturing base, leaving England less dependent on its cloth exports.[63]

Falling food prices and the growing manufacturing sector contributed to the transformation of how the poor were viewed. Previously considered a burden, the poor were now reconfigured into a potentially productive resource that, if employed correctly, could contribute substantially to England's wealth and power.[64] The poor could solve the personnel shortage in the navy and in England's commercial fleet, as well as provide much needed manpower for the growing manufacturing industry. The practice of encouraging the surplus population to emigrate to the colonies therefore came to an end, shifting the emphasis towards the Hartlibian project of transforming them into productive assets at home.[65]

The English state continued to rearrange its fiscal administration to meet its growing financial obligations. To pay for the Civil War, Parliament had introduced two new taxes that along with the customs tax would provide the bulk of the state's revenues for the foreseeable future: the excise and the land tax. The excise levied taxes on popular consumption items like beer, meat, salt, soap, and paper, thus serving as a more efficient way to raise money than the recently abolished monopolies.[66] While this tax contributed the greatest share of the state's revenues, the gentry was now for the first time also forced to contribute substantially to the state's revenues via the land tax.[67] Once Charles II was restored to the throne, however, Parliament was pressured to reduce the reliance on this tax, once again putting most of the burden on the customs and excise taxes. The expansion of commerce in the next few decades, coupled with the state's decision to terminate the customs and excise farms, ensured that these two revenue sources raised substantial funds for the government. Yet, since Charles was spending way beyond his means, he was forced to borrow extensively from the goldsmith bankers, who were pleased to obtain such lucrative business.[68]

Although money was still considered scarce during the second half of the seventeenth century, there was now some measure of relief. The well-to-do were able to access different kinds of credit mechanisms to facilitate their transactions, while the poorer sorts were able to purchase goods using trade tokens.[69] Goldsmith bankers and scriveners, although they had been developing their operations for some time, emerged as an important source of lending during the interregnum.[70] Prominent bankers like Sir Thomas Vyner, Edward Backwell, John Colville, Jeremiah Snow, and the Meynell brothers developed large-scale banking operations serving the landed gentry, merchants, and the government.[71] In addition to lending money, goldsmith bankers and scriveners also discounted bills of exchange and exchanged foreign coin, as well as issued checks (running cash notes) and promissory notes.[72] The latter would soon enjoy significant negotiability among merchants, leading some historians to suggest that they deserve to be thought of as currency.[73] Yet, regardless of how widely these goldsmith notes circulated, their liquidity and prevalence was not sufficient to put an end to the perception that England needed a more elastic money supply. Few, if any, political economists were convinced that England was already equipped with a monetary system sophisticated enough to answer the demands of its rapidly expanding commerce or that it would suffice to copy any of the continental banking schemes.[74]

Credit Currency Proposals

A number of proposals for how to best design a credit currency were published between the Restoration of Charles II and the foundation of the Bank of England. Many, but not all, of these proposals were influenced and inspired by Hartlibian ideas. Yet even if they did not accept every principle of Hartlibian political economy, they all agreed that it was possible to generate enough trust in credit instruments for them to circulate as money. While some of the pamphlets discussed in the following were written as much as thirty years apart and therefore responded most immediately to very different economic and political conditions, there is a sense that in many cases these proposals were written in conversation with each other.

In moving beyond the existing network of personal credit to a system of generally circulating anonymous credit instruments, political economists sought ways to move from what sociologist Niklas Luhmann calls personal trust to system trust, or from what Anthony Giddens refers to as facework commitments to faceless commitments.[75] Some credit proponents argued that a mechanism's reliance on the integrity and skill of a particular person was an advantage, while others viewed it as weakness, a source of precariousness. A few pamphleteers proclaimed to have discovered a way to generate system trust, thus obviating anyone in possession of credit money from having to trust any other specific person. Such a credit currency would thus operate similarly to modern money, as described by Luhmann: "Anyone who trusts in the stability of the value of money, and the continuity of a multiplicity of opportunities for spending it, basically assumes that a system is functioning and places his trust in that function, not in people."[76] Nevertheless, in the end, most of the proposed schemes relied on trust in particular individuals, in one way or another.

Much of the discussion about credit therefore focused on the importance of people's reputation, skills, manners, character, virtue, and honesty. But since people were not always able to directly gauge the reputation of those in whom they were deciding to put their trust, markers or indicia of propriety and virtue—such as wealth, education, and gentility—were emphasized. However, since a trusted party always had the freedom to mislead, lie, or renege, as both Hobbes and Locke pointed out, it was essential that the government was willing and capable of prosecuting those engaged in activities that undermined trust, such as corruption, overissuance, forgery, counterfeiting, or other fraudulent practices. The idea of using the death penalty to deter people from manipulating credit was an integral part of nearly all of the period's credit money proposals. Hence, as much as seventeenth-century political economists believed that it was possible to generate trust in credit money by designing a transparent mechanism with impeccable security, managed by men of the highest reputation, the gallows nevertheless constituted an important ingredient in the formation of trust.

ASSIGNABLE DEBT INSTRUMENTS. The most straightforward way to establish a credit currency was to make personal debts universally assignable. As noted earlier, by revising the nation's legal code it was possible to monetize all personal debts. John Bland, who described himself as a "wel-wisher to the Nation and its Prosperity," proclaimed just before the Restoration that in order to "Nourish, Improve, and Strengthen" the merchant corps, it was necessary to make bonds and bills fully assignable and transferable.[77] Until the beginning of the eighteenth century, only the initial creditor had the right to sue the debtor. The crucial legal change was therefore to allow any holder of a bill to sue the initial debtor. Only then could holders of the debt instruments be assured that they would be able to convert their bill or bond into the money or merchandise initially offered as security for the loan.[78]

Making personal debts transferable would generate a number of benefits. By monetizing debts owed to them, merchants would no longer have to wait for payment before they could reinvest their capital, thus increasing their turnover. The merchants' capital would also become safer, as they were no longer exposed to the risks of asynchronous cash flows. As an anonymous pamphleteer promoting increased assignability of bills and bonds declared:

> Tradesmen live upon Credit, buy much upon Trust, are obliged to pay on certain days on which if they fail, their Credit is lost; and as they buy upon Credit, so they must sell upon Trust: And if the person trusted by them, pay not at the time limited, yet are they that trust them obliged to observe punctually their days of payments, because the credit of those Merchants that trust them, depends thereupon.[79]

The most important benefit of monetizing personal debts, however, was that the money stock was enlarged and that some of the social and economic ills associated with the scarcity of money problem could be eliminated.[80]

In addition to the legal changes required for debt instruments to circulate widely, John Bland added that people had to commit themselves to maintaining the "Reputation of their Bills" by being "extream[ly] punctual in their payment."[81] Yet, even if people became more punctual, the integrity of the bills was still in jeopardy because of the general dishonesty that Bland detected among the English. He asked, "among a people so apt and ready to deceive, as we of this Nation be, and to counterfeit mens hands, what course is to be taken to prevent such a mischief?"[82] First, he proposed to enhance transparency by making sure that all bills and bonds were standardized so that forgeries and counterfeits could be more readily detected. Second, the original debtor issuing the credit instrument should be forced to do so in the presence of a notary public to ensure that all bills and bonds were backed by an actual person with access to property. Third, Bland added that the punishment for counterfeiting had to become harsher to reflect the severity of the crime. He insisted that "it be made Felony in the highest degree to Counterfeit any mans hand to any Bill, or Bond, or other writing whatever, and to profer the same as a true Deed, Bill, or Bond."[83] He also noted that if the forger is "not punished with death, at least lose his hand for the fact, which strict punishment will undoubtedly deter all from presuming to advantage themselves by such fraud."[84] The key ingredients of a well-functioning credit mechanism were thus reputation for honesty and punctuality, transparency, and severe punishment. Together, these ingredients would contribute to the formation of an environment in which people were able to overcome doubt and anxiety and develop the proper kind and degree of trust for the new currency to circulate.

The river engineer and agricultural improver Andrew Yarranton (1619–1684) also advocated that personal debt instruments become negotiable. He insisted that such instruments could circulate widely as long as the general level of honesty in England was improved. In an ambitious book reminiscent of the Hartlibians' universal reform project, *England's Improvement by Sea and Land, To Out-Do the Dutch without Fighting* (1677), Yarranton proposed that England must build a new culture of honesty so that all agreements could be trusted. He argued that in "All Kingdoms and Common-wealths in the World that depend upon Trades, common *Honesty* is as necessary and needful in them, as Discipline is in an Army, and where is want of common Honesty in a Kingdom or Commonwealth, from thence Trade shall depart."[85] He further called on the government to dedicate itself to honest dealings. "For as the Honesty of all Governments is so shall be their *Riches;* And as their *Honour, Honesty,* and *Riches* are, so will be their *Strength*; And as their *Honour, Honesty, Riches,* and *Strength* are, so will be their *Trade*."[86]

In addition to promoting a culture of honesty and trust, Yarranton proposed five improvements that he believed would strengthen England economically and geopolitically—most immediately allowing England to prevail over the Dutch without having to fight a fourth Anglo-Dutch war. Of the five necessary improvements, one—making all rivers navigable—involved an ambitious engineering project, while the remaining innovations were essentially designed to enhance trust in credit. Yarranton argued that England ought to establish a public bank for merchants similar to that of the Bank of Amsterdam, a Lombard bank operating as a pawnshop for the poor, a Court of Merchants to swiftly settle all claims and disagreements, and a public register for all lands and houses. The creation of a public register was particularly important to Yarranton. Land and estates could only serve efficiently as security if they were well defined and adequately secured, which was not currently the case. Yarranton lamented the fact that landed gentlemen were often unable to borrow money from scriveners against their land because "no man can know a Title by Writings, there being so many ways to incumber the Land privately."[87] The fact that there was no official register of who owned a piece of land, estate, or house meant that even men of great fortunes were forced to present a third party willing to pose as security for a loan.

Yarranton argued that two dominant reasons for why the Dutch were so commercially successful, despite the size of their population and limited resources, were their land registry, in which all sales of lands and houses were publicly registered, and their legal system, which supported the circulation of credit instruments. This allowed the Dutch to easily borrow against their property and to conveniently trade the resulting debt instruments. Yarranton proclaimed: "Reader, I pray Observe, that every Acre of Land in the Seven Provinces [of the Dutch Republic] trades all the world over, and it is as good as ready Money."[88] Hence, if England learned from the Dutch and created a public register and allowed for the transfer of all bills and bonds, land and houses would "be equal with ready Moneys at all times."[89] This reform would not only quicken trade and vastly increase the prosperity and strength of England, it might also prevent a continued cycle of Anglo-Dutch Wars. Hence, similar to Bland, Yarranton highlighted the need for a new culture of honesty, as well as the importance of improving the integrity and transparency of the security backing the credit notes.

BANK OF LONDON. The London merchant Samuel Lambe also motivated his proposals for a more sophisticated credit system by referring to England's geopolitical interests. He argued during the interregnum that England had no other choice but to establish a credit currency in order to keep up with the Dutch, economically and militarily.[90] He suggested that a number of prominent merchants should bond together and create a Bank of London, with the authority to accept deposits and extend loans. The directors should be drawn in equal numbers from the great London merchant companies, including the "East India, Turky, *Merchant Adventurers, East Countrey, Muscovia,* Greenland & Guynne *Companies,*" but most importantly they had to be "men of estates and credit" in order to instill a sense of confidence among the public.[91] Drawing inspiration from the design of the Italian merchant banks, the Bank of London's primary purpose was to facilitate transactions between traders.[92] The bank would accept deposits from merchants, who could then conduct most of their transactions by assignation, thus saving "much trouble in receiving and paying of money."[93] In addition to the money deposited, the merchants would also be able to trade on a line of credit granted by the bank on good security, amounting to two or three times the size of the merchant's deposits.[94] By having access to such bank money, merchants guaranteed that transactions would not only become safer and more convenient, but they would be able to invest and transact beyond their liquid capital. This would effectively expand the amount of money in circulation, even though the bank would not issue any physical paper notes.[95] This alternative to a physical currency would also eliminate "fraudulent payments in counterfeit and clipt Coyn, or mis-telling money, rectifying errours in Accounts, which occasion Law suits, preventing theft, and breaking open houses, where money is suspected to lie, and robbing on the high-ways Graziers, Carriers, or others that use to carry money from Fairs."[96] The elimination of these sources of anxiety, insecurity, and crime, combined with the expansion of the money stock would "wonderfully encrease all manner of Trade."[97]

In order to ensure that the "imaginary money" created by the Bank of London would be widely accepted, Lambe specified a number of measures to ensure that people trusted the bank and the money it issued. First, as mentioned above, the bank's managers needed to be men of "estates and credit," meaning that ideally they were landed gentlemen of impeccable reputation. They, in turn, were responsible for selecting prudent officers, who would manage the bank's affairs in accordance with strict rules. Only by engaging men of character was it possible for people to trust the managers' testimonies about the condition of the bank. To ensure that the managers did not succumb to the temptation of misusing or embezzling money, Lambe insisted that the directors had to institute "such great penalties as shall be thought fitting" to deter improprieties among the managers.[98] Lambe furthermore proposed that officials were made responsible for preparing the bank's accounts and make them available to the public at least once per year. The hope was, consonant with Locke's focus on personal observations, that people would be able to form a more robust opinion if they were able to witness firsthand how the credit currency was designed and secured. The publication of the accounts was meant not only to inform the public about the state of the company's affairs, but also to indicate rule-boundedness, expertise, and honesty—virtues that signaled to the public that the bank was safe and secure.[99] Transparent accounting thus revealed the character of the bankers, not just the bank's financial position.

Lambe's use of the term "imaginary money" followed a long tradition going back to the Middle Ages, when the term was minted to refer to the kinds of money existing only in the bankers' accounts. While the seventeenth-century meaning of *imagination* often denoted something that existed solely in peoples' minds, it also had a different meaning. For Hobbes, imagination was a *"decaying sense."*[100] He suggested that every conception in the human mind originates as a sensory impression. Once the object is removed from our senses, we still retain an image of that object. This, according to Hobbes, is our imagination; a memory of a personal observation or experience.[101] Hence, for Hobbes, imagination had nothing to do with fantasies or mental concoctions, but referred to how sensory impressions are stored in people's minds. Hobbes's definition fits well with Lambe's concept of imaginary money. Unlike a coin or a note with a physical presence circulating in and out of people's hands, generating a continuous impression on people's senses, imaginary money only existed in people's minds and in the bank's accounts. It was for this purpose that Lambe insisted on transparent accounting rules, so that people could observe the accounts and thus form a vivid imagination.

CIRCULATING GOVERNMENT BONDS. While Lambe hoped to reduce the complexity of credit by designing a scheme that only required people to trust the bank, Sir William Killigrew (d. 1695), politician, projector, financial advisor to Charles II, and a moderately successful playwright, posited a credit mechanism that focused all the trust on the state. Inspired by the Dutch *renten* and *obligaties*, he proposed three years after Charles's Restoration that the government should issue £2,000,000 worth of bonds and pass a yearly tax of £300,000 to service the interest and gradually pay off the loan.[102] Creditors willing to lend to the government would be issued a bond either with "his Name in the Bonds, or Blank; saying, Payable to *A.B.* or to the Bearer . . . this last is best, because of transferring them."[103] The bonds would be issued in denominations from £5 to £100, with a preference for the lower denominations as they circulated more readily. In order to further enhance liquidity, the government would guarantee that the bonds "shall not only be transferable, but currant, as Mony in all Payments whatsoever, even into the Exchequer."[104] The government was thus the focal point of this entire mechanism. Not only did the bonds raise money for the state, but the state also provided the primary security. The state would maintain a legal framework guaranteeing transferability, as well as secure the debt through its authority to tax. The power to tax and to punish was thus the primary source of people's trust in the continued exchangeability of these bonds.

Killigrew added a number of other measures intended to ensure the integrity of the bonds. First, he suggested that an act should be passed that made it treason for officers to issue more bonds than Parliament had authorized. Comparing such fraud to currency debasement, whereby the holders of money were robbed, he hoped that the fear of harsh punishments would keep the officers from overissuing bonds. He also suggested that each bond should be signed by the secretary and three commissioners to reduce the possibility of fraud. To further eliminate the officers' discretionary power in favoring certain investors, Killigrew advised that interest on the bonds should always be paid in sequence of issuance and that the priority of payment should be recorded in the official books. Through these measures, Killigrew sought to marginalize the risk of unprincipled management that might undermine trust.

Killigrew envisioned that these bonds would be both more liquid and more secure than coin. Since all bonds would be numbered and registered, any bond that was lost, stolen, or burned could be recovered. These instruments would also, by law, be accepted everywhere. In fact, Killigrew wanted to make it a treasonous offense for anyone to refuse bonds in payment for any debt or obligation. He also proposed that counterfeiting bonds should become a capital offense so that any seed of doubt in the public's mind that a bond might be inauthentic could be minimized. If all of these security measures were implemented, he asserted that:

> these Bonds will be superior to Gold and Silver, because these Bonds cannot be counterfeited, lost, stoln, or burnt without recovery; they will be a new *Species* of Mony that will grow in our Coffers, every day increasing, which Gold nor Silver does not, but is liable to many Inconveniences, as Thieves, false and clipt Mony, counterfeiting, loss of time in counting, and chargeable to carry in large Sums.[105]

Insisting that the measures he outlined would generate the requisite trust for his proposed currency to circulate widely, he proudly proclaimed, "All mankind must confess, that Credit grounded on a good and solid Security, if it can be made currant, is not only as good, but better than Mony it self."[106] Estimating that England at the time had no more than £7 million in circulation, Killigrew was convinced that a £2 million increase in the money stock would greatly expand the nation's trade and employment. It would also ease the fiscal pressures on the state and facilitate the raising of the requisite funds for the Royal Navy.

Contrary to many of the other schemes proposed during the second half of the seventeenth century, a version of Killigrew's proposal was actually implemented in the 1660s. Dissatisfied with the power that the goldsmith bankers enjoyed as the king's primary creditors, Sir George Downing (1623-1684), Secretary of the Treasury, sought to circumvent their influence by introducing Treasury Orders, an alternative means of borrowing for the Crown.[107] Almost indistinguishable from Killigrew's proposal, the Orders were made legally assignable and redeemable for cash in strict sequence. Holders of these securities could then decide whether to keep them until they came due or sell them to a discounter, frequently a goldsmith banker. Most investors pursued the latter option, generating a situation by 1672 where the bulk of the Orders were in the hands of a small number of bankers. Hence, Downing's scheme inadvertently served to further strengthen the goldsmith bankers' position as public creditors.

England's financial architecture was famously rattled at the start of 1672, when Charles decided to suspend interest payments on approximately half of his debt. Although he had accumulated a total debt of £3 million, his decision to halt payments was not due to an inability to actually service the outstanding debt. Instead he suspended payments in anticipation of another costly war with the Dutch. Although Charles intended for the moratorium to be temporary, Parliament's refusal to grant him additional revenues to service the old debt made many depositors nervous about keeping their money with the goldsmith bankers, many of whom were stuck with bad debts on their books. Substantial withdrawals were made during subsequent months, eventually forcing some of the banks to close down.[108] This series of events not only undermined the established banking system, it also damaged the Crown's ability to borrow. The Crown once again had to rely on corporate bodies, like the East India Company and the City of London, and on the nascent system of annuities to raise funds. Fortunately for Charles, however, the nation's flourishing commerce generated soaring excise and customs receipts, reducing his need to borrow. Nevertheless, the Stop of the Exchequer had revealed the backwardness of England's financial system, intensifying the call for a universally negotiable paper currency and a national banking system.[109]

OFFICE OF CREDIT. Killigrew's proposal to issue circulating government bonds and Lambe's design for the Bank of London were criticized for relying too much on trust in particular people—managers, directors, or public officials. This not only led to a dangerous dependency on certain key figures, which created problems when they died or left government, but it also exposed the schemes to the risk that the trusted figures might not live up to their reputed skill, prudence, and propriety. Hoping to avoid reliance on any particular individual, plans for the formation of an Office of Credit, or Bank of Credit, were hatched during Charles II's reign. One of its earliest proponents, Hugh Chamberlen (1630–ca 1720)—fellow of the Royal Society, famous court physician, and an active pamphleteer on financial matters—described the Office as a hybrid between the Bank of Amsterdam and a Lombard Bank. While the Bank of Amsterdam issued notes backed by coin, and the Lombards allowed people to borrow money against property, the Office of Credit would issue notes on the security of goods and merchandise. Chamberlen described the Office as serving as "a generall *Store-house*, receiving all parties Goods, and delivering out their Tickets."[110] He compared it to the common practice "in *Virginia, Barbadoes* and other Plantations, where the Planters bring in their *Tobacco* and *Sugar* to the *Store-house* (in the absence of Ships) and receive a Note; (there being no Money) from the *Storekeeper*, who is but a private person, and with that Note, as far as the *Storekeeper* is known, can they purchase any other Commodity."[111] As soon as the merchants and manufacturers had built up an inventory of goods they could bring it to the warehouse where they received credit up to a certain value. This allowed merchants to effectively monetize their goods and to reinvest their wealth before the sale of their inventories. This accelerated the turnover of the merchants' capital and thus enriched both the merchants and the nation.

Chamberlen's proposal approached the challenge of establishing trust differently from the previous proponents of credit money. In trying to reduce the anxiety surrounding credit, Chamberlen deflected attention away from the potentially corruptible human element involved in the issuance of credit and instead highlighted the materiality of the security backing credit. In defining credit as "the reputation of Mans honesty, or abilitie, or of a things intrinsick value," he underscored the importance of the latter.[112] He pointed out that in "this Office will be always sufficient Pledges of intrinsick value, to answer the full credit [outstanding]."[113] The fact that credit issued by the Office was fully backed by merchandise in the storehouse meant that the goods played the active role in generating trust and the Office played only a passive role in the issuance of credit. "For the Goods lodged in the *Office*," he argued, "are the reall Debitor, and the person possessing the Credit of them (although a hundred times, by Assignment, transferred) is the Creditor."[114] The security lodged in the storehouse of the Office was far greater than that of the proposed Bank of London, which would never have enough security available at any one time to redeem all outstanding claims. The Office actually maintained a greater than full reserve, in that it only issued credit on a fraction of the merchandise deposited in its warehouse. Hence, even if the price of the goods in the warehouse suddenly dropped, the Office would still be able to sell the goods in the marketplace and redeem the notes presented.

To reduce the exposure to severe price volatility, Chamberlen proposed that most goods should not be kept in the warehouse for more than a month. During the time the merchandize was in the possession of the Office, the merchant would have complete access to the goods, allowing him to "take care of them, and prevent any damage that may happen to them."[115] There would also be servants on hand who, for a small fee, would "use all means of preserving the Goods: from Mould, Mildew, Canker, Rust, Rats, Mice, Mothes, Spots, Staines, Wet, Dust, Rot, &c."[116] If the goods were not redeemed by the depositing merchant, either by returning the initial credit instrument, some other bill or bond, or coin, by the time agreed on, they would be offered up for sale. If the goods fetched a higher price than the credit issued, the merchant would receive all of the revenues, minus a small fee. This meant that whoever was holding the initial credit instrument was now able to redeem it for ready money and that the holders of the credit notes could always be confident that the notes were adequately backed.

Since his proposed credit mechanism was backed by a more than adequate security, Chamberlen confidently projected that "in the future there will be no need of Trusting."[117] Credit's dependency on trust, he argued, had arisen because the scarcity of money had forced people to rely on personal bills and bonds, which often lacked adequate security. The resulting chain of personal credit had worked well as long as every person involved committed themselves to punctual payments. However, since it was enough for "one slow or dishonest man, for want of payment, [to] . . . obstruct the Trade of 100, or more persons" there was always a great deal of anxiety associated with this precarious chain. But, since the Office would only issue credit on the basis of solid security, merchants did not expose themselves to any discernable risk and therefore did not need to develop a culture of trust.[118]

Chamberlen was exuberantly optimistic about his proposed scheme, offering a long list of private and public benefits. First and foremost, he believed that trade would receive a monumental boost, increasing by a factor of twenty to forty. This would provide a massive stimulus to fishing, manufacturing, land improvement, plantations, and innovations in all fields. The well-to-do would be further enriched, while the poor would now be able to find employment and thus a steady income. All this commercial activity would furthermore lower the price of goods and thus allow England to become the *Emporium* of Europe, if not of the World."[119] The government would also benefit, as its revenues from the excise and customs would steadily grow. In addition to contributing to the quantity of money in circulation, the new medium of exchange would also enhance the quality of the currency. No longer would merchants be bothered by the necessity of carefully counting and assessing diverse and tattered coins or the possibility of incurring losses due to the receipt of counterfeit and clipped money. The number of bad debts and associated lawsuits also would drop, and this would soon drastically reduce the number of people in debtor's jail.

Mark Lewis (1621–1681), a Church of England clergyman and Hartlibian-influenced schoolmaster, also supported the establishment of an Office of Credit. Arguing that its credit notes were "as good as Mony," the Office had the potential to "advance the Riches and Honour of the Nation, beyond any thing the *Spanish Indies* could have done, if we had possessed our selves of them."[120] He predicted that the only constituencies that would lament the introduction of such new money were "Thieves, Brokers, and griping Usurers."[121] Lewis reassured his readers that the Office was safe from both counterfeiting and monarchical expropriation. He insisted that it "shall be Felony without Clergy to counterfeit, or steal a Bill, or by force to attempt the violating any of these Banks."[122] While a monarch might be tempted to abuse his power, Lewis was confident that the many benefits the Office might provide to the monarch and the nation would ultimately deter him. A prince would be no more interested in ruining a properly functioning credit system than he would be likely to pass up the philosopher's stone, if indeed it could ever be found. In fact, if the monarch were to obtain the magic tincture, he would ideally employ it in the same manner that a well-functioning credit system regulates the money stock. Lewis explained:

> The best use any Prince could make of such a Stone (if such a thing was), would be to put it into safe hands that they might make so much Gold and Silver as would supply his own occasions, ordinary and extraordinary; and furnish his People with so much stock as might quicken Trade, improve Husbandry, and set up all kinds of Manufactures; for a People thus exercised, would be in a better condition to defende their Prince and themselves, and to offend their Enemies; than if Gold was as plentiful as Stones, and Silver as the Sands; when all would degenerate into effeminacie, and be a prey to their Neighbours for their Riches.[123]

Of the many proposals for an Office of Credit that circulated during the 1680s, arguably the most convincing proposition was the anonymous submission, *Bank-Credit: or the Usefulness & Security of the Bank of Credit Examined* (1683).[124] Staged as a conversation between a merchant and a gentleman, the pamphlet dramatizes a debate in which the former sought and ultimately managed to convince the latter of the safety of an Office of Credit. The author focused in equal measure on the security of the merchandise backing credit and the incorruptibility of the directors of the proposed bank. He argued that if the bank always followed its bylaws, dictating that the bank would never issue credit to the full value of the merchandise deposited in the warehouse, the credit would always be perfectly secure. Of course, the directors or officers of the bank might bend the rules and issue credit beyond the security in the warehouse. However, the merchant assured the gentleman, "I am very certain the Officers of the *Bank* will run as great hazard of being discovered in issuing any Bill of Credit where there is not always a Fund to make it good."[125] Not only were the officers involved in the day-to-day running of the bank "under their Oaths, and give[n] Security for the faithful discharge of their Places," but they were also under explicit orders to uphold "the Honour, Credit, and Interest of the Governours of the *Bank,* whose Estates and Reputation in the World, render them above such Fraud."[126] Hence, for the managers, being men of character, retaining their reputation was more important than any temporary pecuniary gains.

While the gentleman acknowledged to the merchant that "*You have satisfied me in this,*" he moved on to inquire about counterfeiting, a threat to the safety of the bills that neither the goods in the warehouse nor the incorruptible officers could do much about. The gentleman added that if the merchant could account for this risk, "*you will go very near to satisfie most men.*"[127] Contrary to most of the pamphlets advocating harsh punishments for monetary crimes, this author focused on eliminating counterfeiting by issuing bills that were near-impossible to manipulate. He suggested that by printing the bills with "Indented Knots" and "Marks," fakes would be easily discovered. The only way that counterfeiters would then be able to continue their trade was if they gained access to the actual technology used by the bank itself. However, not even the officers would be able to "come by any of the Stamps, Seals, Plates, Indenting Instruments, or Paper, . . . those things being always under three Locks and Keys, in the Possession of known Persons for Reputation, and impossible to be come at, but in the Presence of the Governours."[128] This apparently satisfied the gentleman, who proclaimed that he was:

> fully convinced, that so Great and Good an Undertaking deserves, and will find the Applause and Assistance of all Prudent, Industrious and Good Men, and in fine, of all such as have any value for the publick Prosperity, or regard to their own Private Advantage.[129]

BANK OF ENGLAND. The Glorious Revolution of 1688 fundamentally transformed England's fiscal and financial system. After James II's short reign, during which soaring custom and excise revenues essentially allowed him to govern independently of Parliament, William III was forced to accept a strict financial settlement. Parliament granted the monarch a yearly revenue of £1.2 million, a sum that was far below the £5.5 million that the war against France would end up costing on average per year. This deficiency forced William to call frequent

Parliaments, thus ensuring that he had to govern jointly with Parliament. To pay for the war, Parliament added a number of new taxes and increased the reliance on the land tax. Yet, as the downturn in trade reduced the customs and excise receipts, total revenues still fell far short of expenditures. To make up the difference, the government issued more tallies and undertook additional borrowing from the City of London.[130] The Treasury also introduced three new devices, lotteries, tontines, and annuities, which provided the foundation for England's first system of long-term borrowing.[131]

The financial innovation that ultimately enabled England to pursue the war on Louis XIV without going bankrupt was the Bank of England. A 1694 parliamentary act allowed the Bank to raise a capital stock of £1.2 million, the full value of which was to be lent to the government, paid out in notes or sealed bills, rather than coin, in exchange for tallies. In return, the government committed £140,000 per year to the Bank from a new tax on shipping and liquor, which was enough to pay subscribers an 8 percent dividend (£100,000 payable in cash and Exchequer Orders), provide a management fee to the Bank (£4,000), and allow the Bank to improve the returns on its reserves by acquiring annuities.[132] The Bank's capital was subscribed in ten days by some thirteen hundred people and the Bank swiftly commenced its operations.[133] In addition to lending interest-bearing bills to the government, the Bank discounted bills of exchange, accepted deposits, and issued loans. Depositors could either choose to have an account book or to be issued notes payable to the person or bearer. The Bank also issued paper notes to borrowers, on the security of goods, like silver plate and jewels.[134] By 1696, the Bank had lent £1,240,000 in sealed bills to the Treasury and issued £887,000 of notes to its private customers. The Bank's notes were redeemable for coin on demand, made possible by keeping a portion of the coin paid in by the subscribers and some of the deposits in the Bank on hand. The Bank's notes circulated at par from the start, signaling the arrival of England's and Europe's first widely circulating credit currency.[135]

In addition to the new types of government borrowing and the new currency, the explosion in joint-stock companies and the formation of a better organized securities market contributed to making the 1690s the epicenter of the Financial Revolution.[136] Dubbed the "Age of Projectors" by Daniel Defoe, the first half of the decade saw the number of publicly traded stocks increase by at least a hundred.[137] The Royal

Exchange initially housed the trade in securities, along with its vibrant trade in commodities, but as the controversy surrounding the practice of stock trading intensified, a limit was put on the number of jobbers and brokers welcomed there. Soon, however, stock traders were expelled *en masse*.[138] The trade then moved to the coffeehouses, most famously Jonathan's and Garraway's, located in the alleys between Cornhill and Lombard Street, a stone's throw away from the Royal Exchange.

The creation of a liquid securities market in which long-term bonds could be traded, alongside company stocks and various derivatives, reduced the cost of borrowing for the government and substantially lowered the risk for investors. Since the new bonds would mature long into the future, the government effectively did not have to pay back the principal of the loan, leaving them to worry only about servicing the interest payments. These payments were now lower as it had become safer to lend to the government, and lenders had the added flexibility of being able to sell their bonds and thus end their tenure as government creditors at their own discretion.

The Bank of England was the brainchild of William Paterson (1658-1719), a Scottish-born projector, West Indies merchant, and later one of the originators of the fateful Darien scheme.[139] Lamenting that England did not have a bank that could "facilitate the circulation of Money . . . by which Trade hath been exceedingly discourag'd and obstructed," Paterson advocated a bank that issued notes backed by a fractional reserve of silver.[140] Paterson insisted that any bank not grounded on the security of metallic money had no real chance of surviving. Since silver operated as the standard of value, he argued, *"Credit not founded on the Universal Species of Gold and Silver, is* [therefore] *impracticable."*[141] He even added that credit not secured by coin was "false and counterfeit."[142] But with a sufficient amount of silver in the vault—Paterson noted that a reserve of 15–25 percent would suffice—the notes issued by the Bank would be perfectly secure.[143] Further adding to the security backing the notes were the profits from the Bank's commercial operations, which had "as good and great a probability" for profits as any other company, and, most importantly, the revenue flow from the government "that cannot fail" as it was secured by its power to tax.[144] Paterson pointed out that "the Security of the *Bank* . . . will be clear and visible, and every way equal to, if not exceeding the best in *Christendom*."[145] Unlike many of the other credit money proposals, Paterson did not emphasize the character and reputation of the Bank's managers and directors.[146] Instead he focused on the safety of the silver in the vault and the comfort of knowing that the government had the requisite power to raise enough revenues to meets its obligations to the Bank.

In promoting the safety of the Bank, Paterson addressed the contemporary fear that it was too risky to establish a bank in a monarchy—a suspicion strengthened by the recent Stop of the Exchequer. Paterson saw no basis for this worry. In fact, he claimed that property was safer in England than anywhere else. Given that William had agreed to govern in unison with Parliament, the only danger, in Paterson's mind, was if England fell victim to the Jacobite threat. He argued that since "there being no Country in *Christendom* where Property hath been more sacred and secure for some Ages past, notwithstanding all our Revolutions, than in *England,* it must needs follow, that nothing less than a Conquest, wherein all Property, Justice, and Right must fail, can any way affect this Foundation."[147] Paterson thus linked the success of the Bank with the survival of the new monarch and, even more importantly, England's national security and its long-cherished ideals of property and freedom.[148]

Paterson also highlighted how the Bank would improve the state's fiscal health and greatly contribute to the nation's commerce. He proclaimed that "none can reasonably apprehend any other Consequences of this Design to the Government and Nation, but that it will make Money plentiful, Trade easie and secure, raise the Price of Lands, draw the Species of Gold and Silver into the Hands of the Common People."[149] He believed that the long-term borrowing facilitated by the Bank was far more beneficial than the recently introduced annuities and lotteries. In fact, had the money that was allocated to lotteries been invested in the Bank, the same funds would have generated more than double the money to the government and would have had a vastly different qualitative impact on society; the money would have turned into "Funds beneficial to Trade and the Industry of the Nation; whereas the other are quite contrary, Nurses of Idleness, Baits of Vanity, possessing the People with a certain sort of Levity and Giddiness, and filling them with fond Expectations, destructive to their Welfare and future Improvements."[150]

Paterson's partner, the London financier, wine merchant, and the first deputy governor of the Bank, Michael Godfrey (1659–1695), also contributed a pamphlet in defense of the Bank, calling it "one of the best Establishments that ever was made for the *Good of the Kingdom*."[151] Godfrey agreed with Paterson that the Bank would lower the cost of public and private borrowing, which would encourage "*Industry and Improvements*," as well as raise the value of land and promote the expansion of commerce.[152] Godfrey noted that finally all English people with good security who were in need of money would now "know where to Apply themselves and be Supplied."[153] And those who deposit their money in the Bank "have it as much at their disposal as if it were in the hands of *the Goldsmiths*, or in their own *Cash-Chest*."[154] Godfrey also tried to win the support of the landed men, pointing out that the value of land in England would increase by some £100 million, thereby compensating them for all the land taxes they had paid to fund the war. He also addressed the landed elite's concern that the Bank would make the monarch financially independent, which would nullify the financial settlement of the Glorious Revolution. Godfrey assured them that this would not be the case. The Bank could not extend more money to the Crown than Parliament legislated and it was certainly not in the interest of the Bank to promote the power of the monarch, since it was Parliament that provided the security for the Bank.

Like Paterson, Godfrey also insisted that the reason why the Bank's notes would circulate without any problems was because they were redeemable on demand for silver coin. Notes backed by anything but silver, such as land or merchandise, would not work; it would "soon end *in Confusion*."[155] Since there is always a cost incurred when notes are redeemed for anything but silver, such notes would always trade at a slight discount, eventually eroding the value of such a currency. Contrary to the Bank's notes, which he believed would soon circulate internationally, any other form of paper currency would not only be unable to circulate outside the nation, but would broadcast to the world that England no longer had enough money to conduct the war.

After the formation of the Bank of England, its supporters kept up the propaganda campaign to promote the Bank and its notes. A number of people rushed to the defense of the Bank, including Sir Humphrey Mackworth (1657–1727), the industrial entrepreneur, well-connected politician, and the cofounder of the moral reform group the Society for the Promotion of Christian Knowledge (SPCK). Noting that England already possessed all the natural, economic, and human resources required for great prosperity and geopolitical strength, Mackworth argued that with the establishment of the Bank, the nation was now capable of capitalizing on this potential. *"Our Country,"* he argued, *"thus accomplish'd with all Blessings, as to Fertility and Ingenuity, a little help* [from the Bank] *will make it the most Glorious Place in the World, and His Majesty the most Potent Prince in* Christendom."[156] He argued that the bank was first to settle *"the Great Question . . .* [of] *How to raise a Stock or Fund that shall be credited by all."*[157] The fact that the Bank's notes were assignable by law and secured by Parliament's power to tax ensured that the notes would retain their value and thus be able to serve as a pledge in market exchanges.[158] The availability of this new currency, Mackworth argued, "will make the King *great*, the Gentry *rich*, the Farmers *flourish*, the Merchant *trade*, Ships *encrease*, Seamen to be *employed*, *set up* New Manufactures, and *encourage* the Old. What may not such a King be and do, that reigns over such a People, who are not inferiour to any in Courage, and doubtless their Spirits will rise higher, when they find they have Purses superiour to all."[159]

Another pamphlet that compared the Bank favorably against its continental counterparts claimed that the Bank had the capacity to expand credit on an altogether different scale than the Bank of Amsterdam. The anonymous author noted that the Dutch bank maintained two divisions: the primary operation that issued paper notes on deposited coin and plate and the much smaller Lombard division that lent money on the security of property. Since only the latter effectively extended credit, the author pointed out that the *"Bank of Amsterdam* is only a *Deposite* of Ready Money, for the security of Trade, and for the Convenience of writing off, instead of paying out."[160] As such, the note-issuing division of the Bank of Amsterdam did not, the author contended, deserve to be called a bank. The Lombard, or lending, division, on the other hand, did expand the money stock by lending money to people who could present good security. However, in comparison to the Bank of England, the capacity of the Bank of Amsterdam to expand credit was miniscule. Not only did the Bank of England issue notes to depositors and borrowers, but it also lent more than £1.2 million in banknotes to the government. As these notes entered circulation, the bank significantly contributed to the expansion of the money stock, expanding it by what he estimated to be 15 percent. All of these benefits led the author to proclaim exuberantly, "After so many Difficulties, and so much Opposition from Malice and Ignorance, we see the *Bank of England*, not only brought to some degree of Perfection, *but crowned with so glorious Success*, as are not only surprizing at home, but sufficient to amaze all *Europe*."[161]

LAND BANKS. Soon after the establishment of the Bank of England, many landed men in Parliament became discontent with the Bank's violations of traditional country values, such as the centralization of authority, land as the essence of power, and the inherent moral superiority of landed men.[162] The country leadership, one historian points out, "saw the centralization of finance, controlled by a junto-led commercial oligarchy, as little better than an absolute monarchy."[163] Moreover, the landed men were disgruntled by the fact that the now increased land tax forced them to pay for the new political administration, at the same time that they saw their political influence wane. This discontentedness led to a febrile effort to launch a national land bank that could rival the Bank of England.

The land bank scheme proposed by William Potter in the 1650s, initiating the entire debate about a generally circulating credit currency in England, never quite disappeared from consideration. Writing in the immediate aftermath of the Great Plague and the Great Fire of London, and during the concluding phase of the disastrous second Anglo-Dutch War, Sir Edward Forde (d. 1670), a former royalist army officer and prominent inventor of hydraulic equipment, called for a major overhaul of the financial architecture to help England rebuild. He argued that since "Bills, Bonds, Book Accompts, and even verball promises" had revealed their capacity to mediate transactions, there was no good reason why credit on good security could not substitute for coin altogether. Since credit was more convenient and "supplyes and contents us as well as Money," Forde argued that the advantages of credit money were obvious.[164] He asked, "who would not rather have a Straw, or a piece of Paper, then a hundred pounds, if he were sure it would at all times yield him as much as he took it for."[165] He favored the creation of a number of different credit currencies, each designed for a particular segment of the population. He first suggested the creation of a land bank, since "Land security is evidently, of all, the surest, and most satisfying, where the Title is cleer, and no danger of Counterfeits."[166] Next, he suggested that the government should issue interest-bearing bonds, backed by future tax receipts, similar to the Treasury Orders discussed earlier. These debt instruments would circulate without problems, as "No Money can be surer than Taxes by Act of Parliament."[167] Lastly, Forde also advocated the formation of a Lombard bank that would provide loans to the poor on the security of personal property. This would allow the poor to borrow at rates substantially lower than the 40–60 percent interest they were often forced to pay.

Also writing during the early phase of the Restoration, the merchant Francis Cradocke offered Charles II a method to discover *"Richer Mines then any the King of* Spain *is Owner of; and for wealth not much inferior to what* Solomon *possessed in all his Glory."*[168] After providing an overview of the different types of money used throughout history, Cradocke concluded that it is not the "manner or figure, solidicy or dust of metals, that necessarily make it current, but the certainty and security of value by which it may be current from one to another."[169] For Cradocke, land was the ideal security because it "is as sure and certain a security and pledge as Plate or any other Goods of a mans own mark or making."[170] And, since the value of all lands in England exceeded that of coin by a factor of twenty, a land bank would be able to issue far more credit than a bank using precious metals as security.

One of the Bank of England proponents acknowledged the land bank's superior capacity to create credit. This, however, he regarded as a source of great volatility. The author pointed out that if the proposed land banks were actually successfully implemented, they would have the capacity to expand the money stock by somewhere between £20 million to £800 million. In light of the estimation by John Cary (1649–1719), a prominent British sugar merchant and well-known political economic writer, that the annual expenditures undertaken by English consumers, tradesmen, and government authorities together amounted to only about £1 billion per year, such an enormous expansion in the money stock would bring about complete chaos.[171] "The *Projectors of China,*" Cradocke suggested, "are in fresh pursuit of the *Universal Medicine*; those in *Germany* and elsewhere in *Europe* are within an *Ace* of the *Transmutation* or *Philosopher's Stone*; and those in *England* are fixing of *Banks* beyond the *Moon*; and should they all succeed to expectation, the Question would rather be, Which should do least Mischeif, than which should do most Good."[172] As opposed to these high-flying projects, the anonymous author argued that the Bank of England provided just the right mix of security and flexibility—enough to facilitate all commercial undertakings, to finance the government's operations, and to limit opportunities for scruple-free financiers to take advantage of desperate borrowers.

Cradocke, however, insisted that money issued by land banks constituted the most secure form of credit. The key, as many credit money proponents had already pointed out, was to establish a land registry that could remove the confusion surrounding landownership that had been caused by centuries of alternating property regimes, and thus to make sure that two people could not use the same piece of land as security for two different loans. By combining the bank and the land registry, owners of land and houses would have constant access to credit, which they could either decide to let lay dormant or use to pay for goods and services. The key to ensuring that people would trust the bank's credit was to make sure that the registration of land and houses was conducted in the most accurate, transparent, and responsible manner. To that effect, the plan for a land registry should be announced in all cities and towns, read in all parish churches throughout England and Wales, and broadcasted to "all Governors of Plantations abroad, Ambassadours in foraign Kingdoms, and Consuls or other publique Ministers."[173] The registration itself should be conducted by "twelve of the most able honest men" from each parish, who would not only sort out who had legitimate ownership claims on the land, but also estimate the value of the holdings. To ensure transparency, or that "all things appear plain and easie to be found or seen" in the registry, Cradocke called for consistency in the manner in which each bank recorded ownership and transactions. Once all encumbrances on the land had been clarified, a process that would take about a year to conclude, the bank would be able to commence the issuance of credit notes. Any landowner should be entitled to obtain credit amounting to half of the value of their estate, or more in the case of "reputed, known, honest or able men."[174] Borrowers would obtain a line of credit on which the bank charged 3 percent interest, payable in coin to the government. To reduce the likelihood that the bank's money was compromised, Cradocke stated, "That no man shall personate another to obtain Credit in Bank, nor counterfeit any Bill or Seal of Office, upon pain of death."[175]

A vast number of benefits would follow the implementation of this proposal, Cradocke insisted. In addition to the benefits of expanding trade, fishing, manufacturing, and increasing the ease and convenience of commerce, Cradocke highlighted that the land bank would provide an excellent source of funds for the king. Not only would Charles II receive the 3 percent interest charged on all loans, projected to be at least £2 million per year, but he would also gain access to loanable funds at an interest rate far below that currently charged by goldsmith bankers.[176] The plethora of private and public benefits that a land bank would bring about led Cradocke to conclude, using a verbatim quotation from Potter (without attribution), that "it plainly appears, that the way to remove Poverty, Taxes and most publique grievances, and to make this Nation abound in Wealth, Trade, Cities, Shipping, People and Renown, in neither upracticable nor difficult."[177]

Many of the land bank proposals were clearly influenced by Potter and the Hartlibians. Not only did they follow the basic design laid out by Potter, but the Hartlibians' general conceptualization of credit as an instrument of infinite improvement motivated much of the thinking about land banks. For example, Nicholas Barbon, physician, builder, insurer, and famous economic writer, used the idea of an infinitely expanding commerce to challenge Thomas Mun's orthodox conviction that the path to national prosperity went through parsimony, frugality, and sumptuary laws.[178] While frugality and thrift might be advantageous for an individual whose "Estate is Finite," Barbon wrote, it does not hold true for a nation whose stock is potentially infinite.[179] He added, "For what is Infinite, can neither Receive Addition by Parsimony, nor suffer Diminution, by Prodigality."[180] Instead, he argued that people's insatiable desires should be recognized as providing a critical impetus behind the infinite expansion of the economy.[181] While the basic wants of the body are finite and can thus be satisfied relatively easily, Barbon insisted, "The Wants of the Mind are infinite."[182] He continued:

> Man naturally Aspires, and as his Mind is elevated, his Senses grow more refined, and more capable of Delight; his Desires are inlarged, and his Wants increase with his Wishes, which is for every thing that is rare, can gratifie his Senses, adorn his Body, and promote the Ease, Pleasure, and Pomp of Life.[183]

For Barbon, mankind's desire for refinement, enjoyment, and extravagance expressed itself primarily in the realm of fashionable clothing. In addition to the aesthetic enjoyment of fineries, the always elegantly-clad Barbon proclaimed that people engaged in an ever-escalating sartorial

competition because the "decking of the Body . . . is the Mark of Difference and Superiority betwixt Man and Man."[184] Also fueling the infinite
expansion of the economy was the building trade, a sphere of particular
interest to Barbon. He argued that as buildings were erected and cities
grew, not only would the consumption of fashionable clothing increase,
but conspicuous consumption would extend to other areas. He wrote,
"Man being Naturally Ambitious, the Living together, occasion Emulation, which is seen by Out-Vying one another in Apparel, Equipage, and
Furniture of the House."[185] Hence, the insatiable demand for goods and
services was grounded partly in people's actual enjoyment and partly in
their desire for status vis-à-vis others in society.

Barbon combined his idea of infinite desires driving an infinitely
expandable economy with the insistence that the money stock should
be kept appropriately scarce. Using the now common definition of
money, Barbon claimed that it served as a "Pawn for the Value of all
other Things."[186] Although Barbon recognized that gold and silver had
been particularly popular as pawns in exchange because they were more
difficult to counterfeit, he was essentially open to any material serving as money, as long as it could be kept scarce.[187] This was the reason
why the pursuit of alchemy would always be fruitless. "How greatly,"
he asked, "would those Gentlemen be disappointed, that are searching
after the *Philosopher's Stone*, if they should at last happen to find it?"[188]
He continued, "For, if they should make but so great a Quantity of Gold
and Silver, as they, and their Predecessors have spent in search after
it, it would so later, and bring down the Price of those Metals, that it
might be a Question, whether they would get so much *Over-plus* by it,
as would pay for the Metal they change into Gold and Silver."[189]

Barbon's insistence that the currency be kept scarce did not, however,
imply that the money stock should be held fixed. In fact, Barbon was
an avid supporter of land banks and even participated with John Asgill
(d. 1738), a prolific writer on both financial and theological issues, in
launching one of the period's most high-profile land banks in 1695.[190]
Asgill argued that a land bank would be more advantageous and secure
than the Bank of England, because land provides a more elastic, yet
safer, security. While he argued that land offered a definite check on
the amount of credit created, credit issued by the Bank of England was
far more unpredictable. Most importantly, since the Bank's security
was partially dictated by the profits of its banking operations, it could

potentially vary widely. As such, the Bank's security therefore differed "little from the Trust or Credit that is given to private Traders, which is good or bad, as they are fortunate or unfortunate."[191] Since a land bank, on the other hand, rested on the solidity of land, the price of which was comparatively stable, it was not exposed to the same level of risk as the Bank of England. The land bank therefore combined an impeccable security with the capacity of expanding the money stock in a way that could facilitate infinite economic progress and make the Hartlibian dream of universal reformation come true.

Hugh Chamberlen, who had previously been a staunch advocate for the establishment of an Office of Credit, joined the campaign for land banks in the 1690s and in 1695 launched his own land bank as a rival to that of Barbon and Asgill.[192] In a series of pamphlets, Chamberlen pointed out that the great bulk of all commerce in the world was now conducted with the aid of credit, but lamented that much of this credit was still based on the merchants' personal trustworthiness, that is, "the Reputation and Opinion of the great Profits made in the course of a prosperous Trade."[193] England, he argued, could leapfrog its rivals in wealth and prosperity by launching a land bank, whereby "the want of a sufficient Stock of Money" could be ameliorated "by a Credit grounded upon a more Real and Substantial Fund, than the Credit of any other Nation."[194] Hence, similar to his earlier interventions, Chamberlen argued that a solid security could transcend the need to rely on trust and opinion. He concluded, "Bills of Credit thus founded upon Land, and Strengthened by the Sanction of Law, and made in a form incapable of Forgery, will be found an excellent instrument or Medium of Trade, equal in all respects to Gold and Silver, and Superior to them in divers regards."[195]

The only writer who could rival Chamberlen's enthusiasm and prolific support of land banks during the 1690s was merchant and entrepreneur John Briscoe (d. 1697), who also formed a short-lived land bank venture in 1695, called the National Land Bank.[196] He maintained that the "Scarcity of Money" was so persistent that England must "create some new *Species* of Money" in order to avoid a serious decay in commerce. For Briscoe, land constituted the best possible asset to back credit since it was "the most undoubted security."[197] By grounding the currency in land, not only was the currency backed by one of the most stable commodities, the land bank made "the lands of England, or rather England itself a Medium of Trade and Commerce."[198] The very essence of the nation—its land, soil, and landscape—was thus marshaled in support of the new currency.

While most of the land bank advocates felt that they had convincingly showed that land was a far superior security, they still had to find a way to ensure that the managers and directors were sufficiently incorruptible to ensure people's trust. Briscoe admitted that "it will not be an easie thing to perswade the multitude to trust, *their All* in the hands of Men, of whom they have not any personal knowledge, doubts will arise whether these Commissioners or Agents, may be honest, or able."[199] Crucial to overcoming this doubt was to make sure both directors and managers were carefully selected landed gentlemen. The landed elites' reputation for greater virtue, morals, and patriotism would lend stability and credibility to the land bank. And since the bank would issue credit on the security of land it meant that landed men would be the primary recipients of credit money. This meant that the new money entering society would be invested and employed by men of the same high moral fiber as the leadership of the land bank. The virtues associated with landownership were thus coupled with the materiality of land to generate the best possible circumstances for trust to develop. Finally, Briscoe expressed a concern with the dangers of counterfeiting. His solution, like that of most others, was to let the hangman do the job. But instead of limiting the charge of high treason to the actual counterfeiters of notes, he suggested that it should be extended to anyone who offers "them in Payment, knowing them to be Counterfeited."[200]

After a brief, but intense, debate about the preferred design for a land bank and a number of unsuccessful launches, Parliament incorporated the Land Bank United in 1696. The bank was allowed to raise £2.5 million in specie from landowners, in return for a 7 percent annual dividend to the subscribers and the right to borrow money on the security of their landholdings. The bank would lend £500,000 per year on mortgages, as well as lend substantial sums to the government.[201] The bank, however, failed miserably in its attempt to attract subscribers. While the king committed to subscribe £5,000, the Bank only managed to raise another £2,100 from the public.[202] Many reasons for this failure can be identified, including the success of the Bank of England's publicity campaign, the lack of proven financial experience of the land bank directors, the instability following the 1696 assassination attempt on William, and the dearth of silver coin in circulation caused by the Great Recoinage. It was in any case a devastating blow to the Tories' first attempt at establishing a financial apparatus favoring their general political, societal, and economic ideals. One of the primary Tory supporters of the land bank, Robert Harley, would soon be back with another financial scheme designed to challenge the Bank of England and to support the party's interest.

The failure of the land bank allowed the Bank of England to strengthen its position, expand its capital stock by another million pounds, obtain monopoly privileges on certain types of banking activities, and prolong its charter until 1711. After weathering another challenge in 1707, the Bank's charter was extended for an additional twenty-one years. The Bank also assisted in the Treasury's issuance of Exchequer Bills—the next generation of Treasury Orders. Issued in denominations of £5 and £10, the interest-bearing Exchequer Bills provided a way for the government to raise more money and to expand the quantity of money in circulation. When the bills fell into discount for the first time in 1697, the Bank's swift actions bolstered the bills and brought them back up to par again.

Conclusion

Advocates for the establishment of a credit currency unanimously agreed that credit had the potential to usher in a new era of prosperity and power. The key challenge was to design a mechanism that allowed people to trust that the credit instruments would circulate indefinitely. One of the period's more reflective writers on political economy, Charles Davenant, explored the importance of trust for money to circulate:

> Trust and Confidence in each other, are as necessary to link and hold a People together; as Obedience, Love, Friendship, or the Intercourse of Speech. And when Experience has taught each Man how weak he is, depending only upon himself, he will be willing to help Others, and call upon the Assistance of his neighbours, which of course, by degrees, must set Credit again afloat.[203]

Hence, as long as a solid culture of trust was developed, credit would always rebound from a crisis. Davenant added, "Credit, though it may be for a while obscured, and labour under some difficulties, yet it may, in some measure, recover, where there is a safe and good foundation at the bottom."[204] Davenant thus joined the chorus of voices supporting the formation of a new culture of credit in England.

As England entered the last decade of the seventeenth century, the most persistent concern regarding credit was the threat posed by counterfeiters and forgers. The problem was that once the debt instruments entered circulation, the issuer no longer had control over the instruments and was therefore unable to protect the integrity of the notes and bills. This anxiety peaked during the middle of the 1690s. At a moment when the Bank of England's notes had just entered circulation, it was absolutely crucial that the public not only trusted the integrity of the notes, but also the solidity of the silver coin backing the notes. The fact that the coin had been badly clipped and often counterfeited during the last few decades—a trend that intensified in the 1690s—threatened confidence in the new paper currency and thus the success of both the Financial Revolution and the Glorious Revolution. The resulting national crisis gave rise to a vibrant pamphlet debate on how to address the problem. It is to this debate and in particular the role of the death penalty in securing trust that I turn to in the next chapter.

— 4 —

Capital Punishment in Defense of Credit

Introduction

The successful launch of the Bank of England in 1694 opened a new chapter in the history of money. The Bank's paper notes—secured by a fractional reserve of silver coin, profits from its banking operations, and a stream of interest payments from the government—constituted Europe's first widely circulating credit currency. Although the Bank's capital stock was subscribed instantaneously and its notes entered circulation smoothly, the Bank's launch coincided with a severe monetary crisis. Counterfeiting, clipping, and coining had substantially eroded the amount of silver in the English coin to the point where it was no longer able to circulate at par. Although such monetary manipulations had been an irritant for centuries, the reduction of the coin's silver content suddenly emerged as a significant threat to England's power and prosperity.[1] John Locke, for example, wrote in a letter in 1696 to the Irish philosopher William Molyneux, "The business of our money has so near brought us to ruin, that . . . it was every body's talk, every body's uneasiness."[2] Locke even suggested that the clippers and counterfeiters constituted a greater threat to England's safety than Louis XIV's military might.[3] The negative impact of a tarnished silver coinage was especially harmful during the ongoing war against France, making it difficult for England to remit funds to its forces fighting on the continent. Yet, even though financing the war was a crucial concern, I argue that the reason why counterfeiting, clipping, and coining emerged as such a serious threat to England at this particular moment was because it undermined trust in the nascent Financial Revolution. Since Parliament had opted to institute a bank that issued credit notes on the security of silver coin, instead of other securities like land or merchandise, it was now more important than ever that the coin remained incorruptible and inviolable. In order for the Bank's notes to circulate widely, people not only had to be able to trust the authenticity of the notes, but also the security assigned to them. Clipping and counterfeiting therefore constituted what philosopher George Caffentzis calls an epistemological crime, in that they introduced "a continuously deepening obscurity into our reality and into our ideas."[4] If confidence in the coin evaporated, the success of the Bank's notes and indeed the future of the Bank itself would be in jeopardy. Even worse, if the Financial Revolution faltered, the Glorious Revolution would surely fail and England would most certainly face a second Stuart Restoration and an inevitable strengthening of Catholicism. It was therefore of utmost importance that the integrity of the coin be restored.

Surprisingly few scholars have examined the relationship between the Financial Revolution and the Great Recoinage; their focus tends to be on one or the other.[5] I argue in this chapter that by exploring the interrelationship between the Financial Revolution and the Great Recoinage, a new understanding of one of England's most turbulent decades emerges: the kind of government pursuing these measures and institutional innovations was not just the modern "fiscal-military" state but also the early modern "Thanatocratic" state.[6] Looking through the analytical prism in this way reveals a new understanding of how political economists perceived, explained, and facilitated the origins of credit money and the ways in which the state actively and violently regulated its new financial system.

While the debate about England's monetary system famously shifted its focus to the coinage during the monetary crisis of 1694–1697, I argue that credit was still the protagonist of the debate. Contributing to the ongoing conversation about England's monetary future, hundreds of pamphlets were published during the 1690s by political economists who explored the philosophy of money and credit and the essential features of a well-functioning monetary system.[7] A few writers focused exclusively on the importance of a sound coinage for England to flourish commercially and to carry on a successful ground war on the continent. Increasingly, however, commentators recognized that credit and coin were now intertwined and that one could not be considered in the absence of the other. Writing at the tail end of the crisis, the pamphle-teer James Hodges (fl. 1695–1705), for example, argued that "CREDIT being so far sunk at present, through the general Scarcity of Money," that the only way credit could recover was if it were "nourished by a Free Stock of Money . . . always ready to answer all its Demands."[8] Conceiv-ing of credit, similar to his predecessors, as an opinion in a probabilistic framework, Hodges concluded that since "CREDIT being of the Nature of BELIEF, which taketh its Being altogether from free and satisfying PERSWASION, that the thing will be performed, for which Credit is given," it was absolutely essential that the integrity of the coin serving as security for the paper notes was maintained at all times.[9]

There was an overwhelming consensus among contemporaries that the solution to the monetary crisis was a general recoinage—calling in all coins and reminting them using the latest technology. They dis-agreed as to the temporality and terms of the recoinage: whether to remint immediately or wait for the war to end and whether to apply the old standard of silver in each coin or remint the coin with 20 percent less silver to reflect the fact that all outstanding coins were clipped. In any event, they all agreed that it was essential to make it more diffi-cult to clip and counterfeit the coin. Limiting the extent to which the skilful hands of the clippers and counterfeiters made contact with the coin was considered crucial. Drawing, as we saw in the previous chap-ter, on a long tradition of advocating that the manipulation of money should be considered treason, many political economists insisted that the death penalty for clipping and counterfeiting constituted an essen-tial ingredient of the formation of trust in money. The hangman was thus charged with the responsibility of preventing money manipulators from engaging in further crimes either by physically removing them from the world or by deterring them from future acts. The application of the death penalty also reassured the broader public that credit rested on the foundation of a sound coinage and that the government was fully committed to its defense. The hope was that the public would then be able to put their doubts aside and form a favorable opinion of the integrity of both the coin of the realm and the Bank of England notes.

The problem, however, was that even though counterfeiting and clip-ping had been capital crimes for centuries, the threat of death had not sufficiently deterred people from engaging in this potentially lucrative craft. Not only was it extremely difficult to detect who had actually applied their shears, files, and hammers to the nation's coin, many clippers and counterfeiters were pardoned or acquitted because juries often found death too harsh a penalty for a crime that was considered by many to have no specific victim.[10] A number of pamphleteers therefore suggested that relatively milder punishments such as facial disfiguration and hard labor be instituted, as jurors might then be more likely to reach a guilty verdict.

Also adding to the lack of prosecutorial success was the fact that juries often discounted testimonies of witnesses because they were believed to be motivated by the £40 reward paid to informers leading to successful convictions. Convicted felons could also receive pardons if they offered information that led to the conviction of at least two other felons. Commentators consequently insisted that the judicial system had to become stricter and more conscientious in convicting monetary criminals. As part of the effort to increase the deterrence of the death penalty and improve the credibility of the judicial system, John Locke and the Chancellor of the Exchequer Charles Montagu (1661–1715), who along with William Paterson and Michael Godfrey constituted the dominant force behind the Bank of England, recruited the by then already famous natural philosopher Sir Isaac Newton (1642–1727) to become the new Warden of the Mint. Newton was thus put in charge of investigating, detecting, and prosecuting crimes against the currency. By bringing in a person of such impeccable integrity and unmatched intelligence, the government intended to convey to the public the seriousness with which they viewed the safeguarding of the currency and the success of the Financial Revolution. In Chapter 3, I showed that political economists employed various methods that had been developed in natural philosophy for establishing trust. In this chapter the case of Newton joining the Mint exemplifies the transfer of method and practice from natural philosophy to political economy in the 1690s.

Lowndes, Locke, and the Recoinage Debate

Historical Context

The 1690s was a tempestuous decade for England. Not only was the Glorious Revolution subject to challenges and uncertainty, but William III had committed England to fight his archenemy Louis XIV.[11] England now faced an enemy who had four times as many people, enjoyed much greater resources, and had more experience fighting land battles.[12] Victory, or at least an honorable peace, was considered absolutely essential for the protection of the Glorious Revolution, Protestantism, and England's long-cherished liberties. A defeat would most certainly lead to a Stuart Restoration and thus a strengthening of the bond between the Church of England and the papacy. While England had successfully pursued its blue-water strategy for the last century, the nation's armed forces were now fighting alongside soldiers from the Dutch Republic, Austria, Spain, and Savoy, both at sea and on the ground. This required a massive engagement. On average, England employed around forty thousand sailors and seventy-six thousand army troops, at a cost of an average of £5.5 million per year.[13] In addition to paying for bread, beer, and meat for all of its soldiers, enormous expenditures were required to maintain diplomatic alliances, pay for foreign mercenaries, and outfit ships and armies with proper weaponry.

Fighting such a costly war was particularly challenging considering the ill state of England's leading economic sectors; the war had caused a drop in demand for wool and the "Little Ice Age" had produced a series of bad harvests.[14] Apart from a small trade boom during the early part of the war generated by the remittances England paid to its allies, the war caused a rapid fall in trade, both European and extra-European. Blockades and privateering interfered with trade routes, ships and sailors were commandeered by the navy, young men left port towns in fear of the notorious press gangs, and armed hostilities with the Mughals contributed to the retardation of England's long-haul trade.[15] The commercial downturn generated a dip in customs receipts and put an end to the favorable trade balance England had enjoyed for some time. The expanding quantities of sugar, tobacco, dyestuff, silk, and cottons that had lately fueled England's reexport industry could no longer be relied upon to pay for the war and to keep the Mint running. Considering that a large share of England's silver was already being sent abroad in remittance payments and speculators were melting down silver coin and exporting it as bullion, it was only a matter of time before England would face a serious shortage of silver and a consequent scarcity of money.[16]

These dire economic conditions forced England to be fiscally creative. Drawing on a half-a-century debate about the best institutional design for a new system of credit, Parliament finally established England's first national bank, the Bank of England, in 1694.[17] Considering that in "no decade between 1680 and 1790 were there more crises than in the 1690s," the success of the Bank has impressed many historians.[18] R. D. Richards, for example, marveled at the Bank's capacity to thrive in the midst "of financial chaos, of war, of bad harvests, of deplorable coinage conditions, of 'golden' lotteries, of rivaling banking projects, of 'bubble' companies, of Tory antagonism, and of Jacobite 'art and artifice.'"[19]

Yet, despite the early success of the Bank, the nation's nascent financial infrastructure was still fragile. To protect the Bank, it was therefore critical that all mechanisms designed to secure its notes were properly maintained. Most importantly, since the Bank's credit notes were backed by silver coin—Paterson mentioned in passing that the reserve ratio ought to be 15 percent to 20 percent while one historian estimates that the actual ratio varied between 2.8 percent and 14.2 percent—it was now of utmost importance that people were able to completely trust the integrity of the coin.[20] The fact that circulating notes did not have a one-to-one backing of coin in the vault, like the Bank of Amsterdam, already challenged people's ability to trust, but to add uncertainty about the integrity of the few coins actually available for redemption was an even greater obstacle.

The Recoinage Debate

Despite being badly clipped and hammered prior to the 1690s, the English coin had continued to circulate around par.[21] But as the clipping accelerated and the scrutiny of the coin intensified with the founding of the Bank, confidence in the silver coin quickly evaporated.[22] It was now increasingly inconvenient to engage in cash transactions.[23] The question of how to best put a stop to the pervasive manipulation of the coin sparked a vibrant debate among government officials and political economists. Nearly all contributors agreed that England had to call in all of its coin and remint it using new technologies that made clipping and counterfeiting more difficult. This included the use of a mechanical device that turned out coins of precise thickness and circumference and horse-driven presses to deeply imprint the government's seal on all coins. The most important innovation, however, was the edging of the coin. To make sure that clipping was easily detected, the edge of the

coin was either milled or impressed with the words *Decus et Tutamen*—
"a decoration and a safeguard."[24] Treasury Secretary William Lowndes
(1652–1724) was optimistic that the new technology would suffice to
eliminate or at least minimize the problem. He observed that the "Practice of Clipping has never been Exercis'd upon the Mill'd Money, and
I think never can be, because of its Thickness and Edging."[25] He later
added that while it was impossible to completely guard against counterfeiting, the new milled money was so sophisticated that "for every single Piece of Mill'd Money, that has been Counterfeited, or rather been
attempted to be Resembled, there have been more than One thousand
of the Hammer'd Moneys not only Counterfeited, but actually Impos'd
upon the People."[26]

Lowndes's proposal was to recoin the nation's currency, using the
most up-to-date technology, but with 20 percent less silver in each coin.
He argued that the most expeditious option was to remint the coin
with a silver content that reflected the fact that nearly all circulating
coin were badly clipped. He acknowledged that some people would be
hurt by such a recoinage, in particular creditors who would be paid
back in coin with less silver than that which they had been contracted.
However, this was a small price to pay for the restoration of the coin's
integrity and for avoiding a drastic fall in the quantity of coin, which
would be the consequence of reminting the coin at the old full-weight
standard.[27] If the present monetary confusion were allowed to continue,
in addition to the "great Contentions [that] do daily arise amongst the
King's Subjects, in Fairs, Markets, Shops, and other Places throughout
the Kingdom, . . . many Bargains, Doings and Dealings are totally prevented and laid aside."[28] He argued that a stable and standardized currency would ultimately be beneficial to everyone as it would facilitate
both cash transactions and credit contracts, like "Mortgages, Bonds,
Contracts, or other Legal Securities."[29]

Before acting on Lowndes's advice, the Lord Justice invited a distinguished panel of intellectuals to respond to Lowndes's 1695 proposal.[30]
The panel consisted of the political economist Charles Davenant, the
architect Sir Christopher Wren (1632-1723), the natural philosopher Sir
Isaac Newton, and the prominent merchants Sir Josiah Child (d. 1699)
and Sir Gilbert Heathcote (1652-1733).[31] The most influential member of
the panel, however, was John Locke. His primary concern with clipping
and counterfeiting was grounded in his fear that money manipulators

undermined the capacity of money to serve as the universal standard for commercial agreements, which included cash transactions and all kinds of credit arrangements. For Locke, Lowndes's recoinage proposal would only exacerbate the crisis. It was therefore, Locke argued, essential that the coin was reminted at the old standard, because only then would people at home and abroad be able to trust and respect the integrity of England's monetary system. This was the only way to properly protect the architecture of the Financial Revolution and thus the Glorious Revolution, which he stanchly defended.

Locke's position on the recoinage was grounded in his theory of money, an often complex and subtle body of thought, that he had developed over the course of a few decades. His treatment of money in the famous chapter on property in *Two Treatises of Government* (1689) suggests that he subscribed to the traditional notion that money circulates on the basis of its intrinsic value; people part with their commodities because they are offered silver coin embodying equivalent value.[32] This notion, however, only accounts for part of Locke's thinking on money. In addition to the intrinsic value notion, he also embraced the idea that people accept silver on the basis of the belief that it can be exchanged for other goods in the future. Money's exchangeability thus depends on "the tacit Agreement of Men to put a value on [silver]."[33] Phrased in yet another way, once people have "consented to put an imaginary Value upon Gold and Silver . . . [they] have made them by general consent the common Pledges, whereby Men are assured, in Exchange for them to receive equally valuable things to those they parted with for any *quantity* of these Metals."[34] Hence, by placing a certain "Phantastical imaginary value" on silver and making it equivalent to all other things, the silver congeals into the coin's intrinsic value.[35] Silver thus becomes "the Instrument and Measure of Commerce in all the Civilized and Trading parts of the World."[36] Any reduction in the coin's silver content thus robs it of its agreed-upon value and therefore violates the bonds that keep society together. The integrity of the tacit agreement was so crucial to the stability of society, Locke argued, that governments in most nations announce their support of the agreement by stamping the coin with their seal, vouching that "a piece of such a denomination is of such a weight, and such a fineness, i.e. has so much Silver in it."[37] As such, the full authority of the government is marshaled in defense of money's exchangeability.

This implies that when the clippers and coiners manipulated the coin's silver content, they not only threw off "the quantity of Silver which Men contract for," but also undermine the "Authority of the publick Stamp" and thus "the publick Faith" in the government.[38] This breach of trust is what "hightens the Robbery into Treason," and thus makes the perpetrator deserving of death.[39]

Public decisions to lower the silver content of the coin–Lowndes's proposal—were as damaging as private clipping, Locke argued.[40] While clipping essentially debases the coin without public authority—or rather in violation of public authority—a government "Altering the Standard, by Coining pieces under the same denomination with less Silver in them than they formerly had, is doing the same thing by publick Authority."[41] Lowndes's proposition to remint the nation's currency with 20 percent less silver therefore effectively meant that the government would violate all private contracts and undermine its own authority, a decision that no Whig Williamite supporter could approve.

While the effects of a public alteration of the coin would be felt immediately, clipping was a gradual process that left the exchange value of the coin unaffected for long stretches of time, thus delaying the impact of the fraud. However, at some point a critical threshold would be reached, after which a coin deficient in silver would no longer circulate at face value.[42] Since it was impossible to predict when such a fall in the exchange value of the coin would occur, people committed to long-term credit contracts were particularly exposed to the risk. In normal circumstances, "Men are absolved from the performance of their legal contracts, if the quantity of Silver, under settled and legal denominations be altred," but since it was inconceivable to void all contracts agreed upon before the value of the coin dropped, Locke insisted that the only way to maintain the integrity of commercial agreements was to put an immediate stop to both clipping and devaluations.[43]

Locke often insisted that a sound and inviolable standard was necessary for the measurement and mediation of commerce.[44] He claimed, "*Men make their Estimate and Contracts according to the Standard*, upon Supposition they shall receive good and lawful Money, which is that of full Weight."[45] Contrary to Lowndes, who advocated for the importance of a sound coinage in that all coins were standardized at any one point in time, Locke insisted that the standard could not uphold its status as such if it did not remain fixed through time. It was particularly important for the metallic standard to be upheld over time for people to be comfortable engaging in credit transactions. Since "*Credit* being nothing but the expectation of Money within some limited time," Locke concluded that sound "Money must be had or *Credit* will fail."[46] Hence, for the English monetary system to function well, there had to be enough good money in circulation, so "as to keep up the Landholders, Labourers and Brokers Credit," as well as that of the government.[47]

If the silver content were lowered, either by a Lowndes-type devaluation or by letting clipping continue, people receiving the coin or contracting to receive a future payment would obtain less than expected and would therefore be defrauded. Landlords and creditors would be particularly hard hit.[48] Landowners receiving rent payments and creditors collecting interest payments and principal would receive less silver than they had contracted for, thus undermining two types of transactions essential to any market economy. Among the landowners, the king and the church stood to lose the most, while among the creditors, because of the magnitude of its loans, the Bank of England would suffer the greatest loss. By extension, subscribers to the Bank of England would also suffer as they relied on a fixed dividend payment from the Bank. This would hurt Locke personally, as he was one of the original subscribers, first investing the nontrivial sum of £500 and later expanding his holdings to £1,100.[49]

It should be noted that even though Locke invested in the Bank and, as a Whig concerned with the success of the Glorious Revolution, maintained an interest in the Bank's survival, his private journal reveals a certain hesitation about the Bank.[50] Using many of the same criteria to assess credit that had been employed in the debates leading up to the founding of the Bank (explored in Chapter 3), Locke was first and foremost concerned about the security of the Bank. Given that the Bank earned its profits from lending, he questioned whether it would be disciplined enough to always retain enough reserves to redeem its notes on demand. And, in the event that the Bank actually resisted the temptation to extend ever more loans and kept a large share of its capital in the vault, "What should they doe," Locke asked, "if the seamen mutinying for pay or the army for a money should clamour at their dores & say They kept the money from them."[51] The problem here was the Bank's transparency. Contrary to the goldsmith bankers, who "were masters of their books & kept every thing private the Bank books must be open to multitudes."[52] Indeed, anyone could find out at any point how much cash was in the Bank's vault. While this design was intended to generate confidence in the Bank by allowing members of the public to personally observe the Bank's accounts, Locke worried that "A great Treasure heaped to geather in view may make many peoples fingers itch."[53] Lastly, Locke, like most other political economists assessing the prospects of credit, also inquired about the "skill and honesty" of the Bank's managers. While he expressed confidence that the present managers, many of whom were his friends, have "the Characters of fair men," he added that one might never be certain "who will succeed them & . . . [be] secured of their skill & integrity."[54]

Yet, despite his concerns about the Bank, he nevertheless wanted to protect it from the clippers and from Lowndes's recoinage proposal.[55] If indeed the government were to raise the value of the coin, all contracts would be undermined and the foundational trust upon which the Financial Revolution was built would be shaken. Long-term borrowing, whether through lottery loans or the Bank of England, would then become more difficult, once again forcing the government to rely on expensive short-term loans. Locke stated that such a recoinage "will weaken, if not totally destroy the publick Faith, when all that have trusted the Publick, and assisted our present necessities, upon Acts of Parliament, in the *Million Lottery, Bank* [of England] *Act,* and other *Loans,* shall be defrauded of 20 *per Cent.* of what those Acts of Parliament were security for."[56] Indeed, Lowndes's proposal would simultaneously undermine the two primary mechanisms designed to secure the circulation of the Bank of England's notes: the government's authority and the coin in the Bank's vault.

Armed with Locke's dire warnings, the Whig Junto supported by the Bank of England successfully persuaded enough MPs to vote in favor of an immediate recoinage that closely resembled Locke's proposal.[57] The decision to call in the nation's coins and remint them at the old standard has baffled many modern scholars. The idea that Parliament would agree to a solution that would drastically reduce the number of coins in circulation—perhaps by as much as half—is certainly surprising in light of the fact that England had suffered such hardship from its scarcity of money for a century or more.[58] Most historians believe that Lowndes's proposal would have made more sense in that the quantity of money in circulation would have remained roughly the same and any economic dislocation caused by a fall in the quantity of money could have been avoided. I submit, however, that it was precisely *because* England had been laboring under a scarcity of money for so long that Parliament opted for Locke's plan. Even though his recoinage would reduce the number of coins in circulation, members of Parliament nevertheless were willing to accept the temporary commercial and geopolitical inconveniences, because they believed that the Bank had revealed its capacity to solve the scarcity of money problem. They therefore desperately wanted to save the Bank and hold on to the prospect of finally putting an end to the scarcity of money problem.

Joyce Appleby, among others, admonishes Locke for employing an outdated argument that would only bring "folly and disaster."[59] Because Locke undoubtedly was aware of the disastrous economic consequences that would follow from the implementation of his plan, she argues that he must have been motivated by something other than the immediate economic circumstances. According to Appleby, Locke was seeking to make an ideological point: namely, to prove that the government lacked authority over the economy.[60] This, she argues, was part of Locke's general crusade against "arbitrary, unlimited power."[61] While Locke's theory of money certainly played an important role in his larger ideological project, it is unlikely, I belive, that such a dedicated public servant as Locke would have so flagrantly ignored the mandate given to him by Lord Keeper Somers—to find a solution to the present monetary calamity—in order to score an ideological point.[62] In addition to the fact that Locke may not have believed that a recoinage would necessarily lead to a decrease in the circulation of coin—it could be avoided if enough plate were brought to the mint—it is much more plausible, I contend, that Locke was willing to accept the risk of a temporary commercial downturn in order to once and for all put an end to the scarcity of money—a problem that had plagued England for too long.[63] For Locke, this was not a moment to ignore England's troubles in order to promote his own ideology. This was a moment that called for drastic measures to rescue the coin, safeguard the Financial Revolution, and protect the Glorious Revolution.

Appleby also criticizes Locke's preoccupation with the distributional effects of a Lowndes-inspired recoinage. Drawing on comments from some of Locke's contemporaries, Appleby points out that Locke's recoinage plan eventually would have been as damaging to the landed and moneyed interests as Lowndes's plan, since they would end up paying most of the taxes required to cover the cost of the recoinage.[64] I argue, to the contrary, that Locke was not concerned with the distributional consequences per se, but rather with what would happen to the public's trust in credit—in particular public credit—if present creditors were defrauded by 20 percent.[65] Hence, even though Locke may have had a long-standing prejudice against certain segments of the financial community, mostly notably the goldsmith bankers, he realized that credit contracts must be honored and justice between creditors and debtors upheld if the new culture of credit were to have a chance of surviving. Indeed, while Appleby points out that "if Locke wrote about money with one eye on the political implications of his definition, his readers read him with their minds on banking schemes," I believe it is likely that Locke too had his eyes trained on the stability of the new system of credit.[66]

The Great Recoinage and the Financial Revolution

The recoinage debate focused most directly on the nation's metallic currency, yet concerns regarding the Financial Revolution were rarely absent. Not only did many commentators highlight the link between the integrity of the coin and the stability of credit, many others argued that credit money might actually be able to aid in the restoration of the coin. Still others sought to exploit the currency crisis to advocate for an overhaul of the nation's credit system—unsurprisingly the land bank proponents were particularly vociferous.

A number of participants on the panel brought together to evaluate Lowndes's proposal supported Locke's plan, in particular if credit money could be used to augment the money stock during the time it took to carry out the recoinage. The polymathic Sir Christopher Wren, for example, offered his support for Locke's recoinage plan and reiterated that the monetary standard had to be upheld at all cost. He opined that if a nation is considered in isolation from the rest of the trading world, any object—including silver coin of any weight and fineness—might serve as money as long as it is enacted and stamped by the government. But this was not, of course, how the world functioned. "We stand not by ourselves," he argued, "but our Seas, that seem to divide us, make us the more a part of the Commercial World."[67] An English nation situated within a vibrant Atlantic trade was consequently forced to adhere to the international standard, otherwise its coin would not readily circulate around the world. Recoining at the old standard, he believed, although it might create some temporary hardship, would nevertheless be the best strategy, in particular if the government issued enough transferable notes to compensate for the reduction in the quantity of circulating coin. He added, "I Confess this is a Shift, like an Opiat in a Wasting Disease, to gain time for the Operation of Remedies; but it is necessary, to give the People Ease, and stop the Growth of the Disease."[68]

Another member of the panel evaluating Lowndes's proposal, Charles Davenant, also preferred Locke's plan. He too focused on the importance of protecting the status of England's money abroad.[69] Like Wren, he believed that credit money could be used to resolve England's present troubles. In fact, he argued that credit money had already, *de facto*, successfully substituted for coin during the present crisis, well enough that there was no need to jeopardize the war effort by undertaking a recoinage right away. Reflecting on recent conditions, he argued that "the badness of the Species . . . had soe enlarged Creditt that wee hardly felt the want of Money."[70] He continued, "as Some Serpents bear in their head a Stone which cures the venome of their biting, Soe this mischief of the Coyne did in a manner produce its owne Remedy."[71] Not only did paper credit prove that it could substitute for coin in almost all essential transactions, it also served as a bulwark in support of the coin. Davenant argued that since credit notes were denominated in the coin of the old standard, by paying for most purchases with such notes, the value of the coin was upheld. If the present circumstances continued, with "the Species of Money Seldome Intervening . . . the coyne may passe in the Retailing Trade at the rate wholly from Law and Custome."[72] The proof of credit's capacity to protect the value of the coin could be seen in the exchange rate of the English coin. While it had been at par before the war, it was now trading at a discount anywhere from 20 to 30 percent. Yet, he claimed, "there is not yet that Difference in the exchange as the badness of our Silver does really deserve . . . indeed it ought to be near 50 p. cent the lightnesse of our Silver coyne duely considered."[73] Davenant thus concluded that the nation's silver currency, combined with some £40 million of paper credit, would suffice to see the nation through the present war, thus allowing for a postponement of the inevitable recoinage.[74]

Also championing credit money's capacity to rescue England from the crisis was John Blackwell (1624–1701), a prominent Cromwellian government official and later a deputy governor of Pennsylvania. Noting that the condition of the coin was unbearable, Blackwell insisted that the nation's coin must be called in and reminted at the old standard. Similar to Wren, Blackwell suggested that the resulting reduction in coin could be compensated for by an expansion in credit notes. England would "By this *Medium* of Bills of Credit, added to Our Money-Stock," be able to carry out "Vast Improvements, both of Wealth and Power," at the same time that they were able to properly conduct "this Expensive War."[75] Blackwell doubted not that these notes would "Answer Our Expectations as effectually as Moneys in *Specie*."[76] Indeed, he argued that they "will be of such General Use and Great Conveniency, when understood and further experimented, as, People will chuse to have them rather than moneys in *Specie*; as is found true in fact amongst Our Selves, to the value of many Hundreds of thousands Pounds already given out by the 'foremention'd Banks erected."[77]

An author who signed his pamphlet L. R. also suggested that paper money could be used to restore the nation's coinage. He averred that people delivering unmilled crowns and half crowns to the special recoinage commission should be issued interest-bearing bills equal to the face value of the coin. These bills should be declared legal tender, and because they eventually would be redeemed with newly minted full-weight coin, within a year or two, the author saw no reason why they would not circulate at par.[78] In fact, the paper notes would be more advantageous than coin, he claimed, "For though it is true, that . . . [the coin called in] will be converted into Paper; yet it cannot be denied, but it will pass better in Payments than the present Crowns and Half crowns unmill'd."[79] Indeed, the Bank of England had already shown that paper notes "are rather made choice of in Payments than Money."[80]

A special duty on salt was proposed to ensure that the government had the means to pay interest on the bills semiannually and to retire them with full-bodied coin as soon as possible. The bills would be brought into the commission every six months; if there were enough newly minted coins available all bills presented would be retired, but if the revenues from the salt tax were exhausted, new bills would be issued as replacements. This last feature was designed to increase the security of the bill, challenging counterfeiters to produce new plates every six months and making sure that all spurious notes were detected after at most six months in circulation.

L. R. further argued that paper money not only had the capacity to aid the nation's monetary system, it could also contribute more directly to the stability of the new political order established by the Glorious Revolution. Since most people in England would be in possession of paper notes, they would develop a vested interest in the protection of William and his administration, as they could only count on the notes' exchange-ability as long as the present government survived. Credit thus created stronger bonds between the monarch and his subjects than an explicit declaration of allegiance. As the author noted, "it's not to be doubted but that in this Selfish Age, Interest binds more than all the Sacred Bands of Oaths."[81] The subversion of credit consequently would have the opposite effect. Worrying that money manipulators would directly undermine the authority of the king, an anonymous commentator warned that "the debasing and horrible abusing our Coin, has cut a Cloud on our Glorious Deliverance by His Sacred Majesty, and makes unquiet Men take an occasion to open their Mouths against His Government."[82] The safety of coin, credit, and the state itself had become fused into one.

The clipping of the coin could be perceived as a symbolic decapitation of the king; a Jacobite economic plot to destroy the Glorious Revolution. As Steve Pincus has recently argued, many Williamite Whigs blamed the Tories for engineering the crisis in order to, at a minimum, force the establishment of a land bank or, more ambitiously, to undermine the Whig Junto and perhaps even force a Stuart Restoration.[83] Both Wren and Locke seem to have recognized that the attack on the currency may have been part of a Jacobite plot. Wren wrote of the clipping of coin and exporting of bullion, "We need not Doubt, but our Enemies had a Vigorous hand in this Contrivance by Correspondence, more Usefull to them than the Gain of Battels & Towns. Thus we Slept, and the Laws Slept, till this Terrible Wound was inflicted."[84] For Locke, clipping was understood as an act of war, in that it threatened England's capacity to field a well-equipped and properly provisioned military. He proclaimed that "*Clipping* by English Men is robbing the honest Man who receives clip'd Money . . . *Clipping* by Foreigners is robbing *England* it self."[85]

Most Tories were not, of course, Jacobites, and consequently limited their oppositional strategy to undermining the political and economic infrastructure William and the Whig Junto were building.[86] They would be delighted to see the Bank dismantled. Yet, many of the Tories did not want to do away with banking and credit money altogether; they just wanted to see a different form of credit implemented. In most instances, they supported land banks. One land bank proponent claimed that England had no choice but to charter a new national bank as the ill state of the coin had damaged confidence in the Bank of England beyond all repair. Although the resourcefulness of the English people had allowed them to carry on their business with whatever medium of exchange was available, there was no denying that the monetary system had to be fundamentally reformed to restore order to commerce. "Because when there is no Money," the author explained, "all Hands are Idle, and Poverty comes upon the Country like an Armed Man: But false and clipt Money raising the Value of Money, and weak Credit, still keeps many Hands at Work; tho' all cann't or will not."[87] Although the Bank's "weak credit" was better than no medium of exchange at all, the author argued that a sound credit currency backed by land would be that much more beneficial. "Because there is little Money current, if any left," the author argued, "all other Credit is justly clouded; necessities for Money are great, and nothing can Prosper without it, or some sound Credit, which only Land can afford."[88] The author then added, "Land, especially in *England,* is the best Funds, upon which to raise an unquestionable Credit in Banks . . . [Indeed,] these Bills are as truely Money, as that made of Gold or Silver, and Virtually are Gold and Silver Money."[89] The money issued by a land bank would thus be so well received that it could almost completely substitute for metallic money, obviating the need for a recoinage.

John Briscoe and Hugh Chamberlen, whom I discussed in Chapter 3, argued that this was the perfect moment to replace the inherently precarious "Reputation-Credit" and "Money-Credit" for "Land-Credit."[90] Not only would a land bank be able to solve England's long-term fiscal and financial challenges, but it could also facilitate the recoinage itself. If land secured the credit currency, all available silver could be brought to the Mint. In addition to the coin in circulation and in hoards, people should also be required to bring in their silver plate. This would supply the Mint with plenty of silver to produce full-bodied coin; "It is supposed, by most People, that the value of *Plate,* in this Kingdom, exceeds that of our *Coin*; and considering the great Numbers of Silver Tankards, and other Plate, in all Taverns, Victualling-Houses, and Publick Houses of all sorts, there may be a sufficient Supply from thence (without having regard to greater Quantities in Private Houses) to Coin several Millions, when so brought in."[91]

While many commentators advocated for the use of credit money to help solve the coinage crisis, there were others, however, who cautioned that even though credit money had a role to play, its usefulness should not be overstated. The most pressing need was still to restore a sound metallic coinage. The pamphleteer James Hodges, for example, criticized many of his contemporaries for exaggerating the capacity of credit to substitute for coin. He noted that there are those:

> who are of Opinion, that all the present Difficulties may be helped by some special ways of advancing *Credit*, which they project without minding the necessary thing, *Money*; but this Notion must run in a Circle, and so never come to an end, seeing there is an equal need of *Money* for obtaining *Credit*, as there is of *Credit* for obtaining *Money*.[92]

Yet, in the last instance, while it was possible "that Money can make Credit," it was more difficult for credit to make money.[93] As such, for the Bank of England to survive and for its notes to circulate at par it had to find a way to increase its silver reserves. "For let all apparent Reasons pretend and please what they will," he argued, "this will always be found to be the true Touchstone of valuable Paper-Money, that it can be turned into the same Quantity of real Money in lieu of which it is received, whenever the Owner pleaseth."[94] The Bank's ability to attract more coin depended, in turn, on the overall expansion of coin in circulation. He concluded, "if at least so much more Money can be procured, as will be able to give such an Advance to *Credit*, as that these two together by themselves . . . shall prove sufficient to extricate the Nation out of those publick and private Difficulties, which at present do so much call for some speedy and effectual Relief."[95]

The affluent wine merchant and influential political economist John Pollexfen (1636–1715), who served with Locke on the Board of Trade, largely agreed with Hodges on credit's ability to augment the money stock, but that it would never be able to fully substitute for coin. "Credits," he noted, "as far as may be necessary to supply the want of *Coyn*, may be very useful, but if it should be practiced to jostle out the use of *Coyn*, as some have proposed, is most dangerous."[96] Conceiving of credit explicitly within a probabilistic framework, he argued:

Paper Credit may come in, as an aid, in case of want, but not to be depended on, either [as Sinews of War] . . . or carrying on of Commerce, as principal; its original and existence being from Credit, and Opinion, that must be obtained, with a prospect that it will continue, before any use can be made of it, but impossible to prevent its being subject to Chance. Wherefore seeing it must be our *Coyn* that in all cases of extremity must be our refuge, it ought to be preferred, that care may be taken how it may be increased and preserved.[97]

Pollexfen thus concluded that a sound and plentiful coinage constituted the most essential condition for a solid credit mechanism. "Nothing but having a prospect that *Coyn* will be ready to pay such Bills at their respective times, can make them be preferred to Money, nor preserve the Reputation of such Bills, or of any Bills, Notes or *Paper* Credit whatsoever, but the having Money ready to make a punctual payment at the time prefixt and agreed."[98]

The need for a recoinage was obvious to most observers. Like Locke and Lowndes, most commentators focused on the necessity of reestablishing a sound and stable coinage as a precondition for commerce and credit to flourish. Others argued that credit was already more stable than coin and that it was therefore expedient to use credit to support the coin. However, regardless of which form of money was considered the most secure, it was now clear to all that coin and credit were intertwined in a symbiotic relationship; it was therefore impossible to talk about one without the other.[99] However, as will be discussed next, many commentators were not convinced that a general recoinage or the issuance of new credit notes would suffice to restore the integrity of the monetary system. For many, it was also necessary to try to eliminate the very source of the monetary turmoil: the clippers and counterfeiters.

Restoring Trust through Punishment

The success of the Financial Revolution could only be sustained if the integrity of the nation's coin was restored. The injuries clipping and counterfeiting had inflicted on the public's confidence in coin and credit were obvious to any observer. The pamphleteer R. J. proclaimed that "the Inconveniences and Mischiefs that the currency of clipt and counterfeit Money necessarily occasions, are so manifest to every

Body, (even of the meanest capacity) that it is as needless to remonstrate any of them, as it is impossible to enumerate them all."[100] To restore confidence in both coin and credit, it was therefore necessary to find a way to halt the ongoing intensification of clipping and counterfeiting. As we have seen, many contributors proposed ways to make it more difficult to manipulate and circulate false coins, most commonly by only accepting coins by weight and by reminting all coin using the most recent technology. Another way to end clipping and counterfeiting was to stop prospective perpetrators from carrying out their crimes, either by letting the hangman put an end to the money manipulators' lives or by letting highly public and symbolic executions serve as a deterrent.

William Fleetwood (1656–1723), the Bishop of Ely and a regular preacher before King William, Queen Anne, and Parliament, was one of many advocates of draconian punishments for monetary criminals. Subscribing to a similar understanding of money as that of Locke, Fleetwood argued that the silver content and the public stamp combined to provide security in the minds of people to accept the coin of the realm in exchange for their goods. As such, "the Publick Faith and Conscience, Interest and Honour, all engag'd to secure to the Receiver the Weight and Fineness of every single Piece of Money."[101] However, if the government's stamp were debauched, an injury is done to all users of money. Fleetwood wrote, "the World would fall again into distrust and fear, into suspicion and uncertainty about their Money."[102] The problem, however, in putting an end to this heinous crime was that many "Common People" did not recognize the severity of the injury inflicted on the nation. Historian Malcolm Gaskill called it a "'social crime' akin to poaching, wrecking, smuggling, and rioting—activities which, although technically illegal, were sanctioned by popular notions of legality."[103] Gaskill even suggests that the counterfeiters may have argued, on good grounds, that they were offering a service to society by increasing the quantity of coin in circulation.[104] Fleetwood, however, hoped that the dissemination of his sermon would awaken the general population to the severity of the crime committed by clippers and counterfeiters. "They will find," Fleetwood wrote, "that Clippers are as truly Thieves and Robbers, as those they find upon the High-ways, or breaking up their Houses, and do as well deserve their Chains and Halters."[105]

The only way to reduce the numbers of clippers and counterfeiters, according to Fleetwood, was to execute them and let the gruesome sight of the dangling corpses at the gallows deter others from committing similar crimes. He argued that the severity of the crime was such that the very security and honor of the nation was at stake. The death penalty was thus the only punishment that fit the crime and it was therefore justified as "neither Cruel nor Unjust."[106] Indeed, after exploring how clipping and counterfeiting had been punished in the past, Fleetwood called for the abolishment of hanging and a return to more draconian forms of executions. He lamented that punishments had been "chang'd into the Modern Executions, and have so continued ever since, altho' 'tis probable that Punishments of *greater Pain* and *constant Shame*, such as they heretofore were, would secure us better, than putting Men to a short and easie Death."[107]

Counterfeiting of money had been a capital offense in England since at least the fourteenth century and clipping, rounding, or filing coins was pronounced high treason in 1562.[108] The primary shortcoming of these laws was that only the actual clippers and counterfeiters were subject to prosecution. Since money is anonymous and universal, once the clipped or counterfeited money left the hands of the perpetrator it was almost impossible to retrace its steps and prosecute the original crime.[109] It was therefore notoriously difficult to detect, which meant that many perpetrators were never caught. William Chaloner (d. 1699) acknowledged that "Counterfeiting of money is very much Practiced, to the great abuse of His Majesty and Subjects, for want of a method to prevent and discover the Persons offending therein."[110] And Chaloner would know: himself a notorious clipper and counterfeiter of both coin and notes, he offered his suggestions partly as a playful gesture to the authorities and partly as a strategy of diversion.[111]

The little known Joseph Aicken agreed with Chaloner's point of view, observing that since the probability of being detected for clipping and counterfeiting was rather low, the death penalty did not serve as much of a deterrent.[112] Aicken wrote, "it is not the fear of Death that will hinder some Men from this Vice; want is a greater Evil than Death, in the Opinion of such Men; they must therefore be deprived of the Means of committing it."[113] Clippers and counterfeiters required a number of tools and supplies to carry out their trade, all of which they could not possibly produce on their own. They therefore had to rely on a number of different manufacturers to secure the necessary tools.[114] In order to stop this flow of tools and instruments, Chaloner and Aicken both proposed that all tools that might be used in the counterfeiting process should be marked with a seal and only be allowed in the possession of certified tradesmen. Any tradesman found selling or lending his tools to counterfeiters could then be considered an accomplice. Aicken warned, "no Man in England shall dare to sell, make, buy or use any such things, under pain of Death; for such things in Dishonest hands may be converted unto *Counterfeiting the Coin*; which hath brought great Calamities on this Nation, and if not effectually prevented, will bring it again into the like calamitous Condition."[115] Anyone selling tools and materials to clippers and counterfeiters "ought therefore to be hang'd."[116]

Chaloner also suggested that the Mint had to make it more challenging, iconographically and technically, to counterfeit the coin. "The *Heads, Letters,* and *Arms* should be so curiously done," he said, "that few in the Kingdom could do it so well; and rise up so high that it could not be Stampt but with and Engine of a Tun Weight, or by the strength of *Horses, Wind,* or *Water,* and then it would be morally impossible to Counterfeit Money without being discovered."[117] By requiring greater skills and the possession of specialized technology, it would be easier to narrow down the number of suspects capable of counterfeiting the coin.

Another method to stop counterfeiting was to eliminate some of the primary paths that led to this kind of criminal behavior. Echoing Sir Robert Cotton's comment half a century earlier that the alchemists were the foster fathers of the counterfeiters, Aicken claimed, "The chief Cause of the prevailing of this Vice, is the Study of *Experimental Philosophy, Alchimy,* and *Chymistry.*"[118] Aicken suggested that "this Age is so much addicted [to these studies] that almost all other Learning is despised."[119] Since the people who spend all their resources trying to transmute base metals into silver and gold will always be disappointed by the results, they often use their acquired knowledge of metals to manipulate the coin for private gain. He predicted confidently that "when our *Chymist* has spent all his Estate in endeavouring to find out the *Philosophers Stone,* but instead thereof, finds little else but broken Pots and Glasses, with the consumption of a good Estate; afterwards, for a Livelyhood, he falls to Counterfeiting the Coin of the Nation, for his former Study is a great help and assistance to him in this."[120] Aicken consequently suggested that the possession of alchemical books and manuscripts, as well as tools, like "Chymical Furnaces" and "Crucibles," and ingredients, like "Regulus of Antimony," "Corrosive Sublimate," "Sal-armoniack," and "Aqua-fortis," should be added to the list of objects only allowed in the possession of licensed professionals.[121]

Some authors wanted to tackle the problem by extending the death penalty to additional activities, such as the passing of counterfeit money. For example, Simon Clement (1654–1730), a stockbroker and merchant and later in life an influential Tory propagandist, proposed that "the Government should Issue a Proclamation, Declaring, That for the putting a stop to the abuses of the Money, the Laws should be put in Execution against any person that should presume to offer any Clipt Money after a certain prefixt Day."[122] In a similar statement for the inclusion of utterance of false money as a treasonable offence, R. J. suggested that "if any Person utter'd counterfeit or dimhished Money, knowing it to be false or dimhished, he might be indicted, and punished as guilty *of a great Misprision*; and if he knew the Counterfeiters, or Diminishers of it, or utter'd it for them, *he was partaker of their Crime, and guilty of High-Treason*."[123]

An alternative to making it a capital crime to circulate clipped or counterfeit coin was to impose severe punishments on those who knowingly accepted manipulated coins. John Lewis, for example, proposed that Parliament ought to pass an act that compelled "*all Persons whatsoever, under some severe Penalty, to* Cut *and* Deface *all Pieces of Money that should be tender'd in Payment, and discover'd to be* Counterfeit."[124] People who frequently dealt with money, such as anyone concerned with the king's revenues, the Exchequer, the Bank of England, cashiers of companies, merchants, and shopkeepers, should be forced to take a solemn oath and commit to never knowingly accepting any false coin. An anonymous author concurred with this proposal, proclaiming that "the Bankers and great Officers ought to suffer, for it has been the Receivers that have made the Thieves."[125] He added, "tho' the Clipper has been Hang'd and Dy'd Poor, yet there are others that Deserve to be Hang'd, that Live Rich."[126]

At the start of 1695, the Chancellor of the Exchequer, Charles Montagu, established a committee to consider how to put an end to clipping and counterfeiting. Two months later, the chair of the committee,

Francis Scobel, delivered a proposal to the House of Commons, suggesting that the "present Laws against clipping be enforced by some Additions."[127] The report provided the basis for the 1695–1696 *Act to prevent counterfeiting and clipping the Coine of this Kingdom* and the 1696–1697 *Act for the better preventing the counterfeiting the current Coine of this Kingdom*.[128] While the former statute was relatively unambitious, limiting the extension of the death penalty to those found guilty of counterfeiting Spanish coin and those in possession of clippings or filings, the latter statute significantly transformed the legal code regarding counterfeiting.[129] Section one pronounced:

> notwithstanding the good Laws still in force against the counterfeiting of the Moneys and Coins of the Realme yet the said Offence doth and is like daily to increase to the manifest Wrong and Injury both of his Majesty and all his loving Subjects being very much occasioned for want of a due and condigne Punishment to be inflicted upon such Artificers and others who without any lawful Authority do make or use Puncheons Stamps Dyes & other Engines and Instruments which are commonly used or may be made use of in or about the coining of Money.[130]

Unlicensed possessors—including aiders and abettors—of tools and equipments used for clipping or counterfeiting were thus hereafter considered perpetrators of high treason and would be hanged if found guilty. The statute also declared it high treason to mark, mill, or grain the edges of any current or diminished coin and to blanch, case, or wash copper in order to pass it off as silver.[131] Utterance, however, only became a capital crime in 1742, when the court decided that the pursuit of those who uttered false coin might lead investigators to the core of the counterfeiting ring.[132]

New provisions safeguarding Bank of England notes were also implemented. The Bank's directors were fully cognizant of the risks involved in issuing paper money. They recognized clearly that the "notes for Running Cash being considered as liable to be counterfeit for preventing thereof it was Ordered That they be done on Marble paper Indented."[133] While this made it more difficult to produce forged notes of high enough quality to enter circulation, the Bank soon became witness to the counterfeiters' skill when it discovered "one of the said Bank marbled notes to have been counterfeited."[134] As a result, the directors appointed a special committee to "prosecute the discovery of the frauds on the Bank."[135] The committee considered a number of proposals for how to best prevent the counterfeiting of their notes, including one by William Chaloner. Yet by August of 1696 they were still searching for better methods.[136] They were aided in their fight by Parliament, which passed an act in 1696 making it a felony to forge or counterfeit any Bank of England note and to present any such notes for redemption at the Bank. The directors quickly ordered that "the Counterfeiting and Forging of Bank Notes be officially prosecuted according to Law against such as are guilty thereof."[137]

The state was now armed with the requisite weapons to go after the clippers, counterfeiters, and forgers and thus to declare to the public, through the work of the hangman, that England was fully committed to the defense of the nation's monetary system.

Despite the preponderance of support for the death penalty, there were a significant number of commentators who argued that the death penalty was not the appropriate penalty for clipping and counterfeiting. For example, in a pamphlet the Treasury paid to print, the dean of Rochester, Samuel Pratt (1658–1723), claimed that "the laws are severe enough made, and put in Execution, and yet *NewGate* is perhaps now as full of Clippers as it was Three or Four Years ago."[138] And, what is even worse, the ordinary at Newgate revealed that the "Guilt of Clipping" had almost no effect on "the Criminal's Conscience."[139] While Pratt believed that a sense of religion might help put an end to the "gainfulest Sin that ever was invented," he acknowledged that preaching did not have much of an effect on those who never attended church.[140] Hence, for Pratt, neither the death penalty nor religion could put an end to clipping and counterfeiting since the ruffians committing these crimes were afraid neither of dying nor of God's judgment.

The anonymous author of the tract *Further Proposals for Amending and Settling the Coyn* questioned the effectiveness of the death penalty on the grounds that juries often viewed it as too harsh a punishment and therefore acquitted many accused clippers. The author therefore concluded that the remedy for clipping and counterfeiting "must be endeavoured by such Punishments as will deter more, than what is at present, and yet will not prevail with Juries to be too easie and compassionate in *Acquitting Clippers.*"[141] The proper punishment for clipping and counterfeiting should therefore be "to stand one Hour in the Pillory, then to have one half of his Nose cut off; and after, to be either sold to the *Plantations* for Seven Years, or emply'd in Work-Houses at home; which would deter *English Men* more than Death, and save the labour of so many *Men*, as well as so many *Lives*."[142]

Although Locke was certainly not averse to capital punishment, he too did not believe that the hangman alone could put an end to money manipulations. The potential income from clipping and counterfeiting was simply too high. He claimed that "*Clipping* is so gainful, and so secret a Robbery, that penalties cannot restrain it . . . Nothing I humbly conceive, can put a stop to *Clipping*, now it is grown so universal, and Men become so skilful in it, but making it unprofitable."[143] In Locke's mind, the only method whereby clipping could be made unprofitable was to remint all coin at the old standard and only allow coin to pass by weight while the recoinage was under way. Although it would force people to bring out their scales when conducting business during the interim period before all coins had been reminted, Locke believed that it was the only means whereby the coinage could be fully protected.

Locke also argued that the death penalty was ineffective because the clippers and counterfeiters had lost their respect for the gibbet. It was therefore necessary to restore people's respect, which required a concentrated effort to educate the public about the injuriousness of money manipulations. Locke agreed with the pronouncement of his friend John Pollexfen, that it was necessary to establish "stricter prosecutions . . . to strike the greatest terrour into such Offenders, that they may no longer be incouraged to go on, by depending upon the favour of Juries, niceties of Law, or hopes of Pardons."[144] In setting out to correct these problems, Locke followed the prevailing prescription for improving credibility, already discussed in Chapter 3, of selecting managers of the highest integrity, expertise, and reputation. This led Locke, in conjunction with Charles Montagu, to recruit one of the period's brightest minds, Isaac Newton, to assume the responsibility of the wardenship of the Royal Mint.[145] Newton's meteoric rise to fame had whetted the Cambridge natural philosopher's appetite for a more dynamic life that only the nation's capital could offer. So when the official invitation came from Montagu in March of 1696, Newton did not hesitate.[146] He left his studies of physics, mathematics, optics, and alchemy in Cambridge and dedicated himself to the restoration of the nation's currency, which included the responsibility for investigating, interrogating, and prosecuting clippers and organizing the Great Recoinage.

While the wardenship had previously been a sinecure requiring limited involvement, Newton committed himself to the task with the same level of diligence and perseverance that he had famously employed in his scientific investigations.[147] Consonant with the prevailing spirit of empiricism, Newton gathered as much firsthand information as possible, working through the Mint records of the last two hundred years. He refused, as much as possible, to rely on others' testimonies and calculations, and instructed his deputies to trust no "other eyes then your own."[148] Newton spent long hours at the Mint managing a network of agents and informers with whom he cooperated to interrogate and prosecute suspects. There are signs from early on in his tenure, however, that Newton was not entirely pleased with the responsibilities of his new position, and he petitioned the Treasury to relieve him of his duty to prosecute the money offenders. The reason for this petition was neither morality nor compassion. Instead he cited a lack of proper rewards to his office for the detection of counterfeiting operations; the flight of clippers and counterfeiters to the countryside, "where I cannot reach them"; and the juries' lack of confidence in witnesses after the state began offering cash rewards to informants who provided intelligence.[149]

Once his request was denied, however, he spared little effort in carrying out his charge. Newton personally traveled to prisons, taverns, and inns—often in disguise—to investigate counterfeiting rings.[150] He methodically investigated his cases and painstakingly interrogated witnesses, employing means that sometimes bordered on torture.[151] Once he had found his man, or woman, he prosecuted his cases with vigor and then, if successful in obtaining a conviction, ruthlessly denied pardons or remissions. For example, when the convicted counterfeiter William Chaloner desperately pleaded to be pardon by Newton—"O dear Sr no body can save me but you O God my God I shall be murderd unless you save me O I hope God will move your heart with mercy and pitty to do this thing for me"—Newton replied with silence.[152] Chaloner was hanged by the neck at Tyburn two weeks later. Newton's rationale for denying pardons was reportedly that "these dogs always return to their vomit."[153] An example of such a serial counterfeiter was Jane Housden. In an appeal to the court to finally execute her, Newton writes:

> Jane Housden was committed to prison . . . in the year of 1696 for clipping the coin of this kingdom . . . Newstead her pretended husband . . .

used indirect practices to . . . procure ye liberty to the said Jane Newstead. About two years after, the said Jane Newstead was again committed
to prison . . . for putting of counterfeit money & suspicion of coining the
same, & about four pounds of counterfeit money were then taken upon
her & three files with some sand found in her house . . . Afterwards in
the years 1702 she was again committed to prison & convicted of counterfeiting the coyn of this kingdom & pardoned by her Maty in order to
be transported, & was set at liberty upon giving security to transport
herself & therefore being now found in England . . . And this present year
[1710] being again accused of high Treason in counterfeiting the coyn
of this kingdom when she was apprehended she dropt a parcel into the
Thames wch was found to be a parcel of counterfeit money.[154]

Repeat offenders such as Housden strengthened Newton's resolve not
to grant pardons. In 1724, when asked whether he wanted a counterfeiter named Edmund Metcalfe hanged, he replied: "I know nothing
of Edmund Metcalfe convicted at Derby Assizes of counterfeiting the
coin; but since he is very evidently convicted, I am humbly of opinion
that it's better to let him suffer, than to venture his going on to counterfeit the coin & teach others to do so until he can be convicted again, for
these people very seldom leave off. And it's difficult to detect them."[155]

Newton commuted death sentences only when a convicted criminal
agreed to become a witness against other counterfeiters. For example,
a convicted counterfeiter named Peter Cooke bought himself a respite
by providing evidence that allowed Newton to successfully prosecute
Chaloner.[156] In another case, Newton ordered the keeper of New Prison
to keep Charles Ecclestone, an informer "charged upon Oath wth High
Treason in Counterfeiting the Current Coyne of this Kingdom . . . [in]
safe custody . . . [as] he being now intended for one of his Maties evi-
dences against several clippers & coyners of false & counterfeit money."[157]

Executions had to be highly visible and public in order for the death
penalty to serve as a mechanism for deterring prospective clippers and
counterfeiters and to signal to money users in general that the state
was taking serious measures to ensure the continued exchangeability
of notes and coin.[158] Although spared the more heinous punishment
of drawing and quartering that was normally reserved for the execution of high treason convicts, male clippers and counterfeiters were
hanged, while women were often burned. On the day of execution,

offenders were driven in public procession from Newgate Prison to the gallows at Tyburn.[159] These occasions, known as "Tyburn Fair" or "Hanging Match," were notable public events that people from all walks of life observed: "from early morning the factories and work-shops were deserted, while at the coffee-houses and taverns parties even formed the previous day."[160] Some prisoners, such as highwaymen, were allowed to stop along the route to drink with friends, allowing them to arrive at the gallows suitably sedated by alcohol. Clippers and counter-feiters, on the other hand, since their crimes constituted high treason, enjoyed no such comforts, but were dragged on a sledge without wheels through the sewage accumulated along the London streets, ending up at the intersection of Oxford Street and Edgeware Road, known then as Tyburn Tree and now as Marble Arch. The actual hangings were the-atrical, featuring the dramatic last words of the condemned, the rela-tives' tear-filled farewell, the hangman's often flamboyant performance, the actual moment of hanging, the macabre hangman's dance—which could go on for minutes, especially since the trapdoor had yet to be implemented—and the chaotic aftermath, when relatives and body snatchers struggled to recover the body.[161] This spectacle of terror and the theatrical performance of death situated the onlookers within a web of coercion with the explicit intent of establishing respect for and com-pliance with the rules of the monetary system.

The well-attended execution of convicted coiner Eleanor Elsom, here described by one of the onlookers, provides a glimpse of how the execu-tions were carried out:

> She was . . . saturated with tar, and her limbs were also smeared with the same inflammable substance, while a tarred bonnet had been placed on her head. She was brought out of the prison bare-foot, and being put on a hurdle, was drawn on a sledge to the place of execution near the gallows. Upon arrival, some time was passed in prayer, after which the executioner placed her on a tarr barrel, a height of three feet, against the stake. A rope ran through a pulley in the stake, and was placed around her neck, she herself fixing it with her hands. Three irons also held her body to the stake, and the rope being pulled tight, the tar barrel was taken aside and the fire lighted . . . She was probably dead before the fire reached her, as the executioner pulled upon the rope several times whiles the irons were being fixed.[162]

Newton imprisoned more than a hundred suspected clippers and counterfeiters during the height of the monetary crisis. In his first year at the mint (1696), there were twenty-three capital convictions out of seventy-one prosecutions for crimes against the currency.[163] The rate of prosecutorial success had improved greatly from the previous year (1695), when twenty-two people were convicted in 114 trials. The Old Bailey records further indicate that twelve people were found guilty in forty-four trials in 1697 and that there were seven guilty verdicts in twenty trials in 1698. After that, when the monetary crisis had passed, the number of annual prosecutions dropped into single digits for the next two decades.[164] According to the historian John Craig, Newton's success in detecting and prosecuting the clippers and counterfeiters, combined with his unwillingness to give amnesty to convicted criminals, reestablished the death penalty as an effective deterrent. For that reason, Newton's tenure at the Mint deserves "significant credit for a great reduction in the volume of counterfeiting."[165] This apparent success encouraged authorities to continue applying the death penalty for clippers and counterfeiters throughout the next century and a half.[166]

Weathering the Storm

In November of 1695, a version of Locke's recoinage proposal was adopted and soon thereafter approved by Parliament. No clipped coins were allowed to pass current after May 4, 1696. Holders of clipped coin who owed taxes (property, excise, and customs) or who had lent money to the government would receive compensation for bringing in their coin from a new tax on windows. Landowners and merchants (who owed taxes and lent to the government), bankers and jobbers (who discounted the coin), and tax collectors were quick to turn in their tarnished coin and thus benefited from the recoinage. By contrast, wage earners and the poor who did not pay taxes, and thus were not indebted to the government, had to find a taxpayer willing to buy their money. Soon they found that store owners would not accept their money at par. This created a great deal of unrest among the general population, as witnessed by a letter sent to John Ellis in the office of the Secretary of State. Thomas Power of Bideforde in Devon writes, "I thought it my duty to inform you that the proclamation issued out to hinder the currency of clipt moneys hath causes great disturbances here in the country in so much that (as it is reported) several here have been murdered in some market towns about it, and people speak very hard of the government because of it; and tis supposed by all except some speedy care be taken there will be an uproar."[167] This is indeed what happened in many parts of the country once the deadline passed and clipped coin ceased to be accepted in payment to the government. While the government successfully managed to put down these riots by force, it was compelled to delay the deadline for bringing the coin to the Mint by a month, thus giving more people a chance to exchange their old coins.[168]

The reminting of nearly £7 million was a Herculean enterprise that would have taken nine years to complete at the rate that the Mint was turning out new coin. Although he was not formally responsible for the coining operations—the Master of the Mint was—Newton analyzed and reorganized the minting process using the same precision he had employed in his scientific pursuits. In addition to establishing a number of temporary mints in the provinces, he brought additional machines to the London Mint and conducted time-motion studies of its employees. He managed to increase the production from fifteen thousand pounds of coin per week to one hundred thousand pounds of coin per week.[169] The Mint was at work six days a week, twenty hours per day, tirelessly turning out new coin. So, by the end of 1697, the vast majority of the nation's coin had been reminted and the entire project was brought to conclusion by the middle of 1698. Yet, even though the Great Recoinage was considered a marvelous success, its immediate effect, as predicted, was to worsen the monetary crisis. During the summer of 1696, when the Treasury had ceased to accept the old hammered coins as payment for taxes there was almost no cash to be found, a situation that only gradually improved in the autumn. The value of the silver coin in circulation dropped from £12 million in December of 1695 to £4.2 million in June of the following year, only to climb slowly back up to £6.2 million by December.[170] The scarcity of money problem had thus reemerged, this time more devastating than ever. Add to this, the fact that the war against France had taken an unfavorable turn, and England's prosperity and power looked all the more precarious.[171]

As expected, the sudden drop in the quantity of coin dangerously threatened the nascent culture of credit. The Bank of England was unable to redeem all notes presented, leading to a discount of 16 percent, which soon grew to 24 percent.[172] The historian Patrick Kelly notes that the correspondence between William III and his secretary of state, the Duke of Shrewsbury, reveals that the king was increasingly frustrated with the recoinage and anxious about the state of credit.[173] The lack of both money and credit contributed significantly to the massive failure of the National Land Bank in August of 1696 and the disastrous Malt Lottery in April of 1697.[174] However, credit had not completely evaporated. The Bank granted the government a loan of £200,000 in specie in August of 1696, which combined with the Bank's engraftment of £800,000 of discounted tallies in 1697, signaled an improvement in credit conditions. Once the Treaty of Ryswick was signed in the early autumn of 1697, ending the Nine Years' War, credit was fully restored and the money stock expanded rapidly.[175] In 1698, Charles Davenant gave testament to the fact that "this huge Engine [of credit], which for some time has stood still, [now] begins to be in Motion."[176] He noted that the conditions may not yet be as favorable as they were a few years earlier, when "the Bulk of Trade, here at Home, was carried on almost without the Species of Money," but conditions were certainly improving.[177] Looking back at credit's recent oscillations, Davenant offered the words with which this book began:

> Of all Beings that have Existence only in the Minds of Men, nothing is more fantastical and nice than Credit; 'tis never to be forc'd; it hangs upon Opinion; it depends upon our Passions of Hope and Fear; it comes many times unsought for, and often goes away without Reason; and when once lost, is hardly to be quite recover'd.[178]

Writing once again about credit a few years later, he succinctly summarized the events of the previous decade, saying, "the ill State of the Silver Coyne, and the necessity there was of Calling it in, in order to its Amendment, gave the great Blow to Credit, and made a considerable addition to the Deficiencies."[179] He acknowledged that the recoinage had been necessary, even though it had led to a situation in which "there was scarce any such thing as Credit Existing."[180] Yet, he amended this claim by suggesting that "Tho' Credit, through the Scarcity of Mony, has been in an ill posture, yet 'twill be absur'd to affirm, That it was ever quite extinguish'd; for no People could have subsisted a single Week without it, 'tis the principal Mover in all Business; and if there should be a total Stagnation in this nerval Juice, a dead Palsie would forthwith seize the Body Politick."[181] He praised the Bank of England for its contribution to the restoration of credit. While the Bank lost its credit "in the common Wreck," it managed to conduct its affairs, with the help of the government, in ways that lifted not just its own credit but that of the entire nation.[182] Davenant noted that twelve months after the recoinage, the Bank was once again redeeming its notes at par, an achievement that ought to be viewed as sufficiently impressive to convince people to support the Bank in the future.

Yet all was not perfect. Davenant recognized that the nation had a mounting public debt that sooner or later would come due, and once it did, it would create an enormous strain on public finances. He also expressed a deep concern with the increased vulnerability to national emergencies that this debt burden created. Borrowing a metaphor from Wren, Davenant warned that paper credit is "an opiate that quiets the patient for a time, but it is no cure for the disease their ill combat has brought upon us: can this imaginary wealth stand the shock of any sudden calamity?"[183] Moreover, he proclaimed that most ministers were too focused on raising money for the future and did not pay proper attention to the servicing of the debt contracted in years past. Noting that "if some of the Time was spent in looking after Old Funds, that is, employ'd in procuring fresh Supplies, Governments would not be in such Distress for Mony."[184] He then added, this "huge Engine of Credit, . . . in all probability is not to be put in order, by patching here and there; and can never have true Motion, till the Legislative Power interpose in setting all the Springs right, and in mending the whole."[185] The best way to make credit flourish was therefore not to borrow sporadically to meet each new eventuality, but rather, "by wise Arts of Government, to give a Value and Reputation to the Fourteen Millions already depending on the Public Faith."[186] Although it would take a decade before the public debt would become a serious problem, Davenant presciently predicted the arrival of a fiscal crisis and hinted at the type of solution that eventually would be employed. It is to this episode we turn in the last two chapters.

Conclusion

The interrelatedness between coin and credit was widely recognized in the 1690s. Many commentators noted that the circulation of both coin and credit was based fundamentally on people's opinion about their security and continued exchangeability. Although he did not write extensively on credit, Isaac Newton argued cogently that "'Tis mere opinion that sets a value upon money; we value it because with it we can purchase all sorts of commodities and the same opinion sets a like value upon paper security."[187] Newton cautioned, however, that credit must never be issued in excess: "Credit is a present remedy against poverty & like the best remedies in Physick works strongly & has a poisonous quality."[188] As discussed in Chapter 3, in confronting these issues political economists explored numerous ways to enhance people's opinion of credit—impeccable security, honorable and competent management, transparency, and harsh punishments for any activities that might tarnish trust and confidence. Since Bank of England notes were backed by a fractional reserve of silver coin, the importance of an impeccable coinage became all the more important. If people could not trust the integrity of the coin, people's opinion of the banknotes would surely suffer. The first order of business was therefore to make sure that the coinage was restored to its former standard and purity; this the government did by undertaking a massive recoinage using the latest technology in order to make it significantly more challenging to counterfeit the coin. In addition to the Great Recoinage, the government also adhered to the advice of Newton and others to enforce draconian punishments on those who jeopardized trust.

The ill state of the coin and the consequent anxiety about the exchangeability of Bank of England notes attracted a large number of public service–minded intellectuals to aid the government in its fight against these near-invisible enemies of state. Firmly committed to the defense of the Glorious Revolution, John Locke and Isaac Newton reoriented their philosophical and scientific pursuits in the service of the nation. Although they were not always pleased with their respective roles in fighting the counterfeiters—both Locke and Newton expressed frustration with their work on behalf of the state in this matter—they nevertheless remained dedicated to the cause. Newton communicated his commitment to public service in a letter to the astronomer John Flamsteed, "I do not love to be printed on every occasion, much less to be dunned and teased by foreigners about mathematical things, or to be thought by our own people to be trifling away my time about them, when I am about the King's business."[189] Locke, in a letter to Molyneux, similarly expressed his dedication to public service, despite his growing disinterest in political economy:

Though I can never bethink any pains or time of mine, in the service of my country, as far as I may be of any use, yet I must own to you, this, and the like subjects, are not those which I now relish, or that do, with most pleasure, employ my thoughts; and therefoe shall not be sorry if I scape a very honourable employment [Board of Trade], with a thousand pounds a year salary annex'd to it, to which the king was pleased to nominate me some time since.[190]

Some historians proclaim that the "recoinage was a failure" or, like Appleby, that "no intended goal of recoinage was achieved."[191] I have shown, on the contrary, that since the restoration of the coin was a necessary component of safeguarding the nascent Financial Revolution, the Great Recoinage must be considered a success. Even if the "recoinage caused immense inconvenience, and was grossly unfair," it contributed importantly to credit's recovery and a quick drop in clipping and counterfeiting.[192] Also suggestive of the recoinage's success was the fact that England was able to secure a peace with France in 1697, which would have been unlikely had England not managed to adequately restore its finances. This success led the famous diarist John Evelyn to suggest that both Newton and Locke should be honored by having their silhouettes adorn the English coin.[193] While Locke never received this honor, Newton's day came some three centuries later in 1978, when the Bank of England issued a £1 note with an image of Sir Isaac Newton on the back. The natural philosopher was depicted with his *Principia*, a telescope, a prism, and a map of the solar system. Unsurprisingly, the iconography contained no trace of Newton's more direct link to the nation's first credit currency.

— III —

Slavery and Credit

— 5 —

Public Credit and the Public Sphere

Introduction

A profound crisis disrupted the English Financial Revolution in 1710. Public credit was in a tailspin, with government bonds trading at a heavy discount, forcing the Treasury to borrow on increasingly unfavorable terms.[1] The rapidly deteriorating trust in public credit jeopardized the sustainability of the still developing Financial Revolution and thus the stability of the fiscal-military state. The crisis—called by contemporaries the "Loss of the City"—was particularly disturbing because it revealed the extent to which public credit was no longer an exclusive affair between the Crown and a small number of wealthy financiers. It was now subject to the fickle judgment of the public.[2] Since public debt instruments were now actively traded, the status of the national debt was dictated by an amorphous public's decentralized judgment of the prospects of a disembodied and depersonalized state administration. The recognition that an intractable public opinion now dictated public credit was deeply unsettling to traditional elites.[3] While John Locke and others had earlier argued that it was possible for people to derive well-informed opinions that could accurately guide them in a world of uncertainty, the consensus among philosophers was that the collective opinion of the multitude was never accurate and therefore should not be trusted. Locke wrote, "there cannot be a more dangerous thing to rely on, nor more likely to mislead, one; since there is so much more Falshood and Errour amongst Men, than Truth and Knowledge."[4]

The power of public opinion to dictate public credit was seen as a threat to the traditional political economic authority. That an anonymous public was able to influence England's political and geopolitical options, including its ability to wage war and thus its capacity to defend its borders and its cherished liberties, was deeply unsettling.[5] To the governing elite, decisions about politics, war, and the succession were the sole responsibility of people properly educated and experienced in political affairs.[6] Yet, despite their shared discomfort with the political influence of the public, both Whigs and Tories soon realized that the fickleness and instability of public opinion could be wielded as a political weapon. Both parties consequently used the public sphere to manipulate public opinion for their own ends. The incumbent ministry tried to shape public opinion of England's political, economic, and military administration in order to shore up public credit, while the opposition sought to undermine public opinion in order to sink public credit and thus force a ministerial shift. As such, public opinion, the public sphere, and public credit became intricately linked as the financial innovations introduced as part of the Glorious and Financial Revolutions became permanent fixtures of English society.[7]

In exploring the politically inflected discourse on credit sparked by the 1710 crisis, I seek to address historian Mark Knights's grievance that the early eighteenth-century "link between opinion, credit, and *partisan politics* remains under-explored."[8] Not only were numerous prominent writers, such as Daniel Defoe, Jonathan Swift, and Joseph Addison, paid to produce texts intended to shape the public's opinion about the state of credit, but the ways in which these writers conceived and theorized credit were deeply influenced by their party-political agendas. By controlling the language by which the public gained financial literacy, these writers tried to frame people's basic understanding of what credit was and how it worked and, in that way, to ensure that people would invest in ways that inadvertently supported their party's interest. In this chapter I argue that ideas about credit, which came to influence the economic discourse for the rest of the century, cannot be properly understood in isolation from the party-political wrangling of 1710.

The Political and Geopolitical Context
of the 1710 Credit Crisis

The unprecedented spending associated with the War of Spanish Succession (1701–1714) was primarily responsible for generating the 1710 credit crisis. But it was the intensity of the party wars between Whigs and Tories that elevated the crisis to a national emergency. The war, pitting England, the Dutch Republic, Austria, and Portugal against France and Spain, was largely a continuation of the Nine Years' War. The main strategic aim of the Alliance was to check France's expansion by making sure that Louis XIV's grandson, the Duke of Anjou, was prevented from laying claim to the now vacant Spanish throne. Instead, the Alliance supported Emperor Leopold I's son, Charles of Austria, as the new Spanish king. If France gained control over Spain it would then be able to take advantage of the entire Spanish empire, making France the most powerful nation both in Europe and the Americas. The Dutch and the English already had developed a strong imperial presence, and had even greater aspirations, making them unwilling to stand idly by while the French pursued their aim of universal monarchy.

England's success in this war made it the "military *Wunderkind* of the age" and signaled its emergence as a world power.[9] For the first time, England was able to mobilize a military that could rival any other European nation, in size and firepower, both on land and at sea. During the war, England had on average ninety-three thousand men in the army and forty-three thousand men in the navy, compared to around twenty thousand in the army and navy respectively during the second Anglo-Dutch war in the 1660s.[10] Also contributing to England's success was the legendary command of John Churchill, Duke of Marlborough (1650–1722), who skillfully managed the British redcoats and Jack Tars.[11] Success, however, did not come cheaply. Maintaining armies at war in both Flanders and Spain, as well as on the oceans, was enormously expensive. In addition to the sheer increase in enlisted men, new types of firepower and fortifications introduced during the seventeenth-century military revolution added greatly to the basic expenditures of waging war.[12]

The expansion of England's armed forces would not have been possible without the Financial Revolution.[13] While the Stuart monarchs had developed a permanent Crown debt, the establishment of a perpetual public debt with the tontine and lottery loans and the formation of the Bank of England in the 1690s enabled the government to borrow on a greater scale and at a lower interest than ever before.[14] The debt was also considered more secure now that the government had substantially improved its system of revenue collection. In addition to the further development and use of both indirect (excise and customs) and direct (land and hearth) taxes, the government had also put an end to the notoriously inefficient system of tax farming.[15] A relatively efficient corps of civil servants was now in charge of the collection of taxes.[16] Collectively, these fiscal reforms enabled the Treasury to raise more money faster and the state to carry a much greater debt burden, contributing substantially to England's financial flexibility.[17]

In the political realm, the already sharp hostility between Whigs and Tories intensified. The two parties had originated during the Exclusion Crisis of the 1670s over the issue of whether a Catholic monarch, in this case Duke of York, should be allowed to succeed to the throne. The two-party system emerged in an even more prominent role when Parliament's authority was enhanced as a result of the financial settlement of the Glorious Revolution and the passing of the Triennial Act in 1694. Debates on controversial issues like religion, foreign policy, military strategy, and public finance were increasingly staged within this binary opposition, the vehemence of which occasionally conjured up fears of another civil war.[18] While the electorate decided on the composition of the House of Commons, the monarch selected the ministry. Since the ministry had to work closely with the Commons, which now controlled the fiscal machinery, the monarch's choice was circumscribed by political pragmatism. The Whigs were generally better organized than the Tories. The so-called Whig Junto successfully coordinated and managed the party so that even though the Tories won four out of five elections during Anne's reign, the Whigs maintained significant influence.[19] In general, Anne tried to select political moderates for her ministry to ensure that the party conflict did not cripple the political administration. This led to her selection of Sir Sidney Godolphin (1645–1712) as Lord Treasurer in 1702, who together with Marlborough successfully governed the country for the next eight years.[20] While both of them started out as moderate Tories, they soon became allied with the Whig Junto, as they found the Whigs more supportive of the war effort.

The debate on public credit was mostly conducted along party lines. Although actually composed of numerous layers of complex ideological conflict, the Whig–Tory opposition generally mapped well onto the divide between the landed and moneyed interests.[21] While the Tory landed interest included some traditionalists who advocated a mostly agrarian-based civic republican society, free from a standing army, national debt, and moneyed men, most of the landed men had by this time become favorably inclined towards commercially oriented agriculture, wide-reaching domestic markets, and active colonial expansion.[22] Moreover, they were increasingly accepting of the new financial configuration or at least certain parts of it.[23] As long as a Tory-friendly alternative to the Whig Bank of England was implemented and the recent increases in the land tax used to service the state's deficits were rolled back, the landed interest seemed to have transcended its aversion to elaborate financial schemes.[24] The landed interest had been trying for some time to establish a land bank, but the failure of John Asgill's and Nicholas Barbon's project in 1695 had forced them to look for other solutions compatible with their political and economic interests. They now concentrated on establishing a joint-stock company with the capacity to lend to the government on the same scale as the Bank of England and the East India Company, hoping that such large-scale lending would earn the Tories greater leverage over public policy.[25]

The moneyed interest was comprised mostly of merchants, bankers, and financiers. Often viewed as *arrivistes* or parvenus, Whig merchants and financiers often had landed roots. While they could not rival the accumulated wealth of landed men, their rapid commercial gains and the liquidity of their wealth was nevertheless intimidating to traditional elites. The moneyed interests were in general supportive of commercial and financial undertakings. Some preferred particular types of commerce, for example, domestic industry over the reexport trade, while others valorized trade over finance, in particular speculation and stockjobbing. Most were pleased with recent political and financial transformations and viewed the Glorious Revolution and the formation of the Bank of England as conducive to their aims. Predictably, they were also supportive of the shift from a heavy reliance on the hearth tax to the land tax to finance the wars. Because of the lucrative lending opportunities the war provided, many of the moneyed men believed that it was worthwhile to continue fighting until the French were definitively defeated and English merchants were in a position to take over the bulk of French colonial commerce.[26]

For much of the War of Spanish Succession, the Godolphin–Marlborough ministry enjoyed great military and political success. It transformed what had initially been a defensive military strategy into one in which Britain scored a number of decisive victories that significantly changed the European balance of power. This accomplishment was made even more impressive by the fact that it was achieved without bankrupting the nation. In fact, the ministry harnessed the nation's resources in a way that left state finances in better shape than they had been during the previous war and, more importantly, in better shape than those of its enemy.[27] By 1709, however, England's string of military successes were replaced by a failed peace at The Hague and a bloody battle at Malplaquet, and the escalating expenses of the war had pushed the nascent fiscal apparatus to its limits. With spending averaging £7 million per year, the total public debt had skyrocketed from £14 million to £36 million during the course of the war.[28] Short-term military departmental debts had begun to spiral out of control, with the navy, army, ordnance, and transportation debentures—most of which were short-term loans unsecured by specific revenue flows—trading at an alarming discount.[29] The largest component, the navy bonds, traded at a 35 percent discount in 1710 and the army and transport debentures reached a 40 percent discount in the beginning of 1711, signaling the public's eroding confidence in the government's capacity to adequately service its debts.[30] In addition, Exchequer Bills, considered the most secure financial instruments at the time, with liquidity almost as high as coin itself, had also begun to drop below par. To darken the economic horizon further, there was a general disruption in European financial markets and a string of failed insurance companies that centered on London.[31]

Also contributing to the political crisis of the ministry in 1710 was the Sacheverell affair. The Reverend Dr. Henry Sacheverell (d. 1724), a High Church clergyman, used the pulpit to question the legitimacy of the political order established by the Glorious Revolution. His sermons were attended by large crowds and printed versions sold more than one hundred thousand copies, igniting an intense public debate about the present division of power between Parliament and the Crown. To discredit the Tory attacks, the Whigs decided to impeach Sacheverell before the House of Lords. But instead of gaining public support, the trial generated widespread support for Sacheverell and the Tory cause.[32] In the rioting that followed, angry mobs attacked dissenters' meetinghouses, as well as the Bank of England, which constituted a powerful symbol of the new political order.[33] The sermons, trial, riots, and surrounding debates generated an adverse political climate for the ministry, at the same time that it galvanized the Tory party.

Further political controversy was stirred up by the ministry's failure to secure an honorable peace with France. The Tories blamed the Whigs for intentionally making excessive demands on the French in order to ensure that the war was prolonged and that the moneyed interest could continue benefiting from lending to the government. The landed interest was understandably troubled, considering that taxes on their land paid for much of the war and thus also served to enrich the bondholders.[34] The political and financial climate in England during the summer of 1710 pointed towards a serious crisis for the ministry.

The political turmoil reached a crescendo in June of 1710, when the queen dismissed the Earl of Sunderland, Marlborough's son-in-law, from the office of secretary of state and replaced him with a Tory. Sensing that even more radical changes were underway, the Whigs embarked on a campaign to convince the queen that an overhaul of the ministry would have disastrous consequences, in particular for public credit. The prominent merchant and director of the Bank of England, Sir Gilbert Heathcote (1652–1733), who staunchly supported the Whig battle cry of "No Peace without Spain," wielded his political clout to help the Godolphin ministry weather the storm. On the day after Sunderland's dismissal, Heathcote paid the queen a visit to obtain an assurance that no further political changes were pending. The resulting commitment by the queen was of course nothing more than a stalling tactic to keep the channels of credit from the Bank open, if only until the more radical changes were unveiled. In addition, her former advisor and confidant, Sarah Churchill (1660–1744), the Duchess of Marlborough, sent the queen a warning of the financial implications of a ministerial change: "I may tell your Majesty what I have lately heard for the honour of my Lord Treasurer [Godolphin] from all the considerable men in the city, which is, that if he should be removed, they would not lend a farthing of money."[35] The queen had now been duly warned that any further political reforms would occasion a "Loss of the City."

The final undoing of Godolphin came in August. When the Bank was asked by the military pay offices to discount a number of bills of exchange—normally a routine line of short-term credit that the Bank provided to the Treasury—the Bank declined on the basis that it could not afford to take on such risks in the midst of political instability and sinking credit. Heathcote told Godolphin that the Bank now needed an assurance in writing from the queen that no further ministerial changes were forthcoming. This move turned out to be a serious miscalculation and on August 8, 1710, the queen dismissed Godolphin. Two days later she announced Robert Harley as the new Chancellor of the Exchequer, effectively making him the new first minister.[36]

England was now in a state of political and financial crisis. What would the consequences of this ministerial change be on domestic politics and how would this alter England's approach to the war? How would financial markets react to the turbulence? Would a ministry favoring the landed interests honor the government's outstanding debts to the commercial and moneyed interests? Worst of all, the Whigs warned, would an impoverished English military have to capitulate to its long-time enemy and face a French invasion with its resulting absolutism and papal tyranny? While all of these concerns were foisted on Harley from the very beginning of his tenure, the most immediate challenge he faced was to find a way to shore up public credit. The future of Harley's ministry, the stability of the fiscal-military state, the continuity of the financial apparatus, and indeed the security of England relied on a rapid solution to the crisis of public credit.

Harley promptly went to work to raise enough funds to keep credit afloat and the armed forces at war. Contrary to the advice from some of the more radical Tories who tried to convince him to rely solely on money from the landed interests, he wisely did not give up on courting the Whig moneyed interest. Although the Bank of England did not grant him all the funds he requested on the terms he had hoped for, the fact that they were willing to extend any loans at all sent important signals that the established channels of government finance were still open.[37] Encouraged by their success in managing the reaction to the ministerial change, the new ministry and the queen launched the next phase of their political agenda and dissolved the Whig-dominated Parliament at the end of September; a new election was called for October. This brought about a sell-off of government bonds and stocks in the Bank of England and East India Company, causing prices to fall and nervous foreign investors to withdraw funds and smuggle specie abroad, noticeably reducing the circulation of coin in England. While the ministry and the queen repeatedly tried to reassure the city that they were committed to political and religious moderation, and that they would do everything in their power to uphold public credit, fears that the ministry would default on—or use a *sponge* to wipe out—the entire national debt kept on escalated, thus contributing to the severity of the financial crisis.

Public Opinion, Public Sphere, and Public Credit

The crisis of 1710 sparked a vigorous debate about the nature of credit and the most appropriate way to restore it to its former glory. It was clear to all observers that the transformation of public credit during the Financial Revolution had significantly altered the composition of both creditors and debtors. The institutionalization and bureaucratization of the state, combined with the increased transferability of government bonds, generated an increasingly anonymous and detached relationship between the two poles of the credit relationship. Since the state no longer raised money on the personal reputation of the monarch and his connections to specific goldsmith bankers, tax-farmers, landed men, and wealthy merchants, but rather on the investing public's opinion of the effectiveness of the state's management of the fiscal apparatus, the state-as-public-debtor became more abstract and disembodied.[38] At the same time, lending to the government no longer locked creditors into a long-term personal relationship with the state. The increased transferability of government securities and the resulting market in these instruments enabled government creditors to unload their financial assets whenever their opinion of the investment changed.[39] Public credit thus came to depend on how public opinion perceived the state's current capacity to service the interest payments and its imaginary ability to repay the debt in some distant, theoretical future.[40] In this new culture of credit, public opinion became the arbiter of public credit, dictating everything from England's imperial campaigns, fiscal administration, and legislative decisions to the choice of ministers.[41]

The number of people who translated public opinion into a rising or falling credit by trading bonds was rapidly expanding, reaching approximately eleven thousand in 1710 and close to forty thousand a decade later.[42] The vast majority of these investors held only a small number of bonds and the practice of joint, multiple, and corporate holdings of securities was rare.[43] This made it unlikely that any person or body had the capacity to consistently exert influence over financial markets.[44] The majority of the investors were metropolitan British merchants, along with significant numbers of French, Dutch, Huguenot, and Jewish

investors. Women also played a major role: alongside wealthy merchants, peers, gentry, civil servants, and professional men, rich widows were counted among the major proprietors of financial assets.[45]
The middling sorts came into contact with the new financial instruments as well, attracted by the mounting spirit of investment, speculation, and gambling.[46] Even people of more modest means invested in
financial markets by buying a share—one-tenth or one-twentieth—of a
£10 lottery loan ticket. Opportunities to invest in these securities were
plentiful, as the government issued more than half a million £10 tickets
and thirty thousand £100 tickets between 1711 and 1714, sold partly in
well-frequented pubs.[47] With aspirations of winning the grand prize,
thousands of investors showed up at Guildhall for the public drawings,
turning these events into major public spectacles, which William Hog-
arth would later satirize in his painting *The Lottery* (1724).

The investing public thus constituted a remarkably large and diverse
body of people.[48] And, these investors channeled the opinion of an even
wider non-investing public. Since the issues pertaining to public credit
were deeply intertwined with other major issues of the day—party
politics, foreign policy, the succession, and religious controversy—the
opinion of the investing public was formed within a much broader
public sphere, informing many tens, if not hundreds, of thousands of
people. This public significantly overlapped with the parliamentary
electorate—consisting of an estimated three hundred thousand men at
this point—but arguably represented a broader and more diverse political force.[49]

The fact that public opinion was based on the beliefs and sentiments
of such a decentered and fragmented public made it almost impossible
to control. Propagandists nevertheless tried to access this public and
influence its thinking by flooding the public sphere with their writings.[50]
In so doing, they took advantage of an already vibrant print culture
that had developed as a result of increasing literacy rates, a burgeoning
commerce in cheap print, frequent electioneering, an expansion in the
number of public petitions, and the lapse of the Licensing Act in 1695.[51]
This flourishing print culture was particularly useful to political chal-
lengers, who were now able to orchestrate elaborate campaigns against
incumbents.[52] However, the reigning ministry, although often forced
to defend itself against its critics, also used the public sphere to try to
shape public opinion.

Experimenting with different mediums and messages, and widely disseminating their publications, propaganda writers primarily targeted people operating in urban public spaces like pleasure gardens, the Royal Exchange, Exchange Alley, alehouses, and coffeehouses. Providing access to people of most social groups, political leanings, economic standing, and religious convictions, London's approximately five hundred coffeehouses played a particularly important role as spaces in which public opinion was formed. And, since much of the trade in stocks and bonds was carried out in coffeehouses located in Exchange Alley, in particular Jonathan's and Garraway's, changes in public opinion informed by coffeehouse conversations often translated immediately into rising or falling credit. The spatial and conceptual proximity between Exchange Alley and the coffeehouse thus ensured that the public sphere and the new system of public credit mutually conditioned each other during the Financial Revolution.[53] Hence, the public sphere not only promoted a more democratic political discourse, as the philosopher Jürgen Habermas famously proposed, it also contributed to the democratization of public credit.[54]

Yet, it should be noted that the public sphere informing decisions regarding public credit at the turn of the eighteenth century differed in important ways from that theorized by Habermas.[55] The seventeenth-century English version of the public sphere was not exclusively a space for rational public criticism of the state. Instead, the ministry was trying to shape public opinion as much as was the opposition, making the public sphere a forum for debate between multiple oppositional forces and the state, rather than solely an avenue for criticism of the state.[56] Furthermore, the conversation about public credit was not exclusively based on rational critical arguments, in which equal individuals recognized "the better argument."[57] Instead, since the debate was designed to sway the public's sentiment, imagination, or expectations, rational arguments were not always preferred. Instead, propaganda writers used multiple types of arguments, rhetoric, and evidence, the epistemic content of which occasionally promoted rational discourse, while oftentimes relying instead on satire, humor, distraction, and obfuscation.[58]

The fact that these debates were conducted in multiple types of media, including newsprint, pamphlets, broadsides, and ballads, raises the question of whether it might be more accurate to think in terms of multiple separate and partially overlapping public spheres, rather than one larger public sphere.[59] The Whig historian John Oldmixon, for example, argued in 1714 that the content and audience of different forms of propaganda yielded radically different reactions. "Pamphlets work slowly," he wrote, "and the Operation of one Pamphlet is often spoil'd by that of another," while the "Crying and Singing" of the balladeers "warms the Minds of the Rabble, who are more capable of Action than Speculation."[60] Although all spaces for public discussion were not open to every person and all publications were not intended for every audience, the fact that pamphlets, newspapers, and ballads tended to share the same general concerns meant that even disjointed social groups were exposed to largely the same set of ideas and arguments. Since similar conversations were carried on in many different spheres, it therefore seems plausible to think in terms of one diverse, yet unified, public sphere. In fact, it was this heterogeneity and amorphousness of the public sphere that intrigued and threatened contemporaries. To them, the public exercised a palpable political force, yet it was impossible to pinpoint its exact social location. Hence, by trying to disaggregate the public sphere and pin down its specific location there is a risk of losing the very quality that linked public opinion to the views of the multitude and thus made it such an enigmatic and intimidating social phenomenon to those who tried to manage it.

The fluidity, elasticity, and open-endedness of opinion allowed for the simultaneous presence of different, often conflicting, public opinions. That is, contrary to the singularity and coherence that Habermas argues public opinion developed later in the eighteenth century, public opinion did not denote a general agreement at this point, but rather represented a multiplicity of opinions, ranging from different nuances of the same general idea to diametrically opposing views.[61] The very fact that public opinion was not firmly grounded in reason or a careful empirical assessment meant that it also had the capacity to change suddenly and with little warning. In the midst of this general fear of the precariousness of opinion, Whig and Tory writers sought to exploit this fickleness to further their respective political agendas.

Propaganda and the Shaping of Public Opinion

Party politics informed every facet of the debate on credit. As Mark Knights points out, partisanship "ensured that everything political could be seen in two ways—the same words, phrases, people, and events were routinely represented differently according to party allegiance."[62] The challenge for propagandists was therefore to construct a convincing theory, or narrative, that enabled people to comprehend the world from a particular point of view. As Knights notes, the "political struggle was thus a competition between and over rival representations and truth-claims."[63] In the realm of finance, the challenge was to shape people's economic literacy and their understanding of the present financial crisis, partly so that they would invest in ways that promoted the party cause. That is, both Whig and Tory writers offered theories and analyses aimed at improving financial conditions, at the same time that they sought to promote their party's political interests.

The Whig position on public credit was most clearly articulated by the prolific propagandist Benjamin Hoadly (1676–1761).[64] Writing at the time of Godolphin's dismissal, he warned of the multiple disasters that a ministerial and parliamentary rearrangement would bring about. Adopting the voice of a Tory who recognized the damages his party was inflicting on the nation, in his *Thoughts of an Honest Tory* (1710) Hoadly warned against the sinister aims of Tory politicians. His fictitious persona claimed he had always supported the Tories and worked for a Tory majority, but that now he was "quite sick at the review of the Methods our Friends have used to gain this happy Prospect."[65] Warning that a continuation of party conflict was jeopardizing the status of public credit at a particularly inopportune moment, he queried ominously:

> Is this a time for such a Total Alternation [in the ministry], as must shake the confidence of Friends, and inspire the Enemy with Hopes? Is this the Season for an entire change of Hands, when *Publick Credit* must be sunk into nothing, before the rest of *Europe* can have time to know whom they are to depend upon, and the people at home whom they are to trust?[66]

A political rearrangement would completely undermine public credit and would thus force England to accept an inglorious peace with France and a return of the Pretender—James II's son James Francis Stuart— who had already made an attempt to invade England in 1708. And, if the present party hostilities were not quickly brought under control, nothing prevented that "the *field* of *Election* should become a *field* of *Battle*."[67]

The potentially disastrous consequence of an implosion of public credit continued to be Hoadly's main theme in *Fears and Sentiments*

of all True Britains; With Respect to National Credit, Interest and Reli-
gion (1710). Instead of using the rhetorical technique of impersonat-
ing his opponents, he now pretended to tone down the partisan tenor
by defending the interests of all Englishmen, another common literary
device. In exploring the nature of credit and its importance to England's
power and prosperity, he sought to form a better understanding of how
credit crises occured and what could be done to prevent them in the
future. Like many of his contemporaries, Hoadly located the essence of
credit in trust. He argued that one of the most essential components of
trust is the borrower's reputation for prudence, which can only be built
up over time. "*Publick Credit,*" he wrote, is "like *Private Reputation*;
obtained by a *Series* of *good Conduct* made up of a multitude of *good*
Actions."[68] The splendid reputation that Godolphin had built up over
the years thus constituted an indispensable asset to the state. But now
that he had been dismissed, trust had to be rebuilt from scratch.

Hoadly highlighted that the past was not the only component that
dictated trust. Expectations of the future and imaginations of the
unknown were at least as important in deciding the status of credit.
This is exactly what made credit such an enigmatic and unpredictable
phenomenon. Since expectations and the imagination could never be
firmly grounded in certainty or controlled by authority, Hoadly noted
that a certain anxiety inevitably accompanied credit. Credit's capacity
to transfer the implications of an event through space and time and to
generate real implications of an imagined event meant that the mere
suspicion of an unfavorable future or distant event had the capacity to
become a serious threat to credit in the present. For Hoadly, the current
prospects of a dissolution of Parliament exemplified how such "an ugly
fear" of the future might cause public credit to sink in the present.[69]

Because of its sensitivity to speculations about the future, credit
was particularly vulnerable to the ongoing party strife. Hoadly consequently lambasted the Tories for jeopardizing public credit by ceaselessly scheming for their own political advantage. He accused them
of opportunistically putting their own fortunes ahead of the national
interest. He called for a greater sense of mutual responsibility among
the feuding political actors in order to stabilize credit and thus secure
the continuity of the political order created by the Glorious Revolution.
While political parties should be allowed to freely squabble over most
things, they should resolve to treat public credit as a national concern,

transcending the pettiness of party politicking.[70] The Tories ought to realize, he wrote, that a fall in public credit would severely damage England's national security. A falling credit would not only weaken the nation in itself, it would also worsen England's relative position as England's loss of credit would be France's gain. He wrote, "as the first raising our *Credit* to such a pitch, was the *Entire ruine* of the *French King's Credit*; so the *Death* of *ours* must necessarily give a *New Life* to *his*."[71] The only reasonable solution to the present problem, therefore, was to invite Godolphin back to once again manage public credit.

Hoadly ended his pamphlet by reminding the Tory landed interest that in the event that the October elections granted them a parliamentary majority, they ought to prudently manage the national debt. He suggested that they should refrain from mismanaging or defaulting on the national debt, ultimately in order to protect their own wealth. Because if the government were to default on its debt and thus erase the property of the moneyed interest, there should never be any surety in the minds of the landed interest that the government would not, at some point, seize their lands and estates as well. In that circumstance, he asked, "What can be secure? What can be a *Title*, or a *Right*? Or, what can become of *Property*?"[72] In Hoadly's mind, even though financial wealth was grounded in immaterial and abstract future-oriented notions—like trust, confidence, and opinion—it nevertheless carried the same legitimacy as the most real and concrete forms of property. Consequently, Hoadly argued, if financial property were violated it would constitute a full-on attack on the long-celebrated English ideals of property and liberty, and would thus undermine the very foundation of society.[73]

Hoadly's Whig intervention was quickly challenged by the Tories. The new Lord Treasurer Robert Harley assembled an impressive propaganda team, including Simon Clement (1654–1730), Abel Boyer (1667–1729), Jonathan Swift (1667–1745), and Daniel Defoe (1660–1731).[74] Once in control of the ministry, Harley and the Tories were intent on managing expectations and imaginations in a manner that kept public credit afloat. With the help of these writers, Harley sought to establish a uniquely Tory understanding of the nascent culture of credit. Written under the direct supervision of Harley himself, Clement's *Faults on Both Sides: Or, An Essay upon the Original Cause, Progress, and Mischevious Consequences of the Factions in this Nation* (1710) commented on recent English political history through the lens of the Whig–Tory divide.[75] His historical analysis culminated in a discussion of the contemporary challenges facing England, including a point-by-point refutation of Hoadly.

Clement had much to say on the issue of credit, offering the Tories both a different analysis of the financial crisis and a different way of assessing the imaginary component of credit. First, he criticized the directors of the Bank of England for interfering with the queen's choice of ministers and thus acquiescing to becoming an instrument of party. While his criticism of the Whig Bank was harshly worded, he took great pains to flatter and praise individual directors of the Bank, most likely to avoid jeopardizing Harley's continued relationship with them. Clement also addressed the threat of a "Loss of the City," or that "this change of the Ministers will fall the Stocks, Foreigners will draw their Money out of our publick Funds, and both publick and private Credit will be ruin'd."[76] To Clement, these scenarios were mere fabrications and empty speculations designed to "frighten ignorant and unthinking People."[77] He nevertheless spent a great deal of effort trying to dispel the fears of such a loss.

On the issue of falling securities prices, Clement offered a different interpretation of how public opinion influences credit. While Hoadly argued that expectations and imagination formed by the public were unavoidable and integral to the determination of securities prices, Clement claimed that the only true measure of a stock's value was its intrinsic worth, which was determined by the size of the company's capital stock, the performance of its managers, and its recent profits and losses. Similarly, the price of government bonds ought to be dictated by the revenues of the state, the character of the fiscal managers, and the recent history of the debt. The key ingredients in the formation of trust, according to Clement, were thus transparency, managers with reputations for integrity and propriety, and financial instruments backed by impeccable security. Apart from making the manipulation of credit a capital offense, he highlighted the very same ingredients of trust that earlier writers, discussed in Chapter 3, had posited.

If stock or bond prices would increase beyond that which the fundamentals dictated, it could only be attributed to an increase in what Clement called "*imaginary wealth*."[78] By portraying the value generated by a favorable public opinion as fictitious, unreal, or imaginary, Clement dismissed the public's newfound capacity to dictate credit as largely irrelevant and irrational. That is, public opinion was not the expression of the general population's careful assessment, but rather a confused, uninformed, and unfounded sense that must be acknowledged as such. Moreover, he blamed the most recent run-up of the "imaginary value" on the sordid dealings of the stockjobbers, a group that had long been vilified for their contributions to the destabilization of credit.[79] He consequently regarded the fall in stock and bond prices after the ousting of Godolphin as an inconsequential adjustment in the public's imagination or opinion, unworthy of serious attention.

The difference between Hoadly's and Clement's understandings of credit captures an important tension between the Whig proponents of the new financial system and the more conservative landed Tory tradition. For Clement, the intrinsic value is the "true" value, while the "imaginary value" is based on unsubstantiated beliefs and conjectures. The latter is seen as dangerously precarious in that it is liable to speculation, rumors, manipulations, and lies. Every investor knew and tacitly accepted that credit was inherently risky and uncertain. However, as Locke and others had already explored, it was nevertheless possible to form a sound opinion that a person could trust.[80] The key was for every person to remain informed of the relevant conditions and only trust the most skilled witnesses.[81] But this was hardly the case in reality, Clement and the Tories insisted. In practice, most people based their opinion on what the multitude believed, which meant that opinion did not approximate true knowledge and therefore did not serve as a reliable guide for action. Clement thus viewed the abstract and immaterial component of financial assets with much greater suspicion than Hoadly. The Tories were consequently much more comfortable, at least for the moment, with real existing assets, like land and merchandise, serving as security for financial assets. Hoadly, on the other hand, while also recognizing the precariousness of public opinion, did not ascribe any particular normative qualities to opinion and expectations, viewing them instead as natural and unavoidable features of all credit instruments.

Lurking beneath the surface of this debate about expectations and opinion was a deeper controversy over political and economic authority. Was society still under the rational, skillful, and just leadership of the landed elites or had the commercial and moneyed interests acquired a greater political influence through the public debt? Even worse, was it possible that no one was really in clear control of the economy and that it was now dictated by an amorphous and anarchic public opinion? The commonplace concern among the landed interest that the expansion of public credit would introduce rampant speculation and corruption had now been augmented by the fear that important political and economic decisions were dictated by people who did not even understand what the impact of their actions would be on England's political and geopolitical future.

Clement's intervention generated a series of Whig responses, including Joseph Trapp's *Most Faults on One Side* (1710), an anonymous author's *Faults in the Fault-Finder* (1710) and *A Supplement to Faults in the Fault-Finder* (1711), and a series of articles by Arthur Maynwaring (1668–1712) in the Whig newspaper *The Medley*. To address these, Clement wrote a rejoinder titled *A Vindication of the Faults on Both Sides* (1710), in which he further explored the issue of public credit. He once again revealed his discomfort with credit's dependency on expectations, opinion, and imagination. To combat this inherent fickleness, he reiterated the importance of good securities backing debt instruments and transparent bookkeeping so that security prices accurately reflected existing conditions.[82] In addition to his discussion of the importance of prudence and probity in issuing debt instruments, he restated his views on the distinction between intrinsic and imaginary value. He advised that "People ought never to value them [stocks] by the Rates they may go at in *Exchange-Ally*, but to inform themselves truly of the certain Sum that has been paid into the Stock, and of the Dividend that is constantly made, together with the probable Success of the Management."[83] Clement thus suggested that the best way to manage the imaginary component was to devalue its importance so that people would simply ignore it. People should look at the empirical facts, not follow the confusion generated by rumors, propaganda, and lies.

Sensing that a massive propaganda campaign would be necessary for his ministry to sway public opinion, Harley employed the prolific writer Abel Boyer to write for his cause.[84] Boyer had collaborated with Harley in the past, but it was only in the autumn of 1710 that Harley invited him to officially produce propaganda in his service. In *An Essay towards the History of the Last Ministry and Parliament* (1710), Boyer laid out a series of arguments designed to influence the public's opinion of Harley's stewardship of the government and thus their assessment of public credit. In building his case, Boyer explored the centrality of credit to the modern state and economy. Without credit, he argued, only a fraction of desired commercial transactions would be carried out and the state would find itself unable to fulfill its most basic responsibilities. As such, "Credit is become the very *Heart* and *Soul* of all *Trade* and *Commerce,* either *private* or *publick.*"[85] In fact, public credit had become so important, he argued, that any activity that threatened to undermine it should be considered high treason.

In order to pinpoint its essential workings, Boyer sketched a rudimentary definition of credit. He claimed that credit is *"The Opinion or Confidence we have in another's Ability, Honour,* and *Punctuality to Discharge or Pay a Debt."*[86] Public credit, by extension, is "the same *Opinion* or *Confidence,* with respect to the State or Government, founded on the Experience of its *Ability, Honesty,* and *Punctuality."*[87] Boyer recognized that a mix of reputation and expectation dictated the status of credit. However, uncomfortable with the role played by public opinion as the arbiter of credit, he tried, like Clement, to make credit more stable by grounding it in something less precarious and ephemeral. Similar to many of the seventeenth-century political economic writers, Boyer proposed that if the managers of public credit were men of impeccable honor and character, as well as sufficient means, their ingrained moral virtues might stabilize public opinion and therefore infuse credit with a greater sense of surety and constancy. This argument was pleasing to the landed interest, who believed that their pedigree and socialization made them uniquely suited and equipped for political authority. Because, according to Boyer, such men had England's long-term interest in mind, they would not succumb to the same temptations as the profit-thirsty moneyed classes, which meant that the financial system would be placed on a firmer footing.

Boyer moreover refuted Hoadly's claim that the elimination of Godolphin had caused credit to collapse. He developed an argument to show that public credit never depends on one person alone and that the dismissal of Godolphin in favor of Harley could not have been the cause of credit's collapse.[88] Does the public's confidence, he asked, reside in the state administration, or with the specific individuals in charge of managing the fiscal apparatus? On the most basic level, he argued, opinion about the state's capacity to service its debt should be dictated by the wealth of the nation and Parliament's ability and willingness to channel this wealth towards the public debt. This suggested to Boyer that public credit depends firstly on Parliament, as this body was responsible for the requisitioning of funds to service the debt, and secondarily on the queen, as she was responsible for selecting "Able, Honest, and Faithful Officers in the Government of the Treasury and Exchequer."[89] No particular public official was therefore responsible for public credit, which meant that credit ought not to sink as a result of a ministerial change.

Boyer was trying to come to grips with the depersonalization of public credit created by the disembodiment of the state and the increased transferability of government bonds. He challenged the Whig position, earlier articulated by Hoadly, that since public credit is "like *Private Reputation*," and since Godolphin had already established himself as having an impeccable integrity, he should be allowed to continue serving as Lord Treasurer.[90] Instead of recognizing that the monarch no longer was the main symbol and guarantor of the state's credibility and that public credit consequently had become depersonalized, Hoadly claimed that the Lord Treasurer had replaced the monarch as the personal guarantor of the state's credit. Boyer, on the other hand, argued that the traditional notion of public credit as lodged in the monarch's— or any other public person's—reputation no longer captured the realities of public credit. The state administrators' honor, probity, and respectability were still of utmost importance to the formation of trust, but it did not matter who specifically served in these positions of power. For the public to be able to trust, public credit had to be managed by men of virtue. Virtue was thus not removed from the concept of credit, but it was powerfully depersonalized.

Even though Boyer showed that public credit does not rely on any particular person, the fact that the price of government securities had indeed fallen in the immediate aftermath of Godolphin's dismissal required Boyer to provide an alternative explanation. He argued that part of the reason was that Godolphin had run up such a staggering debt, making people doubt whether it could be adequately serviced. He also suggested that the Exchequer had mismanaged the collection of taxes, that England's foreign trade was overburdened by excessive duties, and that a negligent colonial administration had squandered lucrative trading opportunities. However, the primary reason for the fall in public credit was the precariousness and fickleness inherent in public opinion. He remarked that even though the fiscal apparatus was impeccably organized and the new Treasury officers were indeed honest, able, and punctual, what mattered most was "the *Opinion* or *Confidence*, we have that they are really Honest, Able, and Punctual."[91] This led Boyer to conclude that "the *Excellency of Credit* rests on a slippery Bottom, I mean, OPINION; which being Nice, Tender, and easily Affected and Byass'd, so *Credit* either rises or falls with it."[92] Boyer here echoes Charles Davenant's famous reflection on the irrationality of public opinion and the threat to political stability that it constituted. Boyer, however, believed that this was just a momentary instability and that once Harley and his administration were given a chance to prove themselves, public opinion would turn in their favor and credit would soon rise again. That is, as long as people focused on the soundness of the security of financial assets and the integrity of the managers, public opinion did not have to be destabilizing.

The writer who would end up playing the most active and arguably most effective role in Harley's propaganda machinery was Daniel Defoe.[93] Defoe had previously written for Harley when he was a member of the Godolphin ministry, but when Harley was dismissed from the ministry in 1708, Defoe stayed on and continued working for him until the fall of the Whig Junto was imminent. On July 17, 1710, Defoe wrote to Harley asking him to renew his patronage. He proclaimed that "It would be a Double honour to Me to have my Gratitude Mixt with the Service of My Country."[94] Harley was naturally delighted to add such a prolific pen to his cause. After a couple of months of guarded or tepid support, Defoe's triweekly *Review of the State of the British Nation* took on an increasingly Harleyian bias, and after another few months Defoe began producing pamphlets in explicit support of Harley's ideas and policies.

In August of 1710, the same month in which Queen Anne replaced Godolphin with Harley, Defoe published *An Essay upon Publick Credit*, one of the period's most intriguing reflections on credit.[95] While the central aim of this essay was to show, similar to Boyer, that public credit was never lodged in one person alone, the most fascinating feature of this pamphlet was Defoe's recognition of the difficulties of grasping the essence of credit.[96] He announced at the outset:

> I am to speak of what all People are busie about, but not one in Forty understands: Every Man has a Concern in it, few know what it is, nor

is it easy to define or describe it. If a Man goes about to explain it by
Words, he rather struggles to lose himself *in the Wood*, than bring others out of it. It is best describ'd by it self; 'tis like the Wind that blows
where it lists, we hear the *sound* thereof, but hardly know *whence it
come*, or *whither it goes*.[97]

For Defoe, credit was a deeply mysterious phenomenon, the ontology of
which could not be determined analytically. While credit is clearly recognizable when it makes its appearance, it is near impossible to completely
articulate exactly where it comes from and how it can exist. Defoe continued in the same spirit, "*Like the Soul* in the Body, it acts all Substance,
yet is it self Immaterial; it gives Motion, yet it self cannot be said to Exist;
it creates *Forms*, yet has it self *no Form*; it is neither Quantity or Quality;
it has no *Whereness,* or *Whenness, Scite,* or *Habit*."[98] Defoe offered a similarly ambivalent reflection on credit in his *Review.* He wrote:

> Credit, seems to have a distinct Essence (*if nothing can be said to exist*)
> from all the Phaenomena in Nature: it is in it self the lightest and most
> volatile Body in the World, moveable beyond the Swiftness of Lightning;
> the greatest Alchymist could never fix its Mercury, or find out its Quality;
> it is neither a Soul or a Body; it is neither visible or invisible; . . . A perfect
> free Agent acting by Wheels and Springs absolutely undiscover'd.[99]

Given these qualities, Defoe resorted to a more pragmatic understanding based on the ways that credit had functioned in practice.

Defoe explored the roots of the English credit system, tracing it back
to the scarcity of money that resulted from the rapid expansion of world
commerce in the sixteenth century. Because the world supply of gold
and silver was relatively fixed, when trade steadily increased there came
a point when all desired transactions could no longer be undertaken.
To address this problem, merchants allowed buyers to take possession
of goods in return for a promise of repayment in the future. Despite the
obvious risks involved, merchants were willing to extend this favor as
long as they could be convinced of the buyer's "Integrity and Ability for
Payment."[100] According to Defoe, this was the first appearance of credit
and it possessed all its mysterious qualities right from the start. He writes:

> CREDIT is a Consequence, not a Cause; the Effect of a Substance, not a
> Substance; 'tis the *Sun-shine*, not the Sun; the quickning SOMETHING,

Call it what you will, that gives Life to *Trade*, gives Being to the Branches, and Moisture to the Root; 'tis the *Oil* of the Wheel, the *Marrow* in the Bones, the *Blood* in the Veins, and the *Spirits* in the Heart of all the Negoce, Trade, Cash, and Commerce in the World.[101]

Here he combined discourses of metaphysics, natural philosophy, mechanics, and medicine, and even invited readers to provide their own metaphors for this "quickning SOMETHING, *Call it what you will*." While this confusing mix of metaphors highlighted the essential, but mysterious, role of credit in society, he did not pretend to contribute towards a more precise definition.[102] Defoe's primary aim here was to establish that even though the phenomenon of credit escapes human intelligibility, it was nevertheless absolutely essential to modern society and should therefore be protected at all cost.

Having established that credit is capable of generating great benefits to a modern commercial society, Defoe proceeded to investigate the conditions under which credit thrives. The most essential feature required for credit to flourish was "universal Probity."[103] For Defoe, credit grows steadily as long as people commit themselves to "fair and upright Dealing, punctual Compliance, honourable Performance of Contracts and Covenants."[104] All the ingenuity in the world cannot conjure up credit in the absence of such probity, and all the money in the world will not raise credit in the absence of honesty and punctuality. Moreover, where there is probity and justice, all other barriers to establishing trust and credit are superseded. He exemplified this by asking, "How do we Trade among the *Turks,* and Trust the *Mahometans,* one of whose Doctrines, in the *Alchoran,* is, not to keep Faith with Christians?"[105] Defoe answered that "They have obtain'd it by a just, punctual, and honourable Practice *in Trade,* and you *Credit them without Scruple*; nay, rather than a Christian."[106] In singling out probity as the universal and exclusive criterion for trust and credit, Defoe reiterated the point that public credit was not tied to any specific minister, but could be raised by any able and prudent person. After all, he insisted, if an Englishman can trust a prudent Muslim, it should not be that difficult for him to trust one of his own, so long as he exhibited proper virtues and character. Hence, similar to Boyer, Defoe believed that if people of honor, probity, and character were put in charge of the Treasury and Exchequer, the precariousness of public opinion would be reduced and so would the instability of credit. For Defoe, Godolphin provided an excellent example of the kind of person it would take to stabilize public credit.

Defoe also commented on what he saw as an absurd Whig threat: that the investing public would refuse to purchase government bonds because of loyalty to the former ministry. To predict this outcome was, to Defoe, the same as saying that "Nature will cease [and] Men of Money will abstain from being Men loving to get Money."[107] Defoe shared this sentiment with Clement, who argued that the investing public, regardless of political conviction, would always purchase government bonds as long as they were backed by good security and offered an adequate rate of return. For him, the marketplace was largely impervious to political ideology.

It is possible to reconcile Defoe's and Clement's views that people did not trade against their economic interests with the claim made by sociologist Bruce Carruthers that both Whigs and Tories were observed trading in ways that supported their respective party's political agenda.[108] Since each party's propaganda machinery encouraged investors to internalize a certain set of ideas about the present political situation and particular expectations about the future, the investors' outlook and expectations would be such that their individual economic interest would coincide with the party's overarching aim. Successful propaganda for the Whigs, for example, therefore meant that investors were convinced that it was in their financial interest to sell bonds after the dismissal of Godolphin and thus further sink public credit, while the opposite was the case for the Tories. As such, many investors entered Exchange Alley to transact stocks and bonds primarily to augment their own wealth, while inadvertently ending up contributing to the political interest of the party they supported. This, of course, does not rule out that there were some who intentionally compromised their economic interest to promote political ends in the market for stocks and bonds.

Defoe tried hard to convince his audience that party strife or religious disagreement would not keep investors from buying bonds issued by the government, as long as Parliament secured its loans with a stable revenue flow and prudence and probity informed the management of the public debt. What did matter, however, was that it was clearly conveyed to the public that the state's fiscal administration was indeed managed properly. For this purpose, it was important that the recording of the conditions of the public debt was accurate and transparent.[109] As Simon Schaffer has shown, since Defoe believed that "Social life should be reported the way nature was," he advocated marshalling modern empirical methods in the world of finance so that it would appear intelligible and predictable to investors.[110] If merchants and government officials kept meticulous accounts of their finances and allowed them to be witnessed firsthand by the public, the credibility and trustworthiness of credit instruments could increase and there would be less room for public opinion and imagination to run amok. The focus on firsthand observation as the key to the formation of sound opinion, articulated by Locke and others, continued to constitute one of the cornerstones of credit. The Tories thus tried to ground public opinion in the same principles as private opinion. People should ignore secondhand accounts and propaganda, and instead personally gather as much information as possible on which they would base their own views. Only then would credit rest on a solid foundation. Clearly, Harley's writers were trying to convince the public to dismiss the fact that the government bonds were trading at a discount, attributing this to the confused assessment of public opinion, rather than any underlying weakness in the government or its ministers.

Defoe's treatment of credit was far from universally admired. In the Whig periodical *The Medley*, Arthur Maynwaring put forth a biting critique of Defoe's ideas, the vehemence of which may have been enhanced by Defoe's recent betrayal of the Whigs.[111] Maynwaring ridiculed Defoe's pronouncements that he would clear up the conceptual issues surrounding credit and suggested that he instead led his readers into a maze of obfuscations. He sardonically stated, "what a Scholar he is, where he speaks of something that is *neither Quantity or Quality, has no Whereness or, Whenness, Scite or Habit.* There's Philosophy for you, Sir."[112] He then provided a point-by-point satirical commentary on Defoe's essay, concluding that Defoe failed so miserably in his arguments that he actually ended up undermining his support of Harley. Maynwaring criticized Defoe's exaggerated claim that all of the responsibility for public credit rests exclusively on Parliament and the queen, thus removing all the blame from the ministers themselves and making it largely irrelevant who served in this capacity. This constituted, in Maynwaring's mind, a strikingly lukewarm endorsement of Harley.

A month later, Maynwaring continued his attack on the Tory claim that credit depends on no particular person, using many of the same arguments previously employed by Hoadly. The absurdity of this proposition had become manifest during the autumn, he claimed, when the Exchequer Bills dropped below par as an immediate consequence of the ministerial change. These securities had previously been impeccably managed by people of solid reputation, but now that these managers were removed, the resulting anxiety led the public to shift their wealth elsewhere. Maynwaring concluded, "Interest being the most impatient, as well as the most timorous thing in nature," uncertainty, regardless of cause, will always make money change location.[113] Maynwaring also addressed Clement's critique of "imaginary value," suggesting that it was ridiculous to claim that something was worth less than its price. He dismissed this notion as a complete misunderstanding of the very nature of credit, which enables expectations and the imagination to generate values greater than that which is immediately present.

Unfazed by Maynwaring's criticism, Defoe continued to defend the Tory position, now with even more elaborate imagery. In a series of articles in the *Review* during the autumn of 1710, Defoe famously revived the figure of Lady Credit, which he had introduced a few years earlier.[114] He described Lady Credit as the younger sister of money, who has the capacity to take money's place in trade, as long as "her Sister constantly and punctually relieves her."[115] Using a set of gendered stereotypes, he portrayed Lady Credit as temperamental, coy, fickle, overemotional, prone to hysteria, but also beautiful, charming, and capable of great wonders.

Part of Lady Credit's volatility and irrationality stemmed from her faulty empirical assessment of the world. Instead of observing and recording events and phenomena in a rational manner, she filtered her impressions through her imagination. As Pocock observes, "not only were the data on which opinion was formed at least partly imaginary, but even those well founded in concrete reality figured to the imagination . . . as features of a mobile . . . universe in which every object was potentially a source of either profits or loss, a subject of both hope and fear."[116] Whether she would interpret something as a sign of hope or a cause for fear was impossible to gauge for the outside world, leading to a great deal of uncertainty and indeterminacy. It was thus impossible to predict and control her mood swings. If she had once been badly treated by a suitor, she would always take a long time to return. Or, as Defoe put it, recovering lost credit "is almost as Difficult as to restore Virginity, or to make a W___re an Honest Woman."[117] Not even kings or Parliaments could force or bribe her to make an appearance. The best way to ensure that she came around was to pretend that she was not wanted. However, once she arrived she had to be constantly attended to with flattery and praise.

Despite her tendency towards inconstancy and fickleness, when Lady Credit flourished she was capable of bringing great fortunes, which she happily spread throughout society.[118] In an article published on August 8, 1710, the day of Godolphin's dismissal, Defoe recalled how Lady Credit had been exuberantly happy during the last decade under the guidance of Godolphin. He described how she "was always Smiling and Pleased, Gay and in Humour—Her walk was daily between the Bank and the Exchequer, and between the Exchange and the Treasury; she went always Unveil'd, dress'd like a Bride; innumerable were her Attendants, and a general Joy shew'd itself upon the Faces of all People, when they saw her."[119] But now, with the intensification of Whig–Tory hostility, her temper had worsened and it was generally feared that she would experience one of her dreaded epileptic seizures.[120] Unfortunately, her fate was far worse than just the falling sickness.

Here Defoe departed slightly from the established Tory position. Contrary to Clement's and Boyer's, as well as his own efforts to remove the focus from Godolphin's personal role in the flourishing of public credit, he acknowledged the Whig claim that public credit had benefited greatly from Godolphin's reputation and skill. In the very next issue of the *Review*, Defoe explained how with the dismissal of Godolphin, Lady Credit lost her "best Friend, that ever she had in this Nation; a Friend that had restor'd her Languishing Condition many a time, when she was at Deaths Door."[121] Defoe further described how she "is deeply sensible of the Loss, she is almost inconsolable for the Disaster, and how it will go with her."[122] Everywhere people mourned the impeding death of Lady Credit. In his imaginary account, Defoe visited the Bank of England, Exchange Alley, and the Exchequer and found the same desperately somber mood. The only people to express a certain joy at the news of the Lady parting from her best friend were the Tories, who had been responsible for engineering the ministerial shift. But even they felt a mounting uneasiness about what they had done and started to worry about the consequences of their actions. Defoe offered the Tories little solace, telling them: "*if she did die*, they had Murther'd her."[123]

Defoe added to the insult by claiming that the Tories had no one in their camp who could save her. This statement took on an added significance in light of the queen's announcement on that very same day—August 10, 1710—that Harley would become the new Chancellor of the Exchequer. Defoe's lack of public support of Harley is puzzling. If indeed Defoe was already on Harley's payroll, it is surprising that Defoe was so critical of the Tory position and Harley himself. In particular since Defoe wrote in a letter to Harley, "It is with a Satisfaction . . . I can Not Express, That I See you Thus Establish'd Again . . . Providence Sir Seems to Cast me back Upon you (I write that with Joy)."[124] It is conceivable that Harley wanted to keep his patronage of Defoe still secret or perhaps Defoe did not want to appear unrealistically partisan and thus jeopardize his reputation. Two weeks later, however, Defoe started to sound more approving of recent changes. While he still paid tribute to Godolphin—"I could be content to spend a whole Page in his Praise"— his message and tone were now more supportive of Harley.[125] Nevertheless, Defoe's defense of Harley remained lukewarm throughout 1710. This, however, would change the following year when Defoe became the most vociferous champion of Harley's proposed financial panacea.

In closing, public credit constituted one of the primary battle grounds between Whigs and Tories. Yet, there were nevertheless a number of principles that both sides shared. As Pocock points out, "An anatomy of the great debate as between 'landed' and 'monied' interest, conducted by the journalists and publicists of Anne's reign, reveals that there were no pure dogmas or simple antitheses, and few assumptions that were not shared, and employed to differing purposes, by the writers on either side."[126] The landed elites were still anxious about the weakening of the traditional political and moral order in which power and authority originated from property in land. For them, organizing society around land ensured that nature's scarcity reigned in the potential excesses of commerce and finance and that the moral virtues exhibited by the landed men increased the likelihood of a stable polity. Yet, they increasingly acknowledged that trade and mobile property had the capacity to contribute substantially and favorably to the political and economic order, as well as provide a solid security for public credit. In particular, after the failure of the land bank venture in 1695, their notion of credit increasingly came to approximate that of the moneyed interest. Both groupings agreed that public credit was based most fundamentally on reputation for prudence and probity, solid revenue flows earmarked for the service of loans, transparent reporting, and favorable expectations of the future. While the Tory landed interest had earlier favored existing assets like land and merchandise as securities backing financial assets, the Tories were now more open to backing credit with expectations of future profits, even though public opinion would then play a more prominent role. While the Tories approached the Whig position on the issue of what kind of asset is most appropriate as security, the Whigs would soon become increasingly uncomfortable with public opinion. Both sides thus agreed that the influence of an unpredictable public had turned public credit into a dangerous source of instability. The fact that an amorphous and not-quite-real public opinion made credit into a fickle, precarious, and, most importantly, uncontrollable force was perceived as a major threat to the prosperity and security of England.

The Evolution of Harley's Panacea

While the debate about credit raged on, Harley struggled to ensure that Hoadly, Maynwaring, and the rest of his detractors' writings did not go unanswered. He was able to keep credit afloat, if only through temporary measures, by appealing to the Bank of England for short-term loans. Harley knew that these loans served as mere palliatives and that he would soon have to pursue more radical solutions. In October of 1710, he began exchanging ideas with two members of the controversial Sword Blade Bank—John Blunt (d. 1733) and Sir George Caswall (d. 1742)—about an ambitious scheme that would engraft the entire unsecured national debt into the capital stock of a new joint-stock trading company. The shares of this company would be exchanged for the outstanding government bonds, on account of the prospective dividend and capital gains generated by the company's trade. Blunt argued in a letter to Harley that this conversion would eliminate the burden of the national debt and, in so doing, wipe off "entirely that unjust reproach which ill men so industriously spread of the danger of the public funds and credit, but also must encourage all persons to lend their money the more freely."[127] This was a brilliantly clever proposal, according to Caswall, who wrote to Harley that it would "promote the retrieving publick credit and give great honour to those in the Administration who shall appear zealous for its execution."[128] It was not the first time that such a financial technique had been used. In 1697, the Bank of England engrafted some £800,000 of depreciated short-term government bonds. These bonds were incorporated into the capital stock of the Bank by offering its holders stocks in the Bank in return. The Bank carried out another such engraftment in 1709, when it expanded its capital stock and exchanged shares for £1,775,028 of discounted Exchequer Bills.[129] The Sword Blade Bank also engaged in a similar scheme in 1702, when it took in £200,000 of discounted army debentures in exchange for shares in the company.[130]

With the help of Blunt and Caswall, Harley now had the basic outline of what he hoped would become a swift and convenient solution to the nation's most pressing challenge. During the course of the autumn of 1710, he convinced the queen of the necessity of restoring public credit and the importance of relieving the unfunded portion of the debt. In November, during her first address to the newly elected Tory-dominated Parliament, the queen highlighted this problem and impelled the members to act quickly to find a feasible solution.[131] She proclaimed "that the Navy, and other offices, are burdened with heavy debts, which so far affect the public service that I must earnestly desire you to find some way to answer these demands and to prevent the like for time to come."[132] Finding a solution to the ailing public credit had now been elevated to the highest national priority. Harley had to figure out where the new company would obtain the revenues that would service the reconstruction of the unfunded debt. He still had some thinking to do before he could announce his panacea.

After months of teetering on the brink of disaster, the ailing trust and confidence in financial markets finally took a turn for the better in December of 1710. Ironically, it was the announcement of Spain's victory over England at Brihuega that provided the long-sought medicament. This military defeat calmed financial markets because it put an end, at least for the moment, to the Whig strategy of "No Peace without Spain" and thus eliminated a serious cause of friction between the directors of the Bank of England and Harley. After the defeat, a more convivial relationship emerged, facilitating the stabilization of the Exchequer Bills and the renewal of the Bank's discounting of foreign bills of exchange. A further sign of credit's recovery came in

March of 1711, when a Bank-organized lottery loan was oversubscribed on the first day. The lottery loan's offer of a two and a half percentage point higher interest rate than recently issued government bonds was apparently enough to sway the public. The proceeds of £1.5 million were used to alleviate the most pressing claims on the military departments, ensuring that the armed forces were able to properly prepare for the summer campaigns. Considering the desperate condition of public credit that had prevailed just a couple of months earlier, the success of the lottery loan was a significant display of vigor and perhaps a sign that public opinion had shifted in Harley's favor.

Everyone was not convinced that the recovery of credit was real. Defoe remained only cautiously optimistic and once again employed the allegory of Lady Credit to voice his concerns. Writing in the *Review* in February of 1711, he describes how in a recent dream he came across "POOR CREDIT! sunk and dejected, sighing and walking alone; I met her t'other Day in the Fields, I hardly knew her, she was so lean, so pale; look'd so sickly, so faint, and was so meanly dress'd."[133] She had told him that she was contemplating leaving England to go to France where she was hoping to encounter a more conducive atmosphere. She was resentful of the treatment she had received in England, in particular considering all the great gifts she had bestowed on this nation and its people. She complained that "now my Face is Threatened to be wash'd with a Spunge; for which of all my Bounties have I deserv'd these Things?"[134] What frightened her most was that financial property rights may no longer be safe in England. Echoing Hoadly's earlier argument, Defoe suggested that a default on the national debt would constitute a massive violation of private property, which would undoubtedly lead to a complete societal breakdown. Defoe tried as best as he could to assure Lady Credit that the present Parliament, ministry, and queen understood the situation well and that all forms of property would be secure as long as the Pretender was not invited back to impose a rule of absolutist tyranny.

The attempt to convince the public that a return of the Pretender would put public credit at great risk soon became a bipartisan concern. Defoe was joined by the leading Whig periodical, *The Spectator*, in trying to ensure that a newly elected Tory majority would not listen to the party's Jacobite elements and hatch a plan for the restoration of the Pretender to the throne. On March 3, 1711, Joseph Addison (1672–1719) offered an account of a recent dream, in which he had encountered Lady Credit at the Bank of England.[135] She was pictured as a "beautiful Virgin, seated on a Throne of Gold," with the halls around her "covered with such Acts of Parliament as had been made for the Establishment of Publick Funds."[136] She frequently looked at these acts to reassure herself that her health and safety were protected. However, as soon as the news of even the least threatening event reached her, she turned nervous and fidgety. Attributing a similar set of gender stereotypes to Lady Credit as Defoe had done previously, Addison described her as emotionally unstable and easily prone to hysteria. At a moment's notice, "she would fall away from the most florid Complexion, and the most healthful State of Body, and wither into a Skeleton."[137] Addison recalled the dramatic event when the doors of the great hall flew open and in walked a threatening group of ghosts, the most hideous and frightening being the Pretender. To the great despair of Lady Credit, he had "a Sword in his right Hand, which . . . he often brandished at the Act of Settlement; and a Citizen, who stood by me, whisper'd in my Ear, that he saw a Spunge in his left Hand."[138] This ghostly display was too much for the Lady's delicate disposition, causing her to faint promptly.

Jonathan Swift, writing under Harley's patronage, dismissed any concerns about a second Stuart Restoration and instead proclaimed that Lady Credit was in remarkably good condition.[139] While the market in private stocks might be in a sickly state, he argued in *The Examiner* that public credit was perfectly fine: "By the narrowness of their Thoughts, one would imagine they conceiv'd the World to be no wider than Exchange Alley. 'Tis probable they may have such a sickly Dame among them, and 'tis well if she has no worse Diseases, considering what Hands she passes through. But the *National Credit* is of another Complexion; of sound Health, and an even Temper, her life and Existence being a Quintessence drawn from the Vitals of the whole Kingdom."[140] Swift argued that the success of the lottery loan had restored public confidence in credit and that even the most vociferous opponents had started to change their opinion. He observed that "we find these *Mony-Politicians*, after all their Noise, to be of the same Opinion, by the Court they paid Her, when she lately appear'd to them in the form of a *Lottery*."[141]

In addition to credit's portrayal as a lady, opinion was ascribed a similar set of gendered traits. Sir Richard Steele (d. 1729), Addison's journalistic collaborator, offered a vivid Hogarthian dream account of an encounter between the two primary influences on the minds of the multitude: masculine *Errour* and feminine *Popular Opinion*.[142] Sharing explicit character and personality traits with Lady Credit (and her Renaissance precursor *Fortuna*), *Popular Opinion* was described as attractive and charismatic, yet deceptive and unpredictable. Steele tells of a green flowery hill where *Errour* and *Public Opinion* resided. The most self-assertive and delusional people walking up the hill went straight to *Errour*, or mistaken belief, while "others of a softer Nature" went first to *Popular Opinion*, from which she delivered them to *Errour*.[143] Steele recalled how *Popular Opinion* was talking to a group of people who were mesmerized by her charisma and sweet talk. He recalled, "Her Voice was Pleasing; she breathed odours as she spoke: she seemed to have a tongue for every one."[144] With a powerful sway over her audience, she shaped their perceptions of the world, highlighting "the beauties of nature to the eyes of her adorers."[145] *Popular Opinion* offered instructions on how to interpret what they saw and, as such, how to form a sound understanding of the world. According to Steele, this invested *Popular Opinion* with a dangerous capacity to mislead and deceive the public.

Steele continued his walk and soon encountered *Errour*, who was dressed in a white robe to resemble *Truth*. He possessed a magical wand that he used to entertain his onlookers with various delusions. The crowd around him was impressed by his accomplishments and seemed convinced by what he told them. After the encounters with *Popular Opinion* and *Errour*, Steele and his company were prepared to enter the *Palace of Vanity*, which was floating on a set of curling clouds above them. The walkway ascending to the palace was painted as a rainbow, the walls were "gilded all for show," and the "top of the building being rounded bore so far the Resemblance of a Bubble."[146] When entering this *Paradise of Fools*—a thinly veiled representation of the political culture established by Harley—Steele encountered a series of phantoms, including *Decreasing Honor*, *Ostentation*, and *Gallantry*, before reaching *Vanity* herself, decked in peacock feathers and seated on a throne with a glittering canopy. Positioned next to her was *Self-Conceit* and below the throne, its corollaries *Flattery*, *Affectation*, and *Fashion*. As Steele was processing his impressions of this hideous display, he heard an old man's voice "bemoaning the Condition of Mankind, which is thus managed by the breath of Opinion, deluded by Errour, fired by Self-Conceit, and given up to be trained in all the courses of Vanity, 'till Scorn or Poverty come upon us."[147] This frank criticism of England's political authority quickly drew the attention of the guards, who violently brought the man into custody. But, it was already too late. The comments had already unleashed a powerful force that brought the *Palace of Vanity* to an apocalyptic end. As numerous harpies, including *Broken Credit, Poverty, Infamy*, and *Shame*, entered the building, *Vanity* and her entourage were forced to flee. Once they disappeared from sight, the palace slowly descended towards the ground and eventually made contact with earth. Steele was not sure that everyone in the palace was aware of this return to basic grounded principles, but he woke up from his dream before he could find out.

Steele depicted *Popular Opinion* as a dangerous and deceptive force that twisted the minds of the multitude and facilitated the Tory ministry's bubbling and corruption of the nation. He illustrated the dynamic of what happens when political propaganda writers successfully infiltrate public opinion. Once the propaganda was absorbed by public opinion, more and more people were swayed, even without informing themselves about the underlying merits of the claims. As such, public opinion became a force for delusion, irrational speculation, and corruption. Referring to Harley's successful propaganda machinery, Steele claimed that public opinion had of late been systematically manipulated to undermine reason and honesty in politics, as well as to raise the credit of a fundamentally corrupt ministry. Hence, while Hoadly had defended public opinion when it was in favor of the Whigs, now that it had turned in favor of the Tories, Whig supporters such as Addison and Steele harshly criticized it. The only solution, in Steele's mind, was to silence the charismatic rhetoric of *Popular Opinion* and reintroduce the quintessentially English virtue of honest *Plain-dealing*. This was the only way that the power of *Popular Opinion*, delusion of *Errour*, and the corruption in the *Palace of Vanity* could be banished.

Through their allegorizations of *Lady Credit* and *Popular Opinion*, Defoe, Addison, and Steele highlighted the imaginary and insubstantial character of credit and opinion. They portrayed credit and opinion as fictitious phenomena, but with real political and economic power. Since credit, opinion, and fiction operated on the same epistemic plane somewhere between reality and the imaginary, these writers found fictional portrayals of social, political, and economic forces particularly useful in their attempts to shape credit. It was not a coincidence that Defoe and Swift, two of the period's greatest fiction writers, were employed as propagandists to mold public opinion.[148]

Conclusion

England's governing elites recognized the importance of finding a solution to the ongoing crisis of public credit. Some commentators blamed the Godolphin ministry for having abused the nascent system of public credit, while others claimed that it was Harley's inexperience and lack of reputation that had caused the "Loss of the City." Harley's supporters tried to defuse the intense criticism from the Whigs by shifting the blame for the instability of public credit to the inherent precariousness of public opinion. Lacking in reasoned judgment and careful empiricism, public opinion was dangerously fickle and mutable, posing a serious threat to the prosperity and safety of both the state and the nation.[149] Harley's advocates, however, argued that as long as the fiscal apparatus was under the sound stewardship of virtuous, prudent, and principled men, that bookkeeping was impeccable and transparent, and financial securities were adequately backed, public opinion would eventually form a positive judgment of credit and thus enable its many benefits.

While the recently improved conditions of credit served as a sign of the public's growing acceptance of Harley, the ever-present specter of the Pretender led both Defoe and Addison to hoist a warning flag. To Harley, the focus on the Pretender was a most welcome, or perhaps even scripted, distraction. Since neither Defoe's *Review* nor Addison's and Steele's *Spectator* focused on Harley as a burden on public credit, Harley had now gained some valuable room to maneuver. This breathing room, combined with the success of the lottery loan, suggested to Harley that the time was now ripe for him to go public with his financial panacea. The formal announcement was delayed, however, by an unfortunate incident in which Harley was stabbed by Marquis de Guiscard, a French adventurer and spy. The wounds inflicted by the assailant's penknife would ordinarily not have been life-threatening, but because Harley's underlying health was poor, he experienced some serious complications. During his recovery, his supporters took advantage of the favorable public sentiment and published a series of uncontested propaganda pamphlets.[150] Defoe, for example, provided his thus far strongest endorsement of Harley in *A Spectators Address to the Whigs, on the Occasion of the Stabbing Mr. Harley* (1711). He claimed that recent developments had revealed clearly to all that Harley had not only saved the nation from the Whig Junto's mismanagement, but that he alone had the capacity to mediate successfully between extremes in party politics and church affairs. To Defoe, Harley also deserved praise for his vigorous prosecution of the war against the *Great Enemy*, as well as for how "His *Management* restores Credit, confirms past Funds, raises New, banishes the Peoples Jealousies about the Spunge; raises *Money* in spight of Pretences of being Exhausted."[151] Given these accomplishments, only Jacobites, papists, and supporters of French tyranny could oppose Harley. This propaganda campaign was extraordinarily successful, paving the way for Harley to return to the political scene stronger than ever. The timing was now perfect for his grand announcement. On May 2, he presented to the House of Commons his plan for the resolution of the nation's public credit crisis: the South Sea Company.

— 6 —

The South Sea Company and the
Restoration of Public Credit

Introduction

Robert Harley launched the South Sea Company in 1711, hoping it would provide a comprehensive solution to the financial crisis. Whereas he had managed to keep public credit afloat by means of a series of financial palliatives, Harley's new scheme was an ambitious attempt designed to restore stability to the nascent financial structure. The South Sea Company undertook a debt-for-equity and private-for-public swap, exchanging company stocks for a set of deeply discounted unsecured government bonds in hopes of reviving public credit and once again making it affordable for the Treasury to borrow. In order to make this transaction appealing to the bondholders, the government committed to paying 6 percent interest on the debt absorbed by the company and, most importantly, granted the company a monopoly on Britain's commerce to the South Seas. Harley hoped that the security of the government annuity payment combined with the prospects of inexhaustible profits from the South Sea trade would entice the investing public to participate in the conversion.[1]

Since the South Sea Company was charted to undertake England's trade in African captives to Spanish-controlled South America, Harley's solution to the credit crisis relied on the public favorably imagining the prospects of the Atlantic slave trade. As credit became entangled in one of the most brutal and violent moments of early modern capitalism, the discourse on credit incorporated a new set of concerns. While Chapter 5 explored the complex relationship between public credit and public opinion, this chapter focuses on the party political struggles to shape the formation of the public's social imaginary of the Atlantic slave trade.[2] As Harley established the South Sea Company, his propaganda writers worked tirelessly to ensure that the public visualized the trans-Atlantic slave economy as an inexhaustible fountain of riches. Intent on undermining Harley's attempts to restore public credit, the Whig opposition predictably replied with scathing criticisms of the company's commercial and financial prospects. The debate surrounding the South Sea Company therefore came to focus on the extent to which the investing public believed that the company's slave trade would be profitable enough to generate an adequate rate of return. A number of studies have pointed to the importance of the slave trade to the formation of the Atlantic economic system and the subsequent industrial revolution. This chapter shows how the discourse and configuration of credit during the Financial Revolution was also shaped by the slave trade.[3]

The success of the South Sea Company was based on harnessing the English fascination with the Atlantic world. Instead of just earmarking additional taxes to service the debt, Harley provided the company with a source of revenue that, while not providing any guarantees, carried the promise and prospect of great gains. Not only was this an age of projectors and instant fortunes, with investment, speculation, and gambling gripping the nation, it was also an era when English society was obsessed with the distant and exotic.[4] The South Seas, in particular, had for a long time held a special place in the English imagination, dating all the way back to the Elizabethan privateers' forays into the Spanish empire.[5] Richard Hakluyt had carefully chronicled and glorified the voyages of Sir Francis Drake, Sir John Hawkins, and Thomas Cavendish, during which they ruthlessly scavenged ships and port towns to glean some of the vast fortunes of the region.[6] More recently, travel accounts by William Dampier and Woodes Rogers had further intensified the already strong fascination with this vast and unknown world.[7] The Third Earl of Shaftesbury commented on the popularity of voyage narratives, as well as their importance to contemporary imaginative life, noting that they "are the chief materials to furnish out a library." He continued, "These are in our present days what books of chivalry were in those of our forefathers."[8]

By tying the public debt to the profits from the Atlantic slave trade a closer mental association was forged between the urban milieu of London, the slave forts on the African coast, and the colonial towns of New Spain. This sophisticated time-space compression transferred value from the future to the present, from the sphere of commerce to public finance, and from the Atlantic world to the city of London. The mental processes involved in raising this credit positioned the Atlantic slave trade at the very center of English political and economic life.[9] By exploring the debates surrounding the formation of the South Sea Company, this chapter examines the nature of the association between public credit and the slave trade. I will discuss how Tory and Whig propagandists portrayed the company and its prospects, with particular attention to the striking absence in these debates of any recognition of the slaves' agency or subjectivity. This lack of recognition of either the slaves' mortality or their rebelliousness highlights credit's general capacity to obfuscate its underlying social reality—what I will call *credit fetishism*. The complete disregard for the slaves' humanity is not surprising in itself, but it becomes all the more striking in light of the fact that the Whig opposition did not include it in the extensive list of risk factors they brought to the public's attention in order to undermine support for the company. An image of rebelling or dying African captives would only have contributed to the Whig project of raising doubts about the company's profitability.

This chapter also calls into question the scholarly tradition of viewing the South Sea Company as a fraudulent scheme from its inception. When studied from the point of view of the deceit and manipulations committed during the scandalous bubble years (1719–1720), it is indeed tempting to ascribe an inherent pathology to the company. Historians of the company, such as John Carswell and John Sperling, laid the foundation for this interpretative tradition, which has enabled subsequent scholars to summarily dismiss the company's financial innovations as inherently corrupt and its trading efforts as chimerical.[10] However, when studied within the context of the financial crisis of 1710, the company appears as an ingenious innovation built around what contemporaries considered sound financial principles. Moreover, since the company successfully resolved the ongoing financial crisis, it fulfilled its primary purpose remarkably well. It was only towards the end of 1718, when the company's access to the slave trade was terminated by the outbreak of another war with Spain that the company looked to John Law's financial wizardry in Paris for ideas on how to make its stocks appreciate without an underlying revenue source. Indeed, it was the very loss of the slave trade as a source of

revenues that forced the company to become creative in ways that ultimately would backfire.

The Successful Launch of the Company

The South Sea Company, or *The Company of the Merchants of Great
Britain Trading to the South Seas and other parts of America and for
the Encouraging the Fishery*, was chartered for the purposes of restoring public credit and managing Britain's trading interests in Spanish
America.[11] To rid the market of the most heavily discounted bonds—
which included the short-term, unfunded debentures issued by the
navy, army, ordnance, and transportation departments to finance the
wars against France—Harley invited the holders to exchange their
bonds for shares in the South Sea Company.[12] The company was given
the right to create a capital stock of £9,471,325—the exact sum of the
outstanding debt the company was designed to absorb—and the Treasury committed itself to indefinitely paying 6 percent interest on the
debt capitalized by the company, amounting to £568,279 per year, in
addition to a yearly £8,000 management fee.[13] Excise taxes on wine,
vinegar, and tobacco were earmarked to fund the annual payment.[14]
This scheme provided obvious benefits to the Treasury. By incorporating these unsecured, high-interest, heavily discounted debentures
into the capital stock of the company, the Treasury was able to greatly
reduce its expenses for servicing the national debt. The liabilities were
transformed into a long-term debt that would never have to be paid
off and the effective interest rate paid by the Treasury was reduced. A
vastly simplified administration of the liabilities made the scheme all
the more attractive. If successful, these features would ensure that the
existing burden on the national debt would be lifted and the Treasury
would once again be able to raise funds on favorable terms.

The greatest challenge was generating interest among the investors
to participate in the scheme. On its own, the offer to exchange £100
debentures, trading at a 35 percent discount (and therefore worth £65
at the moment), for company shares with a £100 face value was insufficiently attractive. In order for people to give up their debentures, which
paid an annual interest between 5 and 6 percent, they had to be offered
an additional incentive. It was to this end that Harley promised the
company a commercial monopoly to Spanish America, hoping that it

would spark the investors' imagination of great profits and accompanying dividends and capital gains. The trade monopoly gave the company exclusive rights to engage in commerce from the Orinoco River down to Tierra del Fuego and up along the entire western coastline of the Americas.[15] The jewel of this trading privilege was the Assiento, which conferred the right to carry African slaves to Spanish ports, as well as opportunities to sell British goods, legally and illegally, in this vast colonial market.[16] While the Assiento contract was then in the hands of the French, Harley fully expected that England would be able to acquire it in the ongoing peace negotiations.[17]

Harley's innovative plan was well received from the very beginning. Soon after the announcement of the company in May of 1711, the queen knighted Harley as Earl of Oxford and Mortimer and five days later appointed him as the new Lord Treasurer. The investing public also embraced Harley's plan, immediately showing interest in converting their bonds when the subscription books opened on June 27. Just weeks after the subscription process began, £2 million had already been subscribed and had it not been for a temporary halt to arrange some administrative details, the conversion would have continued apace. One voice noted that the public was so impatiently interested in the scheme "that 'tis not doubted but much the greater Part, if not the whole Sum of the 9471325 *l.* will be subscrib'd."[18] This prediction turned out to be accurate. Within a couple of months, two-thirds of the capital stock had been subscribed and by the end of the year nearly the entire outstanding debt had been converted.[19] Harley's propagandist Daniel Defoe celebrated the accomplishment, writing in September of 1711 that, "the Bringing so great an Undertaking so near Perfection, in so short a Time, may well be reckon'd among the Wonders of Her Majesty's glorious Reign."[20] The steady increase in the company's share price served as a further testament to the scheme's favorable reception by the public. Quoted daily in the papers along with the East India Company and the Bank of England, the South Sea Company stock began trading in September around £65, reflecting the heavy discount on the converted debentures. The stock quickly appreciated during the autumn, reaching £81 by mid-November. An increase of 25 percent in just two months was a stunning success by any standard and indicated that Harley had succeeded in piquing the public's curiosity in the Atlantic slave trade. In launching a venture that would raise nearly eight times as much credit as the Bank of England's initial public offer in 1694 and four times the money lent to the government by the new East India Company in 1698, Harley's South Sea Company contributed substantially to the Financial Revolution by expanding the scale and transforming the configuration of public finance.[21]

Harley's scheme addressed most of the concerns that had surfaced in the debates leading up to the launch of the company—explored in Chapters 3 and 5. Most importantly, public credit had been assigned what appeared to be a solid revenue source as security. The potentially lucrative trading rights, combined with the guaranteed annuity from the Treasury, convinced the investing community that the conversion was a safe and likely rewarding transaction. The company furthermore addressed the issue of whether public credit rested in one person or in the government's fiscal apparatus. The scheme actually removed most of the discretionary power from the Treasury, leaving the state responsible only for raising enough excise taxes to pay the fixed yearly annuity. The management of the commercial revenues securing the scheme was assigned to the South Sea Company's directors, a group of merchants, financiers, manufacturers, and politicians with mostly Tory leanings. By putting Harley in charge of the Treasury and inviting a number of Tories to manage the company, the landed men, who had maintained the greatest skepticism about the stability of credit, could now feel more at ease since men of honor, character, and probity were in charge of public credit. Another reason why the scheme appealed to the landed interest was that taxes on commerce, rather than on land, would be used to pay for the venture.[22] Finally, by alleviating the navy's indebtedness and by giving it further responsibilities in the Atlantic and Pacific worlds, the scheme promoted the Tory oceanic imperial policy.[23]

The scheme also appealed to the Whigs on a number of central issues. First and foremost, by encroaching on the French trade to Spanish America, the company interfered with France's ability to finance its military with New World silver and thus reduced the likelihood that the French would be powerful enough to support a second Stuart Restoration. Harley was also careful to appease the Whig moneyed interest by inserting provisions in the charter of the South Sea Company preventing it from infringing on the financial activities of the Bank of England and the trading spheres of the East India Company.

Additionally, he made it illegal for the directors of the other two companies to serve on the board of directors of the South Sea Company. Despite these attempts, however, Harley's scheme was not favorably received by the Whigs.

Shaping the Imagination of the South Sea Company's Financial and Commercial Prospects

The launch of the South Sea Company engendered much debate, from Parliament, the Royal Exchange, and Exchange Alley to London's pleasure gardens and coffeehouses. Whig and Tory propagandists sought to create, influence, and transform public opinion, in hopes of dictating how the market perceived the company's prospects. While detractors tried to infuse an anxiety about the company's viability, Tory supporters tirelessly pointed to the virtues of the South Sea scheme.

In an anonymous pamphlet, sometimes attributed to Defoe, published on the day following Harley's proposal to Parliament in May of 1711, the author jubilantly stated that "Mr. *Harley's* Proposal, of providing effectually for the payment of the Publick Debts of the Nation, and of Establishing a Trade to the South-Sea of *America*, hath fill'd the Hearts of all good Subjects with Joy."[24] Brimming with optimism, the author continued, "The Provisions made for the Payment of the National Debts cannot but produce a lasting Credit; And an Establishment of a South-Sea Trade, must tend exceedingly to the good of all Degrees and Ranks of Men amongst us: The Poor will be more employ'd in Manufactures, the Product of the Estates of our landed Men will become more valuable, and the Trading part of the Nation will be greatly encourag'd."[25] The increased presence of English ships in Spanish America would prevent the French from expanding their commercial presence in the region and bar them from establishing control over the world's "only inexhaustible Fountain" of gold and silver.[26] The author was concerned that while the Spanish, "from their Slothful Temper, and from their innate Pride, or from an inaptness to Manufactures, have not had the Advantages that they might have had, by the Possession of those Treasures," the French might make better use of this silver and gold, furthering their dangerous quest for universal monarchy.[27] It was therefore "high Time for *Great Britain*, for its Safety and its Interest, to vie with *France* in this Matter, before it be too late."[28] By associating the success of the company with England's national security, the author tried to elevate support of the company into an act of patriotism.

Jonathan Swift joined in the chorus of celebratory pronouncements in his periodical *The Examiner.* He praised Harley for restoring the Exchequer Bills to former prominence and for finding a way to bring the skyrocketing national debt under control.[29] For all his contributions, the public ought to acknowledge Harley as a "great Person, whose Thoughts are perpetually employ'd, and always with Success, on the good of his Country."[30] Swift predicted that "in all probability, if duly executed" the South Sea Company would "be of mighty Advantage to the Kingdom, and an everlasting Honour to the present Parliament."[31] He concluded by envisioning that this scheme would "prove the greatest Restoration and Establishment of the Kingdom's Credit."[32]

The geographer and cartographer Herman Moll's (1654–1732) ambitious tract *A View of the Coasts, Countries, and Islands within the Limits of the South Sea Company* (1711), tried to pique the interest of the investing public in a different way. By synthesizing the available knowledge of the region's climate, geography, natural resources, and native populations, and by producing elaborate maps, he made tangible the commercial advantages awaiting the company. This information would have been of limited use to ship captains operating in the region; the primary aim was more likely to feed the public's imagination of the South Seas.[33] By reading Moll's vivid descriptions, readers were provided with enough information to form an elaborate mental picture of the conditions in this part of the world.[34] As a member of a group of geographers and navigators who frequently met at Jonathan's Coffeehouse, one of the main sites for the transaction of financial instruments, Moll was well acquainted with the intellectual atmosphere of Exchange Alley and therefore must have known what it took to incite the imagination of the investing public.[35]

Moll's book repeatedly emphasized the commercial benefits to England of establishing a trade to Spanish America. First he mentioned the advantage of having English ships carry the nation's manufactures to South America. This trade had previously been organized out of Cadiz, with Spanish merchants enjoying a monopoly on the shipping. But now, with an English trade open to the region, profits as high as 3,000 to 4,000 percent might realistically be expected. Second, Moll explored and listed the extensive array of exotic goods that England would be able to import. Not only would this enable a more sophisticated consumption at home, it would also stimulate England's reexport trade. Third, Moll speculated that England would find even greater treasures of gold and silver than had the Spanish, since the persistently mistreated natives had kept the most spectacular mines hidden from the Spaniards.[36] The most promising feature of the South Sea Company scheme, however, was that England would gain access to the slave trade to South America. Moll suggested that "the greatest Trade, and the most beneficial the *English* ever had with the *Spaniards* on the Continent, was for Negroes."[37] While the volume of this traffic had always been limited by the difficulties associated with smuggling, with the trade laid open to the English, extraordinary profits would soon become a reality. Moll tried to associate the success of the company with the prosperity of the nation, thus hoping that the public would realize the importance of supporting the company.

Moll described a world far from the ordinary experience of most Londoners. The extent to which knowledge travelled across such long distances has been extensively studied by historians of science.[38] It is often assumed that distance hinders and interferes with the transmission of information and knowledge. Yet, according to the historian Mario Biagioli, distance was not always an obstacle: in certain circumstances, distance could be viewed as an advantage in that it enabled certain individuals or groups to claim access to, and to shape, authoritative knowledge. This was particularly the case when information was partial "due to the distance between those who are working at producing knowledge claims and those who may or may not decide to take the risk of investing in such claims."[39] In the case of the South Sea Company, it might have been easier to make people believe in claims of inexhaustible riches in the Atlantic world when the audience had no direct access to the region. By feeding investors a selective story, it was easier to convince them to act on the information at their disposal. As Biagioli notes in reference to other investment schemes, "What we see at play are judgments predicated on distance and guided by the investors' desire, interest, and willingness to invest, that is, the situated and partial perception of the potential benefits they might have obtained from those investments."[40]

Since the South Sea Company relied on the public's favorable assessment of a world very few had experienced or witnessed in person, propaganda writers had to offer partly fictional accounts that allowed people to imagine the conditions and opportunities in the Atlantic world. For this purpose, Defoe and Swift used similar literary styles to those they would later employ in their highly successful fictional writings, such as *Robinson Crusoe* (1719), *Captain Singleton* (1720), and *Gulliver's Travels* (1726). The continuity between their propagandistic pamphlets and their novels has not gone unnoticed by literary critics.[41] Robert Markley, for example, notes that because the world of finance is based on expectations and opinions, imagination was essential in that it enabled the public to visualize and assess the future.[42] Catherine Ingrassia adds that credit "was not a 'real' event; rather it was a phenomenon that could be known primarily through print sources."[43] This means, she argues, that "the workings of the new financial economy existed discursively, to be accessed on the page and recreated imaginatively in the mind of the investor."[44] The decision to invest in a stock or a bond necessitated the participation in "an imaginatively based narrative."[45] Moreover, in facilitating credit, the imagination participated in the even larger project of creating a new economy. As Laura Brown points out, Defoe used imaginary writings to convey the idea that the economy was no longer dictated by the past and "the rules of logic, coherence, or order but by the 'Power of the Imagination' to create a world of its own outside those rules."[46]

Fictional narratives were not the only media used in the efforts to access the public's imaginary. Pamphlets and newspapers were joined by ballads. Popular throughout the early modern period, in particular during social and political upheavals, ballads were performed on all levels of society, entertaining the literate elites and serving the illiterate or quasi-literate with news, information, and political commentary.[47] Historian Adam Fox notes that "the practice of inventing ballads and songs in order to ridicule and shame a rival or adversary was one well-known at all social levels."[48] They were generally performed in open public spaces, like taverns, inns, alehouses, coffeehouses, and fairs. In some instances, the ballads were printed on cheap paper and pinned on the walls of these establishments or distributed in the marketplace, sometimes accompanied by illustrations.

During the years surrounding its launch, the South Sea Company was a frequent protagonist in the ballads; some celebrated its glorious future while many more satirized its allegedly dismal prospects. *An Excellent*

New Song, call'd, An End to our Sorrows (1711) glorified the company by praising Harley for engineering his ingenious plan and for tying the company to such a promising trade. Harley was also applauded for having the presence of mind to offer a high enough interest rate—nine or ten rather than the previous six—on the new lottery loans, enough to reinvigorate credit:[49]

> His Capacity's greater by far, than
> > Any Statesman that e'er went before him;
> Having paid a *vast Debt* to a Farthing
> > *Without Money*, for which we adore him.
>
> He'll *Silver* in *Plenty* bring home,
> > By the *Trade* fix'd in the *South-Sea*;
> Which, if it to *any thing* come,
> > No doubt it will *something be*.
>
> Our *Credit* was once at a stand;
> > But now 'tis *Restor'd* again;
> Since *Nine* or *Ten* does command
> > What with *Six* was endeavour'd in vain.[50]

Another ballad, *Oxford and Mortimer's Vindication* (1711), paid further tribute to Harley's fiscal ingenuity. No longer dependent exclusively on the Bank of England, the ministry had acquired an alternative way to restore public credit and thus ensure a well-funded navy. The ballad promised that:

> Our Trade in the *South-Seas* will bring us in Gain,
> > Most pleasing unto the Nation;
> And what still add Glory to th' auspicious Reign,
> > 'Twill better our Navigation.
>
> Our Sea-men, where-ever they be, do not fear
> > Their Pay, for Pay they don't grumble;
> And when the starv'd Squadrons of *Lewis* appear,
> > To fight the *French* Dogs they don't mumble.[51]

The Whig opposition quickly sought to counter the Tory propaganda apparatus, in order to undermine the favorable social imaginary Harley tried to create. The principal Whig complaints against the financial and commercial prospects of the company were summarized in an anonymous broadsheet.[52] The author queried, "Whether giving a Fund of Interest upon the Debt, and then subjecting the whole to a Hazardous and Unlikely Adventure may be properly called securing Our Debts? Or whether it may not more properly be called a putting us into a regular Course of losing both Principal and Interest?"[53] Continuing to heap suspicion over the prospects of trading to the South Seas, the author asked, "Whether Erecting a Company, and Appointing a Stock to Trade to a Place actually in Possession of Our Enemies, and of which we see no Prospect of Dispossessing them, does not Encorporate the Proprietors into the Spectators Worthy Society of *Castle-Builders?*"[54] To underscore just how absurd and unrealistic the scheme was, he added, "Whether a Voyage to the *South-Sea* (where neither Friends or Enemies will Trade with us either now or hereafter) and a Voyage to the *World in the Moon*, are not founded upon the same *Phænomena* of Probabilities?"[55]

Having challenged the claim that a trade to the South Seas would become a cornucopia, the author questioned the manner by which debt-holders were invited, or compelled, to enter the scheme. He asked, "Whether obliging People to subscribe to this Stock, or else not admitting them to share the Security given others for their Debt, is not as much a Force as a High-way Man demanding Money with a Pistol in his Hand, seeing he does not take it by Force, but only tells you what your Condition may be if you refuse it?"[56] With the highly controversial figure of the highwayman, the author suggested that the South Sea scheme was a thinly veiled forced loan violating the investors' rights and integrity. By preventing the bondholders from enjoying the guaranteed 6 percent interest payment from the Treasury without also participating in the trading venture, the architects of the scheme had infringed on the long-celebrated "Liberties and Properties of *Englishmen.*"[57] Similar to Harley's writers, this author turned the South Sea Company controversy into an issue about patriotism. That is, not only should people be informed that the company was likely to fail miserably, they should also recognize that the formation of the company jeopardized the most sacred of English values and principles.[58]

Satirical and witty ballads lent themselves particularly well to the Whig project of subverting the formation of a favorable imaginary.[59] The prolific Whig writer Arthur Maynwaring, discussed in Chapter 5, penned a series of popular ballads in which he ridiculed the South Sea Company.

In *An Excellent New Song, call'd Credit Restor'd* (1711), he sardonically praised the company for its ingenious scheme. Mockingly, he begins:

> All *Britains* rejoice at this Turn of the State,
>> Which rescu'd from Plunder the Nation;
> From this happy year you for ever may date
>> Of Credit the Restoration.

Like the previous anonymous pamphlet, he criticized the conversion scheme as constituting a forced loan and charged that the company's directors—here represented by Samuel Shepeard, John Blunt, and Arthur Moore—were corrupt to the core.

> Next open to all a *Subscription-Book* stood,
>> In which if some Fools would not enter,
> The Statesmen not only *propos'd* what was Good,
>> But they likewise compel'd them to venture.

> And such fair Accounts the *Subscribers* will see,
>> That surely there can be no losing;
> For Shepherd and *Blunt the Directors* shall be,
>> With *More* of her Majesty's choosing.

After a couple of stanzas in which Maynwaring accused Harley's scheme of ultimately being an attempt to restore the Pretender, he suggests that while the South Sea trade might indeed benefit a small number of people, its trading prospects were not significant enough to warrant its £10 million capital stock. Far from providing a solution to the credit crisis, the scheme would only plunge the nation further into the crisis.

> For the Seamen may gain, in the *South-Sea* Trade,
>> Their Pay, since so rudely they crave it:
> And who can complain that a Debt is unpaid,
>> When the Lubbards *for fetching* may have it.

> Thus our Debts being clear'd from the fruitful *South-Seas*,
>> In Wealth we shall daily grow stronger;
> Tho Stock-Jobbing fails, why dismay'd should we be,
>> Since we want to be trusted no longer?[60]

Maynwaring continued the Whig attack on the company's financial features in *The South-Sea Whim* (1711). Referring to the cuckolded investors as *South-Sea Cullies*, he suggested that sailors, bondholders, and tallies were joined together like slaves and forced to serve a despotic master.

> We are a wretched Motly Crew,
> More various than the Weather,
> Made up of Debtors Old, and New,
> Jumbled and tack'd together;
> Tars, Soldiers, Merchants, Transports, Tallies,
> Chain'd in a row like Slaves in Gallies.

While the investors had initially lent their money to the government for the patriotic purpose of furnishing ships, guns, food, and beer for the nation's navy, they were now rewarded with worthless shares in a precarious trade.

> And we poor Grasiers of the Plain,
> Who serv'd them Pork and Beef,
> Must take hard Words instead of Gain,
> And Charters for Relief;
> For sound good Meat without a Hogo,
> They give us Bills on *Terr' del Feugo.*

Maynwaring concluded the ballad by calling for a mutiny against the company:

> But come, my Lads, together stand,
> Let's suffer this no more:
> Shall we that on the Seas command,
> Be Bully'd thus on shore?
> No, no, my Boys, pull th' Helm a-Lee,
> *And Heave the Rogues into the Sea.*[61]

The Whig opposition thus systematically attacked the company, pointing out the multiple ways in which it jeopardized the safety, prosperity, laws, and values of England. Fearing that the public would listen to these charges, Defoe penned two pamphlets in which he defended both the financial and commercial features of the company. In September of 1711, he began a pamphlet by noting that "either the *South-Sea-Trade* as now projected and offered, is a Disease upon the Nation, or the temper with which, and manner how we receive it is a Disease."[62] This approach suggested that the disease resided in the public's perception of the scheme and that it had now grown so severe as to "prove Mortal to that Life of the Nation our Credit."[63] In order to remove the virus of doubt from public opinion, Defoe responded in detail to the criticism leveled against the company's financial configuration. He focused primarily on the often criticized provision in the charter that gave the directors the right to call in additional money from the shareholders—proportional to their ownership but not to exceed 10 percent—to finance the launch of the company's trade. Defoe acknowledged that no one was allowed to benefit from the 6 percent annual interest payment without also becoming part of the trading enterprise. He admitted that in general it is not appropriate to have a benefit forced upon anyone, but only a malevolent Whig opposition could have "insinuated among the Creditors, that this was some snare, that the Government made some advantage by the Proposal, and that the thing might be of ill Consequence to them."[64] Defoe added, "Sugar-plumbs are never Thrust down Childrens Throats, but put into their Hands, as what there is no fear but they will gladly accept; Pills and bitter Draughts indeed require some Art or Force to compel or oblige them to swallow."[65] Through this campaign, the Whig opposition "gain'd their wicked purpose, alarm'd the People, made them Jealous, Uneasy, and ten times more Clamarous than they were before."[66]

Defoe also responded to the charge that the company's trading privileges were worthless. In *A True Account of the Design, and Advantages of the South-Sea Trade* (1711), he praised the "Project, formed with great Wisdom and Publick Spirit by the Prime Minister, for Incorporating the Proprietors of the said Debts to carry on a *Trade to the South-Seas*: Whereby a further Advantage will, in all Probability, accrue to the said Proprietors, and, through their Means, to the Whole Nation."[67] After highlighting the fact that the company served as an important bulwark against France's quest for universal monarchy, he detailed the "infinite Advantages" that could be expected from this trade.[68] It would encourage England's shipping and manufacturing enough to pay for the present war, and England's colonial system would also benefit. In addition to supporting the commerce of the North American colonies, the slave trade would also receive a boost from a booming South Sea commerce. In particular, Defoe thought that the South Sea trade would provide the ailing Royal African Company with much needed encouragement by affording them "an Opportunity of Vending great Numbers of *Negroes* to the *Spaniards*."[69] Nowhere in this debate was there a mention of the risks associated with the trade in slaves.

The Geopolitics of South Sea Commerce

The propaganda war surrounding the formation of the South Sea Company continued apace throughout 1711, with one side trying to promote the idea of infinite riches in the Atlantic world, while the other side did everything conceivable to subvert this imaginary. Increasingly, the hostile climate that prevailed in South America became the central topic of the debate. Defoe tried to reassure his readers that the French and the Spanish military presence in the region would not provide an insurmountable obstacle. A few French fortified colonies would not be able to withstand an attack by the English navy, which had accomplished far greater victories during the last twenty years of war. And Defoe believed that as long as England settled in areas mostly inhabited by the Spanish, they would most likely welcome the English presence as they would provide "them with what they stand most in need of, for that Purpose, *viz. Negroes*; which we may easily do, with no small Advantage to our selves."[70]

Indeed, the company's trading prospects were viewed increasingly as relying on the establishment of fortified colonies in Spanish America. Attention was therefore directed to the drawn-out peace negotiations. Critics of Harley's ministry claimed that it was pursuing a premature peace, one that would leave France in a position of strength. This betrayed the chief end of the Grand Alliance, namely, to prevent the House of Bourbon from gaining control of Spain and the trade to South America. If France were allowed to gain control over the Spanish trading empire, the implications for England's trade would be disastrous. In *A Letter to a Member of the October-Club* (1711), Francis Hare (1671-1740), a former chaplain-general in Marlborough's army, warned that:

> we, no doubt, shall be so narrowly watch'd hereafter, that it will no longer be in our Power to sell Negroes to the *Spaniards*; *France* will undertake that whole Work herself, and we shall consequently be depriv'd of the only Branch of our *African* Trade, which makes any Returns of Bullion into *England*.[71]

Maynwaring seconded Hare's warnings. He asked whether "any Man seriously believe that the *French* and *Spaniards* will give us lasting Settlements in the *South-Sea*?"[72] In his mind, it was sheer foolishness to believe that the French king would honor his promise to allow fortified English ports and unhindered trade. And, even if England would be able to establish a port from which they could carry out this "imaginary Traffick," it would likely prove no more beneficial than the disastrous Darien venture.[73] Maynwaring further addressed the company's prospects of gaining direct access to gold and silver mines in South America. Even if it were possible, it was not in the nation's best interest as it would "only destroy our Industry, and [make] us such a lazy Generation as the *Spaniards*."[74] Maynwaring thus concluded that the South Sea Company was a mere sham and that it had no prospects of alleviating the nation's credit crisis.[75]

After declaring that there was no reasonable basis to the criticism of Harley's policies and that the Whigs offered no further arguments "but what we find in their Ballads," Swift set out to defend Harley's strategy in the peace negotiations. In his famous *Conduct of the Allies* (1711), Swift argued that England ought to put a prompt end to a war that was mistakenly conceived from the very start.[76] Having had little to gain from entering the continental theater as a principal participant, England instead should have focused on obstructing the flow of American gold and silver to Spain and France. In true Tory fashion, Swift argued that England ought to be a maritime power and that it had no business squandering its resources on expensive continental campaigns. England's pursuit of this errant strategy had allowed France to gain a critical edge in the imperial race. For the last decade, he wrote, "*France* hath been wisely engrossing all the Trade of *Peru*, going directly with their Ships to *Lima*, and other Ports, and there receiving Ingots of Gold and Silver for *French* Goods of little Value; which, beside the mighty Advantage to their Nation at present, may divert Channel of that Trade for the future, so beneficial to us, who used to receive annually such vast Sums at *Cadiz*, for our Goods sent thence to the *Spanish West-Indies*."[77] To blame for this disastrous development were the moneyed interests, "whose perpetual Harvest is War, and whose beneficial way of Traffick must very much decline by a Peace."[78] Swift lamented that "We have been fighting to raise the

Wealth and Grandeur of a particular Family; to enrich Usurers and Stock-jobbers; and to cultivate the pernicious Designs of a Faction, by destroying the Landed-Interest."[79] To ensure that the war would not come to an end, the moneyed interests had flooded the public sphere with misinformation, turning coffeehouses into bastions of lies, rumors, and deceit. It was therefore crucial that the public properly realized not to "mistake the Eccho of a *London* Coffee-house for the Voice of the Kingdom."[80]

Instead of continuing to harshly criticize the Whigs, Defoe now tried a more conciliatory approach in *Armageddon: Or, the Necessity of Carrying on the War* (1711). He defended the Whigs against the charge of advocating perpetual war, showing that they actually had more to gain from peace. Not only would commerce recover, but so would credit—the two facets that concerned the moneyed men the most. He also defended the Tories by arguing that the peace treaty presently negotiated by the ministry was indeed an honorable settlement and did not constitute a breach of the Grand Alliance's strategic aims. Soon thereafter, Defoe took an even more radical step in trying to reduce the controversy surrounding the peace negotiations by putting forth the bold claim that it actually made little or no difference to England which foreign power ruled Spain, as long as England was able to maintain a fortified presence in the South Seas.[81] Hence, he argued, the South Sea Company would flourish regardless of whether the House of Bourbon or the House of Austria ruled Spain.

Defoe had similarly highlighted the urgency of establishing fortified colonies in South America in a series of articles in his *Review* during the summer of 1711. He scoffed at the proposal that free trade might be established in the area, proclaiming in an inflammatory manner, "To think of the *Spaniards* giving Consent to a Peace, upon Condition that the *English* shall have FREE TRADE to *New Spain*; is just as if *England* should make Peace with *France*, upon Condition that the *French* should come over hither, and lie with our Wives."[82] He continued, "*New Spain* is the Spouse of the *Old Spain*, and they will no more prostrate her to be debauch'd in Trade by us, than they, *the most Jealous People in the World*, should allow us to come to Bed to their Wives."[83]

In *An Excellent New Song, call'd, Mat's Peace, or the Downfall of Trade,* Maynwaring continued to take aim at Harley. He argued that not only would a premature peace leave France in a position of military and economic strength, it would also have disastrous implications on England's credit and commerce.

> Our Stocks were so high, and our Credit so good,
> (I mean all the while our late Ministry stood)
> That Foreigners hither their Mony did send,
> And Bankers Abroad took a pleasure to lend.
> > But tho all the Serivce was duly supply'd,
> > And nought was *embezzl'd* or *misapply'd*;
> > By all that wise Management what shall we gain,
> > > If now at the last we must give up *Spain*,
> > > > If now at the last we must give up *Spain*?
>
> By giving up *Spain*, we give up all our Trade
> In vain would they tell us a Treaty is made
> For yielding us Forts in the distant South-Sea,
> To manage our Traffick with Safety and Ease.
> > No Lyes are too gross for such *impudent Fellows*,
> > Of Forts in the Moon *as well* they might tell us;
> > Since France at her pleasure may take them again,
> > > If now at the last we must give up *Spain*,
> > > > If now at the last we must give up *Spain*?[84]

By the end of 1711, Defoe announced that the time for propaganda writing had come to an end and it was now up to the public to be the final judge of the company's prospects. He predicted confidently that once the stock appreciated to par, the critics' clamor would cease and public opinion would turn in the company's favor. In fact, Defoe had already begun to detect signs of such a reversal of public opinion. By the autumn of 1711, rising stock prices had started to transform peoples' impressions, making them more favorably disposed towards the scheme. He claimed "that many People who had their Mouths as wide open against the *South-Sea-Stock*, as ever, and that forswore coming into the Subscription, are so far chang'd in their Notions, as not only to Subscribe what they had, but to Purchase more."[85] He even dared the critics of the scheme to sell their stocks, as there were plenty of people interested in buying in. He then stated, in a manner that curiously encapsulated the prevailing race and power dynamic, "he that will not subscribe it, will sell it to him that will; and the Rise of Credit will wash this Blackamore white."[86]

Commercial Setbacks and Mounting Criticism

While the debate in the public sphere raged on during the autumn of 1711, the South Sea Company was busy setting up its corporate structure, formulating its bylaws, organizing the subscription books, setting salaries for employees, designing its coat of arms, and leasing a building to house its offices. The company's thirty directors worked alongside a staff of clerks and accountants to undertake the debt-for-equity conversion.[87] Each subscriber paid a small sum of money at the moment of conversion, providing the company with ready cash for incidental outlays. Once the primary operations of the company were clarified, the directors organized themselves in several standing committees—Shipping, Treasury, Accompts, Correspondence, Buying and Warehouses, and House and Servants.[88] To ensure that the directors attended all meetings, they were forced to deposit 40s., a portion of which was refunded each time they arrived to the meetings on time.[89] The most pressing issue confronting the directors during the first months was to agree on a method for raising money to launch the trade. The directors resolved that they would try to appease their critics by not exercising their right to call in additional money from the proprietors of the company's stock—the privilege Defoe had so staunchly defended. Instead they gave the Committee of Treasury instruction to devise an alternative way of raising working capital, which led to a £200,000 bond issuance a few months later.[90]

By January of 1712, the company, or more precisely the Committee of Buying and Warehouses, was preparing for the launch of the company's trade. They assembled practical information about trading to the South Seas, drew up lists of goods that might be "procured upon Trust," as well as investigated what kind of ships and what crew size would be appropriate to conduct the trade.[91] The company also petitioned the secretary of state, Henry St. John (1678-1751) (soon to become Viscount Bolingbroke), to provide military support for the company's operations. The company requested a force of twenty ships of line, forty transport ships, and four hundred troops to establish a colony. To their delight, in a letter dated March 13, 1711, Bolingbroke wrote, "Your Memorial to my Lord Treasurer concerning a Squadron for making Settlements in America for the Benefit of the South Sea Trade has been laid before the Queen and I am Commanded to let you know that Her Majesty will

give Order for such a Force to be provided as with the Sufficient for carrying on and Securing the said Trade."[92] By the summer, however, the
plans for a major force to settle a colony had been replaced by a much
more limited commitment to furnish a mere three men-of-war for the
carrying of goods and a few ships to secure the convoy.[93] This force was
designated to sail with the company's first shipment of goods. However,
to the great dismay of the directors, by August of 1712 the convoy had
yet to depart. Suspecting that the reason for the delay had to do with
the inability of the navy to spare the ships necessary for the convoy, the
directors wrote a letter to Harley in which they begged him to arrange
for the appropriate ships, as the cargo was starting to decay. When the
cargo was loaded onto two ships, *Anglesea* and *Warwick*, it seemed as
though the launch of the trade was imminent. But by February of 1713,
the ships still had yet to sail and the condition of the cargo was further
deteriorating.[94] The inability of the company to commence trading,
combined with the mounting criticism in the public sphere, left shares
in the company languishing in the £70–80 range throughout 1712.

The continuous delays in the company's trading venture were viewed
as a certain sign of the company's inevitable failure. In *A Letter from
a West-India Merchant to a Gentleman at Turnbridg* (1712), an anonymous author proclaimed that even if England secured the most advantageous Assiento contract, it would still prove to be a drain because
the slave trade to South America had never been particularly profitable.
Based on information from English and Dutch slave traders operating
out of Jamaica and Curaçao, he reported that the Spanish often colluded
to force down the price of slaves and charged extravagant prices for provisions needed to keep them alive while awaiting sale. Furthermore, the
Spanish refused to purchase all of the slaves delivered, claiming that
they did not fulfill the requirements for size, age, strength, or health.
Additionally, the Spanish required that the Assientistas pay duties even
on slaves arriving too sickly to be sold. These considerations led the
author to conjecture that the French had actually lost money on the
Assiento and that they were therefore secretly pleased to transfer the
contract to England.

With the company's reputation under fire, Defoe once again tried to
come to the rescue. He claimed, this time with a great sense of urgency,
that there had never been "an Undertaking of such Consequence," nor
one in which the people involved "have been so uneasie, their Opinions

of it so confused, and their Knowledge of the Manner and Circumstances of it so small."[95] He reiterated that England was far better suited
than France to carry out the South Sea trade and that it was central
to England's national security that this trade be acquired—"a Trade,
which in the Enemies Hand is so fatal to us, and which in our Hands
might be so fatal to them."[96] The key was for England to establish a fortified presence in the region, since the Spanish would never voluntarily
open up trade to its colonies. He unequivocally added:

> unless the *Spaniards* are to be divested of common Sense, Infatuate, and
> given up, abandoning their own Commerce, throwing away the only
> Valuable Stake they have left in the World, and in short, bent to their own
> Ruin, we cannot suggest that they will ever, on any Consideration, or for
> any Equivalent, part with so Valuable, indeed so Inestimable a Jewel, as
> the Exclusive Power of Trade to their own Plantations in *America*.[97]

Defoe concluded by declaring that the South Sea trade "is not only
probable to be Great, but capable of being the Greatest, most Valuable,
most Profitable, and most Encreasing Branch of Trade in our whole
British Commerce."[98]

Launching the Trade

On March 26, 1713, once the peace treaty of Utrecht had been signed,
the company was finally granted the Assiento, an event that served to
mitigate frustration over the lack of commercial activity. The agreement
called for the English to deliver a minimum of forty-eight hundred African slaves—or *Piezas de India*—per year, for the next thirty years, to
Spanish America.[99] In order to qualify as one *pieza*, the slave had to be
healthy, at least fifty-eight inches tall, and between the ages of fifteen
and thirty. If shorter, younger, older, or defective, the slave would only
count as a fraction of a *pieza* and would not command full price. The
payment for a slave could be made in gold or silver, as well as in "fruits
of the country," such as sugar, tobacco, and dyestuff. The contract also
specified that two-thirds of the slaves should be male and nine-tenths
over the age of sixteen.[100] Suggestive of the slave owners' intended use of
their female slaves, the company informed its purchasing agents that it
was desirable that the "Women as near as possible to be all Virgins."[101]
If the company encountered demand for additional slaves, they had the

right to increase its shipments, up to ten thousand per year.[102] Initially
the company was allowed to send only one five-hundred-ton ship per
year to the annual fair in Spanish America, but two licenses for ships of
six hundred tons were soon added. While the limited trade in dry goods
was a setback, the company still voted to accept the contract, hoping
perhaps that additional commerce would be possible through contraband trade. More discouraging, though, the treaty did not allow for England to establish any fortified trading outposts. Even so, judging by the
reaction in the stock market, the public's perception of the company's
trading privileges appears to have been favorable. Immediately after the
details of the Assiento contract were announced, the stock moved above
£90 for the first time and continued to appreciate during the spring and
summer, rising past £97 in the middle of June 1713. While it is impossible to attribute the movement in stock prices to any specific event, the
substantial increase in the share price suggests that the public was at
least not entirely displeased with the prospects of the Assiento.

With the Assiento contract finally signed, the company entered into
an intense period of activity, and its records reveal a palpable excitement about finally being able to engage in the trade it had been chartered to undertake. The queen wished the company "good Success in
all your Undertakings" and promised that they "may depend upon
my Protection and Favour."[103] Harley also stated his excitement about
the company: "I hope the Gentlemen of that Company will go on with
Vigour & Dilligence that no more time may be lost in making effectuall
her Majesty's gracious Intentions to them and that So advantageous a
Trade may be carried on to its full Extent."[104] Additional money was
raised through loans from the Bank of England and from another bond
issuance, enabling the Committee of Buying to start purchasing goods
for the annual merchandise ships and for the slave trading ships.[105] The
newly created Committee of the Assiento started to negotiate for the
supply of slaves.

While the company would lease ships from independent merchants
to transport the slaves, they still needed to contract with a supplier of
slaves on the coast of Africa. The company negotiated with both the
Royal African Company (RAC) and with the separate traders, trying to
secure the most favorable terms. Since Parliament had opened up the
Africa trade in 1698, the RAC had complained that the separate traders
(or interlopers, as the RAC preferred to call them) had undermined a

previously thriving business by both taking advantage of the company's forts on the African coast and forcing up the price of slaves. The RAC argued that the separate traders had provided their African counterparts with too much commercial experience and that this had turned the Africans into "Expert Merchants, if such a Term may be given to Cunning Tricking Villains."[106] Similarly, it had "exalted the naked *Africans, and raised the price of Negroes* to the *Intollerable* rate they are now at."[107] Defoe echoed these views, arguing that because the Africans "were taught to be Hucksters and Brokers for one another; the whole Scale of the Trade was turned, and instead of putting our Price upon them, they learnt now to put their Price upon the *English*."[108] In Defoe's mind, this created a situation in which "the Trade for Negroes to the Plantations became the most precarious and oppressive thing imaginable; the Uncertainty of the Supply put the Colonies often to great Extremities to carry on their Works, and the Dearness of them when they came, became an Excessive Unsufferable Burthen and Grievance to our Plantation Trade."[109] Like Defoe, many commentators were convinced that the RAC monopoly had to be reestablished for Britain to be able to properly carry out the Assiento.[110]

The company eventually reached an agreement with the RAC in August of 1713, to supply "Sound healthy and Merchantable Negroes" on the coast of Africa.[111] Soon thereafter the company dispatched three ships, *St. Marks*, *Windsor*, and *Canada*, to the coast of Africa to procure a total of 1,230 slaves, all of whom were branded with the company's newly designed seal.[112] A couple of months thereafter, the company ordered another three ships to sail, *Elizabeth* to carry five hundred slaves from Whydah, and *Hope* and *Smith* to buy three hundred slaves each on the Gold Coast.[113] This was followed two weeks later by a vote to employ the *Hallifax*, *Hope Gally*, and *Smith* for further slave trading ventures.[114] Although the license ships, *Warwick* and *Anglesea*, were still awaiting orders to sail, the fact that the slave trade had been launched came as a major relief to the directors. To facilitate a further expansion, the directors voted in October of 1713 to establish factories with five to six representatives at each location, in Cartagena, Vera Cruz, Buenos Ayres, Porto Belo, Havana, and Caracas.[115] The company also established agencies in Barbados and Jamaica, which enabled them to refresh ailing slaves as well as purchase additional slaves to make up the annual quota.[116]

Political instability disrupted the trade during the summer of 1714. While the queen's confidence in Harley had been waning for some time and Bolingbroke was emerging as his likely successor, the ascent of George I to the throne dealt the old ministry its final blow. Accused of plotting to restore the Pretender and for negotiating the Peace of Utrecht—which the Committee of Secrecy condemned as treasonous— Bolingbroke was forced to flee to France, while Harley was imprisoned in the Tower of London. The political drama associated with their fall, and the subsequent death of the queen during the summer of 1714, slowed down the company's activities. Just days before she died, the queen had sent the company a stern letter, "I wish you good success in Carrying on your Trade and hope you will make a better use, than you have hitherto done, of what I have bestow'd upon you."[117] Even though the directors were actively pursing new trades—corresponding with the RAC about contracting for another 2,430 slaves and planning for the *Anglesea* to embark on a smuggling voyage—the lack of commercial success and the general uncertainty during 1714 contributed to a drop in the company's share price, which closed at £83 on the day that Harley's tenure as Lord Treasurer came to an end.[118]

But the share price rebounded quickly. The day after the queen's death, it jumped £5 and then gained another £10 during the next fortnight, returning to £97. A general excitement about the ministerial and monarchial overhaul appears to have developed, judging by the fact that the share prices of the Bank of England and East India Company rose as well.[119] Soon after, when George I arrived on English soil, the company sent him a congratulatory note, to which he replied: "The Wealth & Prosperity of My People depend So much upon Commerce, that it shall be always my Care to protect & encourage it."[120] A few months later George was made governor of the company and he soon became a major shareholder, purchasing some £10,000 worth of stock.[121]

Soon after the political turmoil subsided, ships were once again regularly departing London for the Gold Coast and Angola to purchase slaves for Spanish America. Recent estimates suggest that the South Sea Company carried out 22 percent of England's total slave trade in 1714.[122] The demand was so strong that the company had to order its agents in Barbados to purchase an additional thousand slaves on the island to be shipped to Caracas, a pattern that would continue for the next few years.[123] As more and more South Sea Company ships returned to London laden with colonial goods—precious metals, sugar, dyestuff, and hides—the company's share price continued to appreciate. The stock reached £99 in mid-September of 1714 and continued to trade in the high nineties until it finally reached £100 on May 10, 1715. At this point, all indications were that the company had succeeded in the Herculean task of restoring public credit to its former glory. The company's future now looked nothing but bright.[124] The company had attracted approximately six thousand shareholders, including many prominent politicians, nobility, gentry, and merchants.[125] The South Sea Company claimed to have an income of £680,000 per year, allowing for total dividends of nearly 7 percent.[126] This early success of the company's trade and the appreciating stock price almost entirely silenced the discussion in the public sphere regarding the company's commercial and financial prospects.[127] Public opinion apparently deemed the company's slave trade promising enough to support its enormous capital stock. This was, of course, exactly the outcome that Defoe had prophesized two years earlier when he wrote in the *Review*, "Now, should the *South-Sea-Stock* Rise to Par, let your own Humour, or Madness, or Folly, or whatever you please to call it, be the occasion, this is plain; all your Quarrels at the Circumstances die of course, for *Men never find Fault where they get Money.*"[128] This did not necessarily signal that people were pleased with the present performance of the company, but only that they felt sufficiently optimistic about the future of the trade to continue to hold stock.[129] Defoe noted that it was essential to look at how people perceived the future to understand the present and that expectations can generate values that are far beyond present wealth. "Great," Defoe consequently proclaimed, "is the Power of Imagination!"[130]

The company's commercial success continued for the next several years. While there are many different numerical estimates, the most recent statistics suggests that the company shipped 2,090 slaves in 1715, which again made up 20 percent of England's total slave trade. In 1716, this number rose slightly to 2,127 (14 percent of England's slave trade); in 1717 the company transported 3,953 slaves (23 percent); and during its final year before the cessation of the Assiento, the company brought 3,742 slaves (25 percent) to the South American market.[131] The company's trade thus appeared to be in good health, despite numerous obstacles, including the complaint that the Caribbean was "infested with Pyrates."[132] The pirates had intercepted one of the company's sloops operating out of Jamaica, stealing 24,600 pieces of eight, and attacked the company's ship *Royal Africa*, seizing all its provisions, as well as twenty-eight slaves.[133] Despite these obstacles, the company's stock continued to trade around par throughout 1715 and then inched up to £110 in 1716. The following year, it reached £120 before settling back to around £115 in 1718. That autumn, the company's slave trade was suspended when the already antagonistic relations between Britain and Spain erupted into armed hostilities. Soon after the Royal Navy defeated the Spanish navy at the Battle of Cape Passaro in August of 1718, the Spanish government ordered the property of the company to be seized, in defiance of the Assiento. This abruptly terminated the company's trade.[134]

The extent to which the company ever made any profits is unclear. Scholars who have examined this question have been hampered by a lack of accurate financial accounts. While recognizing these challenges, historian Elizabeth Donnan speculates that, "there seems every reason to believe that the negro trade had been carried on at a loss during the years under consideration [1713–1718]."[135] John Sperling reached similar conclusions, arguing, "The negro traffic lost money for the Company and the legitimate trade in the annual ships brought a modest profit."[136] Historian Colin Palmer, on the other hand, after considering all of the company's expenses and revenues, posited that "the company's venture into the slave trade was far from unprofitable. In fact, its profits appear to have been better than good."[137] Whether or not the company was profitable, and despite the fact that it never delivered the forty-eight hundred slaves it was legally allowed, the public nevertheless appeared pleased enough with what they observed to continue buying the company's shares. The stabilization of the share price above par coincided with a lowering in the government's cost of borrowing, which signaled beyond doubt that credit was now restored. The success of Harley's propaganda machinery in developing a favorable imaginary of the Atlantic slave trade had thus succeeded in contributing to the restoration of public credit.[138]

Credit, Risk, and the Denial of Agency

This chapter has argued that the credit crisis of 1710 was resolved by a calculated use of the public's imagination of great colonial riches. As

revealed by the success of the South Sea scheme, the investing public apparently judged that the company's slave trading privilege would
generate high enough profits so that the company could pay substantial
dividends. Harley's propaganda writers had shaped an imaginary that
focused primarily on commercial opportunities, while downplaying
risks, challenges, and obstacles. Also marginalized in this imaginary
were the human implications of the trade. If the directors of the company reflected on the health and well-being of the slaves or the safety
of the traders, it was only insofar as it had an impact on profits. The
directors ordered and read a number of instructional manuals on how
to treat slaves in order to ensure their survival, including *Examination
of the Surgeons and Their Chests, A Method for the Better Preservation
of the Lives of the Negros,* and *A Scheme for the Better Management of
the Negroes & the Negro Trade.*[139] While the company's correspondence
with factors and ship captains did address problems of insurrection
and disease during what would later become known as the Middle Passage, the company records contain no indications that these issues were
ever formally discussed by the directors.[140] The almost complete silence
about the conditions and experiences of the African captives extended
to the public debates surrounding the South Sea Company.

It is far from surprising that the human condition of the slave trade
was ignored at this moment, decades before the early abolitionist
movement was formed. As the historian Kathleen Wilson points out,
newspapers and periodicals covering the empire "effac[ed] the crueler
aspects of empire, colonialism and 'trade' and the subjectivity of the
growing numbers of peoples under English rule."[141] What is remarkable
is that one of the biggest risk factors facing the company—the agency
and resistance, as well as the mortality, of the slaves—was ignored
in the public discussion about the company's prospects. Death from
violence, overwork, and disease was of course pervasive in the world
of Atlantic slavery.[142] While the pamphlets and the ballads written in
opposition to the company frequently warned about the risk posed by
the French and Spanish navies and, in some instances, the threat from
unruly natives or opportunistic pirates, there was barely any mention
of the prevalence of death from disease, frequent suicides, cases of self-
mutilation, or rebellions committed by the captives on board the ships.
While the downplaying of risk would have been in the interest of the
company, the fact that the opposition did not exploit this risk factor in

their attacks reveals the extent to which the African captives' agency, subjectivity, and humanity were left out of the British imaginary of the Atlantic world.

The absence of any reference to the slaves' agency and resistance is particularly noteworthy given the general perception of Africans as barbarously cruel and the abundance of contemporary evidence concerning the slaves' rebelliousness. Africans at the time were often considered subhuman, lacking the capacity for civilization, religion, law, and honesty.[143] One of the few aspects of their humanity that was recognized was their alleged disposition towards violence and cruelty, since these qualities instilled respect and fear in the Europeans. Sir Dalby Thomas, a prominent London merchant who served as the agent-general of the RAC on the Gold Coast, described the Africans as having "neither religion nor law binding them to humanity, good behaviour or honesty."[144] He further added that the Africans "are naturally such rogues and bred up with such roguish principles that what they can get by force or deceit . . . they reckon it as honestly their own."[145] Because of the Africans' alleged intractability and propensity for violence, much of the English population feared them. The stereotype of violent Africans was further fueled by the frequent incidents of rebellions, both on the plantations and on board the slave ships. A recent study estimates that approximately one in every ten slave ships experienced some sort of collective uprising, and accounts or rumors of rebellions, small and large, in Barbados and Jamaica, circulated widely in England.[146]

Published accounts of slave rebellions were available to the investing public in London. For example, the naval surgeon John Atkins suggested in a pamphlet that "there has not been wanting Examples of rising and killing a Ship's Company, distant from Land, tho' not so often as on the Coast."[147] Another person intimately familiar with the slave trade, Captain William Snelgrave, claimed in a pamphlet that "I knew several Voyages had proved unsuccessful by Mutinies; as they occasioned either the total loss of the Ships and the white Mens Lives; or at least by rendring it absolutely necessary to kill or wound a great number of the Slaves, in order to prevent a total Destruction."[148] During such collective uprisings, captives would fashion weapons from their chains and shackles and seek to overwhelm the outnumbered crew. However, since the crew's weapons were always superior, nearly all revolts were put down and the ships eventually reached their destinations, although at times with heavy losses to their cargo. Supercargo James Barbot gave an account of his experience while sailing on the Congo River in 1700, when the captives on board his ship rose up and attacked the crew. The assault commenced when a slave "stabb'd one of the stoutest of us all, who receiv'd fourteen or fifteen wounds of their knives, and so expir'd."[149] He continued, "Next they assaulted our boatswain, and cut one of his legs so round the bone, that he could not move, the nerves being cut through; others cut our cook's throat to the pipe, and others wounded three of the sailors, and threw one of them over-board."[150] The crew arranged a barricade on quarterdeck, where they stood "in arms, firing on the revolted slaves, of whom we kill'd some, and wounded many: which so terrify'd the rest, that they gave way, dispersing themselves some one way and . . . many of the most mutinous, leapt over board, and drown'd themselves in the ocean."[151]

Despite the lack of recognition in the public discourse, everyone who had ever been involved in the slave trade or had encountered a slave trading ship knew about the need to prepare carefully for the possibility of slave rebellions.[152] The ship *Hannibal*, for example, which was involved in several slaving voyages around this time, always kept "centinels upon the hatchways, and [had] a chest full of small arms, ready loaded and prim'd, constantly lying at hand upon the quarter-deck, together with some granada shells; and two of our quarter-deck guns, pointing on the deck."[153] Whenever the slaves were on deck for meals and exercise, the captain ordered that cannons and guns must always be loaded and aimed at the slaves.[154] Recognizing the damage that a shipboard rebellion might cause to the ship's crew and its profitability, some captains sought to avoid mutinies by ordering their crew to treat the captives with respect. William Snelgrave, for example, revealed that "I have always strictly charged my white People to treat them [the Negroes] with Humanity and Tenderness . . . both in keeping them from mutinying, and preserving them in health."[155] However, this courtesy was only extended as long as the slaves remained calm and obedient. In the event that the slaves attempted or were successful in inflicting harm on the ship's crew, draconian punishments awaited. Snelgrave, for example, suggested that quick and violent executions were the best deterrents of further mutinies.[156] John Atkins was also a firm believer in showing to the other slaves the painful consequences of disobedience. For example, he reported that three of the abettors to a rebellion were "sentenced to cruel Deaths; making them first eat the Heart and Liver of one of them killed. The Woman he hoisted up by the Thumbs, whipp'd, and slashed her with Knives, before the other Slaves till she died."[157]

Most often captains sought to reduce the risk of shipboard rebellions by keeping the slaves shackled throughout much of the Middle Passage. These chains also prevented slaves from committing suicide. According to the orders given to Captain William Barry of the ship *Dispatch*, he was to "keep [the slaves] shackled and hand Bolt[ed] fearing their rising or leaping Overboard."[158] The record of the ship *Hannibal*, mentioned earlier, described how "the negroes are so wilful and loth to leave their own country, that they have often leap'd out of the canoes, boat and ship, into the sea, and kept under water till they were drowned."[159] The account goes on to reveal that twelve captives "did wilfully drown themselves, and others starv'd themselves to death; for 'tis their belief that when they die they return home to their own country and friends again."[160] In certain cases the captain cut off the legs and arms of those who committed suicide to terrify the rest of the captives, as they believed that their spirit would not return home again if their bodies were dismembered.[161] Nevertheless, suicide and self-mutilation were common ways for captives to resist becoming slaves in the New World. An indication of the frequency of this sort of private rebellion can be gleaned from the presence of nets hanging over the deck areas where the slaves were brought for fresh air and exercise. There were also specially designed utensils—*speculum oris*—to force-feed captives on hunger strikes, and slavers sometimes smashed out the teeth of the slaves in order to feed them by force.

One of the rare contributions to the debate about the prospects of the South Sea Company that explicitly recognized the rebelliousness of the slaves was William Wood's *The Assiento Contract Consider'd* (1714), mentioned earlier. This publication consisted of a number of letters and petitions written by Wood between 1712 and 1714, in which he tried to convince members of Parliament and the Board of Trade in London of the dismal prospects of the South Sea Company and the ruinous consequences that the Assiento would have on Jamaica.[162] He predicted that a falloff in commerce and the resulting depopulation would further expose the island to insurrections from the slave population and to invasions from the outside, either by the French or by the pirates. He claimed there were already eighty thousand slaves on the island and only two thousand whites, which was far below the ideal ratio of one white person for every ten slaves. Wood proclaimed that under such circumstances, "the Negroes . . . may at any time rise and destroy the white People."[163] Yet, despite his recognition of the problem of slave rebellions and the fact that his primary purpose was to show that the "*Assiento* Contract will be *detrimental and a loss to the* South-Sea Company," he did not put these two pieces of information together to argue that the rebelliousness of the slaves might pose a problem to the profitability of the company.[164] His concern regarding the slaves' agency was solely about the safety and prosperity of Jamaica.

While the costs associated with the slaves' agency and rebelliousness—actual deaths and expenses of carrying a 50 percent larger crew, chains, and weaponry—were significant, the largest losses stemmed from disease.[165] The conditions on the ships during the Middle Passage were ideal for the rapid spread of dysentery, smallpox, ophthalmia, and other illnesses. For example, on one of the voyages of *Hannibal*, 228 of the seven hundred captives perished on account of the "white flux" and smallpox. Among the South Sea Company ships, a couple of ventures stand out as having experienced particularly high levels of mortality during the Middle Passage: on the *Indian Queen*, ninety of the 380 slaves loaded onto the ship died from smallpox and another eighty-eight were in various stages of the illness. The ship *George* lost all but ninety-eight of its 594 captives.[166] Even though some vessels lost as much as 90 percent of their cargo, the estimated average mortality rate during the first couple of decades of the eighteenth century was around 15 percent.[167]

As with rebelliousness, most contributions to the debate about the South Sea Company were silent on the issue of mortality during the Middle Passage. One exception was *The Trade Granted to the South-Sea-Company: Considered with Relations to Jamaica* (1714), which explicitly recognized that mortality was a major obstacle to the company's profitability. During season, the author observed a steady flow of ships arriving from Africa with "*Negroes* of all sorts, whereof hardly ever above Two Thirds are fit for the *Spaniards*."[168] To ensure that the company only brought merchantable slaves to the Spanish, the author proposed that all ships should first call at ports in Jamaica, from which the healthy slaves would be sent in sloops to places where the company knew there was a demand. Sickly slaves could be kept on the island to recuperate and surplus slaves could be put to work awaiting more favorable market conditions. As long as the slaves were not disciplined excessively—"The Beauty and Skin of the Slave is much regarded by the *Spaniards*, and the mark of a Stripe upon the Back, would not only spoil a *Piece de India*, but would often prevent the Sale"—or exposed to dampness and rain, such a period could greatly increase the traders' profits.[169] Refreshed slaves would also be able to cope better with the Spaniards' strategy of letting slave ships linger with their cargo in port before they showed any interest in making a purchase.[170]

Tellingly, both William Wood and the author of this pamphlet were located in Jamaica, an island on which death "was at the center of social experience for everyone."[171] Living in close proximity to the slave trade and the plantations made it impossible to ignore the realities of the slave economy. Conversely, only by being far removed from the daily experience of slavery was it possible for writers situated in London to so completely disregard the humanity of the slaves.[172] As historian Christopher Brown succinctly points out, "Slavery often was out of mind because it was very much out of sight. The British enjoyed the fruits of slavery while incurring few of its social or cultural costs."[173]

The experience of the slaves was certainly far removed from the investing public and the propaganda writers in London, but the slave trade was nevertheless at the center of the social imaginary upon which the South Sea Company was based. In order for the investing public to make up their minds about purchasing the company's shares, it was necessary for them to be able to access a mental image of the present and future conditions of the slave trade. Although this imaginary provided a fairly broad and inclusive image of the Atlantic slave trade, in that both proponents and opponents of the scheme contributed to its formation, it was nevertheless based on a selective description of reality. The practice of abstraction was nothing new to early modern Londoners, who had plenty of experience with the marriage market, the insurance industry, indentured servitude, and the labor market.[174] Karl Marx famously described how the commodity form abstracts from people's essential characteristics and qualities, calling this phenomenon commodity and money fetishism.[175] He argued that capitalism, in appearing as a mass of commodities mediated by money, tends to obfuscate its own underlying social reality. The resulting fetishism allows people to engage in market exchange and consumption without recognizing the ongoing exploitation, alienation, and violence that Marx associated with the capitalist mode of production. For example, fetishism allowed seventeenth-century Londoners to purchase a cup of sweetened coffee for a silver coin without ever considering the social conditions within which silver, porcelain, coffee, and sugar were produced.

The abstraction, or fetishism, facilitated by credit differs in important ways from that which Marx ascribed to money. If money allows people to disregard the origins of value, credit on the other hand necessitates a careful construction of a social imaginary of the reality within which future values will be produced. Money frees people from thinking about the past conditions of production, while credit necessitates that the future conditions are carefully considered and vividly imagined. In other words, money and credit enable different practices of abstraction and different kinds of fetishism.[176] This means that if in the process of constructing a social imaginary particular features of the underlying social condition are excluded, I argue, it is a more deliberate act of omission than just not paying attention or disregarding those very conditions. This is not to suggest that credit fetishism originates in a conscious or conspiratorial attempt to conceal important facts. Instead, the social imaginary of credit reveals what members of a society find important, as well as what they disregard, even after careful deliberation. It is a form of unwilled or built-in blindness grounded in a particular understanding of the world.[177] The fact that the debates about the South Sea Company ignored the agency of the slaves meant that the humanness and rebelliousness of the slaves did not even enter the minds of the public.[178] In denying the captives' agency and capacity for violence—one of the few aspects that instilled fear and respect in the Europeans—Africans were stripped of their last claim on humanity, leaving them as mere bodies capable of hard work and suitable to the climate. Although an essential part of establishing a necessary imaginary, their sacrifice was nevertheless real.

The Success of the South Sea Company

The company's success in restoring England's public credit, partly based on the obfuscation of violence and dehumanization, prompted the ultimate praise—imitation—by the French. As France emerged from the war of Spanish succession, its financial affairs were in even worse shape than those of the England. France's total national debt in 1715 amounted to a debilitating two thousand eight hundred million livres—approximately £800 million— and the entire fiscal apparatus was in a state of flux.[179] At this point, the Scotsman John Law (d. 1729) arrived in Paris, after having traveled the continent trying to convince a number of heads of state to implement his financial ideas. Drawing extensively upon his Hartlibian-inspired ideas about credit, published in 1705, Law pitched a proposal for an ambitious overhaul of the fiscal, financial, and commercial apparatus to the French minister of finance.[180] He encountered only limited success. As a consolation, Law was granted the privilege of opening a private note-issuing bank. Through the success of this bank venture, the Banque Générale, Law established his reputation among the Parisian elites. The fact that he was committed to redeem the notes with coin of a particular fineness, specified at the moment of the note's issuance, made the notes immune to debasements. As a result, the notes became popular and circulated freely, not only in Paris, but throughout Europe. The liquidity of the notes was further enhanced in 1717, when local tax collectors were instructed to use the notes in making remittances to the Treasury. This essentially transformed the notes into an official currency.

Having established his reputation in Paris, Law now sought to emulate the South Sea Company, of which he had been a longtime admirer.[181] His first move was to establish the Company of the West, better known as the Mississippi Company, and acquire a monopoly on commerce to Louisiana, which included most of France's holdings in North America. After having received permission by the state to increase the company's capital stock by one hundred million livres, he offered to exchange these shares for coin and banknotes (one-quarter) and for outstanding government bonds, *billets d'état* (three-quarters), which were trading at an 70 percent discount.[182] Law was fully aware of the importance of generating a favorable public opinion of the new securities and an optimistic imaginary of the company's trade. While historian Thomas Kaiser points out that Law did not, at least early on, pay much attention to public opinion concerning his bank and its notes, historian Antoin Murphy notes that Law did indeed organize a systematic propaganda campaign to shape the imaginary of the Mississippi Company.[183] Louisiana was idyllically portrayed as enjoying a mild climate, an abundance of precious metals, a plethora of game, while its capital, New Orleans, was alleged to be a thriving and healthy colonial town, as opposed to a sparsely populated, disease-ridden wetland.

Law next maneuvered to extend the revenue base of the Mississippi Company by acquiring the Senegal Company (summer of 1718) and the Company of Africa (May 1719). The shares of the Mississippi Company were now backed by revenues from the North American trade in furs and tobacco, as well as the trade in African slaves. This ensured that the Mississippi Company and the South Sea Company not only shared the same basic financial architecture, but that the link between the slave trade and the Financial Revolution was forged on both sides of the channel.[184] Law also added the Company of the Indies, the China Company, and France's tobacco monopoly to his corporate empire, essentially giving him control over France's entire colonial commerce. The most extravagant transaction, however, came in August of 1719, when Law reached an agreement with the French state to incorporate the entire national debt, amounting to 1.5 billion livres—or £400 million— into the capital stock of the Mississippi Company, a maneuver that the South Sea Company would later seek to copy. Hence, while John Law initially imitated the South Sea Company's practice of using the slave trade and a debt-for-equity swap to restore public credit, it was now the company's turn to copy Law's strategy of incorporating the entire national debt into the capital stock of a private monopoly company.

Despite the success of the South Sea Company in restoring Britain's public credit from the brink of disaster, the nation was still burdened by its public debt. In 1714, the total indebtedness amounted to £48 million, consisting of some old debts from Charles II's reign, a significant amount of high-interest irredeemable loans taken up in the 1690s, the recent lottery loans, and the liabilities the state owed to the Bank of England, East India Company, and the South Sea Company.[185] Approximately £40 million of this debt was funded, yet it nevertheless constituted a serious burden. In fact, annual interest payments of £3 million absorbed half of the government's tax receipts. Something had to be done to restructure this debt and reduce the interest rate from the current average of 6.25 percent down at least to the 5 percent rate available to private merchants. As such, the new Lord Treasurer, Robert Walpole, faced serious challenges. In 1717, he was able to convince the three companies to agree on a reduction in the rate of interest to 5 percent on many of the liabilities owed to them. This freed up some funds that the government committed to a Sinking Fund, designed to gradually buy up and cancel its debts.[186]

The Treasury tried to take advantage of the favorable financial conditions that prevailed towards the end of the 1710s to further restructure its debt obligations. After engrafting more of its liabilities into the capital stock of the three companies, the Treasury started to convert its irredeemable annuities, some of which were scheduled to run until 1807. In the spring of 1719, the government launched a program designed to gauge whether investors would be willing to convert their irredeemable annuities for highly liquid company stocks. Because of the South Sea Company's recent success in restoring public credit, the Treasury turned to the company to negotiate a scheme, in which the company would offer to convert a series of lottery annuities, contracted in 1710–1711 and maturing in 1742, into company stock.[187] In addition to increasing its capital stock to incorporate the annuities, the company would also be able to increase its capital stock to pay for overdue interest and to raise money for an additional loan to the government. The amount added to the capital stock to cover the interest in arrears and the loan to the government would be determined by the proportion of annuities presented for conversion. At the end, £1,084,790 worth of annuities was converted, which meant that interest arrears of £117,912 and a £544,142 loan to the government were added to the capital stock. This increased the company's capital stock to £11,746,844, but more importantly revealed an extremely profitable financial scheme.

A windfall profit enriched the proprietors of the annuities. They were provided with £1,202,702 worth of £100 shares, which they could turn around and sell at the market price, which was currently £114.[188] The company also benefited from the discrepancy between the market price and the face value. The government gave them the right to expand their capital stock by £544,142 to provide the government with a loan. To raise this money, they sold fifty-two hundred £100 shares at £114, which netted £592,800. This left the company with £48,658 in cash and another £24,142 in shares that could be sold in the market at a value of £27,522. Hence, the conversion of the annuities and the loan to the government provided the company with a swift profit of £76,522. This gain only whetted the appetite of the company to pursue further conversions—particularly since the Assiento had been canceled and it now lacked a secure revenue base.[189]

Conclusion

In January of 1720, the company submitted a hugely ambitious proposal to Parliament designed to incorporate the entire national debt into the company's capital stock, thus basically copying Law's project.[190] Since the Bank of England and the East India Company refused to surrender their parts of the debt, the South Sea Company ended up making a bid for the remainder of the outstanding national debt, amounting to £30,981,712. The company offered a reduction in the interest rate from 5 percent to 4 percent, starting in 1727, and a lump sum donation to the government of £3,000,000. The Bank of England was so threatened by the prospects of the South Sea Company becoming a gigantic financial corporation that it too entered the bidding to take over the national debt. Eventually, however, the South Sea Company prevailed, by offering to pay the government £7,500,000 for the privilege. The scheme would still be profitable to the company, as long as the new shares could be sold sufficiently higher than the £100 face value. Clearly, the company now had a vested interested in seeing its share prices rise as much as possible, an incentive that led the company to pursue a series of infamous manipulations. These manipulations, combined with the general euphoric conditions that prevailed in financial markets throughout Europe, generated an astonishing boom during the spring and summer of 1720. When the bubble burst the foundation of the English financial system was shaken. This crash would come to have a profound impact on how credit was viewed and understood for the rest of the century on both sides of the channel and the Atlantic.

Epilogue

Comparing the aftermath of the South Sea Bubble to the plague ravaging the south of France in 1720, the famous essayists John Trenchard (1668-1723) and Thomas Gordon (d. 1750) claimed in *Cato's Letters* that England had a "contagion of another sort, more universal, and less merciful, than that of Marseilles: The Latter has destroy'd, we are told, about sixty thousands lives; ours has done worse, it has render'd a much greater number of lives miserable, who want but the sickness to finish their calamity."[1] The author of another pamphlet signed *A Lover of his Country* complained that the post-bubble conditions were so dire that "our middle Sorts of Persons in Multitudes shutting up their Shops; our Artificers and Poor starving; Children cursing their Parents that begot them, and Parents the Hour of their Nativity."[2] The enraged public blamed the company's directors for allowing the nation to be "swallow'd by the damn'd *South Sea*." The author of *News from Hell* wrote about the directors, here personified by Sir John Blunt and John Lambert:

> O *Bl . . . nt! O L . . . mb . . . rt!* When the baleful Sound
> Of your curst Names the tender Ears shall wound
> Of Children yet unborn, when they shall read,
> By what dire Arts you made your Country bleed,
> With Horror startled they will scarce believe
> Villains so great, so infamous cou'd live.[3]

Referring to the directors as "Crocodiles and Cannibals," Trenchard and Gordon advocated that the directors, who had nothing to offer but "their necks and their money," ought to be brought to swift justice at the gallows.[4] Their execution would not encounter any sympathy from the public, not even "a sigh from an old woman, though accustom'd perhaps to shed tears at the untimely demise of a common felon or murderer." It would, however, achieve the aim of "soften[ing] the rage of the people."[5]

While the directors and stockjobbers were singled out as the primary culprits of this mayhem, many critics proclaimed that the entire South Sea Company scheme, from its inception, was corrupt and that the Assiento had never been more than a chimera.[6] An anonymous author charged that it was "notorious" that the South Sea project had "no solid or real Foundation, from which any honest Profit" could be expected.[7] Instead, the author argued, the scheme is "contriv'd and carried on with all the Art and Cunning possible, to amuse People, and draw them in by a false View of immense Gains."[8] The famous Tory satirist Edward Ward added his scorn in *A South-Sea Ballad*, in which he noted:

> Five hundred Millions, Notes and Bonds,
> Our Stocks are worth in Value,
> But neither lie in Goods or Lands,
> Or Money let me tell ye.
> Yet tho' our Foreign Trade is lost,
> Of mighty Wealth we Vapour,
> When all the Riches that we boast
> Consist in Scraps of Paper.[9]

The public also received its share of the blame. Trenchard and Gordon accused the ordinary investor of knowingly participating in and contributing to the formation of the new culture of credit. They argued that self-love:

> beguiles men into false hopes, and they will venture to incur a hundred probable evils, to catch one possible good; nay, they run frequently into distracting pains and expences, to gain advantages which are purely imaginary, and utterly impossible.[10]

For Trenchard and Gordon, the notion that society encouraged people to act on their passions and imagination, not according to their reason, constituted the very source of England's downfall. They added, "Our prevailing passions in England, of late, have been hope, avarice, and ambition; which have had such a headlong force upon the people, that they are become wretched and poor, by a ravenous appetite to grow great and rich."[11] The general public had revealed a complete inability to properly assess the world probabilistically. Every person "hoped that fate would be kinder to him in particular, than to a thousand other; and so this mad hope became general, as are the calamities which it has produced."[12] Commenting on the dynamic between passions and interests, which Montesquieu and Hume would later develop, Trenchard and Gordon claimed that the South Sea debacle had showed "the little power that reason and truth have over the passions of men."[13]

After the bubble burst, even Daniel Defoe, who had so staunchly defended the company during its first few years in operation, began to question the intellectual and institutional foundation of the new culture of credit.[14] Addressing himself directly to John Law, he claimed that:

> you only screw'd up the adventurous Humour of the People by starting every Day new Surprizes, new Oceans for them to launch out into; so supporting one Chimera by another, building Infinite upon Infinite, which it was evident must sink all at last into infinite Confusion.[15]

Thus discrediting the notion of infinite improvement, Defoe jettisoned the need for such a currency. The notion of an infinitely expandable currency was also scorned by Jonathan Swift, Defoe's former partner on Harley's propaganda staff. He argued that an infinitely expandable currency was a serious source of instability and should therefore be eliminated. In *The Bubble: A Poem*, Swift famously described a young Daedalian adventurer:

> On *Paper* Wings he takes his Flight,
> With *Wax* the *Father* bound them fast;
> The *Wax* is melted by the Height,
> And down the tow'ring Boy is cast.
>
> A Moralist might here explain
> The Rashness of the *Cretan* Youth,
> Describe his Fall into the Main,
> And from a Fable form a Truth.
>
> His *Wings* are his *Paternal Rent*,
> He melts his *Wax* at ev'ry Flame;
> His Credit sunk, his Money spent,
> *In* Southern Seas *he leaves his Name.*[16]

With this poem, Swift joined the chorus of critical accounts that used the false hope of alchemy to ridicule the gullibility of the public and the failure of credit. In exploring the correspondence between credit and alchemy, Swift demanded that:

> Ye wise Philosophers explain
> What Magick makes our Money rise,
> When dropt into the *Southern* Main;
> Or do these Juglers cheat our Eyes?
>
> Thus in a Basin drop a Shilling,
> Then fill the Vessel to the Brim;
> You shall observe, as you are filling,
> The pond'rous Metal seems to swim:
>
> It rises both in Bulk and Height,
> Behold it mounting to the Top;
> The liquid Medium cheats your Sight,
> Behold it swelling like a Sop.[17]

Also using alchemy to uncover the inherent dangers of credit money, Edward Ward's *South-Sea Ballad* proclaimed that "'Tis said that *Alchemists* of old / Could turn a Brazen Kettle / Or Leaden Cistern into Gold / . . . But if it here may be allow'd / To bring in great and small Things / Our cunning *South-Sea*, like a God, / Turns Nothing into All Things."[18]

As these accounts make clear, the English perceived and experienced the South Sea Bubble as a traumatic event.[19] Increasingly, however, modern historians maintain that the bubble did not have as deep an impact on the English economy as contemporaries believed and feared. Using statistics on bankruptcy and trade, historian Julian Hoppit concludes that the 1720 crisis was no deeper than those of 1710–1711 and 1727–1729 and the financial historians Ann Carlos and Larry Neal argue that even though the South Sea Bubble momentarily shook the financial system, it caused no lasting damage.[20] Yet, even if there was no profound impact on the economy and the financial system, the bubble nevertheless led to a significant transformation in the discourse on money and credit for the rest of the century, if not longer.[21] From having enjoyed an increasingly uncontested position in the realm of political economy, the Hartlibian understanding of money and credit was now challenged by both old and new monetary theories.

Three broad categories of monetary discourses developed during the aftermath of the South Sea Bubble, each of which will be examined briefly below. On one extreme, in *The Querist* (1735) the Irish philosopher George Berkeley (1685-1753) articulated a theory of money that closely reproduced the Hartlibian endorsement of credit money. According to Berkeley, industry was the essence of wealth and money's primary role was to "stirreth up industry, enabling men mutually to participate the fruits of each other's labour."[22] For this purpose, there was no need for precious metals; credit money could mediate transactions equally well. Following the Hartlibian tradition, Berkeley described money as a ticket or token, the material of which was inconsequential. Indeed, the fact that the bulk of Britain's currency was already made up of paper notes was proof enough of its feasibility.[23] Yet paper money was not immune to potential complications. The Mississippi and South Sea schemes had transformed the essence of credit, turning it into "a means for idleness and gaming, instead of a motive and help to industry."[24] Berkeley, however, believed that such problems might easily be prevented.[25] The solution was to maintain a public land bank that properly managed the issuance of credit money. He queried, "Whether the notes of such public bank would not have a more general circulation than those of private banks, as being less subject to frauds and hazards?"[26]

Berkeley conceived of money within a circular flow framework. He argued that an expansion of paper money promoted trade, which would both augment the nation's capital stock and the value of land. The growth of both mobile and immobile wealth could then serve as potential security for the creation of even more credit money, thus continuing the favorable cycle. While economic activity—employment, land improvement, manufacturing, trade, etc.—was the real determinant of the size of the money stock, human agency nevertheless played an active role in controlling the size and distribution of the new money. Berkeley's scheme thus resembled the many land bank schemes proposed before his time, including that of John Law.

On the other extreme, the bursting of the bubble led a number of political economists to call for an end to the use of credit money and a return to the safety of precious metals. The French-born London merchant Isaac Gervaise, for example, revived a number of neo-Aristotelian principles in arguing for a return to metallic money. Gervaise not only subscribed to the idea that metallic coins circulate because of their intrinsic value, he based his worldview on a notion of balance and harmony that resembled that of the neo-Aristotelians. In a pamphlet intended to show "the ill Consequences of an unnatural Use of Credit," he suggested that a nation is healthy and prosperous insofar as it maintains balance in a number of important spheres. First, the social hierarchy had to be in balance. He noted, "Man naturally loves his Ease, the Possession of a part of [the nation's gold and silver] lessens his Desires, and causes him to labour less; which gives him that hath little or no Possession an opportunity by his Labour to slip into his place."[27] The desire to obtain riches, he argued:

> May be look'd upon as the great Spring that forces Movement or Labour; and the Love of Ease, as the small Spring or Pendulum, that keeps Men in a continual Equilibral Vibration of Rich and Poor: so that the one always balances the other, in such manner, as keeps Labour or Movement continually going, in a certain equal proportion.[28]

Related to this principle, Gervaise insisted that a certain balance must also be maintained between nations. Each nation should have gold and silver proportional to their numbers and industry. If this balance is violated and one nation attracts more than its proper share of the world's gold and silver, "the number of Rich is too great, in proportion to the Poor, so as that Nation cannot furnish unto the World that share of Labour which is proportion'd to that part of the [money] it possesses."[29] As a result, the nation's net exports fall, leading to an outflow of the excess money.

Moreover, when a nation attracts too much money, the excess disturbs the balance of the nation's manufacturing. Gervaise argued that there are manufacturing sectors that produce just the right amount for the nation; sectors that produce less than the nation demands and therefore require additional supplies from abroad; and sectors that produce more than the nation needs and therefore have the capacity to export their surplus. If one sector is encouraged by the imbalances to produce more, it attracts "Workmen from those other Manufactures . . . So that what is transported of the encouraged Manufacture, beyond nature, only balances the Diminution of the others."[30]

Advising the legislator to leave trade and money alone and let the economy's inherent dynamic bring about the balance and harmony best suited for each nation, Gervaise argued that trade "is never in a better condition, than when it's natural and free; the forcing it either by Laws, or Taxes, being always dangerous."[31] For Gervaise, credit constitutes another such external intervention that offered little or no benefits. An expansion of credit would only increase the money stock beyond "that Proportion which by Trade naturally belongs to it, that Increase of Credit will act on that Nation, as if it had drawn an equal Sum from a Gold or Silver Mine."[32] This too would lead to an outflow of coin from the nation, leaving it with as large a decline in silver and gold as the increase in credit. Gervaise therefore concluded that, "Credit is of pernicious consequence."[33]

The Scottish philosopher David Hume struck a middle ground between the two extremes here represented by Berkeley and Gervaise. Hume embraced the Hartlibian notion that the essential ingredient in money is trust and that the material of which money is comprised is of secondary importance. He developed a sophisticated theory of trust applicable to all kinds of commercial contracts, including both coin and credit money.[34] While this made Hume philosophically open to a monetary system based on paper money, he nevertheless believed that a currency based on silver and gold was more practical.[35]

Hume held that the specie flow mechanism efficiently distributed money around the world in accordance with each country's level of economic activity. Countries enjoying economic growth and there-fore in need of more money to circulate its goods, would automati-cally attract the appropriate amount from abroad. By producing more commodities, prices would fall, making the nation's output more com-petitive. As exports increased, money flowed in and thus restored the proper proportion between commodities and money in the nation. The same automatic adjustment mechanism would be triggered in the opposite direction in countries with falling output. For Hume, the inexorable dynamic of the specie flow mechanism thus ensured that each nation's commerce, industry, and manufacturing dictated the size of its money stock.

While the size and industriousness of its population ultimately determined both the nation's wealth and the size of its money stock, Hume did not deny that it mattered whether a nation's money stock was expanding or contracting. Indeed, he acknowledged that an increase in the money stock had beneficial effects on economic activ-ity. Not unlike the Hartlibians, he noted in his 1752 essay *Of Money* that "we find, that, in every kingdom, into which money begins to flow in greater abundance than formerly, every thing takes a new face: labour and industry gain life; the merchant becomes more enterprising, the manufacturer more diligent and skilful, and even the farmer follows his plough with greater alacrity and attention."[36] Yet, an expansion of the money stock also had a tendency to trigger inflation. "It appears," Hume suggested "that great plenty of money is rather disadvantageous, by raising the price of every kind of labour."[37] Although he was rather vague about the relative strengths of these effects, he maintained that only monetary expansions caused by increases in exports should be viewed as favorable. While an inflow of money from abroad was as inflationary as a state-engineered expansion of paper money, the former was "an inconvenience that is unavoidable and the effect of that public wealth and prosperity which are the end of all our wishes." Regarding the latter, however, he noted that "there appears no reason for encreasing that inconvenience by a counterfeit money."[38] Hence, although Hume fully recognized the convenience of paper money and acknowledged that such currencies will always have a "place in every opulent kingdom," he was adamant that for the state to "endeavour artificially to *encrease* such a credit, can never be the interest of any trading nation."[39] If the state were to play any part in fostering economic growth, it should be limited to the safeguarding of the basic institutions of commerce. By ensuring that the basic economic infrastructure was safe and sound, commerce, industry, and the arts would flourish, which Hume believed would bring about the greatest amount of wealth and happiness.

Hume was not only critical of state-issued paper money, he was deeply suspicious of the entire system of public credit. He argued that the primary rationale behind the new system of public finance introduced during the Financial Revolution was to enable the state to raise more money, primarily to support its military ventures. Since war directly undermined the very basis for commercial prosperity and political liberty, any institution that systematically promoted and enabled wars should be removed. Even if a nation managed to survive or even emerged victoriously from an armed conflict, chances were that it would eventually collapse because of its excessive indebtedness. Therefore, Hume famously concluded, "either the nation must destroy public credit, or public credit will destroy the nation."[40] If a burdensome public debt were not eliminated, either by voluntary bankruptcy or payment, Hume warned that, "some daring projector may arise with visionary schemes for their discharge." Referring specifically to John Law, Hume continued, "And as public credit will begin, by that time, to be a little frail, the least touch will destroy it, as happened in FRANCE during the regency; and in this manner it will *die of the doctor*."[41]

Adam Smith occupied the same middle ground in the discourse on money as Hume, his long-time friend.[42] He too argued that money is best left to itself; the specie-flow mechanism ensures that each nation retains the appropriate amount of money to circulate its goods. The notion that there could ever be a scarcity of money problem was thus based on a fallacy. Indeed, for Smith, the fact that no problem was "more common than that of the scarcity of money" spoke to the prevailing lack of proper economic literacy.[43] It was this myopia that motivated the pursuit of "the absurd idea of the philosopher's stone . . . [and] the equally absurd one of immense rich mines of gold and silver."[44] Yet, like Hume, even though Smith was practically oriented towards a metallic currency, he noted that a "well-regulated paper money will supply it, not only without any inconveniency, but, in some cases, with some advantages."[45] The key was that people had to have "confidence in the fortune, probity, and prudence" of bankers and that they could trust the integrity of the assets backing the notes.[46] Yet, echoing Swift's Daedalian metaphor, Smith famously cautioned that matters could easily go awry. He wrote:

> The commerce and industry of the country, however, it must be acknowledged, though they may be somewhat augmented, cannot be altogether so secure, when they are thus, as it were, suspended upon the Daedalian wings of paper money, as when they travel about upon the solid ground of gold and silver. Over and above the accidents to which they are exposed from the unskilfulness of the conductors of this paper money, they are liable to several others, from which no prudence or skill of those conductors can guard them.[47]

By still referring to the South Sea Bubble more than half a century after it burst, Hume and Smith revealed the degree to which the bubble shaped the thinking about money and credit. And the lingering effects of the bubble did not end there. For example, President Andrew Jackson's hostility towards the Second Bank of the United States—an attempt to create an American version of the Bank of England—is said to have been sparked by his awareness of the South Sea Bubble. Allegedly, Jackson told the president of the Second Bank, "I do not dislike your bank any more than all banks. But ever since I read the history of the South Sea Bubble I have been afraid of banks."[48]

Versions of these three discourses on money continued to inform the debate about money and credit for the next two centuries—indeed, until this very day. With each new credit crisis, experts and pundits alike question the stability of credit and its corollaries: expectations, opinion, and imagination. Directors of failed banks and credit schemes are chastised and called names far worse than "crocodiles and cannibals," stockbrokers are vilified and accused of fraud, the public is ridiculed for not recognizing the harbingers of the crisis, and the entire architecture of finance is blamed for being inherently corrupt. A variety of solutions are proposed, often involving the anchoring of the monetary system in precious metals or the establishment of fixed rules for how much money can be issued, as well as the implementation of stricter limits on the creation and securitization of private and public credit. However, once the economy recovers and people begin to look more optimistically at the future, traditional forms of credit rebound and new credit instruments are introduced. Imagination of future wealth is realized in the present, enabling more investments, employment, and production. Opportunities for profit are spotted everywhere, even in distant lands or emerging markets and among people in parts of the social hierarchy with whom the investors themselves would never dream of interacting. As the economy prospers, future risk factors are increasingly discounted, accelerating the creation of credit, which in turn ignites even more economic activity. This continues until the moment arrives when confidence, expectations, and trust in the value of securities is perturbed and credit once again enters a downward spiral. While debates about this dynamic have been staged under the rubric of different schools of thought, such as the "banking school" versus the "currency school" in the nineteenth century, or Keynesianism versus monetarism in the twentieth century, the basic arguments remain very similar to those articulated during the aftermath of the South Sea Bubble.

A number of factors have contributed to making credit less precarious today than it was during the Financial Revolution: financial instruments have become more sophisticated, the probabilistic models employed in managing credit are more advanced, new types of insurance contracts that reduce risk have been introduced, and the state has taken on an active role as the "lender of last resort." Moreover, a greater sense of agreement now guides the monetary discourse. Modern economists have retained both the Hartlibian idea of infinite improvement as part of growth theory and the neo-Aristotelian notion of balance survives in the concept of equilibrium. Most economic thinkers also believe that a monetary authority independent from the political apparatus is capable of managing the monetary system in ways that reduces its intrinsic volatility. Credit fetishism may now be harder to maintain because of human rights groups calling attention to atrocities around the globe; political propaganda writers now face a greater challenge trying to sway a more financially literate public; technology now exists that makes it even harder to counterfeit money; and, government elections often hinge on a broader range of issues than public credit alone. Yet, since the world of credit is still characterized by instability, confusion, misinformation, manipulation, fraud, exploitation, and violence, the themes discussed in this book are still relevant to the modern debate. The casualties of credit thus constitute an inherent and unavoidable feature of modern culture.

Notes

Acknowledgments

Index

Notes

Introduction

1. Charles Davenant, *Discourses on the Publick Revenues, and on The Trade of England* (London, 1698), 38.
2. For a discussion of the role of finance in England's state building and imperial expansion, see John Brewer, *The Sinews of Power: War, Money and the English State, 1688–1783* (New York: Knopf, 1989). For a discussion of the relationship between finance and economic growth, see Peter L. Rousseau and Richard Sylla, "Financial Revolutions and Economic Growth: Introducing this EEH Symposium," *Explorations in Economic History* 43 (2006): 1–12; and Ross Levine, "Financial Development and Economic Growth: Views and Agenda," *Journal of Economic Literature* 35 (1997): 688–726.
3. "Casualty." Def. 3a. *The Oxford English Dictionary*, 2nd ed., 1989.
4. Craig Muldrew, *The Economy of Obligation: The Culture of Credit and Social Relations in Early Modern England* (London: Palgrave, 1998).
5. Although the term "political economy" did not enter common use in England until the second half of the eighteenth century, the term best captures the intellectual project of the authors whose writings are explored in this book. The first use of the term political economy is generally credited to Antoine de Montchrétien, *Traité de l'économie politique* (Rouen, 1615).
6. Since the tracts published in the seventeenth century were exclusively written in response to particular monetary crises, each chapter of this book therefore focuses on a set of texts written in response to the same crisis and engaged in an internal conversation with each other. I thus seek to avoid the problem highlighted by Julian Hoppit, namely that scholarly attention to seventeenth-century thinking about economic issues has been characterized by selectivity, anachronism, and teleology. "The Contexts and Contours of British Economic Literature, 1660–1760," *Historical Journal* 49 (2006): 79–80.

7. This book builds on a number of studies of seventeenth-century conceptions of credit and a number of key analyses of the political context of the Financial Revolution, including J. G. A. Pocock, *The Machiavellian Moment: Florentine Political Thought and the Atlantic Republican Tradition* (Princeton, NJ: Princeton University Press, 1975); Julian Hoppit, "Attitudes to Credit in Britain, 1680–1790," *Historical Journal* 33 (1990): 305–322; Muldrew, *Economy of Obligation*; Bruce G. Carruthers, *City of Capital: Politics and Markets in the English Financial Revolution* (Princeton, NJ: Princeton University Press, 1999); Istvan Hont, *Jealousy of Trade: International Competition and the Nation State in Historical Perspective* (Cambridge, MA: Harvard University Press, 2005); Natasha Glaisyer, "'A Due Circulation in the Veins of the Publick': Imagining Credit in Late Seventeenth- and Early Eighteenth-Century England," *Eighteenth Century: Theory and Interpretation* 46 (2005): 277–297; and Steve Pincus, *1688: The First Modern Revolution* (New Haven, CT: Yale University Press, 2009).

8. An earlier version of this argument was published in Carl Wennerlind, "Credit-Money as the Philosopher's Stone: Alchemy and the Coinage Problem in Seventeenth-Century England," *History of Political Economy* 35 (2003): 235–262. I will use the term *Scientific Revolution* sparingly in this book as many "historians now reject even the notion that there was any single coherent cultural entity called 'science' in the seventeenth-century to undergo revolutionary change." Many scholars also suggest that there was a great deal of continuity between seventeenth-century natural philosophy and its precursors. Steve Shapin, *The Scientific Revolution* (Chicago: University of Chicago Press, 1996), 3.

9. William Letwin, *The Origins of Scientific Economics, 1660–1776* (London: Routledge, 1963); Neal Wood, *Foundations of Political Economy: Some Early Tudor Views on State and Society* (Berkeley: University of California Press, 1994); Deborah A. Redman, *The Rise of Political Economy as a Science: Methodology and the Classical Economists* (Cambridge, MA: MIT Press, 1997); Pamela H. Smith, *The Business of Alchemy: Science and Culture in the Holy Roman Empire* (Princeton, NJ: Princeton University Press, 1997); Andrea Finkelstein, *Harmony and Balance: An Intellectual History of Seventeenth-Century English Economic Thought* (Ann Arbor: University of Michigan Press, 2000); Margaret Schabas, *The Natural Origins of Economics* (Chicago: University of Chicago Press, 2005); Thomas Leng, *Benjamin Worsley (1618–1677): Trade, Interest, and the Spirit in Revolutionary England* (London: Royal Historical Society, 2008); and Ted McCormick, *William Petty and the Ambitions of Political Arithmetic* (Oxford: Oxford University Press, 2009).

10. The traffic of ideas between natural philosophy and political economy was not unidirectional; many important insights into nature and matter were

developed with the use of conceptual models initially applied to the economy. For examples of how the economy influenced natural philosophy, see Julia Robin Solomon, *Objectivity in the Making: Francis Bacon and the Politics of Inquiry* (Baltimore, MD: The Johns Hopkins University Press, 1998); Deborah E. Harkness, *The Jewel House: Elizabethan London and the Scientific Revolution* (New Haven, CT: Yale University Press, 2007); and Harold J. Cook, *Matters of Exchange: Commerce, Medicine, and Science in the Dutch Golden Age* (New Haven, CT: Yale University Press, 2007).

11. Ian Hacking, *The Emergence of Probability* (Cambridge: Cambridge University Press, 1975) Barbara J. Shapiro, *Probability and Certainty in Seventeenth-Century England* (Princeton, NJ: Princeton University Press, 1983); and Lorraine Daston, *Classical Probability in the Enlightenment* (Princeton, NJ: Princeton University Press, 1988).

12. Geoffrey Clark, *Betting on Lives: The Culture of Life Insurance in England, 1695–1775* (Manchester: Manchester University Press, 1999).

13. Steven Shapin and Simon Schaffer, *Leviathan and the Air-Pump: Hobbes, Boyle, and the Experimental Life* (Princeton, NJ: Princeton University Press, 1985); Simon Schaffer, "Defoe's Natural Philosophy and the Worlds of Credit," in *Nature Transfigured: Science and Literature, 1700–1900*, ed. John Christie and Sally Shuttleworth, 13–44 (Manchester: Manchester University Press, 1989); Steve Shapin, *A Social History of Truth: Civility and Science in Seventeenth-Century England* (Chicago: University of Chicago Press, 1994); and Mario Biagioli, *Galileo's Instruments of Credit: Telescopes, Images, Secrecy* (Chicago: University of Chicago Press, 2006).

14. Brewer, *Sinews of Power*; Carruthers, *City of Capital*; Michael J. Braddick, *State Formation in Early Modern England, c. 1550–1700* (Cambridge: Cambridge University Press, 2000); Patrick K. O'Brien, "Fiscal Exceptionalism: Great Britain and its European Rivals from Civil War to Triumph at Trafalgar and Waterloo," in *The Political Economy of British Historical Experience, 1688–1914*, ed. Donald Winch and P. K. O'Brien, 245–265 (Oxford: Oxford University Press, 2002); David Stasavage, *Public Debt and the Birth of the Democratic State: France and Great Britain, 1688–1789* (Cambridge: Cambridge University Press, 2003); James Macdonald, *A Free Nation Deep in Debt: The Financial Roots of Democracy* (New York: Farrar, Straus, and Giroux, 2003); and Pincus, *1688*.

15. An earlier version of this argument was published in Carl Wennerlind, "The Death Penalty as Monetary Policy: The Practice and Punishment of Monetary Crime, 1690–1830," *History of Political Economy* 36 (2004): 129–159.

16. There is a recognition among some modern economists that the key to understanding money is to reintroduce "extrinsic beliefs, or social custom, as well as preferences and technology" to the analysis. Nobuhiro Kiyotaki and Randall Wright, "On Money as a Medium of Exchange," *Journal of Political*

Economy 97 (1989): 928. See also Thomas J. Sargent and François R. Velde, *The Big Problem of Small Change* (Princeton, NJ: Princeton University Press, 2002).

17. Frank H. Hahn, "On Some Problems of Providing the Existence of an Equilibrium in a Monetary Economy," in *The Theory of Interest Rates*, ed. F. H. Hahn and F. P. R. Brechling, 126–135 (London: Macmillan, 1965).

18. Joyce Oldham Appleby, *Economic Thought and Ideology in Seventeenth-Century England* (Princeton, NJ: Princeton University Press, 1978); C. George Caffentzis, *Clipped Coins, Abused Words, and Civil Government: John Locke's Philosophy of Money* (New York: Autonomedia, 1989); Peter Linebaugh, *The London Hanged: Crime and Civil Society in the Eighteenth-Century* (Cambridge: Cambridge University Press, 1993); Margot C. Finn, *The Character of Credit: Personal Debt in English Culture, 1740–1914* (Cambridge: Cambridge University Press, 2003); Marieke de Goede, *Virtue, Fortune, and Faith: A Genealogy of Finance* (Minneapolis: University of Minnesota Press, 2005); Christine Desan, "The Market as a Matter of Money: Denaturalizing Economic Currency in American Constitutional History," *Law and Social Inquiry* 30 (2005): 1–60; and Deborah Valenze, *The Social Life of Money in the English Past* (Cambridge: Cambridge University Press, 2006). This book also shares many common perspectives with the literary analyses in the field of New Economic Criticism, which includes Patrick Brantlinger, *Fictions of State: Culture and Credit in Britain, 1694–1994* (Ithaca, NY: Cornell University Press, 1996); Laura Brown, *Fables of Modernity: Literature and Culture in the English Eighteenth Century* (Ithaca, NY: Cornell University Press, 2003); Ian Baucom, *Specters of the Atlantic: Finance Capital, Slavery, and the Philosophy of History* (Durham, NC: Duke University Press, 2005); Robert Markley, *The Far East and the English Imagination, 1600–1730* (Cambridge: Cambridge University Press, 2006); and Mary Poovey, *Genres of the Credit Economy: Mediating Value in Eighteenth- and Nineteenth-Century Britain* (Chicago: University of Chicago Press, 2008).

19. I explore both canonical and minor works because, as Mark Knights points out, ideas and views published in minor, ephemeral, and anonymous works constituted important ingredients of the discourse; see *Representation and Misrepresentation in Later Stuart Britain: Partisanship and Political Culture* (Cambridge: Cambridge University Press, 2005), 45–46.

20. Pocock, *Machiavellian Moment*, 452.

21. Margaret C. Jacob, *Scientific Culture and the Making of the Industrial West* (Oxford: Oxford University Press, 1997); Joel Mokyr, *The Enlightened Economy: An Economic History of Britain 1700–1850* (New Haven, CT: Yale University Press, 2009).

22. P. G. M. Dickson, *The Financial Revolution in England: A Study in the Development of Public Credit, 1688–1756* (London: Macmillan, 1967); D. W. Jones,

War and Economy in the Age of William III and Marlborough (Oxford: Blackwell, 1988); Brewer, *Sinews of Power.*

23. Keith Horsefield, *British Monetary Experiments, 1650–1710* (New York: Garland Publishing, 1983), xi–xix; Larry Neal, "How It All Began: The Monetary and Financial Architecture of Europe during the First Global Capital Markets, 1648–1815," *Financial History Review* 7 (2000): 123. Anne L. Murphy highlights the creation of the Bank of England, the national debt, and an active secondary market in the resulting debt instruments as the essential ingredients in *The Origins of English Financial Markets: Investment and Speculation before the South Sea Bubble* (Cambridge: Cambridge University Press, 2009), 2.

24. Douglass North and Barry Weingast, "Constitutions and Commitment: The Evolution of Institutions Governing Public Choice in Seventeenth-Century England," *Journal of Economic History* 49 (1989); Stasavage, *Public Debt.*

25. The discourse fundamentally changed after the South Sea Bubble, which I will briefly address in the epilogue.

26. In choosing not to limit the Financial Revolution to the 1690s, I follow in the footsteps of Henry Roseaveare, who noted that "seventeenth-century England had laboured long to produce a radical transformation of it financial system." See *The Financial Revolution, 1660–1760* (London: Longman, 1991), 3.

27. By using the term *English Financial Revolution* I do not rule out the existence of other financial revolutions—there were indeed financial revolutions both before and after. For example, James D. Tracy claims that the Habsburg Netherlands experienced a financial revolution in the sixteenth century—see *A Financial Revolution in the Habsburg Netherlands: Renten and Renteniers in the County of Holland, 1515–1565* (Berkeley: University of California Press, 1985)—while John H. Monroe dates an even earlier financial revolution to the Middle Ages in "The Medieval Origins of the Financial Revolution: Usury, *Rentes,* and Negotiability," *International History Review* 25 (2003): 505–562. Richard Sylla locates yet another financial revolution in the last decades of the eighteenth century in the United States in "Hamilton and the Federalist Financial Revolution, 1789–1795," *New York Journal of American History* 2 (2004): 32–39.

28. See, for example, David Armitage, *The Ideological Origins of the British Empire* (Cambridge: Cambridge University Press, 2000); Tony Claydon, *Europe and the Making of England, 1660–1760* (Cambridge: Cambridge University Press, 2007); Alison Games, *The Web of Empire: English Cosmopolitans in an Age of Expansion, 1560–1660* (Oxford: Oxford University Press, 2008); and Jack P. Greene and Philip D. Morgan, eds., *Atlantic History: A Critical Appraisal* (Oxford: Oxford University Press, 2009).

29. Erik S. Reinert, "Emulating Success: Contemporary Views of the Dutch Economy before 1800," in *The Political Economy of the Dutch Republic,* ed. Oscar Gelderblom, 19–39 (Farnham: Ashgate, 2009). Steve Pincus traces out

how the English were careful to implement only such policies that made its economy "more Dutch than Spanish" (*1688*, 51).

30. Neal, "How It All Began," 123. While the Dutch pioneered some important financial mechanisms, such as *renten*—Tracy, *Financial Revolution*—and certain forms of derivatives trading—Oscar Gelderblom and Joost Jonker, "Amsterdam as the Cradle of Modern Futures Trading and Options Trading, 1550–1650," in *The Origins of Value: The Financial Innovations that Created Modern Capital Markets*, ed. William N. Goetzmann and K. Geert Rouwenhorst, 189–205 (Oxford: Oxford University Press, 2005)—the Dutch financial revolution was much more focused on private finance than public finance. Oscar Gelderblom and Joost Jonker, "Completing a Financial Revolution: The Finance of the Dutch East India Trade and the Rise of the Amsterdam Capital Market, 1595–1612," *Journal of Economic History* 64 (2004): 641–672. Additionally, as Marjolein 't Hart points out, the Bank of Amsterdam was such a fundamentally different institution from the Bank of England that it can hardly be viewed as the latter's inspiration; see "'The Devil or the Dutch': Holland's Impact on the Financial Revolution in England, 1643–1694," *Parliaments, Estates and Representation* 11 (1991): 51.

31. For a discussion of this characteristic of credit, albeit in a later period, see Will Slauter, "Forward-Looking Statements: News and Speculation in the Age of the American Revolution," *Journal of Modern History* 81 (2009): 759–792.

1. The Scarcity of Money Problem and the Birth of English Political Economy

1. The so-called General Crisis of the Seventeenth Century had a complex impact on England. It brought widespread unemployment and poverty, but also changes paving the way towards the emergence of England as a world power. For a recent account of the *General Crisis*, see Jonathan S. Dewald, "Crisis, Chronology, and the Shape of European Social History," *American Historical Review* 113 (2008): 1031–1052. See also Keith Wrightson, *Earthly Necessities: Economic Lives in Early Modern Britain* (New Haven, CT: Yale University Press, 2000).

2. Modern economic theory predicts that prices, wages, interest rates, and rents would self-adjust when the quantity of money grows slower than economic activity. Historian B. E. Supple points out that because prices, wages, interest rates, and rents were often dictated by long-term customary contracts and tradition, significant friction and stickiness prevented markets from adjusting. A shortage of silver, therefore, had the capacity of preventing transactions and generating a great deal of unemployment and dislocation. *Commercial Crisis and Change in England, 1600–1642: A Study in*

the Instability of a Mercantile Economy (Cambridge: Cambridge University Press, 1959), 177.

3. Appleby, *Economic Thought and Ideology*, 199.

4. Rice Vaughan, *A discourse of coin and coinage: the first invention, use, matter, forms, proportions and differences, ancient & modern: with the advantages and disadvantages of the rise or fall thereof, in our own or neighbouring nations: and the reasons. Together with a short account of our Common law therein. As also tables of the value of all sorts of pearls, diamonds, gold, silver, and other metals* (London, 1675), 71.

5. Craig Muldrew generates these figures by synthesizing statistics from a number of historians in *Economy of Obligation*, 100.

6. Eric Kerridge, *Trade and Banking in Early Modern England* (Manchester: Manchester University Press, 1988), 99.

7. Chris Briggs, *Credit and Village: Society in Fourteenth-Century England* (Oxford: Oxford University Press, 2009).

8. Gerard Malynes, *The center of the circle of commerce. Or, a refutation of a treatise, intituled The circle of commerce, or the ballance of trade, lately published by E.M.* (London, 1623), i–ii.

9. Neal Wood, *Foundations of Political Economy: Some Early Tudor Views on State and Society* (Berkeley: University of California Press, 1994); Andrea Finkelstein, *The Grammar of Profit: The Price Revolution in Intellectual Context* (Leiden: Brill, 2006); and Paul Slack, "Material Progress and the Challenge of Affluence in Seventeenth-Century England," *Economic History Review* 62 (2009): 576–603, point to the presence of an Aristotelian-influenced discourse on political economy in England as early as the sixteenth century. However, as Slack points out, "it is only from the 1620s that we can identify something that looks recognizable as an English political economy, with its own founding texts, organizing concepts, and ways of thinking" ("Material Progress," 585). It is, of course, possible to point to an even earlier political economic tradition in the fourteenth century that contained many of the same Aristotelian-inspired ideas. See Joel Kaye, *Economy and Nature in the Fourteenth Century: Money, Market Exchange, and the Emergence of Scientific Thought* (Cambridge: Cambridge University Press, 1998).

10. While most commentators use Malynes, Misselden, and Mun to ridicule pre-Humean political economy, a number of scholars have rejected this approach and considered these thinkers in the proper context of the 1620s crisis. See, for example, William D. Grampp, "The Liberal Elements in English Mercantilism," *Quarterly Journal of Economics* 66 (1952): 465–501; R. W. K. Hinton, "The Mercantile System in the Time of Thomas Mun," *Economic History Review* 7 (1955): 277–290; and J. D. Gould, "The Trade Crisis of the Early 1620's and English Economic Thought," *Journal of Economic History* 15 (1955): 121–133.

11. Adam Smith, *An Inquiry into the Nature and Causes of the Wealth of Nations*, ed. E. Cannan (Chicago: University of Chicago Press, [1776] 1976), 450. John Stuart Mill seconded this reading claiming that early seventeenth-century thinkers believed that "whatever tended to heap up money or bullion in a country added to its wealth." *Principles of Political Economy* (London: Parker and Son, 1852), vol. I, 2–3. Jacob Viner reiterates that they believed "in the desirability of an indefinite accumulation of . . . precious metals." "English Theories of Foreign Trade Before Adam Smith," *Journal of Political Economy*, 38 (1930), 264.

12. While Richard H. Britnell, *The Commercialisation of English society, 1000–1500* (Cambridge: Cambridge University Press, 1993) and Christopher Dyer, *Standards of Living in the Later Middle Ages: Social Change in England, 1200–1500* (Cambridge: Cambridge University Press, 1989) claim that English society was already highly commercialized by the fourteenth century, Keith Wrightson cautions that England was primarily rural by the fourteenth century. The truly transformative commercialization, he argues, occurred between the turn of the sixteenth century and the Civil War, when England went from a relatively limited commercial society, in which "Most of the population . . . had limited involvement with larger markets as either producers or consumers," to a more integrated market society in which "many rural households were linked as producers, or as consumers, or as both, to England's major cities" (*Earthly Necessities*, 108–109, 175).

13. R. B. Outhwaite estimates that the price index (base period between 1451 and 1475) stood at 298 in 1561, 527 in 1601, and 687 in 1651; see *Inflation in Tudor and early Stuart England* (London: Macmillan, 1969), 10.

14. C. G. A. Clay estimates that the share of people in England living in urban areas exceeding five thousand people increased from 5.5 percent in 1520 to 8 percent in 1600 and 13.5 percent by 1670; see *Economic Expansion and Social Change: England 1500–1700, Vol. I* (Cambridge: Cambridge University Press, 1984).

15. While the sheep enclosures undoubtedly displaced many people, it should be noted that much of the land affected by this wave of enclosures had already been abandoned during the aftermath of the Black Death. J. R. Wordie estimates that approximately 45 percent of England's cultivable area had already been enclosed by 1500 in "The Chronology of English Enclosure, 1500–1914," *Economic History Review* 36 (1983): 485–505.

16. Charles Wilson, *England's Apprenticeship, 1603–1763* (New York: St. Martin's Press, 1965), 25; Wordie, "Chronology of English Enclosure," 492.

17. Robert P. Brenner, "Agrarian Class Structure and Economic Development in Pre-Industrial Europe," in *The Brenner Debate: Agrarian Class Structure and Economic Development in Pre-Industrial Europe*, ed. T. H. Ashton and C. H. E. Philpin, 10–63 (Cambridge: Cambridge University Press, 1985);

J. M. Neeson, *Commoners: Common Right, Enclosure and Social Change in England, 1700–1820* (Cambridge: Cambridge University Press, 1993).

18. Francis Bacon, "Advice to the King, Touching Mr. Sutton's Estate," in *The Letters and the Life of Francis Bacon*, ed. James Spedding, 252 (London: Longman, Green, Reader, and Dyer, 1868).

19. As petrified as people were of vagrancy culture, they were in equal measure tantalized by it. The fact that the vagrants fashioned their own language, sociability, hierarchy, and norms, and dared to confront and subvert the ideals and morals promoted by Puritan social reformers made them fascinating to the rest of society. Paul Slack, *Poverty and Policy in Tudor and Stuart England* (London: Longman, 1988), 91–107.

20. A. L. Beier, "Social Problems in Elizabethan London," *Journal of Interdisciplinary History* 9 (1978): 204–205. Slack estimates similar relative growth rates of the London population to the number of vagrants in *Poverty and Policy*, 93.

21. The Tudor Poor Laws consisted of a variety of legislations introduced during the course of half a century. See Chapters 3 and 4 in Braddick, *State Formation*; and Paul Slack, *From Reformation to Improvement: Public Welfare in Early Modern England* (Oxford: Clarendon Press, 1999).

22. As Margot Todd shows, "The sanctification of work, the exaltation of discipline and the drive to repress idleness and frivolity have been properly labeled hallmarks of Puritanism"; see *Christian Humanism and the Puritan Social Order* (Cambridge: Cambridge University Press, 1987), 147.

23. Edgar S. Furniss, *The Position of the Laborer in a System of Nationalism: A Study in the Labor Theories of the Later English Mercantilists* (New York: Sentry Press, 1965).

24. While Supple's *Commercial Crisis and Change* highlights the importance of the textile industry for England's prosperity, Joan Thirsk, *Economic Policy and Projects: The Development of a Consumer Society in Early Modern England* (Oxford: Clarendon Press, 1978), notes that early Stuart economic expansion cannot be adequately explained without reference to various new projects, such as pins and starch making.

25. Edward Misselden, *Free Trade. Or, the meanes to make trade florish. Wherein, the causes of the decay of trade in this Kingdome, are discouered: And the remedies also to remooue the same, are represented. The second edition with some addition* (London, 1622), 40.

26. Other manufacturing sectors, such as iron and glassmaking, and trading areas, such as the Levant and the Mediterranean, were also considered for their ability to bring in additional silver and thus ease the employment problem. But since the woolen industry comprised 75 percent of exports and the Low Countries and Northern Europe constituted 75 percent of London's cloth exports, other sectors and regions were of lesser concern. Robert F.

Brenner, *Merchants and Revolution: Commercial Change, Political Conflict, and London's Overseas Traders, 1550–1653* (London: Verso, 2003), 3.

27. Although James has traditionally been viewed as a reckless spender, recent scholarship suggests that he was "hardly more extravagant than his Tudor predecessors or his early modern contemporaries"; see John Cramsie, *Kingship and Crown Finance under James VI and I* (Suffolk: St. Edmundsbury Press, 2002), 40.

28. The military revolution pioneered new battlefield techniques that required better trained soldiers, horses bred for battle, increased use of firepower, and new types of fortifications. Although England managed to avoid large-scale land-based campaigns until the 1690s, the Stuarts spent large sums of money on expanding England's naval capacities. Braddick, *State Formation*, 202–213.

29. Walter Raleigh, "A Discourse of the Invention of Ships, Anchors, Compass, &c," in *The Works of Sir Walter Raleigh*, ed. Thomas Birch and William Oldys (Oxford: Oxford University Press, [1615] 1829), 8:325.

30. Wilson, *England's Apprenticeship*, 89.

31. After a famous debate in 1601, in which monopolies were blamed for breaching the liberties of the English, limiting production and trade, and deteriorating the quality of goods, Elizabeth acquiesced and removed a number of monopolies. David Harris Sacks, "The Countervailing of Benefits: Monopoly, Liberty and Benevolence in Elizabethan England," in *Tudor Political Culture*, ed. Dale Hoak, 7–66 (Cambridge: Cambridge University Press, 1995).

32. Slack, *From Reformation to Improvement*, 53.

33. Christopher Hill estimates that there were approximately seven hundred monopoly patents by 1621 in *The Century of Revolution, 1603–1714* (New York: W.W. Norton, [1961] 1980), 25–26.

34. John Ulric Nef, *Industry and Government in France and England, 1540–1640* (Ithaca, NY: Cornell University Press, 1964), 129.

35. The proposal would have provided James with a guaranteed annual income of £200,000 in return for the abolishment of wardships and purveyance. Cramsie, *Kingship and Crown Finance*, 95.

36. The customs was a complicated mechanism levied on both imports and exports, raising between 30 and 40 percent of the state's total revenues. Michael Braddick, *The Nerves of State: Taxation and the Financing of the English State, 1558–1714* (Manchester: Manchester University Press, 1996), 49.

37. Theodore K. Raab, *Enterprise and Empire: Merchant and Gentry Investment in the Expansion of England, 1575–1630* (Cambridge, MA: Harvard University Press, 1967).

38. For a discussion of the intellectual backdrop to the early English colonization efforts, see David Armitage, *The Ideological Origins of the British Empire* (Cambridge: Cambridge University Press, 2000); and Andrew Fitzmaurice,

Humanism and America: An Intellectual History of English Colonisation, 1500–1625 (Cambridge: Cambridge University Press, 2003).

39. Kenneth R. Andrews, *Trade, Plunder, and Settlements: Maritime Enterprise and the Genesis of the British Empire, 1480–1630* (Cambridge: Cambridge University Press, 1984), 313–314.

40. John C. Appleby, "War, Politics, and Colonization, 1558–1625," in *The Oxford History of the British Empire Vol. 1, The Origins of Empire*, ed. Nicholas Canny, 64, 71, 73 (Oxford: Oxford University Press, 1998).

41. James Horn, "Tobacco Colonies: The Shaping of English Society in the Seventeenth-Century Chesapeake," in *The Origins of Empire*, ed. Nicholas Canny, 183 (Oxford: Oxford University Press, 1998).

42. In addition to Virginia and Barbados, English settlers were also engaged in the relatively successful colonization of Bermuda, St. Kitts, Nevis, Antigua, and New England, as well as the failed projects in Guiana, the Amazon delta, and Newfoundland.

43. Nuala Zahedieh estimates that between 70 and 90 percent of purchases in India were made with bullion in "Credit, Risk and Reputation in Late Seventeenth-Century Colonial Trade," in *Merchant Organization and Maritime Trade in the North Atlantic, 1660–1815*, ed. Olaf Uwe Janzen, 401 (St. John's, Newfoundland: International Maritime Economic History Association, 1998).

44. Clay, *Economic Expansion and Social Change, V. II*, 207.

45. Ibid.

46. Kerridge, *Trade and Banking*; Muldrew, *Economy of Obligation*.

47. Muldrew, *Economy of Obligation*, 95.

48. According to Muldrew, "every household in the country, from those of paupers to the royal household, was to some degree enmeshed within the increasingly complicated webs of credit" (*Economy of Obligation*, 95).

49. Ibid., 101.

50. Robert Ashton, *The Crown and the Money Market, 1603–1640* (Oxford: Clarendon Press, 1960), 1–30.

51. An inland bill of exchange operated similarly to its international counterpart and was mostly used by wholesale traders in London and by large landowners transferring rental income to London. Kerridge, *Trade and Banking*, 45–75.

52. Ashton, *Crown and the Money Market*, 16.

53. James Steven Rogers, *The Early History of the Law of Bills and Notes: A Study of the Origins of Anglo-American Commercial Law* (Cambridge: Cambridge University Press, 1995).

54. This is not to suggest that merchants did not habitually assign bills and bonds to other merchants as payment or to cancel other debts. Yet, Kerridge clarifies that "full negotiability had not been achieved" because of legal restrictions; see Kerridge, *Trade and Banking*, 71.

55. Ashton, *Crown and the Money Market*, 5.

56. Ibid., 24–25; R. H. Tawney, *Business and Politics Under James I: Lionel Cranfield as Merchant and Minister* (Cambridge: Cambridge University Press, 1958).

57. Ashton, *Crown and the Money Market*, 2.

58. In addition to the destabilizing effects of war, English cloth exports were further hurt by the widespread German debasement. This so-called *Kipper-und-Wipper-Zeit* increased the price of foreign imports, making it more difficult for English merchants to sell their goods on the continent. Supple, *Commercial Crisis and Change*, 76.

59. Ibid., 174.

60. Gerard Malynes, *The maintenance of free trade, according to the three essentiall parts of traffique; namely, commodities, moneys, and exchange of moneys, by bills of exchanges for other countries, or, an answer to a treatise of free trade, or the meanes to make trade flourish, lately published* (London, 1622)., 2; Thomas Mun, *A Discourse of Trade, From England unto the East Indies: Answering to diverse Objections which are usually made against the same* (London, 1621), 3; Misselden, *Free Trade*, 28.

61. Gerard Malynes, or de Malynes (d. 1641) was born in Antwerp but spent most of his life in England. In addition to his work as assay master and trade commissioner, he engaged in a large number of merchant ventures, pursued mining projects in Yorkshire and Durham, and cooperated with William Cockayne in an attempt to mint lead farthings to expand the availability of small denomination coin. The latter venture landed him in Fleet Prison in 1609. For further biographical details, see Finkelstein, *Harmony and Balance*; and E. A. J. Johnson, *Predecessors of Adam Smith* (New York: Augustus M. Kelley, [1937] 1965)

62. Malynes, *The maintenance of free trade*.

63. Gerard Malynes, *A Treatise of the Canker of Englands Common wealth. Divided into three parts: Wherein the Author imitating the rule of good Phisitions, First, declareth the disease. Secondarily, sheweth the efficient cause thereof. Lastly, a remedy for the same* (London, 1601), 14.

64. Edward Misselden (d. 1654) gained prominence as a merchant in the Merchant Adventurers' Company. He later served as deputy-governor of this company at Delft and also negotiated on behalf of the East India Company with authorities at The Hague. For further bibliographical details, see Finkelstein, *Harmony and Balance*; and Johnson, *Predecessors of Adam Smith*.

65. While Misselden highlighted the trade deficit in *The Circle of Commerce. Or, The Balance of Trade, in defence of free trade: Opposed to Malynes Little Fish and his Great Whale, and poised against them in Scale. Wherein also, Exchanges in generall are considered: and therein the whole Trade of this Kingdome with forraine Countires, is digested into a Balance of Trade, for the benefite of the Publique* (London, 1623), he emphasized the mint ratio

between silver and gold in *Free Trade*, 11, as the primary cause of the out-flow of money. Since silver was undervalued vis-à-vis gold at the mint, silver flowed out of the country and gold flowed in. However, since silver was the primary monetary metal it meant that the quantity of money in circulation fell. The low price for silver at the mint also led to many people keeping their silver in plate.

66. Misselden, *Free Trade*, 13, 14, 18, 35, 73. Malynes, in the *Maintenance of Free Trade*, agreed with Misselden about a series of causes for the outflow of money, such as excessive imports, the asymmetric East India trade, and the continental wars. Misselden, however, accused Malynes of plagiarism. See Misselden, *Circle of Commerce*, 30.

67. Misselden, *Free Trade*, 77, 95, 98, 101; Misselden, *Circle of Commerce*, 137.

68. Thomas Mun (d. 1641) made his fortune as a merchant trading primarily to Italy. In 1619, he was elected director of the East India Company. He managed important diplomatic concerns for the company, as well as audited the accounts of many members. For further biographical details, see Finkelstein, *Harmony and Balance*; Johnson, *Predecessors of Adam Smith*.

69. Mun, *A Discourse of Trade*, 50–51.

70. Thomas Mun, *England's Treasure by Forraign Trade. Or, The Balance of our Forraign Trade is The Rule of our Treasure* (London, 1664), 99.

71. Mun, *Discourse of Trade*, 55.

72. Mun, *England's Treasure by Forraign Trade*, 89. Permission to export bullion was particularly important to the East India Company, which Mun represented, as their business relied on using silver to purchase raw materials and unfinished goods that could be processed and finished in England and then exported at a profit.

73. Mun, *England's Treasure by Forraign Trade*, 35.

74. Aristotle, *Politics*, ed. Stephen Everson (Cambridge: Cambridge University Press, 1988), 167.

75. Aristotle, *Nicomachean Ethics*, trans. Martin Ostwald (New York: Macmillan Publishing Company, 1962), 124.

76. Ibid., 125.

77. Hinting at an early version of Montesquieu's notion of *doux commerce*, Aristotle points out that that the state "erects a sanctuary of the Graces" in the market place in order to promote the kinds of reciprocal interactions necessary for justice and sociability (ibid., 124).

78. Ibid., 127.

79. Keith Thomas, *The Ends of Life: Roads to Fulfillment in Early Modern England* (Oxford: Oxford University Press, 2009), 16.

80. Finkelstein, *Grammar of Profit*, 12. In describing this worldview, Neil Wood notes, "From their perspective social order was and should be inegalitarian, dependent on a hierarchy of ranks and stations from the lowest to the

highest, each with its differential duties and privileges. Every member of society of whatever rank should industriously pursue his vocation and strive in friendship and cooperation with fellow citizens to subordinate particular advantage to the promotion of the common interest" (*Foundations of Political Economy*, 4).

81. Malynes, *Maintenance of Free Trade*, 2.
82. Gerard Malynes, *Saint George for England, Allegorically described* (London, 1601), 16.
83. Ibid.
84. See Appleby, *Economic Thought and Ideology*, chap. 3.
85. Thomas, *Ends of Life*, 111.
86. Misselden, *Free Trade*, 12.
87. Aristotle, *Politics*, 15.
88. Malynes, *Saint George for England*, 42.
89. Ibid., ix.
90. Ibid., 45.
91. Aristotle clarifies that "external goods have a limit, like any other instrument, and all things useful are useful for a purpose, and where there is too much of them they must either do harm, or at any rate be of no use, to their possessors" (*Politics*, 157).
92. Ibid., 11.
93. Mun, *Discourse of Trade*, 48.
94. Ibid., 49.
95. Mun, *England's Treasure by Forraign Trade*, 31.
96. Malynes, *Saint George for England*, xi.
97. Malynes, *Maintenance of Free Trade*, 4.
98. Mary Poovey points out that "the intrinsic worth of precious metals was to be the ground of value, and this worth both reflected and reflected upon the authority of the king, whose power, in turn, derived from God and was the foundation for the nation's greatness"; see *A History of the Modern Fact: Problems of Knowledge in the Sciences of Wealth and Society* (Chicago: University of Chicago Press, 1998), 72.
99. Mun, *Discourse of Trade*, 1–3.
100. Mun, *England's Treasure by Forraign Trade*, 180.
101. Malynes, *Treatise of the Canker of England's Common Wealth*, 5–6.
102. Gerard Malynes, *Consvetvdo, vel lex mercatoria, or The Ancient Law-merchant. Diuided into three parts: According to the essentiall parts of trafficke. Necessarie for all statesmen, iudges, magistrates, temporall and ciuile lawyers, mint-men, merchants, marriners, and all others negotiating in all places of the world* (London, 1622), 253.
103. Bernard Davanzati, *A Discourse upon Coins*, trans. John Toland (London, [1588] 1696), 18.

104. C. George Caffentiz, among others, notes a vibrant "conceptual commerce between medicine and economic thought" in "Medical Metaphors and Monetary Strategies in the Political Economy of Locke and Berkeley," *History of Political Economy* 35 (2003): 204. See also Alain Clément and Ludovic Desmedt, "Medicine and Economics in Pre-Classical Economics," in *Open Economics: Economics in Relation to other Disciplines*, ed. Richard Arena, Sheila Dow, and Matthias Klaes, 108–124 (London: Routledge, 2009).

105. Malynes, *The center of the circle of commerce*, i–ii.

106. Vaughan, *A discourse of coin and coinage*, 58.

107. Ralph Maddison, *Englands Looking in and out. Presented to the High Court of Parliament now assembled* (London, 1640), 12.

108. Ralph Maddison, *Great Britains remembrancer, looking in and out. Tending to the increase of the monies of the Commonwealth. Presented to his highness the Lord protector, and to the High court of Parliament now assembled* (London, 1655), 12.

109. Ibid., 21.

110. Malynes, *Maintenance of Free Trade*, 2; Mun, *England's Treasure by Forraign Trade*, 72.

111. Mun, *England's Treasure by Forraign Trade*, 42; Misselden, *Free Trade*, 118; Malynes, *Maintenance of Free Trade*, 98.

112. Mun, *England's Treasure by Forraign Trade*, 42.

113. Misselden, *Free Trade*, 118.

114. Malynes, *Maintenance of Free Trade*, 98.

115. Ibid.

116. Ibid., 102–103.

117. Mun argued that loans were absolutely central to the success of the merchants, in particular young merchants and shopkeepers starting without any capital of their own. Malynes and Misselden also advocated for the establishment of a network of Lombard banks—or pawnshops—in London and in the textile districts. By extending credit to the poor, it would be possible to encourage the labor of the poor and "set on worke many fatherlesse children that are ready to sterve" (Misselden, *Free Trade*, 118).

118. Malynes, *Lex Mercatoria*, 254; Mun, *England's Treasure by Forraign Trade*, 72.

119. Paul Slack notes that while the neo-Aristotelians were influential intellectually, they had little immediate impact on government policy in "Material Progress," 586.

120. Supple, *Commercial Crisis and Change*, 190.

121. Robert Cotton, *A Speech made by Sir Robert Cotton, Knight, and Baronet. Before the Lords of His Majesty's most Honorable Privy Council, At the Concil-Table: Being Thither called to deliver his Opinion. Touching the Alteration of Coin* (London, [1626] 1679), 4.

122. Henry Peacham, *The Worth of a Penny, or, A Caution to Keep Money. With the causes of the scarcity and misery of the want thereof, in these hard and mercilesse Times: As also how to save it, in our Diet, Apparrell, Recreations, etc. And also what honest Courses men in want may take to live* (London, [1642] 1664), 5.

123. Peacham, *Worth of a Penny*, 3.

124. These authors borrowed heavily from the 1620s debates, the most extreme case being that of Thomas Roe publishing Robert Cotton's speech to Parliament under the title *Sir Thomas Rowe's Speech at the Councel Table about the Alteration of the Coyn* (1640) and Maddison's reproduction of lengthy passages from Malynes without attribution in *Englands Looking in and out* (London, 1640).

2. The Alchemical Foundations of Credit

1. In exploring the seventeenth-century Cosmographical revolution, historian of science Alexandre Koyré described it as bringing forth the disappearance of "the conception of the world as a finite, closed, and hierarchically ordered whole . . . and its replacement by an indefinite and even infinite universe." *From the Closed World to the Infinite Universe* (Baltimore, MD: The Johns Hopkins University Press, 1957), 2.

2. Reinhart Koselleck, *Futures Past: On the Semantics of Historical Time*, trans. Keith Tribe (New York: Columbia University Press, 2004), 22.

3. The Baconian influence on economic thinking has been well documented by, for example, Letwin, *The Origins of Scientific Economics*; and Redman, *Rise of Political Economy*. Alchemical thinking, on the other hand, which played an important role in the Scientific Revolution—see, for example, Bruce T. Moran, *Distilling Knowledge: Alchemy, Chemistry, and the Scientific Revolution* (Cambridge, MA: Harvard University Press, 2005)—has rarely been acknowledged as having influenced political economy. The exception being Smith, *The Business of Alchemy*.

4. Walter W. Woodward, *Prospero's America: John Winthrop, Jr., Alchemy and the Creation of New England Culture, 1606–1676* (Chapel Hill: University of North Carolina Press, 2010), 22. For discussions of alchemy's mixed spiritual and utilitarian aims, see for example, B. J. T. Dobbs, *The Foundations of Newton's Alchemy or "The Hunting of the Greene Lyon"* (Cambridge: Cambridge University Press, 1975); J. T. Young, *Faith, Medical Alchemy and Natural Philosophy: Johan Moriaen, Reformed Intelligencer, and the Hartlib Circle* (Aldershot: Ashgate, 1998); Harkness, *Jewel House*; Leng, *Benjamin Worsley*; and Ted McCormick, *William Petty*.

5. Tara Nummedal shows that by the end of the sixteenth century, alchemical knowledge had become a commodity sought primarily by projectors

interested in immediate profit in "Practical Alchemy and Commercial Exchange in the Holy Roman Empire," in *Merchants and Marvels: Commerce, Science, and Art in Early Modern Europe*, ed. Pamela H. Smith and Paula Findlen, 204 (London: Routledge, 2002). For an example of the importance of secrecy in the alchemical community, see Lawrence M. Principe, *The Aspiring Adept: Robert Boyle and his Alchemical Quest* (Princeton, NJ: Princeton University Press, 1998).

6. In *The Business of Alchemy*, Pamela Smith shows that Johann Joachim Becher (1635–1682), a German polymath who authored important works on political economy as well as carried out allegedly successful alchemical transmutations, considered alchemy as a helpful device in facilitating a more general improvement process. Alchemy for Becher, as it was for the Hartlibians, was thus both a framework for understanding nature and society and an art capable of expanding the money stock. While the exact relationship between Becher and the Hartlib Circle has not been fully mapped out, Smith shows that they were aware of each other's writings and projects.

7. Richard Drayton, *Nature's Government: Science, Imperial Britain, and the 'Improvement' of the World* (New Haven: Yale University Press, 2000), 54.

8. The list of continental regents who patronized alchemists was long and distinguished, including Cardinal Richelieu, Queen Christina, Christian IV, Gustav Adolphus, Rudolph II, Ferdinand III, and Leopold I. Robin Briggs, "The Academie Royale des Sciences and the Pursuit of Utility," *Past and Present* 131 (1991): 40–41; Susanna Åkerman, *Queen Christina of Sweden and Her Circle: The Transformation of a Philosophical Libertine* (Leiden: Brill, 1991); Allison Coudert, *Alchemy: The Philosopher's Stone* (Boulder, CO: Shambhala, 1980), 199–200; E. J. Holmyard, *Alchemy* (New York: Dover, 1990), 15; R. J. W. Evans, *Rudolf II and His World: A Study in Intellectual History, 1577–1612* (Oxford: Clarendon Press, 1973); Smith, *Business of Alchemy*, 17, 179, 178.

9. George Ripley dedicated *The Compound of Alchemy; or the Twelve Gates Leading to the Discovery of the Philosopher's Stone* to Edward IV. See Michael White; *Isaac Newton: The Last Sorcerer* (Reading, PA: Helix Books, 1997), 115.

10. Frances A. Yates, *Occult Philosophy in the Elizabethan Age* (London: Routledge, 1979).

11. Holmyard, *Alchemy*, 210.

12. J. Andrew Mendelsohn, "Alchemy and Politics in England 1649–1665," *Past and Present* 135 (1992): 30–78.

13. Eileen Reeves is one of the few commentators who have highlighted Malynes's alchemical discussion in *Lex Mercatoria*; see "As Good as Gold: The Mobile Earth and Early Modern Economics," *Journal of the Warburg and Courtauld Institutes* 62 (1999): 126–166.

14. For a recent summary of the roots of seventeenth-century alchemical knowledge, see Woodward's *Prospero's America*, 16–42.

15. Tara Nummedal quotes Paracelsus proclaiming that he sought information from "barbers, bathers, learned doctors, wives, those who make a habit of black magic, from alchemists, at cloisters, from nobles and commoners, from the clever and the simple" in *Alchemy and Authority in the Holy Roman Empire* (Chicago: University of Chicago Press), 31.

16. That metals grew inside the earth was proven by the fact that metal ores had a treelike shape—the Tree of Diana—and that there were many confirmed reports of new discoveries of precious metals in previously depleted mines. Thomas Heton, *Some account of mines, and the advantages of them to this kingdom. With an appendix relating to the mine-adventure in Wales* (London, 1707), 18–19, 111–115.

17. Arthur O. Lovejoy, *The Great Chain of Being: A Study of the History of an Idea* (Cambridge, MA: Harvard University Press, [1936] 1964).

18. John Henry, "Magic and Science in Sixteenth and Seventeenth Centuries," in *Companion to the History of Modern Science*, ed. R. C. Colby, G. N. Cantor, and M. J. S. Hodge, 584 (London: Routledge, 1990).

19. Ibid., 584.

20. Moran, *Distilling Knowledge*, 26.

21. Ibid., 29.

22. Malynes, *Lex Mercatoria*, 255.

23. Ibid.

24. Ibid. Bruce Moran notes that the seven metals correspond to the seven planets, which included the sun and the moon in *Distilling Knowledge*, 68.

25. Malynes, *Lex Mercatoria*, 256.

26. Charles Webster points out that the new scientific thinking invested mankind with the capacity to manipulate the nature–universe complex for its own benefit. The understanding of natural and cosmic forces "could be turned to operative effect, opening up for man the possibility of achieving by natural means what had hitherto been regarded as miraculous . . . All of this was to be attained by the skillful assistance, imitation, or direction of nature"; see Charles Webster, *From Paracelsus to Newton: Magic and the Making of Modern Science* (Cambridge: Cambridge University Press, 1982), 58.

27. Moran, *Distilling Knowledge*, 29, 70–71.

28. Keith Thomas, *Religion and the Decline of Magic* (New York: Oxford University Press, 1971), 269.

29. Malynes, *Lex Mercatoria*, 256.

30. Ibid.

31. Ibid., 257.

32. Ibid.

33. Ibid., 258.

34. Ibid.

35. Basing his analysis on some eighty coins allegedly produced from alchemical transmutations, Vladimir Karpenko has shown that there are numerous ways to make it appear as though a successful transmutation of base metals into gold has occurred. An apparent transmutation could simply be the result of a deceitful manipulation, wherein a precious metal was secretly introduced to the content of the crucible during the experiment. The appearance of gold could also be produced by isolating the precious metal from an alloy or a mixture of compounds. The third method involves alloying the precious metal with common ones, making it look like there is a greater quantity of gold than when the experiment commenced. The alchemist could also use a technique called cementation, in which a layered composite material was obtained that could pass as gold as long as the outer layer consisted of gold. Similarly, alchemists could also fool people by treating the surface area of a common metal with gold. Finally, alchemists could dupe their audiences by finding ways to treat base metals so that they acquired a golden color. See Vladimir Karpenko, "Coins and Medals Made of Alchemical Metal," *Ambix* 35 (1988): 66–67; and "The Chemistry and Metallurgy of Transmutation," *Ambix* 39 (1992): 47–62.

36. Heton, *Some account of mines*, 127.

37. Holmyard, *Alchemy*, 259–267.

38. As Steven Shapin and Simon Schaffer point out in *Leviathan and the Air-Pump*, 55–56, in order for a matter of fact to be established it was important that the experiment was witnessed by the relevant community so that the results could be "attested by the testimony of eye witnesses."

39. Alan Gabbey, "Spinoza's Natural Science and Methodology," in *The Cambridge Companion to Spinoza*, ed. Don Garrett, 151–152 (Cambridge: Cambridge University Press, 1996).

40. The famous Cambridge Platonist Henry More, for example, claimed that the Hartlibians were doing nothing but laying the "ground work of Luciferan knowledge." Quoted in Mark Greengrass, Michael Leslie, and Timothy Raylor, eds., *Samuel Hartlib and Universal Reformation: Studies in Intellectual Communication* (Cambridge: Cambridge University Press, 1994), 20.

41. Peacham, *Worth of a Penny*, 13.

42. Cotton, *A Speech made by Sir Robert Cotton*, 4.

43. Vaughan, *A discourse of coin and coinage*, 10.

44. Ibid., 6. Bruce Moran shows that the condemnation of alchemy as a form of forgery can be traced back at least to the fourteenth century in *Distilling Knowledge*, 31–32.

45. Ibid., 35.

46. Ibid., 6.

47. Paul Slack notes that the Hartlibians were responsible for generating "confidence in linear material progress" in "Material Progress," 588–589. See also

James Jacob, "The Political Economy of Science in Seventeenth-Century England," in *The Politics of Western Science, 1640–1990*, ed. Margaret C. Jacob, 19-46 (Atlantic Highlands: Humanities Press, 1994).

48. Charles Webster, *The Great Instauration: Science, Medicine, and Reform 1626–1660*, (Oxford: Peter Lang, 2002), xxi.

49. William Eamon notes that the "Baconian ideology of openness appealed to the English Puritans because of its ethical component. The gifts of inventors and discoverers were God-given, they argued, and should therefore be used to benefit everyone"; see *Science and the Secrets of Nature: Books of Secrets in Medieval and Early Modern Culture* (Princeton, NJ: Princeton University Press, 1994), 319.

50. Quoted in McCormick, *William Petty*, 57.

51. Although Hartlib authored a number of tracts himself, his primary role was to coordinate, publish, and disseminate the group's various intellectual, social, and technological pursuits. Many of the books and pamphlets published by Hartlib were the results of collaborations. See Kevin Dunn, "Milton among the Monopolists: *Areopagitica*, Intellectual Property and the Hartlib Circle," in *Samuel Hartlib and Universal Reformation: Studies in Intellectual Communication*, ed. Mark Greengrass, Michael Leslie, and Timothy Raylor, 183 (Cambridge: Cambridge University Press, 1994).

52. For the cosmopolitan nature of the alchemical project, see Margaret C. Jacob, *Strangers Nowhere in the World: The Rise of Cosmopolitanism in Early Modern Europe* (Philadelphia: University of Pennsylvania Press, 2006), chap. 2.

53. Woodward, *Prospero's America*, 3.

54. While there was little in the new science or alchemical tradition that was necessarily or logically radical or Puritan, the vision of spiritual, moral, and social progress that Bacon and the alchemical thinkers promoted resonated with the progressiveness of the new reform groups emerging at the end of the Civil War. Mendelsohn, "Alchemy and Politics," 37.

55. Peter Dear points out in *Revolutionizing the Sciences: European Knowledge and Its Ambitions, 1500–1700* (Princeton, NJ: Princeton University Press, 2001), that William Gilbert, physician to Elizabeth, published his views on the virtues of combining empirical, experimental, and utilitarian natural philosophy a few years prior to Bacon. Yet, it was Bacon's formulation of the basic philosophy of this new epistemic culture that had the greatest impact.

56. Harkness, *Jewel House*, 2.

57. As Mary Poovey points out, "Bacon's natural philosophical project was a royal undertaking not only because it required massive funding but also because it was intended to supply knowledge that would reinforce the king's power to decide what measures would serve his people's interests" (*History of the Modern Fact*, 102).

58. Francis Bacon, *Proemium, of the Interpretation of Nature*, quoted in John Henry, *Knowledge is Power: How Magic, the Government and an Apocalyptic Vision Inspired Francis Bacon to Create Modern Science* (Cambridge: Icon Books, 2002), 2.

59. Eamon, *Science and the Secrets of Nature*, 319.

60. Francis Bacon, *The New Organon*, ed. Lisa Jardine and Michael Silverthorne (Cambridge: Cambridge University Press, 2000), 66.

61. Bacon, *New Organon*, 99.

62. William R. Newman shows that alchemists anticipated Bacon's argument that art can improve on nature by some four centuries in "The Homunculus and His Forebears: Wonders of Art and Nature," in *Natural Particulars: Nature and the Disciplines in Renaissance Europe*, ed. Anthony Grafton and Nancy Siraisi, 324 (Cambridge, MA: MIT Press, 2000). Even though Bacon himself was deeply critical of the alchemical tradition, as Walter Woodward shows, "Bacon and the alchemists shared many fundamental assumptions." He continues, "Both Stressed the importance of experiment and observation of the natural world. Both wanted to free natural philosophy from the stultifying authority of the Scholastics; both stressed the utilitarian value of scientific investigation" (*Prospero's America*, 26).

63. Christopher Hill, *The World Turned Upside Down: Radical Ideas during the English Revolution* (London: Penguin, 1972).

64. Margaret C. Jacob, *Scientific Culture and the Making of the Industrial West* (New York: Oxford University Press, 1997), 51–57.

65. Gabriel Plattes, *A Description of the Famous Kingdome of Macaria; shewing its excellent government: Wherin The Inhabitants live in great Prosperity, Health, and Hapinesse; the King obeyed; the Nobles honoured; and all good men respected, vice punished, and virtue rewarded. An Example to other Nations. In a Dialogue between a Schollar and a Traveller* (London, 1641).

66. Gabriel Plattes, *A discovery of infinite treasure, hidden since the worlds beginning. Whereunto all men, of what degree soever, are friendly invited to be sharers with the discovered* (London, 1639), xiv.

67. Ibid., xv.

68. Plattes, *Kingdome of Macaria*, 11.

69. Plattes, *A discovery of infinite treasure*, ii.

70. Ibid., v.

71. Ibid.

72. Ibid., vi.

73. Ibid.

74. Ibid.

75. Ibid., ii.

76. Ibid.

77. Ibid., iv.

78. Lovejoy, *Great Chain of Being*, 101, 108.

79. Ibid., 109.

80. Both Finkelstein, *Harmony and Balance*, 213–214, and Slack, "Material Progress," 589, recognize the importance of infinitude to Hartlibian political economy.

81. Samuel Hartlib, *Cornu copia. A miscellanium of luciferous and most fructiferous experiments, observations, and discoveries, immethodically distributed; to be really demonstrated and communicated in all sincerity* (London, 1652); and Samuel Hartlib, *Samuel Hartlib his legacy of husbandry. Wherein are bequeathed to the Common-wealth of England, not onely Braband, and Flanders, but also many more outlandish and domestick experiments and secrets (of Gabriel Plats and others) never heretofore divulged in reference to universal husbandry. With a table shewing the general contents of sections of the several augmentations and enriching enlargements in this third edition* (London, 1655).

82. Hartlib, *Samuel Hartlib his legacy of husbandry.*

83. As if positive reinforcement was not enough, Plattes also suggested that non-improvers ought to be punished. Jacob, "Political Economy of Science," 24.

84. Cressy Dymock, *A discoverie for division or setting out of land, as to the best form published by S. Hartlib Esquire . . . And an essay to shew how all lands may be improved in a new way to become the ground of the inerease of trading and revenue to this Common-wealth* (London, 1653), 3.

85. Slack, *From Reformation to Improvement*, 77–92.

86. Samuel Hartlib, *Londons charity inlarged, stilling the orphans cry* (London, 1650), 10.

87. Ted McCormick shows that Petty's social, political, and economic ideas grew out of the Hartlib Circle's notion of improvement, in particular their emphasis on education, training, and employment of the poor (*William Petty*, 72).

88. William Petty, *The Advice of W.P. to Mr. Samuel Hartlib. For the Advancement of some particular Parts of Learning* (London,1648).

89. Slack, *From Reformation to Improvement*, 87–92.

90. Hartlib, *Londons charity inlarged*, 1.

91. Ibid., 2, 9.

92. Henry Robinson, *The office of adresses and encovnters: where all people of each rancke and quality may receive direction and advice for the most cheap and speedy way of attaining whatsoever they can lawfully desire. Or, the only course for poor people to get speedy employment, and to keep others from approaching poverty, for want of emploiment. To the multiplying of trade, the advancement of navigation, and establishing this famous city of London 'n a more plentifull and flourishing condition than ever, as is earnestly desired, and shall be diligently endeavoured by a wel-willer of hers* (London, 1650).

93. Samuel Hartlib, *An essay for advancement of husbandry-learning: or propositions for the errecting Colledge of husbandry; and in order thereunto, for the*

taking in of pupills or apprentices. And also friends or fellowes of the same
colledge or society (London, 1651), ii.

94. Hartlib, *Samuel Hartlib his legacy of husbandry*, 291.
95. Cheney Culpeper, *An essay upon Master W. Potters designe: concerning a
bank of lands to be erected throughout this common-wealth. Whereby lands
may be improved in a new way to become the ground for increase of trading,
and of publique and private revenue* (London, 1653), 28.
96. Ibid.
97. Ibid.
98. Leng, *Benjamin Worsley*; Steve Pincus, *Protestantism and Patriotism: Ideolo-
gies and the Making of English Foreign Policy, 1650–1668* (Cambridge: Cambridge University Press, 1996).
99. Henry Robinson, *Englands safety, in trades encrease. Most humbly presented
to the high court of Parliament* (London, 1641), 4–5.
100. Ibid., 8.
101. Worsley's arguments played an important role in the effort to implement the
Navigation Acts in 1651. For a full contextual discussion of the passing of
the Navigation Act and Worsley's role therein, see Charles Webster, "Benjamin Worsley: Engineering for Universal Reform from the Invisible College
to the Navigation Act," in *Samuel Hartlib and Universal Reformation: Studies in Intellectual Communication*, ed. Mark Greengrass, Michael Leslie, and
Timothy Raylor, 213-235 (Cambridge: Cambridge University Press, 1994);
Pincus, *Protestantism and Patriotism*; and Thomas Leng, "Conflict and Co-
Operation in the Discourse of Trade of Seventeenth-Century England," *Historical Journal* 48 (2005): 933–954.
102. John French, *The art of distillation* (London, 1667), 190.
103. Ibid., 193.
104. Ibid., 194. French proceeded to elaborate on various recipes for the "oyl of
gold," as well as on ways to make gold grow in the earth. To achieve the latter,
the alchemist must: "Take leaves of Gold, and bury them in the Earth which
looks towards the East, and let it be often soiled with mans urine, and doves-
dung, and you shall see that in a short time they will be increased." "The reason for this growth," he explains, "may be the Golds attracting that universal
vapour and Sperm that comes from the center through the earth and by the
heat of putrefecation of the dung purifying and assimilating it to it self" (204).
105. Ibid., i.
106. Ibid., iii.
107. Ibid.
108. Ted McCormick, "Economics and the Decline of Alchemy: Gabriel Plattes's
Discovery of Subterraneall Treasure (1639)" (unpublished).
109. Gabriel Plattes, *A discovery of subterraneall treasure, viz. of all manner of
mines and mineralls, from the gold to the coale; with plaine directions and*

rules for the finding of them in all kingdomes and countries. And also the art of melting, refining, and assaying of them is plainly declared (London, 1639), 42.

110. Ibid., 43.

111. Gabriel Plattes, *Caveat for Alchymists, or, A warning to all ingenious Gentlemen, whether Laicks or Clericks, that study for the finding out of the Philosophers Stone; shewing how that they need not to be cheated of their Estates, either by the perswasion of others, or by their own idle conceits* (London, 1655), 88.

112. Ibid., 87.

113. Charles Webster notes that Worsley "emerged as one of the leading proponents of Baconian experimental philosophy and of mercntilist economic policy of the mid-seventeenth century" ("Benjamin Worsley," 234).

114. Leng, *Benjamin Worsley*, 38.

115. Young, *Faith, Medical Alchemy and Natural Philosophy*, 230.

116. William R. Newman and Lawrence M. Principe, *Alchemy Tried in the Fire: Starkey, Boyle, and the Fate of Helmontian Chymistry* (Chicago: University of Chicago Press, 2002), 12.

117. The frequent correspondence between Moriaen and Worsley in 1651, dealing almost exclusively with their respective alchemical experiments, suggested that progress was being made. Young, *Faith, Medical Alchemy and Natural Philosophy*, 226.

118. Quoted in Young, *Faith, Medical Alchemy and Natural Philosophy*, 229.

119. Ronald Sterne Wilkinson, "The Hartlib Papers and Seventeenth Century Chemistry, Part II: George Starkey," *Ambix* 17 (1970): 85–110.

120. Michael Hunter, Antonio Clericuzio, and Lawrence M. Principe, eds., *The Correspondence of Robert Boyle, Vol. I* (London: Pickering and Chatto, 2001), 93.

121. Ibid., 94.

122. Ibid., 114–115.

123. Ibid., 115.

124. Ibid., 99.

125. Starkey's critique of money and commerce is similar to that of the Puritan radical Gerrard Winstanley. The leader of the Diggers proclaimed that money was a tool of the devil and that once freed from this tyrannical device people would "live freely in the enjoyment of the earth, without bringing the mark of the Best in their hands or in their promise; and that they shall buy wine and milk without money or without price, as Isaiah speaks"; see *A declaration from the poor oppressed people of England, directed to all that call themselves, or are called lords of manors, through this nation; that have begun to cut, or that through fear and covetousness, do intend to cut down the woods and trees that grow upon the commons and waste land* (n.p., 1649), 101. For a discussion of Winstanley's alchemical influences, see David Mulder,

The Alchemy of Revolution: Gerrard Winstanley's Occultism and Seventeenth-Century English Communism (New York: Peter Lang, 1990).

126. Quoted in William R. Newman, "George Starkey and the Selling of Secrets," in *Samuel Hartlib and Universal Reformation: Studies in Intellectual Communication* ed. Mark Greengrass, Michael Leslie, and Timothy Raylor, 11 (Cambridge: Cambridge University Press, 1994).

127. For a discussion about alchemy and secrecy, see Eamon, *Science and the Secrets of Nature.*

128. Quoted in Michael Hunter, "Alchemy, Magic, and Moralism in the Thought of Robert Boyle," *British Journal for the History of Science* 23 (1990): 407. Hunter explores Boyle's puzzling participation in the efforts to repeal the act outlawing the multiplication of silver and gold.

129. Quoted in Young, *Faith, Medical Alchemy and Natural Philosophy*, 233.

130. Hunter, Clericuzio, and Principe, *Correspondence of Robert Boyle*, 155.

131. Newman, "George Starkey and the Selling of Secrets," 204.

132. Starting in 1653, Worsley engaged Frederick Clodius, another prominent Hartlibian alchemist, in a sustained debate on metallic transmutation. See Leng, *Benjamin Worsley*, 99–102.

133. *A Bank of Lands; or, an Improvement of Lands, never thought of in former Ages: Begun to be presented upon most rationable and demonstrable grounds by Mr. William Potter (a Gentleman of great deserts, and of a most Publique Spirit) which being more fully cleared in all its Particulars, and established by publique Authority, may become a standing and setled Meanes to enrich the whole Nation, and also to remove Taxes, and other publique Burdens,* in Hartlib, *Samuel Hartlib his legacy of husbandry*, 290. It is unknown in what year Potter first published his proposal for a land bank. *A Bank of Lands* and *An Essay upon Master W. Potters Designe* (1653) are similar enough that they might have been authored by the same person. However, following the lead of Michael Braddick and Mark Greengrass, I attribute the latter to Cheney Culpeper and keep to the convention of considering William Potter the author of the former. Michael Braddick and Mark Greengrass, eds., *Seventeenth-Century Political and Financial Papers*, 105-402 (Camden: Camden Miscellany xxiii, 1996).

134. Many of Culpeper's letters to Hartlib detail an active involvement in alchemical affairs and a frequent engagement with some of the central figures in the Circle's alchemical pursuits. See "The Letters of Sir Cheney Culpeper (1641–1657)," in *Seventeenth-Century Political and Financial Papers*, ed. Michael Braddick and Mark Greengrass (Camden: Camden Miscellany xxiii, 1996).

135. Potter, *Bank of Lands*, 294.

136. William Potter, *The key of wealth: or, a new way, for improving of trade: lawfull, easie, safe and effectuall: shewing how a few tradesmen agreeing together,*

may (borrow wherewith to) double their stocks, and the increase thereof (London, 1650), 38.

137. The primary obstacle to the circulation of personal debt instruments was that only the initial creditor was allowed to sue the debtor. For more discussion, see Chapter 3.

138. Mun, *England's Treasure by Forraign Trade*; Robinson, *Englands safety*.

139. Henry Robinson, *Certain proposalls in order to the peoples freedome and accommodation in some particulars. With the advancement of trade and navigation of this Commonwealth in generall. Humbly tendered to the view of this prosperous Parliament, in this juncture of time* (London, 1652), 18.

140. Ibid.

141. Culpeper, *An essay upon Master W. Potters designe*, 30.

142. Ibid., 29.

143. Potter, *Bank of Lands*, 295.

144. Robinson, *Englands safety*, 34.

145. For Potter, money served as "an *Evidence* or *Testimony*, to signifie how far forth men (by their joint Agreement to take it, being otherwise of no worth, for Commodities of real value) are Indebted for, and engaged, to recommence the fruits of their labours or possessions, in some other Commodities or Necessaries instead of those, that for such money they parted with" (*The key of wealth*, 7).

146. Ibid., 38.

147. Ibid., 56.

148. Ibid., 46.

149. Ibid., 52.

150. Ibid., 28.

151. Ibid., 10.

152. Ibid., iv.

153. William Potter, *Humble proposalls to the honorable the Councell for trade: And all merchants and others who desire to improve their estates* (London, 1651), 15.

154. Potter, *Bank of Lands*, 293–294.

155. Potter, *Bank of Lands*, 295; Culpeper, *An essay upon Master W. Potters designe*, 30.

156. Potter, *Bank of Lands*, 295.

157. Ibid., 297.

158. Ibid., 299.

159. By offering a condensed version of *The key of wealth*, Potter continued to promote this scheme in *The trades-man's jewel: or a safe, easie, speedy and effectual means, for the incredible advancement of trade, and multiplication of riches; shewing how men of indifferent estates, may abundantly increase both their own and other mens trading and riches, without parting with money,*

or any stock out of their own hands: by making their bills to become current instead of money, and frequently to revolve through their hands, with as much in money as the sums therein mentioned do amount unto (London, 1650).

160. Peter Chamberlen, *The poore mans advocate, or, Englands samaritan. Powring oyle and wyne into the wounds of the nation. By making present provision for the souldier and the poor, by reconciling all parties by paying all arreares to the Parliament army. All publique debts, and all the late kings, queenes, and princes debts due before this session* (London, 1649), v.

161. Ibid., 1.

162. The Rump of the Long Parliament eventually ended up selling the land of approximately seven hundred royalists, in a process that William Potter may have been actively involved in. Christopher Hill, *The Century of Revolution, 1603–1714* (New York: Norton, 1966), 97.

163. Chamberlen, *The poore mans advocate*, 48.

164. Ibid., 9.

165. Ibid., 4.

166. Ibid., v.

167. Culpeper to Hartlib, March 15, 1647–1648, in "The Letters of Sir Cheney Culpeper, 1641–1657," 325.

168. Dunn, "Milton among the Monopolists," 184. See also Gweneth Whitteridge, "William Harvey: A Royalist and No Parliamentarian," in *The Intellectual Revolution of the Seventeenth-Century*, ed. Charles Webster, 182-188 (London: Routledge, 1974).

169. Potter, *The key of wealth*, 2.

170. Chamberlen, *The poore mans advocate*, 31.

171. Joyce Appleby traces the shift in the discourse about the poor from a concern with overpopulation to a focus on a shortage of productive hands in *Economic Thought and Ideology*, 129–157.

172. Culpeper to Hartlib, March 4, 1645–1646, in "The Letters of Sir Cheney Culpeper," 269–270.

173. Charles Webster points out that Hartlib's writings were discredited along with "other reform movements, such as the Leveller tracts and the works of Winstanley," in Charles Webster, ed., *Samuel Hartlib and the Advancement of Learning* (Cambridge: Cambridge University Press, 1970), 64. See also Mendelsohn, "Alchemy and Politics," 30.

174. Lotte Mulligan, "Civil War Politics, Religion, and the Royal Society," in *The Intellectual Revolution of the Seventeenth-Century*, ed. Charles Webster, 342–346 (London: Routledge, 1974).

175. Petty proclaimed that "we must erect a Bank, which well computed, doth almost double the Effect of our coined Money: And we have in *England* Materials for a Bank which shall furnish Stock enough to drive the Trade of the whole Commercial World"; see *Quantulumcunque Concerning Money.*

To the Lord Marquess of Halyfax (London, 1682), 7. Touting the benefits of credit money, Petty suggested elsewhere that land "shall not only become as money, but as a Bank of money, which is farr more safe and commodious than coyness"; see *The Petty Papers: Some Unpublished Writings of Sir William Petty*, ed. Marquis of Lansdowne (London: Constable, 1927), 1:78.
176. Bacon, *New Organon*, 71.

3. The Epistemology of Credit

1. William Petty, *Quantulumcunque Concerning Money* (London, 1682), 7; Nicholas Barbon, *A Discourse of Trade* (London, 1690), 27; Davenant, *Discourses on the Publick Revenues*, 38.
2. Mary Poovey recently highlighted the relative independence of money from the material security it represents, calling it the "problematic of representation" (*Genres of the Credit Economy*, 62).
3. Georg Simmel, *The Philosophy of Money*, ed. David Frisby, trans. Tom Bottomore and David Frisby (London: Routledge [1978] 1991).
4. Ibid., 178.
5. Ibid., 179.
6. Ibid., 180.
7. Ibid.
8. Ibid., 179.
9. On the continent, a number of philosophers contributed to the rise of probabilistic thinking, starting with Antoine Arnold, Pierre Nicole, and Blaise Pascal and continuing with Christiaan Huygens, Gottfried Leibnitz, and Jakob Bernoulli. For synthetic treatments of the emergence of probabilistic thinking, see Hacking, *Emergence of Probability*; Shapiro, *Probability and Certainty*; Daston, *Classical Probability*; Lorraine Daston, "Domestication of Risk: Mathematical Probability and Insurance, 1650–1830," in *The Probabilistic Revolution, Vol. 1*, ed. Lorenz Krüger, Lorraine Daston, Michael Heidelberger, Gerd Gigerenzer, and Mary S. Morgan, 237–260 (Cambridge, MA: MIT Press, 1987); Peter Dear, *Discipline and Experience: The Mathematical Way in the Scientific Revolution* (Chicago: University of Chicago Press, 1995); and James Franklin, *The Science of Conjecture: Evidence and Conjecture before Pascal* (Baltimore, MD: The Johns Hopkins University Press, 2001).
10. For readers interested in a more detailed treatment of the institutional designs of these credit schemes, see R. D. Richards, *The Early History of Banking in England* (London: Frank Cass and Company, 1958); J. Keith Horsefield, *British Monetary Experiments, 1650–1710* (New York: Garland Publishing, 1983). See also the forthcoming essay by Seiichiro Ito, "The Making of Institutional Credit in England, 1600–1688," *European Journal of the History of Economic Thought* 18. Ito explores how various banking proposals dealt with

the central issues of safety, security, and trustworthiness, focusing on many of the same banking proponents discussed in this chapter.

11. Shapiro, *Probability and Certainty*.

12. Some historians of science object to the notion of a rise or an emergence of probability. See Daniel Garber and Sandy Zabell, "On the Emergence of Probability," *Archive for History of Exact Sciences* 21 (1979): 33–53.

13. Daston points out that aleatory contracts, in particular games of chance, attracted attention from mathematicians, like the Bernoulli brothers and Johann De Witt. Yet, their mathematical treatments of these games were not widely implemented. Daston argues that lotteries were so profitable that there was no real need to employ more sophisticated mathematical techniques; see Daston, *Classical Probability*, 168. For a cultural history of aleatory contracts, see Clark, *Betting on Lives*.

14. Hacking, *Emergence of Probability*, 38.

15. Hobbes was, as Steven Shapin and Simon Schaffer point out (*Leviathan and the Air-Pump*, 19), critical of experimental methods, claiming that they could only produce opinion, which never rises to the degree of certainty required to be called philosophical or scientific knowledge.

16. Thomas Hobbes, *Leviathan*, ed. Richard Tuck (Cambridge: Cambridge University Press, [1651] 1991), l.vii, 48.

17. Ibid.

18. Ibid.

19. Ibid.

20. Ibid., 49. Echoing Hobbes's claim, sociologist Georg Simmel argued that the kind of trust on which credit is based is "most clearly embodied in religious faith" (*Philosophy of Money*, 179). Others, such as Thomas M. Kavanagh argue, "Credit has nothing to do with religious belief . . . Credit had to do, not with any dogma anchored in the past, but with a belief in the future"; see *Enlightenment and the Shadows of Chance: The Novel and the Culture of Gambling in Eighteenth-Century France* (Baltimore, MD: The Johns Hopkins University Press, 1993), 69. Although there may be parallels between the manner by which people are encouraged to develop religious faith and trust in money—see, for example, Marc Shell, *Art and Money* (Chicago: University of Chicago Press, 1995), 7–22—considering that the seventeenth-century literature on credit did not frequently employ the analogy between faith in God and trust in money, this chapter will not focus on it. For more on the relationship between faith and money, see Philip Goodchild, *The Theology of Money* (Durham, NC: Duke University Press, 2009).

21. Shapin, *Social History of Truth*, 211.

22. Ibid., chap. 2.

23. Ibid., 42–43. Shapin adds that "constancy, reliability, and truthfulness" followed "the contours of authority and power" (69).

24. Ibid., 212. Other historians of science have challenged the importance of gentility and suggested that skill and expertise were the most important determinants of credibility. Barbara Shapiro, *A Culture of Fact: England 1550–1720* (Ithaca, NY: Cornell University Press, 2000), 165.

25. Simon Schaffer, "Social History of Plausibility: Country, City and Calculations in Augustan Britain," in *Rethinking Social History: English Society 1570–1920 and its Interpretations*, ed. Adrian Wilson (Manchester: Manchester University Press), 137.

26. Craig Muldrew is one of the few scholars who recognizes that Hobbes's discussion of covenants and agreements was "in fact nothing more than a description of a credit exchange in the marketplace" (*Economy of Obligation*, 324).

27. Thomas Hobbes, *On the Citizen*, ed. Richard Tuck and Michael Silverthorne (Cambridge: Cambridge University Press, [1651] 1998), 35.

28. Hobbes, *On the Citizen*, 36. Alternatively, in *Leviathan*, Hobbes claimed that "in buying, and selling, and other acts of Contract, a Promise is equivalent to a Covenant" (l.xiv, 95).

29. Ibid., 96.

30. Margaret J. Osler, "Certainty, Scepticism, and Scientific Optimism: The Roots of Eighteenth-Century Attitudes Toward Scientific Knowledge," in *Probability, Time, and Space in Eighteenth-Century Literature*, ed. Paula R. Backscheider, 13 (New York: AMS Press, 1979). See also Shapiro, *Probability and Certainty*, 17, 32.

31. John Locke, *An Essay Concerning Human* Understanding, ed. Peter H. Nidditch (Oxford: Clarendon Press, 1975), IV.xv.2.

32. Ibid., I.i.5. Locke was not alone in recognizing the necessity of acting on the basis of opinion. Daston notes that writers like Robert Boyle, John Wilkins, Pierre Gassendi, and Hugo Grotius "insisted on the incorrigible uncertainty of almost all human knowledge," yet they "affirmed the existence of rational grounds for belief" (*Classical Probability*, 56–58).

33. Locke, *Essay*, IV.xv.3. I follow David Owen in reading "assent" as "just another term for belief or opinion." David Owen, "Locke on Judgment," in *The Cambridge Companion to Locke's 'Essay Concerning Human Understanding,'* ed. Lex Newman, 423 (Cambridge: Cambridge University Press, 2006).

34. Trust, therefore, as Diego Gambetta points out in "Can We Trust Trust?" in *Trust: Making and Breaking Cooperative Relations*, ed. Diego Gambetta, 233 (Oxford: Blackwell, 1988), cannot exist in the absence of "betrayal, deception, and disappointment." Charles Tilly adds that trust can even be defined as "placing valued outcomes at risk to other's malfeasance, mistakes, or failures"; Charles Tilly, *Trust and Rule* (Cambridge: Cambridge University Press, 2005), 12.

35. Locke, *Essay*, IV.xv.2. For a discussion of gradations of reasonableness or opinion, see Gerd Gigerenzer, Zeno Swijtink, Theodore Porter, Lorraine Daston, John Beatty, and Lorenz Krüger, eds., *Empire of Chance: How Probability Changed Science and Everyday Life* (Cambridge: Cambridge University Press, 1989), 7–8. The lack of clear boundaries between trust and distrust led Gambetta to insist that "trust is better seen as a threshold point, located on a probabilistic distribution of more general expectations, which can take a number of values suspended between complete distrust and complete trust" ("Can We Trust," 218).

36. Locke, *Essay*, IV.xv.4.

37. Ibid.

38. Ibid., IV.xv.5.

39. Ibid., IV.xv.4. See also Shapin, *Social History of Truth*, chap. 3.

40. Hacking, *Emergence of Probability*, 33.

41. Locke, *Essay*, IV.xv.4.

42. As the philosopher Michael Ayers points out, "knowledge and belief are not . . . mutually exclusive categories. Belief is, rather, a condition of knowledge"; see Michael Ayers, *Locke. Vol. 1: Epistemology* (London: Routledge, 1991), 125.

43. Locke, *Essay*, IV.xvi.6.

44. Ibid., IV.xvi.7.

45. Ibid., IV.xvi.8.

46. Contrary to many commentators, Joseph Shieber affirms "the centrality of testimony as a source of evidence" in Locke's discussion of knowledge in "Locke on Testimony: A Reexamination," *History of Philosophy Quarterly* 26 (2009): 31.

47. Locke, *Essay*, IV.xvi.9.

48. Ibid.

49. Ibid.

50. Ibid., IV.xvi.10.

51. Ibid. A few years later John Craig showed mathematically the rate at which the credibility of a testimony declines as the sequence of witnesses, the distance from the place, and the space of time increases, in "Theologiae Christianae Principia Mathematica (1699)," *History and Theory* 4 (1964): 1–31.

52. Locke, *Essay*, IV.xvi.10.

53. Ibid., IV.xv.6.

54. Shapiro, *Probability and Certainty*, 9.

55. Michael Braddick, *God's Fury, England's Fire: A New History of the Civil Wars* (London: Penguin, 2009), 389. Paul Slack notes that since England's wealth expanded and population growth leveled off, "There is no doubt that England's wealth was . . . increasing in per capita terms after 1650"—increasing

by at least a third during the last half of the seventeenth century" ("Material Progress," 577–578).

56. Joel Mokyr notes that the improving agricultural productivity facilitated the rapid urbanization, allowing London to grow into a major city with a population of 575,000 in 1700 in *Enlightened Economy*, 14.

57. Jan de Vries, "Between Purchasing Power and the World of Goods: Understanding the household economy in early modern Europe," in *Consumption and the World of Goods*, ed. John Brewer and Roy Porter, 87 (London: Routledge, 1994). Geoffrey Holmes credits the Royal Society, and thus in extension the Hartlib Circle, for promoting improvements in agricultural techniques and practices in *The Making of a Great Power: Late Stuart and Early Georgian Britain, 1660–1722* (London: Longman, 1993), 51.

58. Joan Thirsk, *Agricultural Change: Policy and Practice 1500–1750* (Cambridge: Cambridge University Press, 1990), 155–161.

59. G. E. Aylmer, "Navy, State, Trade, and Empire," in *The Origins of Empire*, ed. Nicholas Canny, 467–480 (Oxford: Oxford University Press, 1998).

60. Pincus, *1688*, 57–59.

61. Joyce Oldham Appleby, "Consumption in Early Modern Social Thought," in *Consumption and the World of Goods*, ed. John Brewer and Roy Porter, 162–176 (London: Routledge, 1994); Linda Levy Peck, *Consuming Splendour: Society and Culture in Seventeenth-Century England* (Cambridge: Cambridge University Press, 2005); Maxine Berg, *Luxury and Pleasure in Eighteenth-Century Britain* (Oxford: Oxford University Press, 2005).

62. Mokyr suggests that between 1622 and 1700 imports and exports "just about doubled" (*Enlightened Economy*, 18).

63. By the end of the century, cloth only constituted about half of England's exports, while colonial reexports and exports of English-made goods to the colonies made up as much as 40 percent; see Charles Wilson, *England's Apprenticeship, 1603–1763* (New York: St. Martin's Press, 1965), 160–164.

64. Appleby, *Economic Thought and Ideology*, chap. 6.

65. Judging by the findings of Jan de Vries, that starting in the 1650s English households engaged more extensively in market-oriented production and consumed more goods in the marketplace, it appears that the English population began to change its habits and practices around this time; see *The Industrious Revolution: Consumer Behavior and the Household Economy, 1650 to the Present* (Cambridge: Cambridge University Press, 2008).

66. William J. Ashworth, *Customs and Excise: Trade, Production, and Consumption in England 1640–1845* (Oxford: Oxford University Press, 2003).

67. Braddick, *State Formation*.

68. The banks accepted deposits at 5–6 percent and lent to the Crown at 10 percent. This favorable spread led many bankers to focus primarily on public loans. In 1666, for example, Backwell's lending to private clients amounted

to a mere 9 percent of his capital, while the rest was lent to the king. Henry Roseveare, *The Financial Revolution 1660–1760* (London: Longman, 1991), 19–20.

69. Since the English state did not produce an adequate amount of small change, private issuers took the initiative to produce halfpence and farthings—tokens that circulated locally. Liza Picard suggests that London and its surroundings had more than thirty-five hundred producers of tokens in the 1660s, offering small change of various sizes, shapes, and materials, in *Restoration London: Everyday Life in London 1660–1670* (London: Phoenix, 1997), 144. For an extensive discussion of tokens, see J. R. S. Whiting, *Trade Tokens: A Social and Economic History* (Newton Abbot: David and Charles, 1971); and for the implications of the shortage thereof, see Sargent and Velde, *Big Problem*.

70. Robert Ashton, *The Crown and the Money Market, 1603–1640* (Oxford: Oxford University Press, 1960), 14.

71. Frank T. Meton, *Sir Robert Clayton and the Origins of English Deposit Banking 1658–1685* (Cambridge: Cambridge University Press, 1986).

72. Albert Feavearyear suggests that the first definite recorded case of a goldsmith note used for making a payment to a third party was in 1668 in *The Pound Sterling: A History of English Money* (Oxford: Clarendon Press, 1963), 107–108. However, because of the Stop of the Exchequer, goldsmiths' notes "were unacceptable as currency in the 1670s," explains Peter Temin and Hans-Joachim Voth in "Banking as an Emerging Technology: Hoare's Bank, 1702–1742," *Financial History Review* 13 (2006): 149.

73. Larry Neal, for example, argues that during the 1690s the goldsmiths' notes were "the favoured medium of exchange within the City of London" in "How It All Began: The Monetary and Financial Architecture of Europe during the First Global Capital Markets, 1648–1815," *Financial History Review* 7 (2000): 124.

74. The Italian banks were criticized for catering only to merchants, and the Dutch public bank was considered unable to significantly expand the amount of money in circulation due to its commitment to maintaining 100 percent reserve of coin in the vault. Sir Theodore Janssen would later describe the Bank of Amsterdam, as well as the banks of Hamburg and Stockholm, "as only great Chests, for the Conveniency of transferring from one Account to another; and where Merchants deposite their Money, if they think it safer there than in their own Houses" (*Discourse Concerning Banks* [London, 1697], 2). More recently, Marjolein 'T Hart has showed that the Bank of Amsterdam was not a model for the Bank of England, as the former did not issue notes and did not lend to the government, in "'The Devil of the Dutch': Holland's Impact on the Financial Revolution in England, 1643–1694," *Parliaments, Estates and Representation* 11 (1991): 39–52.

75. Niklas Luhmann, *Trust and Power* (Chichester: Wiley, 1979), 39–60; Anthony Giddens, *The Consequences of Modernity* (Stanford, CA: Stanford University Press, 1991), 80.

76. Luhmann, *Trust and Power*, 50.

77. John Bland, *Trade revived, or a way proposed to restore, increase, inrich, strengthen and preserve the decayed and even dying trade of this our English nation, in its manufactories, coin, shiping and revenue* (London, 1659), 6.

78. After more than half a century of advocacy, the Promissory Notes Act was passed in 1704, making all debt instruments negotiable. Richards, *Early History of Banking in England*, 23.

79. *The Grand Concern of England Explained; in several proposals offered to the consideration of the Parliament. 1. For payment of publick debts. 2. For advancement and encouragement of trade. 3. For raising the rents of land* (London, 1673), 56.

80. Bland, *Trade revived*, 7.

81. Ibid.

82. Ibid.

83. Ibid., 8.

84. Ibid.

85. Andrew Yarranton, *England's improvement by sea and land. To out-do the Dutch without fighting, to pay debts without moneys, to set at work all the poor of England with the growth of our own lands* (London, 1677), 6.

86. Ibid.

87. Ibid., 8.

88. Ibid., 11.

89. Ibid., 16.

90. Samuel Lambe, *Seasonable observations humbly offered to His Highness the Lord Protector* (London, 1658).

91. Ibid., 12, 15.

92. Lambe also proposed that the bank should provide capital for a subsidiary Lombard bank, specializing in lending to the poor. While the poor would pay a substantially higher interest rate than the tradesmen, it would still be far lower than the usurious rates presently exacted from the poor.

93. Lambe, *Seasonable observations*, 12.

94. Ibid., 15.

95. Not only would the bank provide lines of credit, but it would also attract the gold and silver that English merchants currently exported to Amsterdam for safekeeping. More precious metals would also flow into England as a result of its increased commercial prosperity.

96. Lambe, *Seasonable observations*, 12.

97. Ibid., 11.

98. Ibid., 16.

99. For a discussion of the epistemological impact of double-entry bookkeeping, see Poovey, *History of the Modern Fact*, chap. 2; Jacob Soll, "Accounting for Government: Holland and the Rise of Political Economy in Seventeenth-Century Europe," *Journal of Interdisciplinary History* 40 (2009): 215–238.

100. Hobbes, *Leviathan*, 15.

101. Joseph Addison, in the *Spectator*, later used a similar definition. What he called secondary pleasures of the imagination, flowed "from the Ideas of visible Objects, when the Objects are not actually before the Eye, but are called up into our Memories, or formed into agreeable Visions of Things that are either Absent or Fictitious." Republished in Gregory Smith, ed., *The Spectator in Four Volumes, Vol. III* (London: Dent, 1945), 277.

102. William Killigrew, *To the King and Queens most excellent majesties; the lords spiritual and temporal; and to the knights, citizens, and burgesses assembled in Parliament. An humble proposal shewing how this nation may be vast gainers by all sums of mony given to the crown, without lessening the prerogative* (London, 1663), 2. For a discussion of the Dutch public loans, see Marjolein 'T Hart, "Mutual Advantages: State Bankers as Brokers between the City of Amsterdam and the Dutch Republic," in *The Political Economy of the Dutch Republic*, ed. Oscar Gelderblom, 116–119 (Farnham: Ashgate, 2009).

103. Killigrew, *To the King and Queens*, 2.

104. Ibid., 3.

105. Ibid., 4.

106. Ibid.

107. Feavearyear, *Pound Sterling*, 110, 117.

108. Far from all goldsmith bankers and scriveners went bankrupt as a consequence of the Stop of the Exchequer, leaving bankers like the Hoares, Childs, Pinckneys, and Stokeses to extend loans to the government. Stephen Quinn notes that there were thirty-two goldsmith bankers in 1670 and forty-four in 1677, while the number went down to forty-two in 1700, in "Goldsmith-Banking: Mutual Acceptance and Interbanker Clearing in Restoration London," *Explorations in Economic History* 34 (1997): 411.

109. While the Treasury Orders failed during the Stop of the Exchequer, a new more successful version, the Exchequer Notes, was issued in 1697. Coincidentally, Killigrew's proposal was republished both in 1690 and 1696.

110. Hugh Chamberlen, *A Description of the Office of Credit; By the use of which, none can possible sustain Loss, but every man may certainly receive great Gain and Wealth* (London, 1665), 1.

111. Ibid. For a discussion of this practice in the Caribbean, see John J. McCusker, *Money and Exchange in Europe and America, 1600–1775: A Handbook* (Chapel Hill: University of North Carolina Press, 1992).

112. Chamberlen, *Description of the Office of Credit*, 18.

113. Ibid., 19.

114. Ibid., 2.
115. Ibid., 3.
116. Ibid., 18.
117. Ibid., 19.
118. Ibid., 19–20. When Chamberlen later revisited his proposal for an Office of Credit, he reluctantly acknowledged the unavoidable presence of the human factor involved in the issuance of credit. He argued, "Security can only be expected for the Fidelity of the Undertaker, for the Goods deposited, make them able; and a small Proportion of Honesty and Discretion, may qualifie men to be trusted with the Care of keeping others mens Goods." Yet, in the end, after having considered all of the compelling reasons for why the human element involved in the creation of credit should not constitute an obstacle to trust, he reiterated that the undertakers are not "trusted so much as the Goods themselves, whereof they are only the Keepers"; see Hugh Chamberlen, *Several Objections Sometimes Made against the Office of Credit Fully Answered* (London, 1682), 6.
119. Ibid., 9.
120. Mark Lewis, *Proposals to the King and Parliament. Or a large model of a bank, shewing how a fund of a bank may be made without much charge, or any hazard, that may give out Bills of credit to a vast extent, that all europe will accept it, rather than mony. Together with some general proposals in order to an Act of Parliament for the establishing this bank. Also many of the great advantages that will accrue to the nation, to the crown, and to the people, are mentioned, with an answer to the objections, that may be made against it* (London, 1678), 3.
121. Ibid.
122. Ibid., 15.
123. Ibid., 28.
124. *Bank-Credit: or the Usefulness and Security of the bank examined; in a dialogue between and gentleman and a London merchant* (London, 1683). Other proposals promoting similar banking schemes include Robert Murray, *An Account of the Constitution and Security of the General Bank of Credit* (London, 1683); Robert Murray, *Corporation—Credit Or, A Bank of Credit made Currant, by Common Consent in London. More Useful and Safe than Money* (London, 1682). John Houghton, *An Account of the Bank of Credit in the City of London* (London, 1683), also promoted similar banking schemes.
125. *Bank-Credit*, 11.
126. Ibid., 11–12.
127. Ibid., 12.
128. Ibid., 13.
129. Ibid., 23.
130. The system of tallies was an age-old system based on using notched wood to represent a debt. At the moment of contracting a debt, the stick would be

notched to show how much money had shifted hands and the loan's maturity. The stick was then split down the middle to create two tallies with exactly similar notches. That way, when a tally stick was presented for redemption, it was easy to ascertain its legitimacy. Feavearyear, *Pound Sterling*, 110, 117.

131. For a discussion of these loans, see Dickson, *The Financial Revolution in England*, 45; and Brewer, *Sinews of Power*, 122–125.

132. England and Wales. *An abstract of the Charter to the governour and company of the Bank of England* (n.p., 1694).

133. Michael Godfrey, *A Short Account of the Bank of England* (London, 1695), 1.

134. Richards, *Early History of Banking in England*, 172–173.

135. The sealed bills were printed, assignable by endorsement, and interest bearing. The running cash notes resembled the goldsmith notes and initially functioned as a deposit receipt in the form of a promissory note. Apart from a few series of running cash notes, they did not bear interest. While the most common denominator of the sealed bills was £100, the running cash notes were normally issued at £20. Acceptable notes, a form of deposit receipt, were issued from the beginning in £5 denomination. Richards, *Early History of Banking in England*, 156–160.

136. Jones, *War and Economy*, 13. Anne L. Murphy notes a number of reasons for the emergence of a financial market in England during the 1690s. Most importantly, England's wealth, industry, and trade had advanced considerably, generating substantial surplus funds. Because of the recent moral relaxation, more people were comfortable investing their surplus funds in the financial market. Also contributing was the improvement in financial institutions and skills, much of which was introduced by Huguenot refugees (Murphy, *Origins of English Financial Markets*, 11–19).

137. W. R. Scott, *The Constitution and Finance of English, Scottish and Irish Joint-Stock Companies to 1720, Vol. 1* (Cambridge: Cambridge University Press, 1910), 327. Murphy, however, cautions that the extent of stock market activity should not be overestimated, as the market was still dominated by relatively few stocks (*Origins of English Financial Markets*, 37).

138. Natasha Glaisyer, *The Culture of Commerce in England, 1660–1720* (Woodbridge, Suffolk: Boydell Press, 2006).

139. Richard Kleer has reconstructed Paterson's original 1691 proposal in "'Fictitious Cash': English Public Finance and Paper Money, 1689–97," in *Money, Power, and Print: Interdisciplinary Studies on the Financial Revolution in the British Isles*, ed. Charles McGrath and Chris Fauske, 75–77 (Newark: University of Delaware Press, 2008).

140. William Paterson, *A Brief Account of the Intended Bank of England* (London, 1694), 1.

141. Paterson, *Brief Account*, 10.

142. Ibid.

143. Ibid., 14.

144. Ibid., 11–12.

145. Ibid.

146. For a statement celebrating the performance of the Bank's directors, see Janssen, *Discourse Concerning Banks*.

147. Ibid., 12.

148. Linda Colley, *Britons: Forging the Nation 1707–1837* (New Haven, CT: Yale University Press, 1992). Paterson's suggestion that property had been secure in England for a long time, but that it was now threatened by a second Stuart Restoration, challenges Douglass C. North's and Barry R. Weingast's later assertion that property first became fully secure in England with the Glorious Revolution in "Constitutions and Commitment," 803–842.

149. Paterson, *Brief Account*, 14–5.

150. Ibid., 16.

151. Godfrey, *Short Account*, 1.

152. Ibid., 2.

153. Ibid.

154. Ibid., 3.

155. Ibid., 4.

156. Humphrey Mackworth, *England's glory; or the great improvement of trade in general, by a royal bank, or office of credit, to be erected in London; wherein many great advantages that will hereby accrue to the nation, to the crown, and to the people, are mentioned; with answers to the objections that may be made against this bank* (London, 1694), iv.

157. Ibid., v.

158. Ibid., 4–5.

159. Ibid., 40.

160. *Some observations upon the Bank of England* (London, 1695), 8.

161. Ibid., 1.

162. Isaac Kramnick, *Bolingbroke and His Circle: The Politics of Nostalgia in the Age of Walpole* (Ithaca, NY: Cornell University Press, 1968).

163. Dennis Rubini, "Politics and the Battle for the Banks, 1688–1697," *English Historical Review* 85 (1970): 697.

164. Sir Edward Forde, *Experimented proposals how the king may have money to pay and maintain his fleets with ease to his people. London may be rebuilt, and all proprietors satisfied. Money be lent at six per cent. on pawns. And, the fishing-trade set up, which alone is able and sure to enrich us all, And all this without altering, straining or thwarting any of our laws or customes now in use* (London, 1666), 1.

165. Ibid., 1–2.

166. Ibid., 2.

167. Ibid.

168. Francis Cradocke, *Wealth discovered: or, An essay upon a late expedient for taking away all impositions, and raising a revenue without taxes* (London, 1661), i.

169. Ibid., 4.

170. Ibid., 9.

171. John Cary, *An Essay on the Coyn and Credit of England: As they stand with Respect to its Trade* (London, 1695), 2–3.

172. *Some Observations*, 25. As the historian J. S. Peters points out, "The idea of an infinitely expandable credit system, which the new paper system seemed to make possible, was both compelling and . . . frightening" in "The Bank, the Press, and the 'Return of Nature': On Currency, Credit, and Literary Property in the 1690s," in *Early Modern Conceptions of Property*, ed. John Brewer and Susan Staves, 371 (London: Routledge, 1996).

173. Cradocke, *Wealth discovered*, 11.

174. Ibid., 12.

175. Ibid., 13.

176. Ibid., 29, 36.

177. Ibid., 43. Proclaiming that he had only heard of, but not read, Potter's land bank scheme, Cradocke submitted a proposal highly reminiscent of that of Potter.

178. For a discussion of Barbon's economic ideas, see Christopher Berry, *The Idea of Luxury: A Conceptual and Historical Investigation* (Cambridge: Cambridge University Press, 1994). See also Paul Slack, "The Politics of Consumption and England's Happiness in the Later Seventeenth Century," *English Historical Review* 497 (2007): 609–631, for an analysis of how Barbon was influenced by the Hartlibian improvement projects.

179. Barbon, *Discourse of Trade*, 6. Andrea Finkelstein points out that "Barbon was not only asserting that labor could create infinite wealth from the limited but renewable resources of a finite earth; he was asserting that the resources (the *natural* stock) were themselves infinite"; see "Nicholas Barbon and the Quality of Infinity," *History of Political Economy* 32 (2000): 92.

180. Barbon, *Discourse of Trade*, 6.

181. As Paul Slack points out, emulation was "a motor of economic growth with perpetual motion and infinite potential" ("Politics of Consumption," 615).

182. Barbon, *Discourse of Trade*, 15.

183. Ibid.

184. Ibid., 16. Paul Slack notes that a contemporary of Barbon described him "as fine and as richly dressed as a lord of the bedchamber on a birthday" ("Politics of Consumption," 615).

185. Barbon, *Discourse of Trade*, 69.

186. Ibid., 21.

187. Ibid., 23.

188. Ibid., 26.

189. Ibid.

190. Horsefield, *British Monetary Experiments*, 196–210.

191. John Asgill, *Several assertions proved, in order to create another species of money than gold and silver* (n.p., 1696), 42.

192. Chamberlen published a significant number of pamphlets advocating for land banks, including *A Proposal for Erecting a General Bank: which may be Fitly Called the Land Bank of England* (London, 1695); *A proposal by Dr. Hugh Chamberlain in Essex-Street, for a bank of secure current credit to be founded upon land. In order to the general good of landed men. To the great increase of the value of land, and the no less benefit and augmentation of trade and commerce* (London, 1695); and *Papers, relating to a bank of credit, upon land-security; proposed to the Parliament of Scotland. published by order of the committee, to which the consideration of the proposal is referred* (Edinburgh, 1693).

193. Chamberlen, *Papers, relating to a bank of credit*, 2.

194. Ibid.

195. Ibid., 3–4.

196. Horsefield, *British Monetary Experiments*, 180–195.

197. John Briscoe, *The Following Proposals for, and Accounts of, a National Land-Bank having been Printed at London* (Edinburgh, 1695), 3.

198. Ibid.

199. John Briscoe, *Proposals for supplying the government with money on easie terms, excusing the nobility and gentry from taxes, enlarging their yearly estates, and enriching all the subjects in the Kingdom . . . With a suplement to his explanatory dialogue thereupon* (London, 1694), 11.

200. Ibid., 4.

201. For a more detailed description of this scheme, see Rubini, "Politics and the Battle for the Banks," 699–700; Kleer, "Fictitious Cash," 92–93.

202. Rubini, "Politics and the Battle for the Banks," 709.

203. Davenant, *Discourses on the Public Revenues*, 40.

204. Ibid., 39.

4. Capital Punishment in Defense of Credit

1. Historian Malcolm Gaskill points out that "counterfeiters and clippers across the land had a history as long as the monetized economy, and therefore had even caused concern to medieval English kings" in *Crime and Mentalities in Early Modern England* (Cambridge: Cambridge University Press, 2000), 125.

2. "Locke to William Molyneux, 1696," in *John Locke: Selected Correspondence*, ed. Mark Goldie, 223 (Oxford: Oxford University Press, 2002).

3. John Locke pointed out that "Clipping is the great Leak, which for some time past has contributed more to Sink us, than all the Force of our Enemies could

do" in *Further considerations concerning raising the value of money* (London, 1695), 100.

4. Caffentzis, *Clipped Coins*, 28.

5. Most scholars tend to limit their commentary to the role of the Great Recoinage in the failure of the National Land Bank. One exception is J. S. Peters, who recognizes that the "troubled nature of monetary representation, which the recoinage debate revealed, highlighted the crisis over the more general nature of monetary representation which the issuing of paper-based credit had spurred" ("The Bank, the Press, and the 'Return of Nature,'" 375). Pierre Vilar also argues that the recoinage cannot be understood in isolation from the founding of the Bank of England in *A History of Gold and Money: 1450 to 1920*, trans. Judith White (London: Verso, 1976), 211–221.

6. For a classic account of the English fiscal-military state, see Brewer, *Sinews of Power*. Peter Linebaugh minted the term "Thanatocracy" to denote the English state's rule "by the frequent exercise of the death penalty" in *London Hanged*, 50. Leon Radzinowicz informs us that 187 new capital statutes were implemented during the long eighteenth century in *A History of English Criminal Law and Its Administration from 1750*. Vol. 1 (London: Henry Bonwick, 1948), 4–5.

7. The Licensing Act lapsed in 1695, enabling an explosion in the number of contributions to the debate about England's economy. Hoppit, "Contexts and Contours," 79–110.

8. James Hodges, *A supplement to The present state of England as to coin and publick charges. Containing some further considerations of the circumstances of the Kingdom, with a proposal of help by raising the value of credit. Most humbly offered to the King and Parliament, by J.H.* (London, 1697), 9.

9. Ibid., 11.

10. Gaskill, *Crime and Mentalities*, 132.

11. For descriptions of the turbulent years surrounding the Glorious Revolution, see Gary Stuart De Krey, *A Fractured Society: The Politics of London in the First Age of Party, 1688–1715* (Oxford: Clarendon Press, 1985); Julian Hoppit, *A Land of Liberty? England 1689–1727* (Oxford: Oxford University Press, 2000); and Pincus, *1688*.

12. Jones, *War and Economy*, 1.

13. Brewer, *Sinews of Power*, 30.

14. Mark Overton, "Weather and Agricultural Change in England, 1660–1739," *Agricultural History* 63 (1989): 77–88.

15. Patrick H. Kelly, *Locke on Money* (Oxford: Clarendon Press, 1991), 55–57.

16. The net bullion loss (almost all silver) doubled from 1693 (£354,302) to 1694 (£703,204). Kelly, *Locke on Money*, 58.

17. Richard A. Kleer offers a detailed account of the political debate leading up to the formation of the Bank of England in "Fictitious Cash," 75–82. Steve

Pincus offers a longer durée analysis of the intellectual and political controversy leading up to the Bank's formation in *1688*, chap. 12.

18. Hoppit, "Attitudes to Credit," 308.

19. R. D. Richards, *The Early History of Banking in England* (London: Frank Cass, 1958), 175.

20. Rubini, "Politics and the Battle for the Banks," 696.

21. For the fiduciary character of the English coin, see Kelly, *Locke on Money*, 45–46; Horsefield, *British Monetary Experiments*, 26.

22. Based on Hopton Haynes's *Brief Memoires Relating to the Silver and Gold Coins of England*, Kelly compiled the following statistics on the silver coin brought to the mint:

Year:	percent of legal weight:	percent loss from preceding year:
1686	88.6	
1687	87.5	1.2
1688	84.7	3.3
1689	84.0	0.8
1690	81.2	3.3
1691	78.9	3.0
1692	72.9	7.5
1693	66.7	8.5
1694	60.1	9.8
1695	50.6	16.0
1696 (April)	45.0	11.0

In *Locke on Money*, 116. Further corroborating these numbers, Richard Westfall reports, "The records of the recoinage showed that of the nearly £5 million received and melted down at the Exchequer weighed less than 54 percent of the legal weight." Westfall further notes that "Newton estimated that nearly 20 percent of the coins taken in [during the recoinage] were counterfeit"; see *Never at Rest: A Biography of Isaac Newton* (Cambridge: Cambridge University Press, 1980), 554.

23. The loss of confidence in the English silver coinage triggered a 35 percent increase in the value of the gold coin, the Guinea, and a 20 percent fall in the English coin's exchange value abroad. Jones, *War and Economy*, 21.

24. These new technologies were introduced in England in 1662. However, because the old coins were not called in and continued to circulate at par the newly minted full-weight coins were quickly taken out of circulation, either hoarded, melted, or exported. This generated a situation in which the majority of the coin in circulation were the old bruised and tattered ones.

25. William Lowndes, *A Report Containing an Essay for the Amendment of the Silver Coins* (London, 1695), 97.

26. Ibid., 98. For a description of both the old and the new method of minting coin, see 93–96.

27. Lowndes mentioned in a private correspondence to the Treasury lords that since his plan essentially entailed a default on some of the government's obligations, it might make it difficult to borrow in the future. Richard Kleer, "'The Ruine of Their Diana': Lowndes, Locke, and the Bankers," *History of Political Economy* 36 (2004): 548. For a detailed discussion of Lowndes's position, see Ming-Hsun Li, *The Great Recoinage of 1696 to 1699* (London: Weidenfeld and Nicolson, 1963), chap. 6.

28. Lowndes, *Report Containing*, 115.

29. Ibid., 84–85. While concerned about the general status of credit, Lowndes was not an advocate of credit money per se. He noted, for example, that "the want of a sufficient Stock of Money, hath been the chief Cause of Introducing so much Paper Credit (which is at best hazardous, and may be carried too far)" (85).

30. Lowndes's *Report Containing* was completed in September of 1695, but did not appear in print until November.

31. The panel also consisted of John Asgill, William Wallis, Abraham Hill, Sir John Houblon, Charles Chamberlain, and Sir Joseph Herne. Kelly, *Locke on Money*, 25.

32. John Locke, *Two Treatises of Government*, ed. Peter Laslett (Cambridge: Cambridge University Press, [1689] 1960), 293–302.

33. Ibid., 293. Karen Vaughn points out that for Locke gold and silver "had no value whatsoever to human life (no intrinsic value) to begin with and so derived a value only from universal agreement" in *John Locke: Economist and Social Scientist* (Chicago: University of Chicago Press, 1980), 33.

34. John Locke, *Some Considerations of the Consequences of the Lowering of Interest and Raising the Value of Money* (London, 1691), 31.

35. Locke, *Two Treatises*, 391. Vaughn acknowledges that "this is a strange use of *intrinsic* in Locke's system since he has already categorized the value of silver as imaginary, but it does reflect a quality of silver that makes it useful as money" (*John Locke*, 35). Patrick Kelly also notes that there is an apparent confusion in Locke's use of *intrinsic value*, in that he sometimes locates the value in the inherent qualities of the metal and sometimes in the imagination of men. Yet, in the end, Kelly is fully convinced that Locke believed that it was the common consent of people that placed value on money, and that once people had agreed to value money, it took on a more objective, immutable, and immovable role, which Locke described as "intrinsick." Patrick Kelly, "'All Things Richly to Enjoy': Economics and Politics in Locke's *Two Treatises of Government*," *Political Studies* 36 (1988): 290.

36. John Locke, *Further Considerations Concerning Raising the Value of Money. Wherein Mr. Lowndes's Argument for it in his late Report Concerning An*

Essay for the Amendment of the Silver Coins, are Particularly Examined (London, 1696), 1.

37. Ibid., 5.
38. Ibid., 8–9.
39. Ibid., 9.
40. For a discussion of the difference between manipulations of the coin carried out by individuals and the state, see Ludovic Desmedt and Jérôme Blan, "Counteracting Counterfeiting? Bodin, Mariana, and Locke on False Money as a Multidimensional Issue," *History of Political Economy* 42 (2010): 323–360.
41. Ibid., 12.
42. Locke argued that this threshold is reached once foreign merchants are no longer able to obtain full-weight coin in England to bring back to their home ports. At that point, all clipped coin would be forced into discount. Locke, *Some Considerations*, 157–158. Daniel Carey expands upon this point in "Locke's Philosophy of Money" (unpublished essay), 6–7.
43. Locke, *Further Considerations*, 9.
44. It should be noted that the disagreement between Locke and Lowndes masks a deeper disagreement between members of Parliament over the recoinage, which Patrick Kelly explores in detail in *Locke on Money*.
45. Locke, *Some Considerations*, 156.
46. Locke, *Further Considerations*, 15. While not an advocate of credit money, he was not adamantly opposed to it either. He believed that with the proper legal changes, it was possible to make private debt instruments universally assignable. Locke, however, did not believe that credit money was the only way to expand the money stock. He suggested that if wages and rents were paid more often, money's velocity would increase, which would have the same effect as an increase in the quantity of money. *Some Considerations*, 32–43.
47. Locke, *Some Considerations*, 33. In supporting Lowndes, Isaac Newton pointed out that Lowndes's recoinage proposal would not impose any more damage on landowners and creditors than the clippers had already done. See Li, *Great Recoinage*, 218.
48. Locke, *Further Considerations*, 12–13.
49. Kelly, *Locke on Money*, 103.
50. I am grateful to Daniel Carey for sharing his transcription of Locke's "Dialogues about Banks," Bodleian MS. Locke b. 3, ff. 33–37.
51. Ibid., 36v. The Bank mandated that its cash "shall be carefully kept under three or more Locks, the Keys whereof shall be kept by such three or more of the Governor, Deputy-Governor, and Directors"; see *Rules, Orders, and By-Laws; For the Good Government of the Corporation of the Governor and Company of the Bank of England* (n.p., 1697).
52. Ibid., 36r.

53. Ibid., 36v.
54. Ibid., 37r.
55. Locke appears agnostic about banks and credit money in his "Dialogues about Banks," offering neither resounding endorsement nor categorical condemnation.
56. Locke, *Further Considerations*, 12–13.
57. Davenant wrote in a memorial to Lord Godolphin that "'twas apparent to all the World, That the Bank of England push'd it on with most vehemence" (quoted in Li, *Great Recoinage*, 79). Peter Laslett claims that "it was because the chief figure in the government of the day, Sir John Somers, was so much under the influence of Locke's opinion that his policy was adopted" in "John Locke, the Great Recoinage, and the Origins of the Board of Trade: 1695–1698," *William and Mary Quarterly* 14 (1957): 378. Patrick Kelly argues that in the end "it was William's personal intervention that finally decided in favour of maintaining the existing monetary standard" (*Locke on Money*, 27). It should be noted that Locke's insistence that coin should only be allowed to circulate by weight until the recoinage was complete was not followed. Some contemporaries viewed this provision as inadvisable, as it would prolong the recoinage because there would be no inducement to bring the coin to the mint. See Li, *Great Recoinage*, 69.
58. Nicholas Barbon, *A Discourse Concerning Coining the New Money Lighter* (London, 1696), preface.
59. Joyce Oldham Appleby, "Locke, Liberalism and the Natural Law of Money," *Past and Present* 71 (1976): 43–69. Thomas J. Sargent and Francois R. Velde are even more critical of Locke's economic reasoning, calling it "an embarrassment" (*Big Problem*, 288). Appleby, "Locke, Liberalism," 55, 60.
60. Appleby, *Economic Thought and Ideology*, 217.
61. Appleby, "Locke, Liberalism," 68.
62. Locke told Molyneux in a letter that "I think every one . . . is bound to labour for the publick good, as far as he is able, or else he has not right to eat" (quoted in Kelly, *Locke on Money*, 16).
63. Although Locke argued for a direct link between the quantity of money and economic activity, Caffentzis, as well as Kelly, claims that Locke actually did not believe that his recoinage would generate a commercial downturn. Caffentzis suggests that Locke's "'ace in the hole' was the existence of a 'Gresham hoard,' a large amount of legal, unclipped coin that was not circulating" (*Clipped Coins*, 41).
64. Appleby, "Locke, Liberalism," 58.
65. Pierre Vilar connects the Great Recoinage and the Bank of England, claiming that it was the latter's issuance of credit money that caused the rise in prices and thus a fall in the value of the coin. He suggests that the value of both notes and the coin dropped by approximately the same percentage

(*History of Gold and Money*, 220). Richard Kleer also recognizes that public finance was at the center of the debate between Locke and Lowndes. Since the Treasury was trying to borrow money from the goldsmith bankers, he suggests that Lowndes "deemed it necessary to afford financiers a quiet subsidy." Kleer then argues that because Locke was negatively disposed towards the goldsmith bankers, for manipulating the currency crisis in their favor, he was opposed to Lowndes's plan. Locke therefore suggested a recoinage plan that would effectively tax the holders of the clipped coin, which included the goldsmith bankers; see "Ruine of Their Diana," 553.

66. Appleby, "Locke, Liberalism," 68.
67. Christopher Wren, untitled manuscript, reprinted in Li, *Great Recoinage*, 184.
68. Ibid., 187.
69. Istvan Hont suggests that Davenant was "probably the most influential English analyst of trade and its implications in the closing years of the seventeenth century" in "Free Trade and the Economic Limits to National Politics: Neo-Machiavellian Political Economy Reconsidered," in *Jealousy of Trade*, 201.
70. Charles Davenant, "Essay on Public Virtue, Part 1. To his Grace the Duke of Shrewsbury and the Rt. Hon:ble Sidney Lord Godolphin," reprinted in Li, *Great Recoinage*, 210.
71. Ibid.
72. Charles Davenant, "Memorial Concerning the Coine of England in which are Handled these 4 Questions," reprinted in Li, *Great Recoinage*, 198.
73. Ibid.
74. Davenant acknowledged that postponing the recoinage might make it more difficult to pay the troops on the continent. However, he believed that this was an inconvenience that a healthy public credit could overcome without too much trouble (ibid., 199).
75. John Blackwell, *An essay towards carrying on the present war against France and other publick occasions. As also, for paying off all debts contracted in the same, or otherwise. And newcoyning of all our moneys, without charge, to the great encrease of the honour, strength, and wealth of the nation. Humbly propos'd, for the Parliament's consideration, and submitted to their great wisdom, and love to their country, &c* (London, 1695), 9–10.
76. Ibid., 19.
77. Ibid., 17.
78. L. R., *A Proposal for Supplying His Majesty with Thewlve Hundred thousand Pounds, by Mending the Coin, and yet Preserve the Ancient Standard of the Kingdom* (London, 1695), 2.
79. Ibid., 9.
80. Ibid.

81. Ibid., 15.

82. *Some of the mischiefs arising from the exportation of gold and silver with the consequences which will follow the continuing of clipping: humbly represented to the Parliament of England* (n.p., 1695), 3.

83. Pincus, *1688*, 459.

84. Wren, untitled manuscript, reprinted in Li, *Great Recoinage*, 185–186.

85. Locke, *Further Considerations*, 13. Peter Bower shows that counterfeiting soon became a common strategy to destabilize an enemy's monetary system in "Economic Warfare: Banknote Forgery as a Deliberate Weapon" in *The Banker's Art; Studies in Paper Money*, ed. Virginia Hewitt, 46-50 (London: British Museum Press, 1995).

86. John Brewer argues for the existence of a shared country discourse during the 1690s. He notes that "there were, of course, peculiarly whig and tory variants of country ideology . . . But, when it came to discussing war, foreign policy, money and the state, [country ideology] was the *lingua franca*" (*Sinews of Power*, 157). Pincus, on the other hand, sees a much more radical party polarization, in particular on the issue of banks (*1688*, 389–393).

87. *Positions Supported by their Reasons Explaining the Office of Land-Credit* (London, 1696), 5.

88. Ibid.

89. Ibid., 2.

90. Hugh Chamberlen, *A collection of some papers writ upon several occasions, concerning clipt and counterfeit money, and trade, so far as it relates to the exportation of bullion* (London, 1696), 9.

91. R. B., *Proposals humbly offered to the honourable House of Commons, first, for a way, or method, to procure bullion. Secondly, that his majesty, and subject, will be gainers thereby. Thirdly, that it will highly tend to the good of trade, and commerce in general, during the time the moneys shall be re-coining* (n.p., 1696), 1.

92. James Hodges, *The present state of England, as to coin and publick charges. In three parts. Treating of the necessity of more money before taxes can be effectual, or trade revived, and of ways and means to procure it: . . . against which the opposite prejudices, as injurious to King, Parliament and people, with Mr. Lock's chief positions, are refuted by demonstrable reason and matter of fact. Most humbly presented to the King and Parliament, by J.H.* (London, 1695), 7.

93. Ibid., 8.

94. Ibid., 10–11. Making notes legal tender would therefore not make much of a difference. Hodges called "the forcing of Credit by Law . . . a thing as unnatural and unreasonable as the forcing of Belief, which is impossible and repugnant, seeing it altogether dependeth upon Perswasion, and that wholly either upon the evidence of Verity, or Credit of the Informer" (12).

95. Ibid., 25.
96. Henry Pollexfen, *A Discourse of Trade, Coyn, and Paper Credit: And of Ways and Means to Gain, and Retain Riches. To which is added The argument of a learned counsel, upon an action of the case brought by the East-India-Company against Mr. Sands an interloper* (London, 1697), 65.
97. Ibid., 75–76.
98. Ibid., 75.
99. Thomas Houghton, for example, complained that many thousands of people have felt the ill effects and "groan under a Burthen they are not able much longer to bear; some by Scarcity of Money, others by Want of Credit" in *A plain and easie method for supplying the scarcity of money, and the promoting of trade, whereby all persons may manage their affairs with ease and profit, and be enabled to make payments in the way of trade, till a sufficient quantity of money can be coin'd. Most humbly offer'd to the consideration of both houses of Parliament* (London, 1696), 3.
100. R. J., *A Letter of Advice to a friend about the currency of cliptmoney wherein all the material clauses contain'd in the several acts made in these two last sessions of Parliament for the cure of that evil, are recited; And now printed for the use of the publick* (London, 1696), 3.
101. William Fleetwood, *A Sermon against Clipping, Preach'd before the right Honourable the Lord Mayor and Court of Aldermen, at Guild-Hall Chappel, on Decemb. 16, 1694* (London, 1694), 6.
102. Ibid.
103. Gaskill, *Crime and Mentalities*, 132.
104. Ibid. Stephen Mihm has shown that counterfeiters in the United States during the second half of the nineteenth century facilitated the nation's industrialization by improving the economy's liquidity; see *A Nation of Counterfeiters: Capitalists, Con Men, and the Making of the United States* (Cambridge, MA: Harvard University Press, 2007). D. W. Jones similarly argues that clipping and counterfeiting may have saved England in the 1690s. He concludes that "Clipping not only saved England from a monetary squeeze, but also staved off that collapse in spending, output and employment which remittances and the failure of trade would otherwise have produced" (*War and Economy*, 228).
105. Fleetwood, *Sermon*, 17.
106. Ibid., 20–21.
107. Ibid., 24.
108. 5 Eliz. c. 11. s. 2. "An Act Against the Clipping, Washing, Rounding and Filing of Coines," *Statutes of the Realm*.
109. Malcolm Gaskill points out that the more conscientious counterfeiters "did not store or spend his or her own coins, but passed them on to a third party. Even then, utterers of counterfeits often worked in pairs—one spending the

other carrying the coins at a distance—so that if the spender were caught, he or she could plead ignorance and the carrier could walk away still carrying the bulk of the evidence" (*Crime and Mentalities*, 155).

110. William Chaloner, *To the honourable, the knights, citizens, and burgesses, in Parliament assembled. Proposals humbly offered, for passing an act to prevent clipping and counterfeiting of money* (London, 1694), 3.

111. For an account of Chaloner's life and writings, see Thomas Levenson, *Newton and the Counterfeiter: The Unknown Detective Career of the World's Greatest Scientist* (Boston: Houghton Mifflin Harcourt, 2009).

112. Joseph Aicken, *The Mysteries of the Counterfeiting of the Coin of the Nation, Fully Detected: and Methods Humbly Offered to both Houses of Parliament, for Preventing the said Abuse for ever, by Easie and Reasonable Laws; and for the Raising the Sum of 200000 l. in Three Months Time, and Augmenting his Majesty's yearly Revenue Considerably* (London, 1696), 4.

113. Ibid.

114. Aicken's list of possible accomplices included the charcoal man, bricklayer, smith, ironmonger, brazier, pewterer, goldsmith, engraver, etc. He adds, "No Man can be so ingenious, as to make all his instruments himself; not so well stockt, as to have all such Variety of Ingredients as are here-unto necessary" (*Mysteries of the Counterfeiting*, 5).

115. Ibid., 7.

116. Ibid., 8.

117. William Chaloner, *The Defects in the Present Constitution of the Mint. Humbly offered to the consideration of the Honourable House of Commons* (London, 1693), 1.

118. Aicken, *Mysteries of the Counterfeiting*, 4.

119. Ibid.

120. Ibid.

121. Ibid., 5.

122. Simon Clement, *A discourse of the general notions of money, trade, & exchanges, as they stand in relation each to other. Attempted by way of aphorism: with a letter to a minister of state, further explaining the aphorisms, and applying them to the present circumstances of this nation. Wherein also some thoughts are suggested for the remedying the abuses of our money. By a merchant* (London, 1695), 20.

123. R. J., *Letter of Advice*, 9.

124. John Lewis, *A Proposal to Prevent the Corruption of the Coyn* (n.p., 1695), 1.

125. *Some Questions Answered, Relating to the Badness of the Now Silver Coin of England* (London, 1695), 2.

126. Ibid.

127. *Journals of the House of Commons, Volume 11*, 265–266 (London: H. M. Stationary Office, 1803). The report contained fourteen resolutions, some dealing

with the proposed recoinage and some with new laws against clipping and counterfeiting. The former were all rejected during the spring of 1695.

128. 6 & 7 Will. 3. c. 17. "Act to prevent counterfeiting and clipping the Coine of this Kingdom," *Statutes of the Realm*, 598–600; 8 & 9 Will. 3. c. 26. "An Act for the Better Preventing the Counterfeiting the Current Coin of this Kingdom," *Statutes of the Realm*, 269–270.

129. The act also announced a £40 reward for information leading to the arrest and conviction of counterfeiters, clippers, or bullion traders. *Statutes of the Realm*, 598–599.

130. 8 & 9 Will. 3. c. 26. s. 1. *Statutes of the Realm*, 269.

131. 8 & 9 Will. 3. c. 26. s. 3–4. *Statutes of the Realm*, 270.

132. 15 Geo. 2. c. 28. "An Act for the More Effectual Preventing the Counterfeiting of the Current Coin of this Kingdom, and the Uttering or Paying of False or Counterfeit Coin," *Statutes of the Realm*, 464. The court declared that "whereas the uttering of false Money . . . is a Crime frequently committed all over the Kingdom, and the offenders therein are not deterred, by reason that it is only a Misdemeanor, and the Punishment very often but small, though there be great Reason to believe, that the common utterers of such false Money are either themselves the Coiners, or in Confederacy with the Coiners thereof." The Utterance Law ensured that the coining laws disproportionably punished women. Nicholas Tosney, "Women and 'False Coining' in Early Modern London," *London Journal* 32 (2007): 103. Since many counterfeiting rings used poor women to pass newly counterfeited coin, women were even more exposed to punishment after the passing of the 1742 Utterance Law.

133. Bank of England, Minutes of the Court of Directors, G4/1/34/August 11, 1694. Randall McGowen, "Making the 'Bloody Code'? Forgery Legislation in Eighteenth-Century England," in *Law, Crime, and English Society, 1660–1840*, ed. Norma Landau, 128 (Cambridge: Cambridge University Press, 2002). The historian Henry Rhodes points out that copying the paper was often the greatest obstacle to the forgers in *The Craft of Forgery* (London: John Murray, 1934), 86.

134. Bank of England, Minutes of the Court of Directors, G4/2/60/August 14, 1695.

135. Ibid.

136. Ibid., G4/2/154/August 11, 1696.

137. 8 & 9 William III. c. 20. *Statues of the Realm*. Bank of England, Minutes of the Court of Directors, G4/2/172/October 21, 1696.

138. Samuel Pratt, *The Regulating Silver Coin, Made Practicable and Easie to the Government and Subject. Humbly submitted to the consideration of both houses of Parliament. By a lover of his country* (London, 1696), 14.

139. Ibid.

140. Ibid.

141. A Person of Honour, *Further Proposals for Amending and Settling the Coyn* (London, 1696), 11.

142. Ibid.

143. Locke, *Further Considerations*, 13.

144. Pollexfen, *Discourse of Trade*, 39–40.

145. Locke had previously asked Somers to be considered for the post himself. Roger Woolhouse, *Locke: A Biography* (Cambridge: Cambridge University Press, 2007), 357. After toiling in relative obscurity for many years, the publication of his *Philosophiæ Naturalis Principia Mathematica* "had established Newton as the smartest man in England and thus a natural figure to be called upon at a time of national crisis" (Levenson, *Newton and the Counterfeiter*, 110).

146. Newton and Montagu had become close friends in the 1680s, when they collaborated in establishing a philosophical society in Cambridge. Westfall, *Never at Rest*, 557–558.

147. In Montagu's offer letter to Newton, he suggests that the Wardenship "has not too much bus'nesse to require more attendance then you may spare"; see J. F. Scott, ed., *The Correspondence of Isaac Newton* (Cambridge: Cambridge University Press, 1967), 4:195.

148. Newton quoted in Westfall, *Never at Rest*, 566.

149. Scott, *Correspondence of Isaac Newton*, 4:209. Ironically, in Newton's contribution to the recoinage debate he listed "great Rewards to any that shall discover a Clipper or Coyner or any of their Confederates" as essential to putting a stop to clipping and coining (reprinted in Li, *Great Recoinage*, 219). This was written, however, before his tenure at the Mint commenced.

150. Newton's expense account reveals that he paid an aide to "buy him a suit to qualify him for conversing with a gang of coiners of note in order to discover them" (John Craig, "Isaac Newton—Crime Investigator," *Nature* 182 [1958]: 150).

151. The Newton biographer Frank Manuel claims that Newton "could hurt and kill [at the Mint] without doing damage to his puritan conscience. The blood of coiners and clippers nourished him"; see Manuel, *A Portrait of Isaac Newton* (Cambridge: Belknap Press, 1980), 244. Levenson, however, claims that Manuel's interpretation "is almost certainly nonsense." He goes on to argue that Newton "was a familiar figure, just doing his job, a bureaucrat using the means that were generally available at the time" (*Newton and the Counterfeiter*, 165).

152. Scott, *Correspondence of Isaac Newton*, 4:308.

153. John Craig, "Isaac Newton and the Counterfeiters," *Notes and Records of the Royal Society of London* 18 (1963): 139.

154. Scott, *Correspondence of Isaac Newton*, 5:68–69.

155. Scott, *Correspondence of Isaac Newton*, 6:289.
156. For the full story of how Newton finally succeeded in sending Chaloner to the gallows, see Craig, "Isaac Newton"; Levenson, *Newton and the Counterfeiter.*
157. Scott, *Correspondence of Isaac Newton*, 4:211.
158. In discussing these issues, Michel Foucault claims that "the aim was to make an example, not only by making people aware that the slightest offence was likely to be punished, but by arousing feelings of terror by the spectacle of power letting its anger fall upon the guilty person . . . Not only must people know, they must see with their own eyes. Because they must be made to be afraid; but also because they must be the witnesses, the guarantors, of the punishments, and because they must to a certain extent take part in it" see *Discipline and Punish: The Birth of the Prison*, trans. Alan Sheridan (New York: Vintage Books, 1979), 58.
159. Tyburn was the most important place of execution, but it was by no means the only one. In fact, there were so many gallows in London that it was given the name City of the Gallows. "No matter by what approach the stranger then entered London, he had the fact of the stringent severity of English criminal law most painfully impressed upon him by a sight of the gallows" (Radzinowicz, *History of English Criminal Law*, 200).
160. Ibid., 171.
161. For a description of the culture of Tyburn, see Simon Devereaux, "Recasting the Theater of Execution: The Abolition of the Tyburn Trial," *Past and Present* 202 (2009): 128.
162. Quoted in Radzinowicz, *History of English Criminal Law,* 211.
163. These figures can be compared to the six capital convictions, out of eleven prosecutions, for highway robbery in 1696.
164. All statistics are from *The Proceedings of the Old Bailey*, www.oldbaileyonline.org (accessed July 21, 2010).
165. Craig, "Isaac Newton," 139. C. R. Josset claims that the recoinage and the new penalties against counterfeiting succeeded in putting an end to the counterfeiting in *Money in Britain: A History of the Currencies of the British Isles* (London: Warne, 1962), 90.
166. For two substantial treatments of eighteenth-century money manipulations, see John Styles, "'Our Traitorous Money Makers': The Yorkshire Coiners and the Law, 1769–83," in *An Ungovernable People: The English and their Law in the Seventeenth and Eighteenth Centuries*, ed. John Brewer and John Styles (New Brunswick, NJ: Rutgers University Press, 1980); Gaskill, *Crime and Mentalities*, chaps. 4 and 5.
167. British Library, Add. Ms. 28,924. I am grateful to Rachel Weil for sharing her archival findings.
168. Feavearyear, *Pound Sterling*, 139–142.
169. Levenson, *Newton and the Counterfeiter*, 140, 143.

170. Horsefield, *British Monetary Experiments*, 14.

171. Jones, *War and Economy*, 24.

172. Feavearyear, *Pound Sterling*, 143.

173. Kelly, *Locke on Money*, 64.

174. The Bank actively contributed to the failure of the Land Bank. The directors decided in January of 1696 to petition the House of Commons and "to use such other prudent methods as they shall think fitt . . . to prevent the setting up a New Bank by Act of Parliament" (Bank of England, Minutes of the Court of Directors, G4/2/102/January 29, 1696).

175. Horsefield, *British Monetary Experiments*, 14.

176. Davenant, *Discourses on the Publick Revenues*, 38.

177. Ibid.

178. Ibid.

179. Charles Davenant, *A Postscript to a Discourse of Credit, and the Means and Methods of Restoring it* (n.p., 1701), 14–15.

180. Ibid., 5.

181. Davenant, *Discourses on the Publick Revenues*, 56.

182. Davenant, *Postscript*, 5.

183. Davenant quoted in Hont, *Jealousy of Trade*, 235.

184. Davenant, *Discourses on the Publick Revenues*, 57.

185. Ibid., 58.

186. Ibid., 59.

187. Isaac Newton quoted in Findlay Shirras and J. H. Craig, "Sir Isaac Newton and the Currency," *Economic Journal* 55 (1945): 231.

188. Mint Papers 19.2, f. 611. Quoted in Westfall, *Never at Rest*, 618.

189. Newton quoted in Shirras and Craig, "Newton and the Currency," 217–218.

190. Mark Goldie, ed., *John Locke: Selected Correspondence*, 223 (Oxford: Oxford University Press, 2002). After resting at his home for the first part of 1696, Locke soon joined the Board of Trade, on which he served for the next four years.

191. Shirras and Craig, "Newton and the Currency," 240; Appleby, "Locke, Liberalism," 61. Feavearyear disagrees and suggests that a "larger measure of justice as between debtors and creditors was probably meted out by recoining at the old denomination." Given the conditions England faced during the 1690s, he concluded that "the country gained far more than it lost from the consequences of Locke's reasoning" (*Pound Sterling*, 147, 149).

192. *The Proceedings of the Old Bailey* show a rapid increase in the people tried for coining offences between 1693–5. The number is still high, but falling, in 1696–1697, only to stabilize at the pre-1693 level after 1697 (www.oldbaileyonline.org, accessed July 21, 2010).

193. John Evelyn, *Numismata. A discourse of medals, antient and modern. Together with some account of heads and effigies of illustrious and famous persons, in*

sculps, and taille-douce, of whom we have no medals extant; and of the use to be derived from them. To which is added a digression concerning physiognomy (London, 1697), 260–261.

5. Public Credit and the Public Sphere

1. John Carswell points out, "The changes of 1710 were the political expression of the first fully-fledged crisis in the commercial and financial revolution through which the nation was still passing" in *The South Sea Bubble* (Stanford, CA: Stanford University Press, 1960), 37.
2. Michael Braddick argues that early seventeenth-century "borrowing had been dependent for its security on the word of the monarch and it had been raised through the good offices of individuals or corporations bribed or coerced into acting" (*State Formation*, 259). In 1672, for example, 97.5 percent of the total royal debt was owed to twelve goldsmith bankers. Carruthers, *City of Capital*, 62.
3. Tim Harris describes the ruling elite as "a small group, comprising the monarch and his or her advisers and ministers at Court, the lords, bishops and the MPs who sat in Parliament, and the judges, lord lieutenants and JPs who were responsible for keeping law and order throughout the realm" in *Politics under the Later Stuarts: Party Conflict in a Divided Society, 1660–1715* (London: Longman, 1993), 14.
4. Locke, *Essay*, IV.xv.6.
5. J. G. A. Pocock notes that public opinion now determined the value of public bonds, which in turn "became the index to the stability or instability of governments" in *Virtue, Commerce, and History: Essays on Political Thought and History, Chiefly in the Eighteenth Century* (Cambridge: Cambridge University Press, 1985), 112–113. Pocock adds that since opinion now dictated the value of property, it "has ceased to be real and has become not merely mobile but imaginary" (ibid.). For a systematic treatment of the emergence of a powerful English extra-parliamentary political culture, see Katherine Wilson, *The Sense of the People: Politics, Culture and Imperialism in England, 1715–1785* (Cambridge: Cambridge University Press, 1998).
6. Julian Hoppit notes that "Credit appeared to them to be a Trojan horse, promising well but in fact catastrophically breaching the walls of a harmonious and moral order" ("Attitudes to Credit," 320).
7. Patrick Brantlinger similarly notes, "Public credit is at once tied to state legitimacy . . . and to the political category of public opinion as an aspect of the democratic public spheres emergent during the Enlightenment" (*Fictions of State*, 22).
8. Knights, *Representation and Misrepresentation*, 316.
9. Brewer, *Sinews of Power*, xiii.

10. Braddick, *State Formation*, 165, 214. Brewer points out that seventeenth-century wartime enlistment was on average below that of the Hundred Years' War (1337–1453). After the Glorious Revolution, however, the military took on a much more significant role. In addition to enlistments increasing drastically, the armed forces also became "the largest borrower and spender, as well as the largest single employer" (*Sinews of Power*, 27).

11. Charles Spencer, *Battle for Europe: How the Duke of Marlborough Masterminded the Defeat of the French at Blenheim* (Hoboken, NJ: Wiley, 2004).

12. Jones, *War and Economy*.

13. As noted in Chapter 3, the Financial Revolution unfolded over the course of the second half of the seventeenth century, or as Brewer notes, "Post-revolutionary finance was built on a pre-revolutionary model" (*Sinews of Power*, 95). While North and Weingast, "Constitutions and Commitment," emphasize the radical importance of the Glorious Revolution for England's financial system, Patrick K. O'Brien offers a more nuanced version of their strong temporal, conceptual, and causal claims. He argues that their work "exaggerates the significance of the Glorious Revolution as a discontinuity" and "neglects an immediately prior, but highly significant history of the Civil War, Republican Interregnum, and Restoration, when the constitutional and administrative foundations for a fiscal state were put in place" ("Fiscal Exceptionalism," 246).

14. Patrick O'Brien and Philip Hunt point out that "the transition from a fiscal regime largely dependent on taxes supplemented with Crown estate and other income to a regime armed with the political support, the administrative capacity and fiscal base required to accumulate and service a perpetual debt deserves to be called a financial revolution" in "The Rise of a Fiscal State in England, 1485–1815," *Historical Research* 66 (1993): 134.

15. Ashworth, *Customs and Excise*, 15–30.

16. Brewer, *Sinews of Power*, 91.

17. The Treasury was able to significantly increase the amount of money it raised. In 1672, the Crown's income was £2.3 million and spending amounted to £2.5 million, compared to 1712, when income was £5.7 million and expenditures £7.9; see Carruthers, *City of Capital*, 54.

18. The earlier political conflict between country and court informed, although did not always overlap with, the Whig–Tory divide. Moreover, it should be noted that neither party was ideologically monolithic. While Linda Colley offers a sense of how diverse the Tory party was in *In Defiance of Oligarchy: The Tory Party, 1714-60* (Cambridge: Cambridge University Press, 1982), Martyn P. Thompson has identified a plethora of different factions among the Whigs, including the First Whigs, Old Whigs, New Whigs, True Whigs, Polite Whigs, Vulgar Whigs, Regime Whigs, Skeptical Whigs, and Scientific Whigs. "Daniel Defoe and the Formation of Early-Eighteenth Century Whig

Ideology," in *Politics, Politeness, and Patriotism*, ed. Gordon J. Schochet, 109–124 (Washington DC: Folger Institute).

19. The Whig Junto included Baron Somers, Baron Wharton, Charles Montagu (Lord Halifax), and Edward Russell (Earl of Orford). Harris, *Politics under the Later Stuarts*, 15.

20. Godolphin enjoyed a long a prosperous career, serving Charles II, James II, William and Mary, as well as Anne in various capacities at the Treasury. As Lord Treasurer during Anne's reign, Godolphin worked successfully to make the fiscal system more efficient.

21. Tim Harris cautions that there was no strict demarcation between a Whig moneyed interest and a Tory landed interest. Reality was far more complex. Harris notes that there "were Tory monied men; indeed, before the financial revolution, the monied interest in the City of London had been predominantly Tory. Tories opposed the new credit system set up in the 1690s not because they objected to this type of economic enterprise, but because the benefits to be accrued from it largely passed them by" (*Politics under the Later Stuarts*, 198).

22. The landed elite's aversion to a standing army was grounded in their fear of its astronomical costs, which inevitably would bring on more loans and eventually higher taxes. Instead, they favored an oceanic empire, based around a strong navy and a thriving global commerce. A large Royal Navy would be able to expand England's presence around the globe, thus generating more commerce and higher customs receipts, part of which could be used to foot the bill for the navy, thus making this imperial strategy largely self-financed. Armitage, *Ideological Origins*, 100–124.

23. In examining the London elites, Gary Stuart De Krey found that although there was a Whig bias among merchants, many merchants, industrialists, and money lenders belonged to the Tory party. *A Fractured Society: The Politics of London in the First Age of Party, 1688-1715* (Oxford: Clarendon Press, 1985).

24. The land tax was extensively used to finance much of the two-decade-long war with France. Brewer remarked that "the overall tax burden in England more than doubled after the Glorious Revolution. And the bulk of that increase, at least until the end of the War of Spanish Succession, was borne by means of the land tax" (*Sinews of Power*, 200).

25. The Bank of England and the East India Company were both considered biased in favor of the Whigs, as evidenced by the fact that there were approximately two Whig shareholders for each Tory shareholder in both companies. Carruthers, *City of Capital*, 155.

26. Pincus, *1688*, 366–399.

27. Godolphin forged a close relationship with the Bank of England, as well as to the London mercantile community, which allowed him to manage the

government's borrowing needs with relative ease. Dickson, *Financial Revolution in England*, 59–62. J. R. Jones praised Godolphin's ministry for its success in managing the Treasury, claiming, "Few, if any, later administrations have ever come near to equaling its triumphs" in *Country and Court: England, 1658–1714* (Cambridge, MA: Harvard University Press, 1979), 316.

28. Braddick, *State Formation*, 265.
29. Dickson, *Financial Revolution in England*, 362.
30. *The Case of the proprietors of the army and transport debentures* (n.p., 1711).
31. Brian W. Hill, "The Change of Government and the 'Loss of the City,' 1710–1711," *Economic History Review* 24 (1971): 395–413.
32. Lee Horsley, "*Vox Populi* in the Political Literature of 1710," *Huntington Library Quarterly* 38 (1975): 335.
33. Harris, *Politics under the Later Stuarts*, 181.
34. Roseveare, *Financial Revolution*, 45.
35. Sarah Jennings Churchill, Duchess of Marlborough, *Private Correspondence of Sarah, Duchess of Marlborough*, Vol. 1 (London: Henry Colburn, 1838), 344.
36. Robert Harley's influential political career was launched with his election to Parliament in 1689. Initially he sided with the Whigs, but he later gravitated towards the Tory camp. Harley served a seven-year apprenticeship in public finance as a Commissioner of Public Accounts during the 1690s and was one of the main supporters of the 1695 Land Bank scheme. Harley became a central member of the Godolphin ministry, serving as Speaker of the House of Commons (1701–1705) and Secretary of State (1704–1708). He was ousted from the ministry in 1708 after he allegedly participated in a plot against Godolphin. He nevertheless maintained his influence with the queen, who later selected him to run the government. For more on Harley, see Brian W. Hill, *Robert Harley: Speaker, Secretary of State and Premier Minister* (New Haven, CT: Yale University Press, 1988).
37. The Bank extended two loans to the Treasury in August and September. The first loan was in the amount of £50,000—Harley had asked for twice that amount—and the second loan was for £100,000. Both of these loans had a shorter maturity than Harley had requested. Hill, "Change of Government," 402–403.
38. According to Henry Roseveare, the depersonalization of public credit, resulting from the simultaneous disembodiment of the state and the marketization of securities, constituted "a truly modern innovation" (*Financial Revolution*, 14).
39. While government bonds had been traded before, the new culture of credit emerging in the 1690s generated a much more active financial market. Attempts at making government securities more transferable originated with Downing's Treasury Orders in the 1660s, but these debt instruments

were only transferable in theory. Since goldsmith bankers held most of them as security, only a limited secondary market developed. The lifetime annuities, another popular long-term loan, were also transferable in theory, but remained illiquid because of the legal and administrative obstacles involved in trading them. Larry Neal, *The Rise of Financial Capitalism: International Capital Markets in the Age of Reason* (Cambridge: Cambridge University Press, 1990), 14.

40. Because many of the long-term debts accrued during the Financial Revolution never had to be paid off, it generated a situation, described by Pocock, in which "Government is . . . maintained by the investor's imagination concerning a moment which will never exist in reality" (*Virtue, Commerce, and History*, 112).

41. Mark Knights shows that public opinion was not only important in dictating public credit, but that it played an increasingly active role in informing, assessing, judging, and legitimizing political decisions across the board in *Representation and Misrepresentation*, 5.

42. Dickson, *Financial Revolution in England*, 260–262. The number of investors holding Bank of England stocks increased in the same proportion, moving from 1,272 in 1694 to 4,419 in 1712. Carruthers, *City of Capital*, 83.

43. Ann M. Carlos and Larry Neal, "The Micro-Foundations of the Early London Capital Market: Bank of England Shareholders during and after the South Sea Bubble, 1720–25," *Economic History Review* 59 (2006): 525.

44. Dickson, *Financial Revolution in England*, 254, 301. It should be noted that both Whigs and Tories tried to influence prices in financial markets. For a discussion of such politically motivated transactions, see the discussion of Defoe that follows.

45. Dickson estimates that approximately 20 percent of the investors in government funds and company stocks were women (*Financial Revolution in England*, 260). Hence, women, in particular widows, but also spinsters, played an important role in emerging financial markets. Although women were formally denied the right to own property, fixed or mobile, after they married, this law could be circumvented by setting up a trust that allowed the woman to hold on to property brought to the marriage. Women's jointures were often comprised of stocks and bonds, because unlike land, they were not subject to taxation and there were no laws against women holding such assets. Catherine Ingrassia, *Authorship, Commerce, and Gender in Early Eighteenth-Century England: A Culture of Paper Credit* (Cambridge: Cambridge University Press, 1998); and Ann M. Carlos and Larry Neal, "Women Investors in Early Capital Markets: 1720–1725," *Financial History Review* 11 (2004): 197–224.

46. Roseveare, *Financial Revolution*, 19.

47. Neal, *Rise of Financial Capitalism*, 14. Anne L. Murphy shows that the lottery loans were specifically targeted at those who could not afford to purchase

government bonds. For a more extensive discussion about the lotteries and their place in the Financial Revolution, see Murphy, "Lotteries in the 1690s: Investment or Gamble?" *Financial History Review* 12 (2005): 227–246.

48. Although Dickson's account remains the most complete exploration on the subject, recent research has expanded our knowledge of the investing public. See, for example, Carlos and Neal, "Women Investors," 197–224; Anne L. Murphy, "Dealing with Uncertainty: Managing Personal Investment in the Early English National Debt," *History* 91 (2006): 200–218; and Glaisyer, *Culture of Commerce*.

49. James Van Horn Melton, *The Rise of the Public in Enlightenment Europe* (New York: Cambridge University Press, 2001), 22.

50. Julian Hoppit notes that along with the debates surrounding the recoinage and the South Sea Bubble, the 1710–1711 debate constituted the most intense periods of pamphleteering around the turn of the eighteenth century ("Contexts and Contours," 79–110).

51. Literacy rates in England at the time were approximately 45 percent for men and 25 percent for women. However, in London the figure might have been as high as 80 percent for men, creating a massive audience for newspapers, broadsides, and pamphlets. David Cressy, *Literacy and the Social Order: Reading and Writing in Tudor and Stuart England* (Cambridge: Cambridge University Press, 1980), 47. The remaining Londoners who were unable to read could obtain news and political commentary from public readings, adding to what was already an impressively informed and politically discursive public.

52. Paul Withington argues that a civic public sphere emerged much earlier in the seventeenth-century. He suggests that by 1640, in the 181 incorporated cities and boroughs people were "more than capable of talking and acting, as citizens, against the fiscal, bureaucratic, or military conceits of central authority and the paternalism of country and urbane gentry"; see "Public Discourse Corporate Citizenship, and State Formation in Early Modern England," *American Historical Review* 112 (2007): 1027.

53. Peter Lake and Steve Pincus highlight that debates about political economic issues provided the foundation for the "post-Revolutionary public sphere" in "Rethinking the Public Sphere in Early Modern England," *Journal of British Studies* 45 (2006): 284. Hoppit adds that of the issues most often discussed, credit was at the forefront. Hoppit, "Contexts and Contours," 94.

54. Jürgen Habermas, *The Structural Transformation of the Public Sphere: An Inquiry into a Category of Bourgeois Society* (Cambridge, M. A.: MIT Press, 1991). The rapid expansion of coffeehouses throughout Britain in the second half of the seventeenth century led to "qualitative improvement as well as a quantitative expansion of the opportunities for public discussion," leading Steve Pincus to conclude, "Coffeehouses provided the social and cultural

locus for an early modern English public sphere" in "'Coffee Politicians Does Create': Coffeehouses and Restoration Political Culture," *Journal of Modern History* 67 (1995): 833. Brian Cowan further points out that "the social intercourse of the coffeehouse allowed for, and indeed encouraged, the social fiction of equal status between patrons" in *The Social Life of Coffee: The Emergence of the British Coffeehouse* (New Haven, CT: Yale University Press, 2005), 104.

55. Habermas's concept of the public sphere has been usefully employed by historical researchers. Lately, however, historians have found it necessary to revise his version. The reason why Habermas's concept has been criticized by historians, Harold Mah argues, is because they tend to think of the public sphere as a geographical space, while Habermas thought of it as a fiction existing only in the political imaginary. See Harold Mah, "Phantasies of the Public Sphere: Rethinking the Habermas of Historians," *Journal of Modern History* 72 (2000): 168. See also Conal Condren, "Public, Private and the Idea of the 'Public Sphere' in Early-Modern England," *Intellectual History Review* 19 (2009): 15–28.

56. Karin Bowie notes that a similar type of government participation in the public sphere occurred around the same time in Scotland in *Scottish Public Opinion and the Anglo-Scottish Union, 1699–1707* (Suffolk: Boydell Press, 2007).

57. Habermas, as quoted in Mah, "Phantasies of the Public Sphere," 156.

58. Historians have noted that many different types of discourses were employed in the public sphere. See, for example, Alan Downie, "*Gulliver's Travels*, the Contemporary Debate on the Financial Revolution, and the Bourgeois Public Sphere," in *Money, Power, and Print: Interdisciplinary Studies on the Financial Revolution in the British Isles*, ed. Charles Ivar McGrath and Chris Fauske, 129 (Newark: University of Delaware Press, 2008); Knights, *Representation and Misrepresentation*, 248, 255.

59. For an extensive discussion of the analytical benefits and problems of using multiple publics, see Michael Warner, "Publics and Counterpublics," *Public Culture* 14 (2002): 49–90.

60. John Oldmixon, *The False steps of the ministry after the revolution . . . with some reflections on the license of the pulpit and press, in a letter to my lord* (London, 1714), 33.

61. Public opinion began to figure more prominently and explicitly in the discussion of popular influences on politics in the 1730s. Before that, alternative terms like *public spirit* and *vox populi* were more commonly used. J. A. W. Gunn, "Court Whiggery—Justifying Innovation," in *Politics, Politeness, and Patriotism*, ed. Gordon J. Schochet, 125–156 (Washington DC: Folger Institute).

62. Knights, *Representation and Misrepresentation*, 7.

63. Ibid., 273.

64. Benjamin Hoadly was successively bishop of Bangor, Hereford, Salisbury, and Winchester. In additional to his extensive writings on theological issues, Hoadly wrote numerous tracts in defense of the Glorious Revolution, answering many of Sacheverell's criticisms. Drawing inspiration from John Locke's political writings, Hoadly became one of the leading Whig and low-church propagandists of Anne's reign. For more on Hoadly, see William Gibson, *The Enlightenment Prelate: Benjamin Hoadly, 1676–1761* (Cambridge: James Clark and Co., 2004).

65. Benjamin Hoadly, *The thoughts of an honest Tory, upon the present proceedings of that party. In a letter to a friend in town* (London, 1710), 4.

66. Ibid., 11.

67. Ibid., 12.

68. Benjamin Hoadly, *The fears and sentiments of all true Britains; with respect to national credit, interest and religion* (London, 1710), 7.

69. Ibid., 5.

70. In addition to the clear limits to ideological politics set by commercial society, finance also put a firm check on political ideas, debates, and practices. Hont, *Jealously of Trade*, 185–266.

71. Hoadly, *The fears and sentiments*, 5.

72. Ibid., 9.

73. Although the Glorious Revolution might have made financial property safer, as North and Weingast argue, Hoadly's concern reveals that property rights were still far from being considered entirely safe.

74. J. A. Downie, *Robert Harley and the Press: Propaganda and Public Opinion in the Age of Swift and Defoe* (Cambridge: Cambridge University Press, 1979), 116.

75. Simon Clement initially worked as a stockjobber and merchant. During the 1690s he wrote for the Whigs on issues pertaining to the recoinage and the formation of the Bank of England. As Harley made his move from the Whigs to the Tories, Clement followed suit.

76. Simon Clement, *Faults on both sides: or, An essay upon the original cause, progress and mischievous consequences of the factions of this nation* (London, 1710), 39.

77. Ibid.

78. Clement, *Faults on both sides*, 40.

79. Daniel Defoe, for example, had earlier recorded his disdain for the stockjobbers in *The Villainy of Stock-Jobbers Detected, and the Causes of the Late Run upon the Bank and Bankers Discovered and Considered* (London, 1701).

80. See Chapter 3 for a discussion of Locke's views on trust and opinion.

81. Anne L. Murphy shows that even if early modern investors wanted to collect as much accurate information as possible, they "faced many barriers that

would have prevented them gaining full information about the prospects for any stock or debt product" (*Origins of English Financial Markets*, 130).

82. Simon Clement, *A vindication of the faults on both sides, from the reflections of the medley, the specimen maker, and a pamphlet, entituled, Most faults on our side. With a dissertation on the nature and use of money and paper-credit in trade, and the true value of joint-stocks, maintaining the assertions of the author, in relation to those matters. By the author of the Faults on both sides* (London, 1710).

83. Ibid., 16.

84. Abel Boyer, a Dutch Huguenot, came to England after the Glorious Revolution. He worked as a lexicographer, journalist, historian, and propagandist. He translated a number of French treatises on manners and morals, but it was his historical writings that earned him a reputation throughout Europe. He began working for Harley as early as 1704, when he became an intelligence agent in his service. After a fallout with Jonathan Swift in 1711, Boyer gravitated away from Harley and Bolingbroke towards the Whigs. In 1718, he published a lengthy challenge to Archibald Hutcheson's critique of the government's financial policies.

85. Abel Boyer, *An Essay towards the history of the last ministry and Parliament: containing seasonable reflections on I. Favourites. II. Ministers of state. III. Parties. IV. Parliaments. and V. Publick credit* (London, 1710), 60.

86. Ibid., 59.

87. Ibid.

88. Boyer described how "[t]he *Junto* were indeed alarm'd at the Removal of the E. of S____, but not entirely Daunted, and having recover'd spirit, they resolv'd to try new Expedients to support their tottering Power. In order to do that, their Emissaries propagated a wild Notion, That the PUBLICK CREDIT of *ENGLAND* wholly depended on the late Lord Treasurer; and the Continuation of the last Parliament" (ibid., 20).

89. Ibid., 64.

90. Hoadly, *The fears and sentiments*, 7.

91. Ibid., 63.

92. Ibid.

93. Daniel Defoe is well known to posterity for contributing to the formation of a new literary genre with his novels *Robinson Crusoe* (1719), *Moll Flanders* (1722), and *Roxana* (1724). Before becoming a novelist, Defoe pursued numerous commercial ventures and made a name for himself as a prolific journalist and propagandist. He maintained a Whig allegiance, supporting the Glorious Revolution, for much of his life. However, after he began working for Harley in 1704, first as an agent and intelligencer, and later as a propaganda writer, his publications took on a more Tory-friendly tone. For more on Defoe, see Paula Backscheider, *Daniel Defoe: His Life* (Baltimore, MD: The Johns Hopkins University Press, 1989).

94. Defoe quoted in Backscheider, *Daniel Defoe*, 269.
95. Daniel Defoe, *An essay upon publick credit: being an enquiry how the publick credit comes to depend upon the change of the ministry, or the dissolutions of Parliaments; and whether it does so or no. With an argument, proving that the publick credit may be upheld and maintain'd in this nation; and perhaps brought to a greater height than it ever yet arriv'd at; tho' all the changes or dissolutions already made, pretended to, and now discours'd of, shou'd come to pass in the world* (London, 1710). This essay was momentarily attributed to Harley.
96. Defoe used the same basic argument as Boyer to show that public credit depends on the institutions of Parliament and the monarchy. Defoe challenged the "strange Suggestion" that the newly elected Parliament and the queen would act in ways contrary to the preservation of public credit. He argued, similar to Boyer, that public credit depends more on the institutional apparatus than the particular individuals who manage it. He would later write that public credit depends on people's confidence in the government, by which he meant "not the Ministry, not this or that Party, no, not the Queen Personally—But the Constitution, the Queen or King for the Time being, and Parliament"; see Daniel Defoe, *The Review of the State of the British Nation*, August 9, 1711, reprinted in *Defoe's Review: Reproduced from the Original Editions, with an Introduction and Bibliographical Notes by Arthur W. Secord* (New York: AMS Press, 1965).
97. Defoe, *An essay upon publick credit*, 6.
98. Ibid.
99. Defoe, *Review*, June 14, 1709.
100. Ibid., 9.
101. Ibid.
102. John F. O'Brien similarly argues that "Defoe's *Essay* seems to insist that credit can only be exchanged into more metaphors rather than related to real causes, which is to place it beyond the power of human intervention, a force of nature whose identity is ambiguous and whose consequences are indeterminate," in "The Character of Credit: Defoe's 'Lady Credit,' The Fortunate Mistress, and the Resources of Inconsistency in Early Eighteenth-Century Britain," *English Literary History* 63 (1996): 613.
103. Defoe, *An essay upon publick credit*, 9.
104. Ibid.
105. Ibid., 13.
106. Ibid.
107. Ibid., 16.
108. Carruthers, *City of Capital*.
109. See Shapin, *Social History of Truth*; Adrian Johns, *The Nature of the Book: Print and Knowledge in the Making* (Chicago: University of Chicago Press, 1998).
110. Schaffer, "Defoe's Natural Philosophy," 14.

111. Arthur Maynwaring was a prolific author and politician. A well-connected member of the Kit-Cat Club, Maynwaring used his connection to Godolphin to secure an office at the Exchequer. A committed Whig his whole life, he was elected to Parliament in 1706, only to lose his seat in the Tory landslide of 1710. Maynwaring was a tireless critic of the Tories. After the political crisis of 1710, Maynwaring unofficially took on the role of director of the press for the Whigs.

112. Arthur Maynwaring, *The Medley*, October 5, 1710.

113. Ibid., January 29, 1711, 202.

114. For a more extensive discussion of *Lady Credit*, see Paula R. Backscheider, "Defoe's Lady Credit," *Huntington Library Quarterly* 44 (1981): 89–100; Sandra Sherman, *Finance and Fictionality in the Early Eighteenth Century: Accounting for Defoe* (Cambridge: Cambridge University Press, 1996), 40–54; O'Brien, "Character of Credit," 603–631; and Laura Brown, *Fables of Modernity: Literature and Culture in the English Eighteenth Century* (Ithaca, NY: Cornell University Press, 2001), 95–131.

115. Defoe, *Review*, January 10, 1706.

116. Pocock, *Machiavellian Moment*, 457.

117. Defoe, *Review*, January 10, 1706.

118. Laura Brown points out, "In the imaginary world of this cultural fable, she [Lady Credit] is the motive power of British history. In this sense, she represents a historical force, a force associated with volatile change" (*Fables of Modernity*, 108). Terry Mulcaire adds that despite the negativity associated with credit in the Augustan writings, credit was also valued as a "potentially infinite resource" in "Public Credit; Or, The Feminization of Virtue in the Marketplace," *PMLA* 114 (1999): 1035.

119. Defoe, *Review*, August 8, 1710.

120. Lady Credit was also prone to hysteria. This condition was caused by "a supersensitive constitution and heightened passions, which were consistently connected with the female physiology and thought to generate symptoms of weakness, weeping, fainting, fits, and even death" (Brown, *Fables of Modernity*, 110).

121. Defoe, *Review*, August 10, 1710.

122. Ibid.

123. Ibid.

124. Defoe quoted in Backscheider, *Daniel Defoe*, 271.

125. Defoe, *An essay upon publick credit*, 14.

126. Pocock, *Machiavellian Moment*, 446. He further clarifies, "The Augustan debate did not oppose agrarian to entrepreneurial interests, the manor to the market," nor was there a "simple antithesis between land and trade, or even land and credit" (448–449).

127. Extract of letter from Blunt to Harley, reprinted in Hill, "Change of Government," 412. This letter was a reply to a previous, still unrecovered, correspondence, in which Blunt provided a more detailed account of his proposal.

128. George Caswall quoted in John G. Sperling, *The South Sea Company: An Historical Essay and Bibliographical Finding List* (Cambridge: Kress Library, 1962), 3–4.

129. The Bank agreed to engraft these discounted securities in return for a prolongation of its charter and a more secure monopoly on banking activities. The statute read: "no other Bank, or any corporation, society, fellowship, company, or constitution in the nature of a bank shall be erected, established, permitted, suffered, countenanced, or allowed by Act of Parliament within this Kingdom" (8 and 9 Will. III, cap. 20).

130. The Sword Blade Bank, emerging out of the Hollow Sword Blade Company, used discounted government debentures to purchase estate lands confiscated from Jacobites in Ireland. The Sword Blade Bank ended up with land holdings, which it then used as capital to launch a banking business, in defiance of the Bank of England's monopoly. The Sword Blade Bank granted mortgages for land purchases, accepted deposits, discounted bills, and issued notes. The Bank of England challenged the legal standing of its new rival, but it would take until 1707 before the Treasury reaffirmed its commitment to the Bank of England's monopoly. Considering that the South Sea Company, founded in 1711, was closely associated with the Sword Blade Bank, the Bank of England was concerned that the company constituted another attempt at challenging their monopoly. For this reason, the Bank of England forced the South Sea Company to insert a provision in its charter that prevented it from engaging in any banking activities. Dickson, *Financial Revolution in England*, 62; Sperling, *South Sea Company*, 4–5.

131. The October election was a resounding success for the Tories. The previous Whig majority of nearly one hundred seats was replaced by a Tory majority of nearly 150 seats.

132. Carswell, *South Sea Bubble*, 41.

133. Defoe, *Review*, February 1, 1711.

134. Ibid.

135. Joseph Addison benefitted from the patronage of powerful Whigs, such as Halifax and Somers, from an early age. In addition to his prominent place in politics, he also enjoyed a prominent position in London's literary world, with membership in the Kit-Cat Club and personal connections to writers like Jonathan Swift and Richard Steele. He contributed actively to Steele's *The Tatler* and later teamed up with Steele to launch *The Spectator*.

136. Joseph Addison, *The Spectator*, March 3, 1711, reprinted in Gregory Smith, ed., *Addison & Steele and Others, The Spectator, In Four Volumes* (London: J.M. Dent and Sons, 1907)

137. Ibid.

138. Ibid.

139. Jonathan Swift was born and educated in Ireland and later became dean of St. Patrick's Cathedral in Dublin. He journeyed back and forth across the

Irish Sea, participating in the political and cultural life of both Dublin and London. In September of 1710, Swift agreed to become a propagandist for Harley. Part of this engagement was to serve as the editor of the Tory weekly *The Examiner*. The work for which Swift is chiefly remembered, *Gulliver's Travels*, was published in 1729.

140. Jonathan Swift, *The Examiner*, April 19, 1711, reprinted in Frank H. Ellis, ed., *Swift vs. Maynwaring: The Examiner and The Medley* (Oxford: Clarendon Press, 1985).

141. Ibid. Maynwaring quickly replied by satirizing Swift. He remarked, "instead of placing her [Lady Credit] on so unstable a *Foundation* as the Pillars of the *Exchange*, he has given her the solid *basis* of a *Lottery*" (Arthur Maynwaring, *The Medley*, April 30, 1711, reprinted in Ellis, *Swift vs. Maynwaring*).

142. Richard Steele was born in Ireland, but educated in England. After volunteering to serve in the army in the 1690s, Steele launched a successful career as a man of letters, gaining fame as a prolific essayist and playwright. He founded the successful periodicals, *The Tatler* and *The Spectator*, and worked diligently to promote a Whig political and cultural agenda. He later became a member of Parliament.

143. Richard Steele, *The Spectator*, August 18, 1712.

144. Ibid.

145. Ibid.

146. Ibid.

147. Ibid.

148. On the relationship between the Financial Revolution and the rise of the novel, see Brantlinger, *Fictions of State*; Colin Nicholson, *Writing and the Rise of Finance: Capital Satires of the Early Eighteenth Century* (Cambridge: Cambridge University Press, 1994); Sherman, *Finance and Fictionality*.

149. The precariousness of public opinion reportedly led Isaac Newton to pronounce some years later that while he could calculate the motions of erratic stars, "he could not calculate the madness of the people" (Westfall, *Never at Rest*, 862).

150. The Whig opposition was muted by charges that they had orchestrated the attempt on Harley's life. See, for example, Swift's *The Examiner* on March 29, 1711.

151. Defoe, *A spectators address to the Whigs, on the occasion of the stabbing Mr. Harley* (London, 1711).

6. The South Sea Company and the Restoration of Public Credit

1. For general background information about the company, see Sperling, *South Sea Company*; Colin A. Palmer, *Human Cargoes: The British Slave Trade to Spanish America, 1700–1739* (Urbana: University of Illinois Press, 1981).

2. The term *social imaginary* is here used to refer to a collective vision, perception, or understanding of a world unobserved by most English people. As the literary critic Robert Mitchell points out, the collective imagination "constituted one of the key resources by means of which society became understood in terms of social systems"; see "'Beings that Have Existence Only in Ye Minds of Men': State Finance and the Origins of the Collective Imagination," *Eighteenth Century* 49 (2008): 119.

3. There is a large literature on how the slave trade was financed and how slavery contributed to the British industrialization process. See, for example, Kenneth Morgan, *Slavery, Atlantic Trade and the British Economy, 1660–1800* (Cambridge: Cambridge University Press, 2000); and Barbara L. Solow and Stanley L. Engerman, *British Capitalism and Caribbean Slavery: The Legacy of Eric Williams* (Cambridge: Cambridge University Press, 1987). This chapter, however, is concerned with how the slave trade contributed to the Financial Revolution by serving as the primary revenue source backing public credit. As such, this episode offers a particularly vivid example of how "the history of modern credit practices is inextricably bound up with the violent histories of European state formation, colonial conquest, and slave trading" (Marieke de Goede, *Virtue, Fortune, and Faith: A Genealogy of Finance* [Minneapolis: University of Minnesota Press, 2005], 21).

4. Dickson, *Financial Revolution in England*, 45; Robert Markley, *The Far East and the English Imagination, 1600–1730* (Cambridge: Cambridge University Press, 2006).

5. For a discussion of how the South Seas figured in the English mind-set during the early modern period, see Glyndwr Williams, *The Great South Sea: English Voyages and Encounters, 1570–1750* (New Haven, CT: Yale University Press, 1997); Jonathan Lamb, *Preserving the Self in the South Seas, 1680–1840* (Chicago: University of Chicago Press, 2001).

6. See Peter C. Mancall, *Hakluyt's Promise: An Elizabethan's Obsession for an English America* (New Haven, C.T.: Yale University Press, 2007).

7. William Dampier, *A new voyage round the world: describing particularly, the isthmus of America, several coasts and islands in the West Indies* (London, 1697); Woodes Rogers, *A Cruising Voyage around the World, First to the South-Seas, thence to the East-Indies, and homewards by the Cape of Good Hope* (London, 1712).

8. Anthony Ashley Cooper, Third Earl of Shaftesbury, *Characteristics of Men, Manners, Opinions, Times*, ed. Lawrence E. Klein (Cambridge: Cambridge University Press, 1999), 153.

9. See Nuala Zahedieh, *The Capital and the Colonies: London and the Atlantic Economy, 1660-1700* (Cambridge: Cambridge University Press, 2010).

10. In his study of the South Sea Company, John Sperling deemphasized the success of the company's trade and the extent to which the public embraced the

company. He asserted that "profits from trade had properly been discounted at nil" (*South Sea Company*, 16). John Carswell similarly proclaimed that the scheme "was from the first a sham" (*South Sea Bubble*, 47), while Henry Roseveare called it "a virtual sham" (*Financial Revolution*, 45). Prior to the publication of Sperling's account, however, many historians acknowledged the early success of the company. Philip Stanhope, for example, wrote that merchants quickly swallowed "this gilded bait, and the fancied Eldorado which shone before them dazzled even their discerning eyes . . . This spirit spread through the whole nation, and many, who scarcely knew whereabouts America lies, felt nevertheless quite certain of its being strewed with gold and gems" in *The History of England from the Peace of Utrecht to the Peace of Versailles, Vol. II* (Leipzig: Tauchnitz, 1853), 3. William T. Morgan also concludes that the company's early years were a success. In fact, had it not been for the out-of-control financial manipulations during the subsequent bubble years, Harley "might perchance have ranked beside Godolphin, the younger Pitt, Peel and Gladstone as one of England's great finance ministers"; see "The Origins of the South Sea Company," *Political Science Quarterly* 44 (1929): 38. This controversy is still ongoing today, with Julian Hoppit, "The Myth of the South Sea Bubble," *Transactions of the Royal Historical Society* 12 (2002): 142, claiming that "trade was always of minor importance to the company"; while Bruce G. Carruthers argues that the early operation of the company "was a success and preserved public creditworthiness" (*City of Capital*, 154).

11. While the charter specified that 1 percent of the capital stock would be dedicated towards fishing, there is little evidence that the company actually undertook any fishing expeditions during its first decade.

12. The navy debt was by far the largest portion, amounting to £5,130,539. These loans were short-term obligations sold to the public in anticipation of future, unspecified, tax revenues. When taxes were collected, creditors turned in their promissory notes in return for principal and earned interests. The problem was that revenues fell far short of expenses during the war, which meant that investors were unable to convert their securities.

13. The charter spelled out that the tallies and debentures exchanged for company shares "shall be Deemed and Called the Common Capital and Principal Stock of the said Company; and all Person concern'd to have a Share in the Annuity or Fund, in Proportion to their Stock, and to become Members of the Company, and be Admitted without Fee or Charge"; see *Abstract of the charter of the Governour and Company of Merchants of Great Britain, trading to the South-Seas, and other parts of America, and for encouraging the fishery* (London, 1711).

14. In order to pay the 6 percent annuity, the House of Lords passed a bill that extended the duties on wine, vinegar, tobacco, and East India goods, as well

as wrought silks and whale fins, originally passed to finance the war against France. Anno 9 Anne, c.21, p. 203.

15. The trading privileges naturally did not include territories in possession of the Portuguese and the Dutch.

16. *Assiento* (or *Asiento*) is a Spanish legal term designating a contract between the government and a private body for the administration of a public service. Since Spain had been barred from access to the African continent by the Treaty of Tordesillas in 1494, they had had to rely on foreign powers to supply them with slaves. While Spain had shipped slaves already employed on the Iberian Peninsula to its American holdings from the beginning of American colonization, they began to contract for slaves shipped directly from Africa in 1528. The initial *Assientistas* were two German merchants, who were well integrated in the colonial trade of Seville. For the next century and a half, the contract was held by merchants from Portugal, Spain, and Italy. In 1685, the Dutch acquired the Assiento and seventeen years later, France was able to obtain it. George Scelle, "The Slave-Trade in the Spanish Colonies of America: The Assiento," *American Journal of International Law* 4 (1910): 612–661.

17. The idea of charting a company to conduct England's trade to Spanish America was not new, neither was England's interest in obtaining the Assiento. England began negotiating in earnest for the contract in 1707, when the prominent army official and diplomat Sir James Stanhope was sent to Spain. Yet it was not until May of 1711 that the English and the French agreed on the basic commercial parameters of the peace treaty. English officials still had to engage in a few more years of diplomacy with the Spanish and the French before it could begin trading. Donnan, "The Early Days of the South Sea Company, 1711-1718," *Journal of economic and business history* 2 (1929): 422.

18. Herman Moll, *A View of the coasts, countries and islands within the limits of the South-Sea-Company. Containing an account of the discoveries, settlements, progress and present state . . . From the River Aranoca to Terra del Fuego, and from thence through the South Sea to the farthest bounds of the late act of Parliament. To which is added, an account of former projects in England for a settlement, and the accomplishment of the last in the establishing the new company; with a list of the commissioners names appointed by her majesty to take the subscriptions. As also some useful observations on the several voyages that have been hitherto publish'd . . . Illus. with a general map* (London, 1711), 220.

19. According to the *Abstract of the Charter* (1711), subscription books were opened on June 27 and by the end of July, £3,405,559 had been subscribed. By the end of the year £9,177,968 had been subscribed. Sperling, *South Sea Company*, 25.

20. Daniel Defoe, *A True account of the design, and advantages of the South-sea trade: with answers to all the objections rais'd against it. A list of the*

commodities proper for that trade: and the progress of the subscription towards the South-sea company (London, 1711), 37. The authorship of this pamphlet has recently been contested by Arne Bialuschewski, who claims that another member of Harley's propaganda team, Abel Boyer (see Chapter 5), was the author. Since Defoe expressed similar views in his *Review* and other pamphlets, I will follow the convention of attributing this pamphlet to Defoe. Ultimately, for the purposes of the argument in this chapter, it does not matter greatly which one of Harley's writers authored any particular piece. See Arne Bialuschewski, "*A True Account of the Design, and Advantages of the South-Sea Trade*: Profits, Propaganda, and the Peace Preliminaries of 1711," *Huntington Library Quarterly* 73 (2010): 273–285. It is notoriously tricky to judge which pamphlets were authored by Defoe. In this chapter I will adhere to the attributions in the Goldsmith's-Kress Library of Economic Literature. I have also consulted John Robert Moore, *A Checklist of the Writings of Daniel Defoe* (Bloomington: Indiana University Press, 1960), and P. N. Furbank and W. R. Owens, *A Critical Bibliography of Daniel Defoe* (London: Pickering and Chatto, 1998).

21. Carruthers, *City of Capital*, 76–78.
22. During the 1690s, the land tax had produced 39 percent of government income, compare with less than 24 percent from customs and 26 percent from excise taxes. After an increase in excise taxes in the first decade of the eighteenth century, the land tax once again generated the biggest share of revenues, although the proportion dropped to 37 percent. Roseveare, *Financial Revolution*, 34, 45. The reigns of William and Anne were anomalous as the only periods when the land tax dominated the state's revenues. Brewer, *Sinews of Power*, 99.
23. Ibid., 168. David Armitage argues, "An empire of the seas would not be prey to the overextension and military dictatorship which had hastened the collapse of the Roman Empire, nor would it bring the tyranny, depopulation and impoverishment which had hastened the decline of Spain" (*Ideological Origins of the British Empire*, 100–101).
24. *A Letter to a member of Parliament, on the settling a trade to the South-sea of America* (London, 1711), 4.
25. Ibid., 4–5.
26. A weakened Spanish navy was unable to prevent the French from trading freely to ports in Chile and Peru. These trading voyages generated lavish profits, reportedly reaching as high as 5,000 percent. William Funnell quoted in Williams, *Great South Sea*, 137. An English merchant jealously attested that the French "go frequently to all the Spanish ports in the West Indies under pretense of carrying niggers, etc., according to their agreement, and at the same time introduce their and other commodities and return the proceeds to France" (quoted in Morgan, "Origins of the South Sea Company," 19). By

using the Royal Navy to harass French slave traders, the English plan was to prevent the French from delivering "the quantity of negroes contracted for, and their Asiento must break the first year and then the Spaniards will be glad to take them of the English" (quoted in Morgan, "Origins of the South Sea Company," 21).

27. *A Letter to a member of Parliament,* 8–9.

28. Ibid., 10.

29. Jonathan Swift, *The Examiner,* June 7, 1711, reprinted in Ellis, *Swift vs. Mainwaring.*

30. Ibid.

31. Ibid.

32. Ibid. Swift was so confident in the ultimate success of the company that he invested £500 in the South Sea Company. Nicholson, *Writing and the Rise of Finance,* 53.

33. Categorizing this type of writing as chorography, Barbara J. Shapiro notes that "even the colonial description most concerned with attracting investment capital and encouraging immigration adopted the language of witnessing and credible testimony" (*Culture of Fact,* 69).

34. Moll's account was later used explicitly by Defoe in his novel *A New Voyage around the World* (1724) to build an imaginary account of the South Seas. Burton J. Fishman, "Defoe, Herman Moll, and the Geography of South America," *Huntington Library Quarterly* 36 (1973): 227–238.

35. Williams, *Great South Sea,* 165.

36. In a 1706 pamphlet, John Le Wright proposed that a colony should be developed in the proximity of Darien. He claimed that this area had been conferred to the English government as a gift by the local prince, Sachem Dego, in gratitude for England saving the villagers from certain massacre by the Spanish. See *Two proposals becoming England at this juncture to undertake* (n.p., 1706).

37. Moll, *A View of the coasts,* 211. Carswell points out that during the first decade of the eighteenth century, the contraband trade of slaves to South America yielded gold and silver at the rate of £200,000 per year (*South Sea Bubble,* 40).

38. For example, Steven Shapin, "Here and Everywhere: Sociology of Scientific Knowledge," *Annual Review of Sociology* 21 (1995): 289–321; Steven J. Harris, "Long-Distance Corporations, Big Sciences, and the Geography of Knowledge," *Configurations* 6 (1998): 269–304; Harold J. Cook, *Matters of Exchange: Commerce, Medicine, and Science in the Dutch Golden Age* (New Haven, CT: Yale University Press, 2007); and Simon Schaffer, *The Information Order of Isaac Newton's Principia Mathematica* (Uppsala: Salvia Småskrifter, 2008).

39. Mario Biagioli, *Galileo's Instruments of Credit: Telescopes, Images, Secrecy* (Chicago: University of Chicago Press, 2006), 22.

40. Ibid., 43.
41. Historian Mark Knights points out that because of the partisan political world of Augustan England was filled with "ambiguities, misrepresentations, and fictions"; political and literary writings had a tendency to converge (*Representation and Misrepresentation*, 7).
42. Markley, *Far East and the English Imagination*, chap. 6.
43. Ingrassia, *Authorship, Commerce, and Gender*, 6.
44. Ibid. Other literary scholars have also pursued the correspondence between credit and textuality. Sandra Sherman, for example, examines the homology between credit and fiction as "a new kind of narrativity" (*Finance and Fictionality*, 5).
45. Ingrassia, *Authorship, Commerce, and Gender*, 7.
46. Brown, *Fables of Modernity*, 101. In addition to Brown, Markley, Sherman, and Ingrassia, other important literary critics have contributed to the field of New Economic Criticism, including Nicholson, *Writing and the Rise of Finance*; Brantlinger, *Fictions of State*; and James Thompson, *Models of Value: Eighteenth-Century Political Economy and the Novel* (Durham, NC: Duke University Press, 1996).
47. Dianne Dugaw argues that the ballads about the South Sea Company "catered to buyers from a higher social level who, hearing the songs in a theatrical or coffeehouse performance, would buy the sheets to sing and hear the songs again accompanied by their own viols, keyboards, and flutes" in "High Change in 'Change Alley': Popular Ballads and Emergent Capitalism in the Eighteenth Century," *Eighteenth-Century Life* 22 (1998): 45.
48. Adam Fox, "Ballads, Libels and Popular Ridicule in Jacobean England," *Past and Present* 45 (1994): 57.
49. There are different estimations of what the effective interest rate was on the lottery loans. Carswell suggests that the interest rate was "an average of something like 8%" (*South Sea Bubble*, 44), while Richard Dale points out that the rate of interest on the lottery loans ranged between 6 and 10 percent in *The First Crash: Lessons from the South Sea Bubble* (Princeton, NJ: Princeton University Press, 2004), 24.
50. *An Excellent New Song Call'd An End to our Sorrows. To the Tune of, I Laugh at the Pope's Deviles* (n.p., 1711).
51. *Oxford and Mortimer's Vindication: Or, Another Song, In Answer to Credit Restor'd. To the Tune, Come Prithee, Horace, hold up thy Head* (London, 1711).
52. *Some Queries, Which being Nicely Answered may tend very much to the Encouragement of the South-Sea Company, and to forwarding that Laudable Undertaking to our greater Satisfaction* (n.p., 1711).
53. Ibid.
54. Ibid.
55. Ibid.

56. Ibid.

57. Ibid.

58. Ibid. The broadside concludes by questioning the respectability and honor of John Blunt, one of the architects of the scheme. Blunt had already earned the scorn of the Whigs in his role as director of the Sword Blade Bank. The author asked, "Whether any thing better could be expected from the Projects of a Stock-Jobber, and a known Cheat, than a Scheme liable to so much Fraud that no honest Man cares to be concern'd in it?" (ibid.).

59. Mark Knights notes that the rage of party often led to a rhetoric based on "the depiction of enemies as laughable; . . . irony, sarcasm, and mocking deference; . . . humourous understatement" (*Representation and Misrepresentation*, 248).

60. Arthur Maynwaring, *An Excellent New Song, called, Credit Restored, in the year of our Lord God, 1711. To the tune of, Come prithee, Horace, hold thy head* (London, 1711).

61. Arthur Maynwaring, *The South Sea Whim. To the tune of —— To you fair ladies now at land, &c.* (London, 1711).

62. Daniel Defoe, *The true state of the case between the government and the creditors of the navy, &c: as it relates to the South-Sea-trade. And the justice of the transactions on either side impartially enquired into* (London, 1711), 3.

63. Ibid.

64. Ibid., 8.

65. Ibid.

66. Ibid., 9. To Defoe, it was only reasonable to ask that a group who had benefited so greatly from the recent acts of the government "should make this small return in Gratitude to the Government *(viz.)* to subscribe, (not *to Give* but only *Hazard*) Ten Pound *per Cent* of their Money upon such a Trade."

67. Defoe, *A true account of the design*, 5.

68. Ibid., 6. Defoe points out that when the company is fully formed it "will have the largest Stock of any Trading-Company in the whole World; and therefore will be best able, with a Small Contribution of each Proprietor; the concurrent Assistance of the National Shipping and Land-Forces, and other Advantages that shall be Specified in their Charter, to dislodge the *French* from the *Spanish West-Indies*; or, at least, to make Settlements there; and carry on a Trade most beneficial to the said Corporation, and to the whole *British* Nation" (10).

69. Ibid., 20. Defoe also added that the South Sea Company would be able to carry on a prosperous trade with the pirates and buccaneers operating in the South Seas. While the East India Company had prevented the South Sea Company from trading to Madagascar, one of the key pirate strongholds, Defoe saw no obstacles to the company taking advantage of favorable bargains offered by these "villains of the world" in the South Seas.

70. Ibid., 29–30.

71. Francis Hare, *A Letter to a member of the October-club: shewing, that to yield Spain to the Duke of Anjou by a peace, wou'd be the ruin of Great Britain*. 2nd ed. (London, 1711), 17.

72. Arthur Maynwaring, *Remarks upon the present negotiations of peace begun between Britain and France* (London, 1711), 25.

73. Ibid.

74. Ibid., 26.

75. Arthur Maynwaring, *The Medley*, March 19, 1711, reprinted in Ellis, *Swift vs. Maynwaring*. Instead he advocated for a resumption of all land granted as favors by the Crown since 1689. Such a solution would raise enough money to retire the entire unsecured debt, at the same time that it would strike a blow at the landed interests.

76. Jonathan Swift, *The conduct of the allies, and of the late ministry, in beginning and carrying on the present war. The fifth edition, corrected* (London, 1711), preface.

77. Ibid., 17.

78. Ibid., 32.

79. Ibid., 44. Swift lamented the present situation in which "the Wealth of the Nation, that used to be reckoned by the Value of Land, is now computed by the Rise and Fall of Stocks." In the same issue of *The Examiner*, he concluded that "Power, which according to the old Maxim, was us'd to follow *Land*, is now gone over to *Money*" (*The Examiner*, November 2, 1710, reprinted in Ellis, *Swift vs. Mainwaring*).

80. Swift, *The conduct of the allies*, 40.

81. Daniel Defoe, *Armageddon: or, the necessity of carrying on the war, if such a peace cannot be obtained as may render Europe safe, and trade secure* (London, 1711), 46–47.

82. Defoe, *Review*, July 17, 1711. A few years earlier, an anonymous author proposed that it was in the interest of England, as well as Spain, for trade to Spanish America to be free and open. Free trade would most benefit England, as its industry and commerce produced more goods suitable for the American market than its main Atlantic competitors. Spain would also benefit by opening up trade to its colonies to foreign merchants, as they would be supplied with all conceivable commodities at competitive prices, while still retaining full control of their mines. *A Letter to Sir William Robinson, in Relation to a Proposal for a Trade to the Spanish West-Indies* (London, 1707), 3.

83. Ibid.

84. Arthur Maynwaring, *An Excellent New Song, call'd Mat's Peace, or the Downfall of Trade. To the Good Old Tune of Green-Sleeves* (London, 1711).

85. Defoe, *Review*, October 5, 1711.

86. Ibid.

87. The company directors included the ex–Bank of England directors James Bateman, Sir Theodore Janssen, and James Dolliffle, and the ex–East India Company directors Sir Matthew Decker and Samuel Shepheard. Robert Benson, the current Chancellor of the Exchequer, and Sir Ambrose Crowley, a major industrialist, were also selected, as well as the prominent financiers Edward Gibbon, Sir Richard Hoare, John Lambert, Samuel Ongley, Francis Stratford, and Thomas Vernon. Additionally, Harley assigned Sir John Blunt, Charles Blunt, George Caswall, Jacob Sawbridge, and Benjamin Todman— all affiliated with the Sword Blade Bank—to the court. Sperling, *South Sea Company*, 6–7. In order to signal the anti-Whig spirit of the company, Harley named himself first governor of the company and James Bateman, who had been Heathcote's main opponent on the Bank of England's Court of Directors, was made the sub-governor.

88. British Library, Additional Manuscript (Add MS), 25,494/34^r/November 14, 1711.

89. Add MS, 25,494/17^r/September 21, 1711. The Bank of England had a similar set of rules and incentives to ensure that its directors showed up on time. Bank of England, Minutes of the Court of Directors, G4/1/54/August 11, 1694

90. Add MS, 25,494/101^r/June 20, 1712.

91. Add MS, 25,494/53^r/January 31, 1712; Add MS, 25,494/69^r/March 19, 1712; Add MS, 25,494/75^r/April 1, 1712.

92. Add MS, 25,494/68^r/March 19, 1712.

93. Add MS, 25,494/99^r/June 20, 1712.

94. Add MS, 25,495/28^r/February 19, 1713.

95. Daniel Defoe, *An essay on the South-Sea trade. With an enquiry into the grounds and reasons of the present dislike and complaint against the settlement of a South-Sea company.* 2nd ed. (London, 1712), 5.

96. Ibid., 6. Defoe suggested that the French had to be attacked at the source of its "Sinews of War . . . Pinching the Enemy in that most sensible Part, *(viz.)* the Fountain of Wealth and Treasure, by which, *as before,* they have been enabled to carry on the War" (13–14).

97. Ibid., 40–41.

98. Ibid., 38.

99. Add MS, 25,495/56^v/June 2, 1713.

100. Healthy slaves between the ages of five and ten counted as half a pieza; slaves between the ages of ten and fifteen amounted to two-thirds of a pieza; and above the age of thirty, they counted as three-quarters of a pieza. Sperling, *South Sea Company*, 22.

101. Add MS, 25,550/83^v/October 10, 1717.

102. William Wood, *The Assiento contract consider'd. As also, the advantages and decay of the trade of Jamaica and the plantations, with the causes and*

consequences thereof. In several letters to a member of Parliament (London, 1714), 38.

103. Add MS. 25,495/63^v/June 23, 1713.

104. Add MS 25,562/6^r/September 15, 1713.

105. Goods purchased by the company for sale in South America included woolens, linens, carpets, dishes, plates, lead, barley, oak boards, doors, medicines, pewter, candles, lace, swords, guns, and gunpowder. Add MS, 25,495/242^r/December 22, 1714.

106. Robert Bleau, *A letter from one of the Royal African-Company's chief agents on the African coasts* (London, 1713), 2.

107. Royal African Company, *The case of the Royal African-Company and of the plantations* (London, 1714), 2.

108. Daniel Defoe, *A Brief Account of the Present State of the African Trade* (London, 1713). Reprinted in John McVeagh, ed., *Political and Economic Writings of Daniel Defoe, Volume 7: Trade* (London: Pickering and Chatto, 2000), 62.

109. Ibid.

110. In a pamphlet written in support of the RAC, Charles Davenant had earlier proclaimed, "While the Trade to *Africa* lies open, we can never settle the *Asciento*, nor make any advantageous Contracts with the *Spaniards* or *Portugueze*, to furnish them with Negroes in their *West-Indies*" (*Reflections upon the constitution and management of the trade to Africa, through the whole course and progress thereof* [London, 1709], 32). For an account of the conflict between the RAC and the separate traders, see William Pettigrew, "Free to Enslave: Politics and the Escalation of Britain's Transatlantic Slave Trade, 1688–1714," *William and Mary Quarterly* 64 (2007): 3–38.

111. Add MS, 25,550/6^v/January 28, 1714. The company's launch was not received well by the Jamaican merchants, whose commercial pursuits included shipping contraband slaves to Spanish America. William Wood, for example, argued that the clandestine slave trade and the associated contraband trade in dry goods out of Jamaica had netted England anywhere between £200,000 and £250,000 per year in gold and silver (*The Assiento contract consider'd*, 2).

112. Add MS, 25,495/96^v/October 28, 1713.

113. Add MS, 25,495/116^v/January 6, 1714.

114. Add MS, 25,495/120^v/January 20, 1714. *Hallifax* never sailed and *Hope* had to wait until the next year to depart.

115. Add MS, 25,495/95^v/October 28, 1713.

116. Palmer, *Human Cargoes*, 59.

117. Add MS, 25,495/188^r/July 21, 1714.

118. Add MS, 25,495/175v–177^r/June 29, 1714.

119. While the South Sea stock increased by approximately 20 percent during this period, the East India stock went up by 18 percent and the Bank of England by 10 percent.

120. Add MS, 25,495/209^v/October 5, 1714.

121. In accepting the honor of being made governor of the company, George I proclaimed, "I have not any thing more at heart than the promoting and Encouraging the Trade of the Nation and therefore thank the Court of Directors for their respect to me and will be sure to promote upon all Occasions the Interest of the Company." He added, "But not being versed in Matters of Commerce I shall always leave the whole Management thereof to the Court of Directors as well as the Choice of all their Officers to the Proprietors." Add MS, 25,495/244^v–245^r/January 3, 1715.

122. David Eltis, Stephen D. Behrendt, David Richardson, and Herbert S. Klein, *The Trans-Atlantic Slave Trade: A Database on CD-ROM* (Cambridge: Cambridge University Press, 2000).

123. Add MS, 25,495/223^v/November 10, 1714.

124. The company had received disappointing news from Madrid about the profit-sharing agreement in November of 1713. The document detailed that the king of Spain was granted 28 percent of the profits, Queen Anne 22.5 percent, a certain Señor Gilligan 7.5 percent, while the company would have control of the remaining 42 percent. The company was outraged and launched a campaign to petition the queen for a better agreement. The political wrangling that followed ended with the queen (June 1714) and Señor Gilligan (September 1715) ceding their parts, leaving the company in charge of 72 percent of the profits. Sperling, *South Sea Company*, 18–19.

125. Add MS, 25,555/41^v/February 1, 1716.

126. Add MS, 25,555/42^r/February 1, 1716.

127. Additional explanations for why the public debate about the South Sea Company petered out in 1713 include the passing of the Stamp Act in 1712, the closure of a number of Whig newspapers, and the death of Arthur Maynwaring. P. B. J. Hyland, "Liberty and Libel: Government and the press during the Succession Crisis in Britain, 1712–1716," *English Historical Review* 101 (1986): 864.

128. Defoe, *Review*, October 1711.

129. For a discussion of factors influencing the movement in stock prices during the early years of the London financial market, see Murphy, *Origins of English Financial Markets*.

130. Defoe, *Review*, October 22, 1706.

131. Eltis et al. *Trans-Atlantic Slave Trade*. Donnan, "Early Days of the South Sea Company," 434–436, estimates that five thousand African captives were shipped by the company in 1715; approximately three thousand in 1716; around sixty-five hundred in 1717; and, during the last year of the Assiento, the company delivered some four thousand slaves. Palmer (*Human Cargoes*, 103–109) suggests that the numbers were 1,530 in 1715; 2,493 in 1716; 2,946 in 1717; and, finally, 3,709 in 1718. Donnan and Palmer base their numbers

on the company's records, which include information about the number of slaves each ship was contracted to deliver. Many of these ships do not appear in the Eltis et al. database, some because they never sailed and others because proper documentation has not been found. Also, complicating the statistics was the fact that the company purchased thousands of slaves on Jamaica and Barbados, which do not show up in the Eltis et al. database as a South Sea Company transaction. The company also bought so-called Prize Negroes, which had been delivered by interlopers, and thus evaded the official record.

132. Add MS, 25,555/72^r/July 11, 1717. The period immediately following the War of Spanish Succession is often referred to as the golden age of piracy. Marcus Rediker, *Villains of All Nations: Atlantic Pirates in the Golden Age* (Boston: Beacon Press, 2004).

133. Add MS, 25,555/72^r/July 11, 1717.

134. On September 25, the company sent letters to their agents at Jamaica and Barbados "prohibiting their sending any more Negroes to the Spanish West Indies till further Order." Add MS, 25,498/61^r/September 25, 1718.

135. Donnan, "Early Days of the South Sea Company," 450.

136. Sperling, *South Sea Company*, 20.

137. Palmer, *Human Cargoes*, 155.

138. Political scientist David Stasavage attributes the improved credit conditions in 1715 to the dawn of the Whig supremacy. He argues that the Whigs were perceived as more trustworthy managers of the public debt; see "Partisan Politics and Public Debt: The Importance of the 'Whig Supremacy' for Britain's Financial Revolution," *European Review of Economic History* 11 (2007): 124.

139. Add MS, 25,495/92^r/October 14, 1713; Add MS, 25,495/120^v/January 20, 1714.

140. The company records are almost entirely silent about the dangers of slaves rebelling. One exception can be found in a letter from the factor in Buenos Aires, who petitioned for money to erect proper buildings "as may Secure the Negroes from running away or falling upon the factories and for their Security against their Insults" (Add MS 25,562/53^r/June 17, 1714). Additionally, in a letter to the factor stationed in St. Iago de Cuba, the company advised against accepting slaves delivered from Congo, as they are "apt to run away" (Add MS, 25,563/83^v/October 31, 1717). The company occasionally instructed its captains to undertake measures to improve the health of the slaves during the Middle Passage. For example, decks should be regularly washed with vinegar and the crew should "Divert [the captives] with Musick and play" (Add MS, 25,567/3^v/January 17, 1723).

141. Kathleen Wilson, *The Island Race: Englishness, Empire and Gender in the Eighteenth Century* (London: Routledge, 2002), 33.

142. As the historian Vincent Brown points out, "The accumulation of property, the reproduction of family and social networks, and the meaningful representation of life all stemmed in significant ways from high mortality and the

lingering presence of the dead" in *The Reaper's Garden: Death and Power in the World of Atlantic Slavery* (Cambridge, MA: Harvard University Press, 2008), 4.

143. Charles Davenant exemplified the prevalent stereotype of Africans. He described the natives on the Gold Coast as "generally so very Poor and Avaricious, and naturally so very Mercenary and Treacherous, even to one another, as well as to the *Europeans*" (*Reflections upon the constitution and management*, 20).

144. Sir Dalby Thomas quoted in Palmer, *Human Cargoes*, 21. Thomas was also a commissioner for the Million Act Lottery in 1694 and the aborted Land Bank in 1696.

145. Quoted in Palmer, *Human Cargoes*, 21.

146. David Richardson, "Shipboard Revolts, African Authority, and the Atlantic Slave Trade," *William and Mary Quarterly* 58 (2001): 72.

147. John Atkins, *A Voyage to Guinea, Brasil, and the West-Indies; in His Majesty's Ships, the Swallow and Weymouth* (1721). Reprinted in Elizabeth Donnan, ed., *Documents Illustrative of the History of the Slave Trade to America* (Washington, DC: Carnegie Institution of Washington, 1930), 2:281–282.

148. William Snelgrave, *A New Account of Some Parts of Guinea, and the Slave Trade* (1734). Reprinted in Donnan, *Documents Illustrative*, 2:355.

149. James Barbot, *An Abstract of a Voyage to Congo River or the Zair, and the Cabinde, in the Year 1700* (1700). Reprinted in Donnan, *Documents Illustrative*, 2:457.

150. Ibid.

151. Ibid. Other personal accounts of revolts include that of the Dutch Chief Factor Willem Bosman, who described in a book translated and published in England in 1705 how he had been part of two such rebellions, one of which "was timely quashed by the master of the ship and my self, by causing the abettor to be shot through the head, after which all was quiet"; see *A New and Accurate Description of the Coast of Guinea, Divided into the Gold, the Slave, and the Ivory Coasts, etc.* (1699). Reprinted in Donnan, ed., *Documents Illustrative*, 1:443. The second rebellion endured by Bosman was more severe, wounding multiple crew members. The captives would most likely have succeeded had it not been for the aid of two other slave ships that happened to be located nearby.

152. See Marcus Rediker, *The Slave Ship: A Human History* (New York: Viking, 2007).

153. Thomas Phillips, *A Journal of a Voyage made in the Hannibal of London, Ann,. 1693–1694, from England, to Cape Monseradoe, in Africa; and thence along the Coast of Guiney to Whidaw, the Island of St. Thomas, and so forward to Barbadoes* (1693–1694). Reprinted in Donnan, *Documents Illustrative*, 1:406.

154. Similarly, James Barbot described how "we cause as many of our men as is convenient to lie in the quarter-deck and gun-room, and our principal officers in the great cabbin, where we keep all our small arms in a readiness, with sentinels constantly at the door and avenues to it; being thus ready to disappoint any attempt our slaves might make on a sudden" (quoted in Donnan, *Documents Illustrative*, 1:462).

155. Snelgrave, *A New Account of Some Parts of Guinea* (1727). Reprinted in Donnan, *Documents Illustrative*, 2:352.

156. Snelgrave tells the story of how he hoisted up a mutineer with a rope and had ten of his men fire at him. Once dead the head was dismembered and thrown overboard. He described how this spectacle "struck a sudden Damp upon our Negroe-Men" and suggested that the latter act was particularly important, "For many Blacks believe, that if they are put to death and not dismembered, they shall return again to their own Country, after they are thrown overboard" (ibid., 359).

157. Atkins, *A Voyage to Guinea* (1721). Reprinted in Donnan, *Documents Illustrative*, 2:266.

158. *Instructions to Captain William Barry* (1725). Reprinted in Donnan, *Documents Illustrative*, 2:327.

159. Phillips, *A Journal of a Voyage made in the Hannibal* (1693–1694). Reprinted in Donnan, *Documents Illustrative*, 1:402.

160. Ibid., 403.

161. Ibid., 402.

162. Wood, who himself was a separate trader, opposed the Assiento since he believed that it might strengthen the RAC's monopoly. Pettigrew, "Free to Enslave," 28–29.

163. Wood, *Assiento contract consider'd*, 21.

164. Ibid., 33.

165. Emma Christopher, *Slave Ships, Sailors and their Captive Cargoes, 1730–1807* (Cambridge: Cambridge University Press, 2006), 182–186.

166. Palmer, *Human Cargoes*, 45, 49.

167. Herbert S. Klein, *The Atlantic Slave Trade* (Cambridge: Cambridge University Press, 1999), 139. According to the Eltis et al. database, the annual mortality rate on the company's ships ranged from 14 percent to 27 percent.

168. *The Trade granted to the South-Sea-Company: considered with relation to Jamaica. In a letter to one of the directors of the South-sea-company; by a gentleman who has resided several years in Jamaica* (London, 1714), 10. The author pointed out, "The demands of the *Spaniards* are generally for compleat Slaves, Men and Women in their Prime of Life, or Boys and Girls, all clean Limb'd, Healthy, without Blemish or Defect, . . . [I]t is very rare that they will Buy any Slave the lest defective or disfigur'd, tho' it be but in the tip of an Ear" (ibid., 9–10).

169. Ibid., 11.
170. Add MS, 25,550/2ᵛ/January 5, 1714.
171. Brown, *Reaper's Garden*, 13. He notes that the death rate for the British was around 10 percent per year, while "Blacks died at slightly lower rates, but in far greater numbers."
172. The denial of the slaves' agency might have been explained by slave merchants insuring their cargo. While the slave trade was one of the pioneers in insuring people, the cargo was only insured against the usual maritime hazards, such as shipwrecks and piracy. Geoffrey Clark points out that the insurance policies "often explicitly excluded their liability for losses stemming from an insurrection by the captives at sea, or as the result of slaves' deaths by means 'either natural, violent, or voluntary.'" Rebellion, suicide, and disease were not insured as they were considered avoidable through proper management and care. See Geoffrey Clark, *Betting on Lives: The Culture of Life Insurance in England, 1695–1775* (Manchester: Manchester University Press, 1999), 16–17. See also Anita Rupprecht, "Excessive Memories: Slavery, Insurance and Resistance," *History Workshop Journal* 64 (2007): 17–22.
173. Christopher L. Brown, *Moral Capital: Foundations of British Abolitionism* (Chapel Hill: University of North Carolina Press, 2006), 51.
174. Robin Blackburn, *The Making of New World Slavery: From the Baroque to the Modern, 1428–1800* (London: Verso, 1997), 386. For an extensive discussion of how money redefined people and human relationships in early modern England, see Deborah Valenze, *The Social Life of Money in the English Past* (Cambridge: Cambridge University Press, 2006).
175. Karl Marx, *Capital: A Critique of Political Economy, Volume 1*, trans. Ben Fowkes (London: Penguin Books, 1976), chap. 1.
176. Writing about insurance and slavery in the context of the famous *Zong* incident of 1781, during which sickly slaves were thrown overboard to collect on the insurance policy, Ian Baucom explores the epistemological changes in value that credit and insurance introduced in the eighteenth century. In insuring the slaves, Baucom argues that finance capital went beyond the commodification of labor inherent in the commodity form. Once the slaves were insured their identity, individuality, and humanity was all but erased and they became imaginary or fictitious beings. For this to be possible, it was necessary to develop "a mutual and system-wide determination to credit the existence of imaginary values." He continues, "Central to that form of value was a reversal of the protocols of value creation proper to commodity capital . . . Such value exists not because a purchase has been made and goods exchange but because two or more parties have agreed to believe in it"; see Ian Baucom, *Specters of the Atlantic: Financial Capital, Slavery, and the Philosophy of History* (Durham, NC: Duke University Press, 2005), 17.

177. The absence of the slaves' subjectivity in the social imaginary of the Atlantic world anticipates the kind of blindness that Uday S. Metha detected in liberal theory in general. Since liberal theory, he argues, assumes that all people are born free, equal, and rational, it is unable to see the subject positions of those who are robbed of these anthropological minimums. Uday S. Metha, "Liberal Strategies of Exclusion," *Politics and Society* 18 (1990): 427–454.

178. While Marx did not comment on the phenomenon that I refer to as credit fetishism, he did offer his thoughts on a different type of abstraction central to credit. He suggested that in credit relations, "Mutual Dissimulation, hypocrisy and cant reach a climax since the man in need of credit is not only defined simply by his poverty but also has to put up with the demoralizing judgment that he does not inspire confidence, that he is unworthy of recognition, that he is, in short, a social pariah and a bad man." Marx continues, "This wholly *ideal* existence of money means then that the *counterfeiting* of man must be carried out on man himself rather than on any other material, i.e. he must make counterfeit coin of himself, obtain credit by lies and underhand means." Marx then concludes that the credit relationship is an object of mutual deception. Karl Marx, "Excerpts from James Mill's *Elements of Political Economy*," in *Early Writings*, introduced by Lucio Colletti and translated by Rodney Livingstone and Gregor Benton (New York: Vintage Books, 1975), 264–265.

179. François R. Velde, "Government Equity and Money: John Law's System in 1720 France," *Federal Reserve Bank of Chicago Working Paper Series* (2003): 12.

180. John Law's *Money and Trade Considered with a Proposal for Supplying the Nation with Money* (Edinburgh, 1705) has been celebrated as a seminal contribution to the theory of money. While his writings may indeed have influenced later thinkers, the discussion in Chapter 3 implicitly shows that there was very little in Law's work that can be called novel.

181. In the congratulatory note that Law sent Harley in June of 1711, he offered to return to England and aid in the management of the South Sea Company. Harley refused his offer and declined to extend him a pardon for his murder conviction from 1694, when he killed Edward Wilson in a duel over a woman. Carswell, *South Sea Bubble*, 65.

182. The success of the Banque Générale led the regent Philippe II, Duc d'Orléans, to rethink Law's proposal for a national bank. He soon granted Law the privilege to establish the Banque Royal, which had the right to issue more than double the quantity of notes than its predecessor. For a detailed account of John Law, his ideas and projects, see Antoin E. Murphy, *John Law: Economic Theorist and Policy-Maker* (Oxford: Clarendon Press, 1997).

183. Thomas E. Kaiser, "Money, Despotism, and Public Opinion in Early Eighteenth-Century France: John Law and the Debate on Royal Credit," *Journal of Modern History* 63 (1991): 10; Antoin E. Murphy, *Richard Cantillon:*

Entrepreneur and Economist (Oxford: Clarendon Press, 1986), 91. Kaiser argues that Law only orchestrated campaigns to promote credit after his system began to falter in 1720. Once Law became desperate, he even prosecuted people who spoke or acted in ways that undermined confidence in the bank notes ("Money, Despotism, and Public Opinion," 17).

184. The link between the South Sea Company and the Mississippi Company was acknowledged by a member of the French ministry of foreign affairs, who wrote, "The Company that it is proposed to form, under the name of the Company of the West, has like the English South Sea Company two objects— that of trade and that of retiring a considerable quantity of *billets d'état*" (quoted in Murphy, *John Law*, 168).

185. Roseveare, *Financial Revolution*, 52.

186. Ibid., 52–53. The following summary of the company's financial dealings leading up to the South Sea Bubble are based primarily on Dickson, *Financial Revolution in England*, 79–89; and Roseveare, *Financial Revolution*, 52–55.

187. Add MS, 25,497/31^v–32^r/May 9, 1717.

188. Add MS, 25,498/123^v/June 25, 1719.

189. The company informed its shareholders in December of 1718 that "it appears obvious the Company cannot in their present circumstance, on the foot of their Trade increase their Dividend above the annuity payable by Parliament" (Add MS 25,498/78^r/December 12, 1718).

190. Add MS, 25498/155^v/January 21, 1719.

Epilogue

1. John Trenchard and Thomas Gordon, "'The Fatal Effect of the South-Sea Scheme, and the Necessity of Punishing the Directors,' No. 2, November 12, 1720," in *Cato's Letters: Or, Essays on Liberty, Civil and Religious, and other Important Subjects*, ed. Ronald Hamowy, 40 (Indianapolis: Liberty Press, 1995).

2. *The South-Sea scheme detected; and the management thereof enquir'd into: with the case of the subscribing annuitants; and a remedy offer'd for our present grievances. In answer to a pamphlet, entitled, The South-sea scheme examin'd, &c. By a lover of his country. The second edition* (London, 1720).

3. Mr. Chamberlen, *News from Hell: or, A match for the directors: a satire. Humbly inscribed to the honourable members of the Secret committee: with a dedication to the Emperour of the Moon* (London, 1721), 7. Silke Statmann explores the ballads sparked by the bubble in *'South Sea's at best a mighty BUBBLE': The Literization of a National Trauma* (Trier: WVT Wissenschaftlicher Verlag Trier, 1996).

4. Trenchard and Gordon, "'Against false Methods of restoring Publick Credit,' No. 4, November 26, 1720," *Cato's Letters*, 50.

5. Trenchard and Gordon added, "The resurrection of honesty and industry can never be hoped for, while this sort of vermin is suffered to crawl about, tainting our air, and putting every thing out of course; subsisting by lies, and practicing vile tricks, low in their nature, and mischievous in the consequences" (ibid., 42).

6. Ibid., 59.

7. *A Letter to a conscientious man: concerning the use and the abuse of riches . . . shewing that stock-jobbing is an unfair way of dealing; and particularly demonstrating the fallaciousness of the South-sea scheme* (London, 1720).

8. Ibid.

9. Edward Ward, *A South-sea ballad: or, merry remarks upon exchange-alley bubbles* (n.p., 1720).

10. Trenchard and Gordon, "How easily the People are bubbled by Deceivers. Further Caution against deceitful Remedies for the publick Sufferings from the wicked Execution of the South-Sea Scheme,' No. 6, December 10, 1720," *Cato's Letters*, 55.

11. Ibid.

12. Ibid.

13. Ibid. Bernard Mandeville published an enlarged version of his *Fable of the Bees* in 1723, partly in response to the vibrant opposition to the new economic climate following the bubble. His intervention, in turn, informed the eighteenth-century conversation about the relationship between the passions, interests, sympathy, faith, politeness, moral sense, and sociability. See Albert O. Hirschman, *The Passions and the Interests: Political Arguments for Capitalism before Its Triumph* (Princeton, NJ: Princeton University Press, 1977).

14. Although he did not criticize the architecture of the scheme directly, he heaped scorn over John Law's system in France, which in many ways was a copy of the South Sea Company. Daniel Defoe, *The Chimera: or, the French way of paying national debts, laid open. Being an impartial account of the proceedings in France, for raising a paper credit, and settling the Mississippi stock* (London, 1720).

15. Daniel Defoe, *The case of Mr. Law, truly stated. In answer to a pamphlet, entitul'd, A letter to Mr. Law* (London, 1721),

16. Jonathan Swift, *The Bubble: A Poem* (London, 1721), 5–6. For a further exploration of Swift's engagement with the South Sea Bubble, see J. T. Klein, "Satirists and South-Sea Baubles in the Age of Hope and Golden Mountains," *Southern Review* 14 (1981): 143–154; Pat Rogers, "Plunging in the Southern Waves: Swift's Poem on the Bubble," *Yearbook of English Studies,* 18 (1988): 41–50; and Sean Moore, "Satiric Norms, Swift's Financial Satires and the Bank of Ireland Controversy of 1720–1," *Eighteenth-Century Ireland* 17 (2002): 26–56.

17. *Discovery of the philosopher's stone. Lately projected by certain dealers in the South-sea* (Dublin, 1720). Swift, *Bubble*, 3–4.

18. Ward, *South-Sea Ballad*. See also, for example, *Discovery of the Philosopher's Stone. Lately projected by certain dealers in the South-sea* (1721).

19. I will not comment on the bubble itself, only its impact on the discourse on credit. For a discussion of how, when, and why the bubble occurred, see Lewis Melville, *The South Sea Bubble* (London: O'Connor, 1921); Carswell, *South Sea Bubble*; Sperling, *South Sea Company*; Dickson, *Financial Revolution in England*; Neal, *Rise of Financial Capitalism*; Niall Ferguson, *The Cash Nexus: Money and Power in the Modern World, 1700–2000* (New York: Basic Books, 2001); Malcolm Balen, *The Secret History of the South Sea Bubble: The World's First Great Financial Scandal* (London: Fourth Estate, 2002); Richard Dale, *The First Crash: Lessons from the South Sea Bubble* (Princeton, NJ: Princeton University Press, 2004); and Helen Paul, *The South Sea Bubble: An Economic History of its Origins and Consequences* (London: Routledge, 2010).

20. Hoppit, "Myth of the South Sea Bubble," 153; Carlos and Neal, "Micro-Foundations of the Early London Capital Market." The same cannot be said for France. While private credit recovered relatively soon after the bubble burst, France did not have a well-functioning system of public credit or a generally circulating credit currency for the rest of the century. Larry Neal, "How it All Began: The Monetary and Financial Architecture of Europe during the First Global Capital Markets, 1648–1815," *Financial History Review* 7 (2000): 133. John Brewer, among others, argues that the resiliency of the British system of credit contra that of France was an important reason why England was able to establish control over the Atlantic world in the eighteenth century (*Sinews of Power*, 29).

21. For a collection of primary and secondary documents reflecting on the events of 1720, see Ross B. Emmett, *Great Bubbles: Reactions to the South Sea Bubble, the Mississippi Scheme and the Tulip Mania Affair*, 3 vols. (London: Pickering and Chatto, 2000).

22. George Berkeley, *The Querist, containing several queries, proposed to the consideration of the public* (Dublin, 1735), query 5, 4. For a discussion of Berkeley's monetary discourse, see C. George Caffentzis, *Exciting the Industry of Mankind: George Berkeley's Philosophy of Money* (Dordrecht: Kluwer, 2000).

23. Berkeley, *Querist*, query 35, 9.

24. Ibid., query 220, 41.

25. Ibid., query 199, 37.

26. Ibid., query 206, 38. While Berkeley noted that the Bank of England exhibited many of the favorable traits of a public bank, he pointed out that it was actually a private bank and therefore not entirely safe from malfeasance and corruption.

27. Issac Gervaise, *The System or Theory of the Trade of the World* (London, 1720), 2.
28. Ibid.
29. Ibid., 5.
30. Ibid., 22.
31. Ibid., 23.
32. Ibid., 8.
33. Ibid., 18.
34. Carl Wennerlind, "The Link between David Hume's *A Treatise of Human Nature* and his Fiduciary Theory of Money," *History of Political Economy* 33 (2001): 139-160.
35. Hume followed Montesquieu's delineation between favorable and unfavorable forms of paper money. Montesquieu argued that paper money backed by silver or future profits could favorably augment the currency, while paper money representing a debt—private or public—have virtually no benefits; see *The Spirit of the Laws* (Cambridge: Cambridge University Press, 1989), part 4, chap. 17, 418. For a discussion of the French debate about credit and Montesquieu's role therein, see Michael Sonenscher, *Before the Deluge: Public Debt, Inequality, and the Intellectual Origins of the French Revolution* (Cambridge: Cambridge University Press, 2007).
36. David Hume, "Of Money" in *Essays Moral, Political, and Literary*, ed. Eugene F. Miller (Indianapolis: Liberty Fund, 1987), 286.
37. Ibid.
38. Ibid.
39. Ibid. For a discussion of Hume's views on the relative merits of different types of monetary expansions, see Carl Wennerlind, "David Hume's Monetary Theory Revisited: Was He Really a Quantity Theorist and an Inflationist?" *Journal of Political Economy* 113 (2005): 223-237. See also Michael I. Duke, "David Hume and Monetary Adjustment," *History of Political Economy* 11 (1979): 572–587; John F. Berdell, "The Present Relevance of Hume's Open-Economy Monetary Dynamics," *Economic Journal,* 105 (1995): 1205–1217; Tatsuya Sakamoto, "Hume's Political Economy as a System of Manners," in *The Rise of Political Economy in the Scottish Enlightenment*, ed. T. Sakamoto and Hideo Tanaka, 86-102 (London: Routledge, 2003); and Margaret Schabas, "Temporal Dimensions in Hume's Monetary Theory," in *David Hume's Political Economy*, ed. Carl Wennerlind and Margaret Schabas, 127-145 (London: Routledge, 2008).
40. David Hume, "Of Public Credit" in *Essays Moral, Political, and Literary*, ed. Eugene F. Miller (Indianapolis: Liberty Fund, 1987), 360-361. For an extensive discussion of Hume's views on public credit, see Istvan Hont, "The Rhapsody of the Public Debt: David Hume and Voluntary State Bankrupcty," in Nicholas Philipson, ed., *Political Discourse in Early Modern Britain*

(Cambridge: Cambridge University Press, 1993): 321-48. Evidence suggests that it may have been the memory of the South Sea Bubble that led to Hume's reluctance to fully embrace a fiduciary theory of money. Ian Simpson Ross, "The Emergence of David Hume as a Political Economist: A Biographical Sketch," in *David Hume's Political Economy*, ed. Carl Wennerlind and Margaret Schabas, 31–48 (London: Routledge, 2008).

41. Hume, "Of Public Credit," 361.

42. For a discussion of the shared features in Hume's and Smith's monetary discourses, see Carl Wennerlind, "The Humean Paternity to Adam Smith's Theory of Money," *History of Economic Ideas* 8 (2000): 77–97.

43. Smith, *Wealth of Nations*, 458.

44. Ibid., 74.

45. Ibid., 458. Smith noted that the banks established in Scotland during the eighteenth century had "contributed a good deal" to Scotland's trade and industry (ibid., 315).

46. Ibid., 310.

47. Ibid., 341.

48. Nicholas Biddle quoted in Robert V. Remini, *Andrew Jackson and the Bank War* (New York: W.W. Norton 1967), 20.

Acknowledgments

Casualties of Credit was written during a particularly rewarding and enjoyable period of my life. For that, I most of all have my wife, Monica Miller, and our amazing children, Langston and Selma, to thank. Monica's human and intellectual brilliance is the foundation of both my general happiness and my enjoyment of academic life. I would not have been the same person without her, nor would this book have been much of anything without her help.

During the writing of this book, I have had the great fortune of teaching in a unique college environment. Barnard College administration, faculty, staff, and students create a truly inspiring and encouraging intellectual milieu. I am forever grateful to the members of the history department for accepting and embracing an interloper into their fold. My Europeanist colleagues, in particular Joel Kaye, Lisa Tiersten, Lars Trägårdh (now at Sköndal University College), and Deborah Valenze have not only become close friends, but they are some of my toughest and most important critics. It is a pleasure to walk up Broadway knowing that intelligent conversations and laughs will be had on a daily basis.

Another virtue of the Barnard College history department is its close relationship to its Columbia University counterpart. In writing a book on the history of ideas regarding the English economy with a focus on culture, politics, slavery, alchemy, and epistemology, one could not have a better set of early modern Europeanist colleagues than David Armitage (now at Harvard), Chris Brown, Pierre Force, Martha Howell, Matt Jones, Susan Pedersen, and Pamela Smith. I am deeply appreciative of their friendly advice and criticisms. I have also benefited from

337

the intellectual breadth and conviviality of the honorary Europeanists Evan Haefeli and Anders Stephanson.

A few people have been instrumental in enabling me to end up in this fortunate position. Harry Clever, Douglas Dacy, Perry Mehrling, and Margaret Schabas have, in their own unique ways, mentored and encouraged me in this process. I am deeply grateful to them.

In writing this book, I have had the pleasure of interacting with many excellent scholars, who have greatly helped in the development of its ideas. In particular, I would like to thank Tim Alborn, Tony Aspromourgos, Chris Berry, Alex Bick, George Caffentzis, Dan Carey, Loic Charles, Ludovic Desmedt, Istvan Hont, Fredrik Albritton-Jonsson, Martin Kragh, Harro Maas, Ted McCormick, Craig Muldrew, Steve Pincus, Johan Sandberg, John Shovlin, Phil Stern, Henry Turner, Rachel Weil, and Anders Ögren.

In presenting the ideas of this book at conferences and workshops, I have received exceptional advice from many people. While I cannot mention them all here, I would like to thank the participants in the Columbia University Seminar on British History, the European History Seminar at Columbia University, the Economic History Seminar at the Stockholm School of Economics, the British Historical Studies Colloquium at Yale University, the European History Seminar at New York University, the Early Modern European History Seminar at the University of Chicago, Séminaire "H2S" Histoires de l'économie at Ecole Normale Superieure de Cachan, and Les Pensées Monétaires dans l'histoire: 1517–1776 at Université Lumière Lyon 2.

Many Barnard and Columbia students have contributed to this project through their participation in seminars and as research assistants. Thanks to Amy Johnson, Embry Owen, Jessica Pulitzer, and, in particular, Angus Lyall, for patiently helping me during different phases of this book.

Numerous librarians and archivists have helped me in my search for documents. I would like to thank the staff at the Rare Books and Manuscript Library at Columbia University, the Baker Library at Harvard University, the Bank of England Archive, and the Manuscripts Reading Room at the British Library. Halfway through this project, Columbia University library acquired the database The Making of the Modern World (Gale Digital Collections), which proved an invaluable resource.

It has been a delightful experience to work with Mike Aronson and his staff at Harvard University Press. Always encouraging and impressively patient, Mike made the writing of this book as stress free as possible.

This project has benefited from the generous financial support of the American Philosophical Society, National Endowment for the Humanities, Columbia University Seminars, Barnard College, Jan Wallanders och Tom Hedelius Stiftelse, Helge Ax:son Johnsons Stiftelse, and Wenner-Gren Stiftelsen. Thanks also to the Institute for Economic and Business History Research (EHFF) at the Stockholm School of Economics for generously providing office space during the completion of this book.

My friends have been enormously important to this project, in their own separate ways. Most of all, thanks to mina bästa kompisar, Bobo Conradi and Peder Hofman-Bang. Thanks also to Sara, Helena, Leia, Micke och Anna, Martin and Amanda, Rebecca and Henry, Åsa och Jakob, Lotta och Greg, Aviva, Betsy, Anu, Nara, Nancy, Herb, Ted, Chip, Chris, Rob, Jompa, Johan, Ubbe, Nico, Nicke, Carl-Johan och Sara, Arne, Nancy, David, Sanjay, Ingmar, Eva och Tobbe, Parsan, Margaret and Lisa, Christian and Russ, Gabriel, Michael and Reggie, Jenny and Heeten, Rachel and Jon, and everyone else.

I want to deeply thank my parents, Olle och Gunilla, for encouraging me to explore the world. I hope this book will make both of you proud. I want to thank my truly exceptional sister, Pernilla, for her unconditional friendship, and her family, Gustav, Albert, och Livia, for their generosity and affection. Lastly, once again and most of all, I want to thank my own family. *Jag älskar er med hela mitt hjärta.*

Index

Harvard University Press is a member of Green Press Initiative (greenpressinitiative.org), a nonprofit organization working to help publishers and printers increase their use of recycled paper and decrease their use of fiber derived from endangered forests. This book was printed on recycled paper containing 30% post-consumer waste and processed chlorine free.